# Training and Development NVQs

A handbook for FAETC Candidates and NVQ trainers

## Les Walklin

## Stanley Thornes (Publishers) Ltd

*By the same author:*
Instructional Techniques and Practice
Instructional Techniques and Practice for Driving Instructors
Teaching and Learning in Further and Adult Education
The Assessment of Performance and Competence
Putting Quality into Practice

96    97    98    99    00    /    10    9    8    7    6    5    4    3    2    1

First published in 1996 by
Stanley Thornes (Publishers) Ltd
Ellenborough House
Wellington Street
Cheltenham
Glos GL50 1YW
UK

ISBN 0 7487 2077 4

Typeset by Action Typesetting Limited, Gloucester
Printed and bound in Great Britain by The Bath Press, Avon

# Contents

# Foreword

The establishment of the Training and Development Lead Body (TDLB) has provided a nationally recognised structure for the identification and monitoring of programmes designed to meet a wide range of needs for teachers, students and others involved in vocational education and training. This TDLB structure has in turn been effectively used as the framework for the new City and Guilds Training and Development NVQ Further and Adult Education Teachers Certificate (FAETC) (C&G 7306). This recently introduced award offers, as an alternative to the original FAETC, a more flexible and in many cases more relevant programme of study and assessment for new teachers and for practitioners who wish to achieve formal recognition of existing skills and experience. The TDLB has also clarified the criteria and responsibilities relating to the processes of assessment within NVQs through the range of assessor units including D11, D21, D32, D33, D34 and D36, and awards based on these and other units are now seen as being essential qualifications for those engaged in managing learning opportunities and assessing NVQs.

Les Walklin has accurately anticipated both the demands and areas of concern for those studying for Training and Development qualifications such as the C&G 7306 and the units referred to above. He has produced, as with previous publications, a timely and comprehensive book which will provide valuable guidance, support and information. Characteristically, the author has ensured that the book includes appropriate reference to essential principles of teaching and learning while providing detailed guidance, in this case to the TDLB units constituting the FAETC programme. As a result the book not only supports the reader with underpinning knowledge but also advises on the selection, accumulation and presentation of evidence for final accreditation. The reader is also greatly assisted by the Introduction (Chapter 1), which establishes the context for subsequent parts of the book so that they can be effectively used in relation to the core and optional units of the various awards covered by the text.

The Government has recently revised the National Targets for Education and Training (NTETs) in order to establish more ambitious levels of NVQ achievement. It is therefore appropriate that an award such as the well-established and highly respected FAETC should now be offered within the NVQ framework. The FAETC 7306 will not only contribute towards the extension of NVQs but will also provide a teaching and training award which itself will promulgate the principles and demonstrate the practices of a competence-based programme. Those achieving the award should be better prepared to guide and support others who are working towards NVQs, thus making an important contribution to the development of competence-based teaching and learning, and indirectly to the achievement of the NTETs' objectives.

The development and introduction of NVQs has required a reappraisal of the traditional roles and responsibilities of teachers and learners, and provided the opportunity for people to widen the context within which skills, knowledge and experience can be developed and related performance is recognised. It is therefore essential that those undertaking the FAETC NVQ should clearly understand the structure, operation and requirements of the award and realistically relate their individual professional responsibilities and experience to the set performance criteria.

I am in no doubt that this book will contribute to the promotion and value of the new 7306, and will provide a comprehensive resource that will promote a successful outcome for the reader while adding to the value of the personal development of those who wish to keep abreast of current matters.

RAY CHAVE
*Vice Principal*
*The Bournemouth and Poole College of Further Education*
*Bournemouth*

# Preface

For professionals working in the field of teaching, training and personal development, the key factors in achieving successful outcomes are to demonstrate consistently the highest personal standards, to facilitate learning opportunities effectively, and, most importantly, to satisfy the expectations of learners. The purpose of this book is to help readers meet these requirements and keep up to date with current developments. It does so by providing an excellent reference and source of guidance and support for people who are seeking information relating to the latest City and Guilds Training and Development (FAETC) NVQ competence-based scheme and other teacher training programmes, and to some of the popular Training and Development Lead Body (TDLB) trainer and assessor units.

Recent experience has revealed that many candidates initially find it difficult to make sense of some award standards and to appreciate the need to provide knowledge evidence by answering relevant questions as well as by demonstrating key 'can do' competences. There is also concern that teacher candidates will not progress very far from their current status if they are expected to demonstrate only limited performance evidence with little knowledge of the 'why' and 'what if' of teaching and learning. In some teacher training programmes, class contact hours have been severely cut to take account of financial constraints imposed, and when hours required for the assessment of units are taken out of available 'learning' time, there may be little time left for course team 'teacher inputs', group learning opportunities and discussing the work of educational researchers and theorists.

There are many excellent texts on general teaching practice available, but candidates and teachers alike have asked for a source of easy reference that can be dipped into so as to gain rapid access to relevant information about training and development award units, and in particular those which the FAETC NVQ comprises. They are seeking a summary of key underpinning knowledge matched to award criteria. This book makes essential reading for anyone involved in such programmes, since it provides the information sought, and gives guidance on identifying, selecting and gathering evidence needed to build a suitably structured folder or similar means of containing and presenting evidence. The layout strictly follows the NVQ award profile and covers all key purposes, related performance criteria, evidence requirements and range statements. It forms an easily accessible reference to the knowledge underpinning performance and serves as a guide to portfolio composition and preparation.

Above all, this text seeks to support candidates at all stages of the Training and Development NVQs and the City and Guilds Further and Adult Education Teachers Certificate process – from initial assessment to final accreditation.

LES WALKLIN
*Charlton Marshall 1996*

# Acknowledgements

The author and publishers are grateful to the following for permission to reproduce copyright material:

Addison-Wesley Publishing Co. Inc. for Flanders' Interaction Analysis Categories (FIAC) from N. Flanders, *Analysing Teaching Behaviour*, 1970.

Bloomsbury Publishing Ltd for a quotation and terms from N. Rees, *The Politically Correct Phrasebook*, 1993.

Lynda Bourne for permission to reproduce the rationale for assessing assignments shown in Figure 14.8.

Malcolm Butcher for providing information and documentation relating to microteaching.

The Care Sector Consortium for permission to reproduce extracts from NVQ Level 2 units Z6 'Enable clients to maintain and improve their mobility' and Z10 'Enable clients to eat and drink'.

The City and Guilds of London Institute for permission to reproduce performance criteria, specimens of current standards and other documentation relating to the City and Guilds Training and Development NVQ Level 3 (Further and Adult Education Teacher's Certificate (C&G 7306) and the C&G 7281 series of assessor, advisor and verifier awards; and the City and Guilds *Access to assessment – candidates with special needs* general policy statement shown in Figure 15.4 (see *Documents Pack*).

William Collins Sons and Co. Ltd. for many references to terms given in the *Collins Dictionary of the English Language*, 1989.

Chris Chrispin-Hobson for permission to reproduce the teaching practice assessment report shown in Figure 16.6 (see *Documents Pack*).

Employment Group – Training, Enterprise and Education Directorate (TEED), formerly the Training Agency, for numerous references to the content of its publications.

Gill French, Dorset School of Nursing, for the task analysis shown in Figure 9.1 (see *Documents Pack*).

D.S. Frith and H.G. Macintosh for extracts from *A Teacher's Guide to Assessment*, published by Stanley Thornes 1984.

Further Education Unit (FEU) (now replaced by the new Further Education Development

Agency (FEDA)) for quotations and numerous references to the content of its publications.

D. Garforth and H. Macintosh for extracts from *Profiling: A User's Manual,* published by Stanley Thornes, 1986.

The Institute of the Motor Industry for permission to reproduce in the *Documents Pack* (relating to Chapter 12) material extracted from Unit 7 of the NVQ Level 3 in Vehicle Mechanical and Electrical Systems Maintenance and Repair (LV).

Richard Laurence Kazimierz Kosior for permission to reproduce in Activity 15.2 the draft questions and answers concerning underpinning knowledge required for Units D32 and D33.

The National Council for Vocational Qualifications for permission to reproduce the NCVQ Assessment Model shown in Figure 13.2.

Penguin Books Ltd for permission to reprint as Figure 10.1 the 'Chart for Bales's Interaction Process Analysis' adapted from W.P. Robinson, *Language and Social Behaviour*, Figure 1, p. 44.

Pergamon Press for quotations and references to the content of *The International Encyclopedia of Teaching and Teacher Education* (ed. M. J. Dunkin), 1987.

Lorraine Poole and Sarah Jayne Farwell, NHS health associate professionals, for permission to reproduce their D32 assessment plan given in Figures 15.2 and 15.3 (see *Documents Pack*).

The Royal Life Saving Society UK (RLSS) for permission to reproduce in Figure 14.7 (see *Documents Pack*) extracts from the Royal Life Saving Society UK National Lifeguard Training Programme provided by Robert Paulley, a qualified RLSS examiner and D32/D33 Vocational Assessor.

TMS Development International Ltd, for a reference made in Chapter 10 to the Margerison-McCann Team Management Wheel.

Christine Ward for extracts from *Designing a Scheme of Assessment*, published by Stanley Thornes, 1980.

Roy Whitlow for permission to reproduce extracts from *Notes for Guidance* in Figures 13.3 and 13.7.

**Special thanks are due to:**

Nikki Glendening, Training Officer, Dorset Community National Health Service (NHS) Trust, and Peter Jordan, Automotive lecturer, Technical Studies Institute, GHQ Armed Forces, United Arab Emirates, for their considerable help and for permission to reproduce the many examples of evidence gathered while they were working with the author towards their Further and Adult Education Teacher's Certificate, C&G 7281/22 (D32 and D33) Vocational Assessor Award, C&G 7281/23 (D36) Advising on Prior Achievement Award, and C&G 7281/24 (D32, D33 and D34) Internal Verifier Award.

Gary Miller and Bryan Rowbotham, two FAETC teacher-candidates who met their teaching practice requirements by facilitating an education and training management programme while working with me. During our frequent reviews and feedback sessions they provided much food for thought about the way mature adults feel about teaching and learning activities, and some of their reflections appear within the text.

I am indebted to the many civilian students and HM Forces' personnel who have collectively over the years taught me a good deal about teaching and learning, and the content of this book reflects some of this knowledge. With this in mind, my very special thanks are due to Colonel David Simpson and Captain Peter Barlow of The Queen's Royal Lancers, Sergeant Major Robbie Williams of The Royal Dragoon Guards, WO2 Chris Greenaway of the Royal Horse Guards Dragoons (the Blues and Royals), and all of the excellent Royal Armoured Corps students past and present that I have had the privilege to work with and learn from, and also to the Dorset NHS Trust FAETC and vocational assessor teams.

Thanks are also due to WO1 Colin Luckham, Yeoman of Signals, and the current Royal School of Signals' Blandford team for their commitment and contribution to our FAETC classes. Their accomplishment has reinforced my faith in the tenacity and resilience of adult learners and their ability to produce the required quantity and quality of work on time whether individually or by promoting effective teamworking.

Every attempt has been made to contact copyright holders, but we apologise if any have been overlooked.

## Disclaimer

Apart from those acknowledged above or elsewhere in the text, the persons named in this book and in the accompanying *Documents Pack* have no existence outside the imagination of the author and have no relation whatsoever with any company or person bearing the same name or names. They are not even distantly inspired by any individual known or unknown to the author, and all incidents are pure invention.

# Testimonial

I have recently obtained the Training and Development Level 3 Further and Adult Education Teachers' Certificate (7306), having qualified in April 1995. At the start it was clearly evident that no specific book relating to this course was available. As a consequence, much time and effort was initially devoted to interpreting and determining what was required for each unit in terms of gathering the evidence needed to meet all specified performance criteria and range statements; and gaining an understanding of the underpinning theories and knowledge.

Having read Les Walklin's finished manuscript, I could immediately see that this book would be an invaluable resource for any student embarking on a City and Guilds TDLB Further and Adult Education Teachers Certificate. The information is set out in such a manner that the reader can jump from chapter to chapter, quickly picking out what they need, depending on which unit (or units) they are working on. I was particularly impressed with the use of self-assessment questions in each section. These step-by-step questions will allow the reader to identify more easily the required underpinning knowledge in a logical manner rather than searching desperately for relevant information. Similarly, the activities in each chapter will assist in knowledge application and act as a guide for students when they are gathering the relevant evidence required for final submission and assessment.

I am sure students embarking on a FAETC course will find that this book will focus their minds on the tasks required at a much earlier stage in their development. I am convinced that by completing each activity suggested and working diligently through the self-assessment questions, readers of this book will be greatly assisted in becoming competent adult education teachers.

G.B. MILLER B.Sc. (Hons)
*Bournemouth 1996*

# How to use this book

This work is presented in the hope that readers will be able to make immediate use of the content. The book can be read from cover to cover or used for spot reference, and it can be 'dipped into' whenever information relating to a particular topic is required.

The book covers all of the core units and optional units for the Training and Development Level 3 (Further and Adult Education Teachers Certificate) and 11 of the Level 4 Training and Development (Learning) units. Each chapter covers all elements and performance criteria of a complete TDLB unit. The text is arranged in a logical sequence: an introduction to each unit followed by all performance criteria with relevant underpinning knowledge and sample documentation; self-assessment questions covering the required knowledge evidence; and sample activities for use when preparing for assessment. Subheadings are given for each element within each chapter, and many sections can be read individually without necessarily referring to what has gone before. Readers may look up matters of particular interest by first consulting the comprehensive index and then retrieving facts from the text.

Although the text is focused on teacher and trainer training and the role of the staff developer, much of the content is readily transferable to others employed elsewhere within the entire education and training occupational area. It is essential reading for those seeking to attain the FAETC and Certificate in Education (FE), and any of the range of the TDLB unit-based NVQ/SVQ Training and Development qualifications now offered, including the D32, D33 and D36 assessor awards.

Note: Several of the Figures referred to in this book are, as indicated in the text, to be found in the accompanying *Documents Pack*. The figures are, however, numbered consecutively throughout each chapter. For example, Figure 2.3 appears in the text, Figure 2.4 in the *Documents Pack*, and Figure 2.5 in the text.

# Introduction: Features of the FAETC NVQ

The aim of this chapter is to examine the City and Guilds Training and Development Level 3 NVQ (Further and Adult Education Teachers Certificate) award structure and features of the C&G 7306 FAETC standards. Ways of gathering, presenting and assessing evidence relating to key roles and competences and the associated terminology will also be discussed.

The 'new' competence-based C&G 7306 Further and Adult Education Teachers Certificate (NVQ Levels 3 and 4) qualification framework was introduced in September 1994, and programmes are currently being offered by a number of colleges and other providers throughout England, Wales and Northern Ireland. The revised 7306 programme is now more user-friendly and much improved on the earlier version available in 1993.

An important feature of the Level 3 version of the FAETC is the designation of 17 TDLB defined units – seven core units and ten optional units (which include the assessor awards) – plus optional Management Charter Initiative (MCI) units. The MCI units can be 'imported' into individual 7306 awards by candidates who have been assessed by qualified MCI assessors and who have already gained these units.

The TDLB units cover five key purposes:

- identifying training and development needs (A)
- planning and designing training and development (B)
- facilitating training and development (C)
- reviewing progress and assessing achievement (D)
- continuously improving the effectiveness of training and development (E).

The Level 3 programme MCI units cover:

- contributing to the planning, monitoring and control of resources
- contributing to the provision of personnel.

The full C&G 7306 NVQ Level 3 qualification now comprises seven core units plus any three optional units, and providers will negotiate attendant assessments of competence and the recording of achievement with individual candidates. For the NVQ Level 4 (Learning) candidates will need seven mandatory core units plus any five from the 19 options offered. A Foundation Certificate in Teaching and Training based on Level 3 NVQ units and unit certification will also be available. However, teaching competence and the ability to effectively facilitate learning remains the essential focus for experience and certification.

Candidates following the 7306 NVQ format will need to demonstrate competences that will be assessed and judged against award performance criteria. Being able to meet unit require-

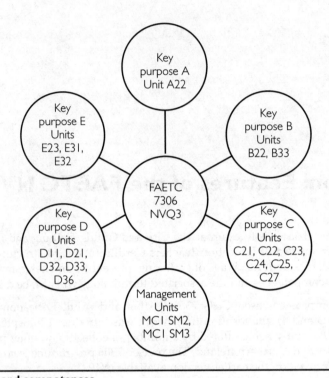

**Key roles and competences**

|  | **Identifying training and development needs** |
|---|---|
| **A22*** | Identify individual learning needs |
|  | **Organising and resourcing learning opportunities** |
| **B22*** | Design training and development sessions |
| **B33*** | Prepare and develop resources to support learning |
|  | **Facilitating and enabling learning** |
| **C21*** | Create a climate conducive to learning |
| **C22** | Agree learning programmes with learners |
| **C23*** | Facilitate learning in groups through presentations and activities |
| **C24** | Facilitate learning through demonstrations and instruction |
| **C25** | Facilitate individual learning through coaching |
| **C27** | Facilitate group learning |
|  | **Assessing achievement** |
| **D11** | Monitor and review progress with learners |
| **D21** | Conduct non-competence-based assessments |
| **D32** | Assess candidate performance |
| **D33** | Assess candidate using differing sources of evidence |
| **D36** | Advise and support candidates to identify prior achievement |
|  | **Evaluating developmental outcomes** |
| **E23*** | Evaluate training and development sessions |
| **E31*** | Evaluate and develop own practice |
| **E32** | Manage relationships with colleagues and customers |
|  | **Management** |
| **MC1 SM2** | Contribute to the planning, monitoring and control of resources |
| **MC1 SM3** | Contribute to the provision of personnel |

*Note:* The full C&G 7306 Level 3 qualification now comprises seven mandatory core units* plus any three units from the options

**Figure 1.1** *C&G 7306 Level 3 (Training and Development) FAETC Award Structure*

ments entails not only the ability to provide performance evidence at the right level but also the ownership of sufficient underpinning knowledge that supports such behaviour. A portfolio of evidence associated with the elements assessed can be built up and used to support performance and knowledge evidence demonstrated during assessments. But care should be taken to ensure that the teacher-candidate is neither encouraged nor required to join in a 'paper chase' or to 'jump through hoops'. In general, alternative sources of evidence are only required when performance evidence does not cover all the specified criteria and contexts defined by range statements. The chapters that follow provide useful information and insight about interpretation and possible approaches to developmental activities concerning all of the new FAETC units.

## Award structure

### Key roles

The key purposes and units shown in Figure 1.1 form a logical approach to the roles of people engaged in teaching and training occupations. The well-established cycle commences with a training **needs analysis** leading to the identification of learning requirements of individuals. This is followed by a strategy for identifying **learning objectives** and planning, developing, organising and resourcing **learning opportunities**; implementing training by selecting methods and facilitating and **enabling learning** to take place; monitoring and **assessing achievement** and reviewing and **evaluating outcomes**.

### Validity and reliability

The number of optional units currently available affords teacher-candidates considerable choice. This should promote valid, reliable and relevant assessments that will (hopefully) meet every candidate's needs. The clusters of units offered fit neatly into the training cycle framework and it is pleasing to note that optional units are now available under the heading 'assessing achievement'. This will make the new award possible to achieve and far more relevant to the many practitioners who work in leisure, non-vocational and non-NVQ/SVQ areas of education and training, many of whom would otherwise be unable to meet the requirements of D32/D33.

The ownership of D32/D33 units carries with it responsibility for maintaining effective and valid assessment of candidates for NVQ/SVQ/GNVQ/GSVQ units. It is therefore important to recognise the central role of the Vocational Assessor and to safeguard the credibility of those who achieve these units by ensuring the valid and reliable accreditation of their competency. This will entail assessment and verification by assessors who are properly trained and qualified to carry out the work. The perceived value to employers of competence-based awards will be influenced by the quality of the assessment process that led to the award of a qualification. In order to maintain standards, assessors must be provided with ongoing advice and support concerning the assessment process and verifiers must continuously monitor and verify assessment practice so as to meet awarding-body criteria. Otherwise NVQs and the like will simply end up as virtually worthless pieces of paper.

# Portfolio building

### Evidence requirements

Many teacher-candidates starting work on NVQs such as the 7306 pose the question: 'What evidence can I collect to meet the assessment criteria for this particular competence?' The FAETC facilitators respond by suggesting certain performance evidence and supplementary evidence but notice that the candidates' eyes are glazing over and frowns are appearing. So they patiently try again and again, slowly digging their own grave. Explaining evidence requirements and range statements can be a very slow process for programme facilitators. Also when the NVQ/SVQ assessment model is new to them and the wording of standards difficult to cope with, trying to grasp what is involved becomes a painful process for candidates. So with this in mind, diagrams giving an overview of the assessment model and showing the types of evidence that may be gathered are given later in the chapter together with brief explanations. More information about evidence and assessment can be found in the section of the book which covers Key Role D, 'Assessing achievement'.

### Gathering evidence against standards

Candidates when preparing for assessment must assemble necessary evidence to cover all **unit criteria** and **range statements**. Much of the evidence needed will fall into two main categories: **performance evidence** and **product evidence**. Candidates will provide performance evidence by demonstrating an activity defined in the performance criteria while being observed by an assessor or perhaps while being videoed at work. Product evidence is gathered for examination, and supplementary or knowledge evidence may also be required. If performance evidence and examination of products and questioning do not alone cover performance criteria the assessor will call for further evidence of **process skills** or **underpinning knowledge**. Evidence presented must confirm competent performance.

### Criteria for evidence presented

All evidence presented for assessment must satisfy five criteria: validity, currency, sufficiency, authenticity and consistency. This is essential, whether the evidence derives from prior achievement, experiential and informal learning, life skills, work experience, simulations or written sources.

**Historical evidence** relates to events of the past . The advisor or assessor concerned will need to check whether or not evidence which the candidate intends to present is up to date, meets current standards and is relevant to the performance criteria being considered. If this can be

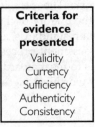

**Criteria for evidence presented**
Validity
Currency
Sufficiency
Authenticity
Consistency

**Figure 1.2** *Criteria for evidence presented*

confirmed then the evidence will meet the requirements of **currency** and **validity**. **Sufficient** evidence must be provided to meet all unit performance criteria and must cover all range statements in terms of context and sources of evidence specified in the standards. Evidence presented must be **authentic**, that is, it must be of undisputed origin. Candidates must 'own' the evidence. It must be genuine and reliable – a valid and accurate representation of facts and clearly the work of the person claiming ownership. When the candidate is working as a team member their contribution must be identified and **confirmed** either by questioning or by a responsible **third party** such as a supervisor. One-off well-rehearsed demonstrations may not reliably reflect ongoing competent performance, and assessors must be convinced that candidates are able to carry out work **consistently** to performance standards before making an assessment decision.

# Assessment model

## *Gathering evidence for assessment*

Features of the evidence-gathering process are given in Figure 1.3. Assessment decisions are made by judging evidence presented against national standards. Plans agreed between candidate and assessor will describe the conditions and circumstances relating to the assessment

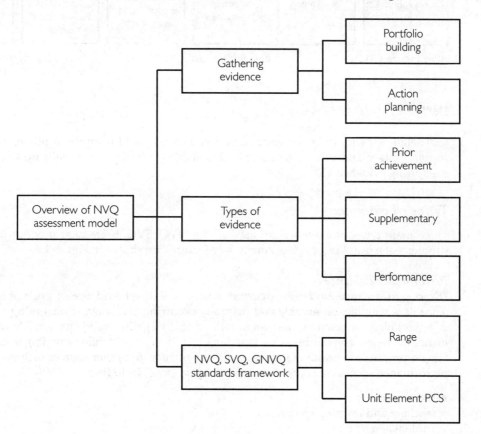

**Figure 1.3** *Gathering evidence*

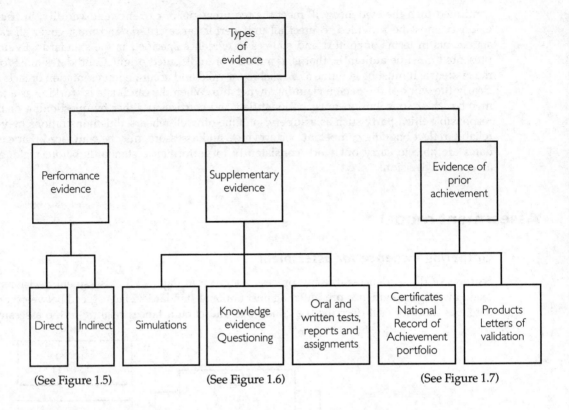

**Figure 1.4** *Types of evidence*

and detail evidence to be gathered. Evidence needed could comprise a mix of performance, supplementary and prior achievement. A suitable portfolio is then built up which contains supporting evidence.

## Types of evidence

Three main types of evidence are used in the NVQ/SVQ assessment process: performance, supplementary and prior achievement. Key features are shown in Figure 1.4.

### Performance evidence
**Direct performance evidence** is current evidence – direct evidence of your present competence. It is tangible, observable and naturally occurring. An assessor **observing** you teaching in a workplace or teaching placement will be able to gather valid and reliable direct performance evidence. The performance you demonstrate unaided while providing a service or creating a product are prime examples of direct evidence. But other sources include **products of performance** – actual outputs of your teaching sessions, including:

● lesson plans
● teaching and learning resources
● student assessments
● student development plans

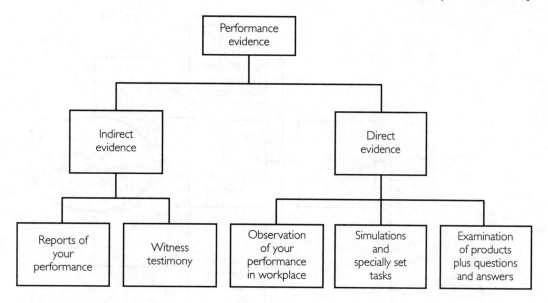

**Figure 1.5** *Performance evidence*

- evaluations of lessons
- lesson preparation notes.

**Indirect performance evidence** includes **witness testimony** – evidence of your teaching performance that is supplied by your line managers, mentors, other tutors, colleagues and candidates. The witness testimony can be oral or written, but it must **directly** relate to the standards and refer specifically to achievements against one or more elements. A witness testimony can be in support of past experience or provide evidence of current performance, but it is very important that your witness is reliable.

### Supplementary evidence

Supplementary evidence is evidence of knowledge and understanding that is associated with vocational skills performed. It can be used to support or supplement performance evidence or indirect evidence presented for assessment, or as 'top up' evidence where prior achievement or current performance alone are insufficient to meet criteria. It may include evidence derived from knowledge testing: oral questioning, written responses to question papers, multiple-choice or computer-based testing, or review of projects and reports. Simulations, skills testing and demonstrations could also be considered, or in fact any relatively recent and current supplementary evidence you can provide that satisfies unit criteria.

Other supplementary evidence may take the form of:

- your employer's letters of confirmation of your current competence at work
- written material or computer-generated products
- your answers to the assessor's questioning
- archive materials that you have produced
- testimonials
- certificates of achievement
- licences

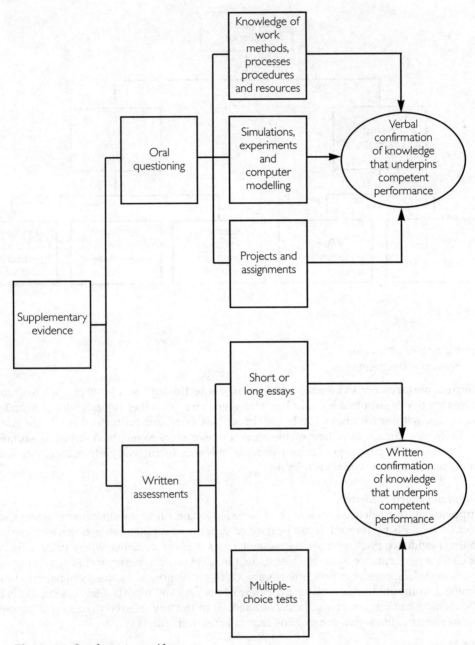

**Figure 1.6** *Supplementary evidence*

- log books and media articles
- references and letters from present and past employers
- accounts of any unwaged work you have carried out
- videoed activity
- computer programming.

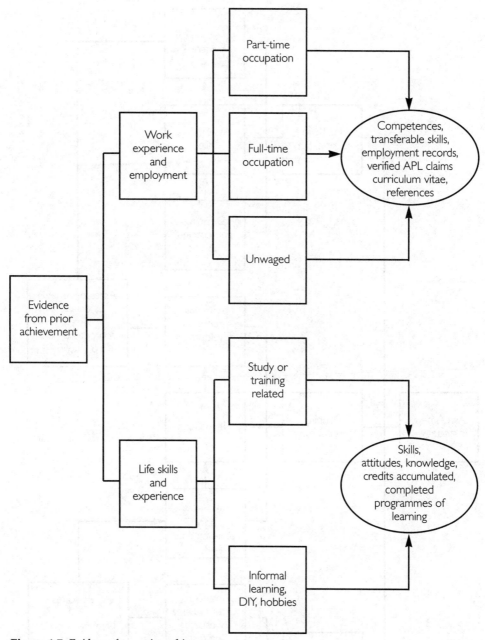

**Figure 1.7** *Evidence from prior achievement*

### *Prior achievement*

Your past experiences may provide a great deal of evidence towards the target award provided that any evidence presented is **authentic** and **relevant** to the units to be claimed. **Prior achievement** derives from relevant past experiences that have resulted in learning and the ability to perform tasks to the required standard. Evidence presented must indicate that the competence claimed has been **retained** to the present day. Typical evidence might comprise

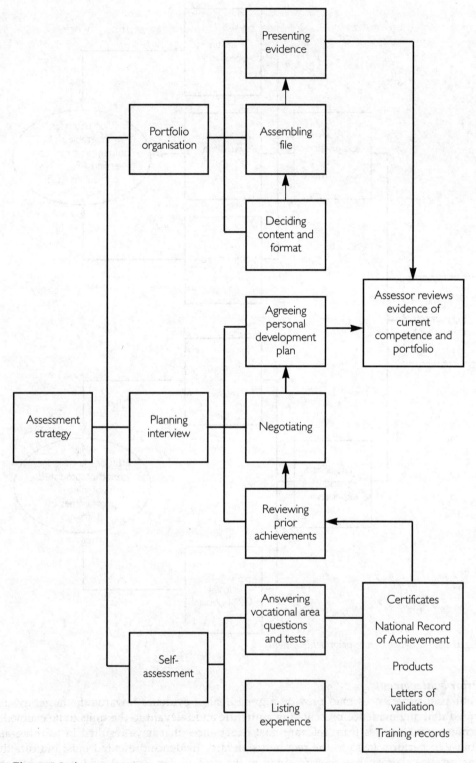

**Figure 1.8** *Assessment strategy*

authenticated letters of validation confirming achievement matched with relevant elements of competence during recent employment or while undertaking unpaid work. Other acceptable evidence might include:

- your curriculum vitae
- role descriptors
- contents of your National Record of Achievement file
- certificates, awards and qualifications.

Chapter 12 is dedicated to a survey and discussion of the process of identifying prior learning and achievement.

# Assessment strategy

An overview of a strategy adopted when preparing for assessment is shown in Figure 1.8. As can be seen, candidates are encouraged to self-assess initially or otherwise establish where they are against unit criteria and range statements, and then create a list of evidence to be gathered before joining an assessment of prior learning (APL) advisor, identification of training needs (ITN) analyst, learning needs identifier or teacher-assessor at a planning interview. A review of prior achievements and any evidence put forward is followed by negotiation and agreement of either a **personal development plan** and **top-up training** or an **assessment plan** (see examples given in Figures 15.1, 15.2 and 15.3 in the *Documents Pack*).

A contents list is drawn up and portfolio content is gathered ready for presentation to the assessor concerned. For ease of identification care must be taken to cross-reference evidence produced against unit criteria.

## Assessing competence for NVQs/SVQs

Assessment outcomes will be based on the performance requirement specified in the statement of unit performance criteria, range statements and evidence specification. Units of competence will be assessed as required by candidates, and open access to assessment, accreditation and certification will be made available by centres offering NVQ/SVQ awards.

The type of assessment method used will be matched to the particular competence to be judged. The guiding factor will be the need to validate properly the candidate's claim to ownership of specified units of competence. Confirmation of competence may derive from a mixture of: **assessed prior achievement, observation of performance** at work or while undertaking predetermined tasks or simulations, and **supplementary evidence** such as written work and tests or face-to-face question and answer sessions. An overview of the NVQ/SVQ assessment model is given in Figure 13.2.

## Assessing achievement

The five optional 7306 assessment units available, D11, D21, D32, D33 and D36, cover important functions concerned with monitoring and reviewing progress and achievement, conducting non-competence-based assessments and assessing candidates using the many different sources of evidence that could be presented. Teachers will need to be able to negotiate assessment plans effectively; collect information on learners' progress and judge performance and knowledge evidence presented by candidates against criteria; make and communicate judgements; give constructive feedback; and record achievement.

*Introduction*

It is well known that account must always be taken of unit standards, range statements, the assessment specification and evidence requirements when considering a valid starting point for any assessment strategy. References to these important concepts are made throughout the book.

# 2

# Establishing learning needs and learning opportunities

The two elements that make up this unit are concerned with **identifying available learning opportunities** and **identifying learning needs with individuals.** This presents us with a 'chicken or egg?' situation. Which element do we tackle first? Do we prefer to have a clear picture of all that is on offer to candidates so that when we meet them we can find out what they need and immediately offer them a range of learning opportunities? Or do we carefully identify their individual needs and then send them away while we seek out opportunities that might fulfil their requirements? There is no universally acceptable answer to the question posed, since individual circumstances vary widely as do the roles and responsibilities of those who are appraising learner needs. Training needs can be established by conducting the identification of learner training needs (ITN) interview. The **ITN principle** is based upon comparison of 'what knowledge and skills are required' with 'what relevant knowledge and skills are currently owned' by the learner concerned. The difference is known as the 'training need'. With this in mind we shall follow the unit sequence and look at the criteria concerning the identification of available learning opportunities before moving on to a consideration of how best to identify learning needs with individuals. But before we do so perhaps it will be helpful to consider some of the main issues within each element.

### Identifying available learning opportunities

**Curriculum entitlement** gives learners the right to participate in suitable learning experiences and to work towards recognised outcomes, such as NVQs and other qualifications. Providers of the service that learners will use have an obligation to deliver quality training and to satisfy action plans agreed. Eligible learners should therefore have access to training opportunities and learning methods that suit them. The minimum entitlement should comprise negotiated content, negotiated and pre-specified outcomes, individual progression opportunities and learning experiences that are open to everyone.

In the training opportunities sphere, the key issues to be considered are: **identifying opportunities** that will match learner needs and expectations, and **auditing** the **feasibility of training**. Then follows a more detailed examination of the **conditions of learning** and available **resources**. When suitable learning opportunities cannot be provided in-house and learner needs cannot be met, a **referral system** should be available to introduce the candidate to others, including alternative providers.

### Identifying and meeting learning needs

A **needs analysis** is candidate-centred and may include training needs relating to an individual or to groups. The outcome is a statement of what candidates **need to learn** based upon a comparison between their job specification or qualification criteria for 'success' and their current achievements and **present level** of ability, training and experience. Such needs can be classified as **demand-led.** Needs may also be anticipated by training providers, simply by referring to awarding body documentation, a syllabus, new legislation or market trends. Programmes made available to meet market trends are described as **supply-led** provision.

Teacher-candidates will need to understand the purposes and techniques of assessing learner needs and identifying available learning opportunities so that needs may be satisfied. They should also adopt the supporting role most appropriate to the learner's experience and requirements. Teachers identify, coordinate and facilitate learning opportunities that are available to learners. But before teachers accept this role they must be competent to carry out each of the key tasks listed below. It will be readily appreciated that none of the tasks stand alone since effective teaching is a technique that integrates multiple skills, knowledge, experience and attitudes. This calls for 'helicopter vision' when meeting with candidates for the first time and seeking to help them identify and clarify their training needs. Teachers must demonstrate ownership of an adequate level of related knowledge and skills backed by a wealth of experience when establishing learner needs. The learning needs assessor will:

- check provision and resources, verify the accuracy and reliability of learner performance standards and discuss associated learning opportunities and teaching programmes with others concerned
- advise learners of the range of opportunities available and explain relevant context, content, procedures and standards
- familiarise learners with the concept of giving credit for relevant knowledge, skills, experience and ability and explain the practice of the accreditation of prior learning and achievement (APL) in terms of recognising the value of awards already held and prior experience gained
- provide information and resources to enable individuals to identify their current competence
- explain techniques of initial self-assessment, assist individuals who wish to gain access to information banks and support learners who may be experiencing difficulties
- define and agree the current competence of individuals
- negotiate developmental action plans and learning programmes in accordance with the needs and abilities of individual learners
- provide the best match reasonably and economically possible either by devising new schemes or by adapting available programmes to meet learner needs and where necessary group or sponsor's requirements.

## Identifying available learning opportunities

*Training and development opportunities available are clearly and accurately identified*

The range of training and development opportunities available must be clearly and accurately identified before a teacher or advisor can recommend ways of meeting their learners' needs. This will involve listing the qualifications on offer or obtaining a current copy of the provider's full-time and part-time prospectus and carefully checking out the facts provided and the availability of relevant course brochures, display posters and leaflets and any other sources of information. Other sources of information about the range and scope of learning opportunities available include promotional materials such as exhibition displays, videos, tape-slide programmes and advertisements used by training providers, local schools and awarding bodies. None of these should be overlooked.

Putting customer requirements first means ensuring that learning opportunities and programmes available are clearly understood by the training provider's representatives and that everything they do is directed towards providing sufficient relevant, current, accurate and detailed information.

*Conditions and characteristics of training and development opportunities available are clearly and accurately identified*

Information about training and development opportunities on offer should be readily available to inquirers, and the ITN advisor or teacher concerned should be able to explain the qualification structure, overall programme coverage, methods and resources involved. Briefings should cover any special features of the learning programme such as the mode of delivery, recommended learning methods, style of facilitation, location, attendance requirements, learning support, resources and facilities available, and any other essential information that candidates may need to help them when making up their mind about joining a programme.

| Training and development opportunities | |
|---|---|
| **Programmes** | **Resources** |
| Qualification structure | People (manpower) |
| Features of learning programmes | Time |
| Entry conditions | Finance |
| Attendance requirements | Materials |
| Time and place | Equipment |
| Mode of delivery | Facilities |
| Training methods | Resource centres |
| Learning methods | Work placements |

**Figure 2.1** *Characteristics of training and development opportunities*

Some important characteristics of training and development opportunities are given in Figure 2.1, and questions that teacher-candidates should be able to answer are:

- What is the qualification structure?
- What are the special features of the learning programmes?
- What are the entry conditions and attendance requirements?
- Where will the programme be based?
- What teaching and learning methods will be used?
- Who will be involved?
- What finance need be provided?
- What materials, equipment and facilities are required?

The quality of advice provided will depend upon the degree of care exercised when collecting and selecting information to be shared with candidates. Relying entirely on prospectuses and other paper-based resources may not alone provide a clear understanding of what is involved in operating the chosen programme, and there may be a need to visit workplaces to observe vocational applications or talk to supervisors and other teachers about what is involved.

*Where learners require more detailed information about learning programmes offered they are referred to the appropriate person*

Candidates seeking information about learning opportunities now expect to receive rather more personal attention than in the past, and if you or someone else in your organisation do not provide it a competitor will. That is the way things are going in education and training today. Competition for 'customers' is intense, and learning to give sufficiently detailed information is a skill forming part of the modern teacher's survival kit. If the teacher or advisor cannot personally provide the required level of information they must find out what the candidate wishes to know and either call in a knowledgeable colleague or send the candidate to someone who can provide help quickly.

Quite often people arrive with problems that cannot easily be resolved by the training provider. They may have particular **learning difficulties** and feel unsure about whether or not to join a training programme. One candidate may have **literacy problems** while **poor numeracy skills** may affect another. Some will have domestic problems and feel anxious or depressed. Others may have a drink, medication or drug-related problem that could affect their decision making or performance on assessment tests. In such instances teachers can **refer** people to either specialist in-house or external agencies who will be able to provide advice. The three main areas where candidates may need help are **educational guidance**, **personal guidance** and **vocational guidance**.

*Resources available and organisational requirements for the delivery of training and development opportunities are accurately identified*

Educational technology embraces any resource that is involved in the design and implementation of teaching and learning, and all that is involved in supporting the learning programme. The five M's cover resources that teachers may be called upon to identify when preparing learning opportunities: materials, machines, methods, milieu (learning environment) and manpower (personpower). The work of facilitators or teachers is currently described by some as **human resource inputs**! They represent the human capital in the form of energy, effort, skills, knowledge and competency that drives the learning programme. Providers should appoint suitable staff who are capable of meeting learner requirements, and should operate a staff development and training programme so as to maintain the quality of the service provided.

**Facilities** provide the means by which a training programme may be implemented, and include the resources needed to support the teacher and learners. However, the planned resource required to operate a perfect programme in the form of **finance**, **materials**, **equipment** and **contact hours** is not always forthcoming. Nowadays, fund-holders with their eye on the 'bottom line' will approve only the most cost-effective solution, and teachers may need to fall back on contingency plans. It is essential that resources available and organisational requirements for the delivery of training and development opportunities are accurately identified. Unrealistic propositions should be talked down and false expectations discouraged, as it would be damaging to raise candidate hopes and subsequently be unable to meet their expectations.

*Where learners require training and development which cannot be met by the organisation they are referred to appropriate alternative providers*

The financial incentive to keep down **unit costs** puts pressure on providers to fill all available places on every course offered. But there will be occasions when candidate requirements cannot properly be fulfilled, and the risk of promising the earth and building up unrealistic expectations during the sales pitch can be considerable. The higher you build candidate expectations the harder it becomes to meet them. In the end you or the system fail the candidate, they lose out and do not come back for more of the same and they tell their friends.

If training providers are not able to meet all candidates' learning needs they should be prepared to suggest one or more courses of action that could be taken. Having outlined possible alternatives the advisor should offer to **refer** or **direct** candidates to someone who meets their requirements. The advisor can be expected to offer only factual information and possibly the names of other providers. The course of action to be taken should be **decided by the candidate**.

## Identifying learning needs with individuals

*Individuals' views about their needs and suitable training and development opportunities are obtained*

The object of **identifying individual learning needs** or carrying out a **training needs analysis** is to identify, prioritise and agree learning needs with candidates. A suitable starting point for any educational or training proposition is the establishment of learners' requirements, and from the onset teachers should aim to develop a sympathetic relationship with candidates. Once a rapport is established and an atmosphere of cooperation prevails the matching of needs with development opportunities can go ahead.

In the past, provision was often heavily supply-led. A menu of courses was offered on a take it or leave it basis, rather than demand-led learning opportunities resulting from market research, data gathered from existing students or inquiries made by prospective customers. Some people have registered for training and development opportunities only to find later that the provision did not really meet their individual requirements. Others realised that they were going over old ground and quickly lost interest or found things too difficult or irrelevant to their needs and made their feelings known by voting with their feet or disrupting other learners.

The importance of the learner's role is recognised by the FAETC award design team, and the designation of units A22 'Identify individual learning needs' and C21 'Create a climate conducive to learning' as essential core units backed by optional unit C22 'Agree learning programmes with learners' reflects this view. This cluster of related units provides an opportunity for teacher-candidates to adopt an integrative approach to gathering evidence that will support claims for recognition of their competency in a number of units, rather than a hotchpotch of bits and pieces that they hope will fit in somewhere.

Matching individual needs and expectations with a personalised training programme is an essential ingredient in any successful learning proposition. The object of **ITN** and **initial assessment** is to help teachers and prospective learners sort out what it is they wish to achieve. Action plans can be produced, and relevant individualised training programmes based upon an analysis of learning need can be arranged.

Quite apart from socially derived needs relating to leisure-based activities and work-related demands, there will be candidates who are directed to the college or other training provider by businesses seeking to invest in training for their people. But whichever route is taken it is the candidate's needs, wants and requirements that matter, not the training provider's. Therefore in order to obtain the best match between what is requested and what is possible, the learning needs assessor will need to ask questions and listen very carefully to the candidate's views about their requirements.

Teachers will need to take account of strategic priorities for action to meet the challenges of the late 1990s that have been identified by the Government.[1] These include the need for businesses to invest in training and to take account of the fact that one million fewer under-25s will be available by 2001 whereas the 25–54 age group will increase by 1.6 million. This could mean that a greater proportion of older people will present themselves for training or upgrading, and their needs will probably differ from those of young people.

People will need help and advice in planning and developing skills to meet the needs of the economy as well as to achieve their own full potential. In this case the teacher will need to be able to encourage those without formal qualifications to take up the challenge of learning so as to help them make their way in life, find a job or satisfy social needs. Motivation might be further promoted by suggesting how self-esteem, status and personal development might be enhanced by accepting training opportunities on offer. There will also be a requirement to give guidance to others with qualifications who are seeking to become more competitive in the labour market by gaining related awards.

Candidates will appreciate advice on how to set about making the most of the chance to use their unfulfilled potential and so move their career along. The initial assessment session provides a setting in which to introduce the concept of being responsible for one's own learning outcomes and career development, and to assist candidates by offering a flexible programme that maximises learning opportunities.

*Identification of needs is based on valid and reliable assessment of all relevant information*

Many new learners will have acquired knowledge and skills either by private practice or experientially through day-to-day living or from work experience. For example, transferable skills may have derived, say, from using a spirit-level or plumb-bob, and these experiences could be formalised and authenticated when assessing a candidate's claims for NVQ credits on the basis of previous experience in the construction trade. Prior learning can be quickly accredited by arranging a 'live performance' or practical assessment that will permit the candidate to validate claims made. Oral assessment will reliably confirm the candidate's status of knowledge evidence against unit or award standards. This enables a better estimate to be obtained of the time needed to meet all NVQ criteria.

## Accreditation of prior learning

The identification of prior achievement is discussed in some detail in Chapter 12, and the City and Guilds definition of APL and guidance for tutors and candidates that now follows gives a clear picture of what is involved:

> The accreditation of a candidate's current competence, based upon evidence of past achievement or past demonstrations of competence. APL allows assessment and certification of competence without the need for candidates to undertake a formal period of study. This open access to assessment simply requires candidates to demonstrate their current competence. APL also allows candidates to put forward evidence of past achievements. This will mean that they will need to keep records of achievements. Current trends are moving towards achievements being kept in a personal portfolio with examples of reports, teaching notes, examples of materials, endorsements from employers and such like.[2]

A review of skills already owned and an estimate of learning needs may be carried out together with the teacher or by **self-analysis**. The analysis should preferably be carried out during the first meeting. Some people will be surprised when asked for their personal views, and for many this will be the first time in their life that they have been actively involved in making an assessment. They will expect to be told what they need to do and ready to take the medicine. Others may be confused because all they will know is that they want to go for a certain qualification and will feel unable to tell the teacher what they need to do about it. But building upon what they can already do will allow feelings of inadequacy to be swept away and a positive **self-image** formed.

## Establishing current achievement

Before writing a **training plan** or **scheme of work** it is necessary for teachers to identify the skills and knowledge required to meet **target award** criteria or the **job description**. This can be achieved either by referring to relevant NVQ units or by analysing the purpose, tasks and competencies needed to perform the job. Once the data is established the candidate's present level of competency can be compared with requirements, and the training needed to bridge the **training gap** identified. The chart given in Figure 2.2 shows the **identification of training needs** (ITN) process. The candidate's **learning needs** will reflect the training needs identified.

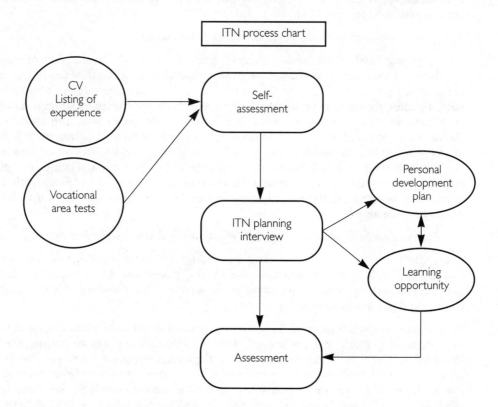

**Figure 2.2** *Flow chart: identifying needs*

In order to establish learning needs, self-assessment methods are often used supported by teacher-advisors who will help them prepare listings of experience, curriculum vitae (CVs) and reviews of prior experience and achievement that can be matched with target award criteria.

## Identifying individual and group needs

Once the interview or self-assessment has been completed it will be possible to agree realistic expectations and make an estimate of learning programme content and duration, although, as already suggested, it will be necessary to confirm any previous achievement claimed. A valid and objective assessment can only be made against a prepared **checklist of award criteria**. The difference between what new learners can do and what they need to learn to do is known as the **training gap**. Once the gap has been agreed, the next stage will be to establish a learning programme and create an **individual development plan** or action plan.

Before the ITN session is concluded, an action plan is agreed and recorded. The form and scope of the plan is a matter for negotiation, and content and context will vary according to the individual needs identified. Teachers should operate a system for managing learning need discussions, collecting relevant information, recording outcomes, categorising and prioritising learners' needs, and compiling reports and action plans. Action planning includes making arrangements for top-up training and where necessary facilitating individual or collaborative learning opportunities within a healthy and safe working environment. The planning process is summarised in Chapter 12, 'Advising and supporting candidates when identifying prior achievement' (see Figures 12.14 and 12.15).

*The use of the information obtained is clearly explained to individuals*

Once learning needs have been identified, information on the availability of training and development opportunities should be readily available to all candidates wishing to gain access to the provider's facilities. This is where an in-depth knowledge of available **learning opportunities**, results of **psychometric** or **selection tests** and the use of suitable **databases** can be helpful to those seeking to match individual requirements with provision. Candidate choices could then either be input to the database, or referred to programme coordinators or to accreditation of prior learning and achievement (APL) advisors who would be able to compare skills owned and skills required with a checklist of criteria relating to their chosen awards. Information gathered would be used to help candidates choose which learning opportunity would be in their best interest to pursue. Confidentiality of sensitive information would be maintained.

*Individuals are encouraged to feel comfortable to ask questions and express their views*

Every effort should be made to ensure that candidates feel at ease during ITN reviews and free to ask questions or clarify doubts. The review process should be carefully explained and interviewers should try to reduce anxiety and encourage candidates to identify current competence and self-assess against ITN criteria.

First impressions are important. How candidates feel about staff when calling at the assessment centre, reception or departmental office, or when telephoning or meeting them for the first time will influence their attitude toward them on subsequent meetings. This is very true when a person is contemplating spending a considerable sum on professional tuition and is also making a big investment in terms of their time. Besides seeking good value for money, candidates will be entitled to expect a friendly and enthusiastic reception. A better attitude will result when a little time is spent welcoming people and giving them a chance to settle down.

Candidates with particular learning difficulties or problems that cannot readily be resolved with the teacher during the initial assessment, and those needing help with organising themselves, may be referred to qualified people in the special needs unit, educational guidance and counselling unit, student support services or specialist training providers as appropriate.

*Identified learning needs and any initial recommendations on ways of meeting them are discussed and agreed with individuals*

Teacher-advisors need to be well prepared for discussions with candidates. A possible starting point could involve **clarifying roles** and developing **trust**. The element of trust is essential to any relationship and should be established before making any recommendations that could affect a candidate's personal or career development. Then follows **confidence building** achieved by **showing respect** for the candidate, making sure that they are not kept waiting and greeting them using the right name!

Thorough **preparation** is an essential prerequisite for successful negotiation. In order to establish credibility and to avoid a nerve-racking experience, teachers who are new to the advisor role should have all necessary information concerning learning opportunities and candidate training needs at their fingertips. Supporting material, brochures and needs analysis should be available for reference if needed.

Once pleasantries have been exchanged, and without appearing too familiar, teacher-advisors should ensure that requirements are clearly described and confirmed. Time-wasting is avoided, and once the discussion is opened a logical sequence is followed in order to reach agreement. Any new information is shared and possible choices of action are assessed. The candidate's attention is directed towards any suggestions or recommendations on ways of meeting their learning needs. Solutions are specified, probable costs are estimated and a way forward agreed. Action plans are sometimes completed on the spot.

When formulating strategies and making recommendations such as those given in Figure 2.3, teachers should be able to:

- behave professionally throughout the interaction
- clarify their own role, and their candidates'
- show respect to their candidates by:
  - greeting them politely
  - addressing them correctly by name
  - recognising their rights and entitlement
  - giving them a fair hearing
- establish rapport and trust
- clarify learning opportunities offered
- negotiate and confirm candidate requirements
- agree a mutually acceptable course of action.

| Strategies | Recommendations |
|---|---|
| Address the client by name | Agree learning requirements |
| Clarify roles | Describe clearly |
| Show respect | Assess possibilities |
| Establish rapport and trust | Specify possible solutions |
| Be confident | Estimate costs |
| Be business-like | Agree way forward |

**Figure 2.3** *Recommending ways of meeting identified needs*

## Non-discriminatory practice

Everyone involved in education and training should uphold the principles of **equal opportunities** and best **non-discriminatory practice**. They should be willing to try very hard to make arrangements for meeting candidates' individual needs and assessment requirements, and they should strive to break down personal and structural barriers obstructing access to learning opportunities.

Teachers may need to develop provision for candidates with **special learning requirements**, and provide equal opportunities with respect to social and religious background, ethnic or national origin, marital status, intellectual or physical capacity, age and gender. Care must be taken to avoid **harassment**, **sex discrimination** and **sexist stereotyping**. In some cases there has been a lack of adequate provision for learners with disabilities, and insufficient thought is given to compensating for serious and minor handicaps and temporary indispositions.

Where a candidate has a handicap that hampers or hinders learning, or a physical disability or disadvantage resulting from either physical or intellectual **impairment**, it may be possible to adapt the learning opportunity so as to overcome the difficulty or provide help to assist cognitive or motor learning. Teachers will certainly be expected to take account of learners' needs and where possible to modify their plans and give advice and relevant guidance.

An **illiterate** person is either unable to read or write or incapable of attaining the standard of reading and writing required for a given purpose. Illiteracy does not mean that a person is 'uneducated' in worldly matters or that they are ignorant or uncultured, but they will need the teacher's help. In the case of new learners the teacher may be required to give help directly or arrange language support for those needing it. This is because new learners will need to meet adequately language requirements pertaining to their chosen learning programme. People can be easily offended if criticised about their written work, and teachers must react in a sensitive manner when seeking to help those affected.

**Dyslexia is** also known as 'word blindness'. It is the name given to an impaired ability to read. Dyslexia is neither caused by nor associated with low intelligence or stupidity and does not reflect a person's IQ. In formal academic situations and when sitting written examinations candidates may be allocated a 'reader' who reads the questions aloud to them. In such cases the examining board concerned must be contacted well in advance so that necessary arrangements may be made to accommodate the candidate.

Teachers should be prepared to suggest ways and means by which illiterate and dyslexic candidates may familiarise themselves with curriculum content and be able to cope with essential written and oral work. Special needs staff can normally diagnose significant **difficulties** in learning and **written communication** and can usually offer specialist support to those who require it.

## Interviewing

Candidates will expect the ITN advisor to be in a position to help them satisfy their learning needs, and if a planning interview cannot be arranged immediately they will appreciate an early appointment. Several important factors should be borne in mind by the advisor when conducting interviews. They are the need to:

- actively listen to the candidate
- give valid information
- use suitable language
- use a range of questioning techniques

- test understanding
- summarise
- agree achievable targets
- maintain confidentiality
- arrange a follow-up meeting.

*Identified learning needs are prioritised and agreed with individuals*

Some learners tend to work very hard doing unproductive things. Some are brimming with energy, impulsive and get going quickly without paying attention to what really needs to be done. When things go wrong they blame others, are quickly distracted and appear not to listen to what team members are saying. Some spend too much time working on detail and as a result miss the big picture. In circumstances such as these, teachers can usefully intervene by suggesting possible courses of action for the learner to consider. A sensible approach to coping with learning needs might be to suggest well-proven time-management techniques such as **prioritising workload** in terms of urgency and importance. Learning opportunities can then be used to best effect when gathering evidence and organising assessments, leading to the successful completion of tasks and enhanced organisational skills.

In order to work more effectively it is helpful for learners to be clear about their learning needs and the tasks and evidence gathering that confront them. Once known, the tasks will be rated for **urgency** and **importance** and then **prioritised** taking account of what **must** be done, what **should** be done and what **could** be done. People new to the NVQ system are unlikely to be able to manage this process alone, especially in the early stages of programmes. This is where teachers acting as advisors can help candidates organise their workload and undertake the top-up training needed to bridge the learning gap.

The teacher's role is to work with their candidate so as to:

- establish current learning needs
- consider how best to enable anticipated needs to be met
- match requirements to available learning opportunities
- arrange necessary top-up training
- support the learner throughout the learning process.

*Initial recommendations on ways of meeting the identified learning needs are passed on to the appropriate people*

In many instances the ITN interviewer role is taken by the course tutor or class teacher. When teachers are working with new learners the most acceptable way of meeting individual and group needs is decided by consensus, preferably before the group assembles for the first time. If an early review is not possible, a tutorial or needs analysis should take place as soon as possible after the initial lesson and again as the course progresses. If advice cannot be given quickly it will probably be too late for learners to opt out of unsuitable programmes and they will be left to make the most of the learning opportunities presented.

People using assessment centres for their ITN reviews will be seen by the provider's specialist advisors who will generate some kind of review document or training and assessment action plan. Copies of ITN documents will be passed to course team leaders who will make the relevant information available to teachers that are in a position to induct the learners concerned and provide further advice and support. Partially trained people will be seen by occupational area assessors who will accredit existing competence.

### Creating personal action plans

During the ITN or initial assessment session a **developmental action plan** may be negotiated that is designed to meet the candidate's present aspirations. The plan gives details of previous experience and achievement and describes how the learner will attain long-term aims and shorter term objectives. Being individually negotiated, the plan lists groupings of compatible learning objectives for each phase of the proposed training programme and a progressive route towards meeting assessment requirements. Obviously, the key long-term aim will be to meet all award performance criteria and accomplish any complementary self-set goals, while shorter term objectives may concern achieving particular elements or units of an NVQ. But teachers will probably agree that learning and achievement does not always go according to plan and it will therefore be necessary to review progress continuously and update the developmental action plan.

A typical planning form is given in Figure 2.4 (see *Documents Pack*) but more detail about action planning is given in Chapter 12, where a suggested procedure for agreeing an action plan with a candidate is outlined in Figure 12.14 and an alternative action plan format is given in Figure 12.15.

An explanation of what is needed to meet assessment performance standards could be given together with an outline of what the candidate needs to do to meet the requirements. Spelling out specific performance criteria in great detail would probably overload and unnerve the candidate and this is best left to later sessions.

If an action plan is produced the teacher will need to check that the content, timing and sequence of learning opportunities agreed will in fact give the best match between the learner's needs and their current status.

*Records are correctly completed and stored in a suitable manner*

The training provider is normally responsible for maintaining relationships with vocational qualification awarding bodies and for arranging for the certification of candidate achievements. Candidates will need to keep their own records and maintain **portfolios** holding evidence gathered. A **training diary** is a personal record of daily events such as work experience and off-the-job training. It can be used as a **formative record** of achievements. Achievement records, log books and diaries enable claims for competence to be checked against award criteria to ensure that candidates have reached the required standard. Entries should be made regularly and examined by the teacher concerned. Awarding body representatives will need to examine records and assessment reports before awards are recommended.

| **Learner records consist of:** | |
|---|---|
| ITN analyses | Log books |
| APL assessments | Diaries |
| Initial assessments | Reviews |
| Training programmes | Award body registrations |
| Action plans | Examination entries |
| Skills tests | Certificates |

**Figure 2.5** *Examples of learner records*

Teachers will be expected to keep records of learners' achievements, and some government-sponsored training schemes insist on this. Elsewhere records are kept of staff skills, qualifications, training and achievements which are used when carrying out skills audits or ITN interviews. Care should be taken to operate within the provisions of the **Data Protection Act 1984.** Some records may be classified as **confidential** and copies will be marked 'confidential' but will be read by all and sundry given the slightest opportunity. When given the responsibility to maintain candidate records teachers need to do better than this. In order to **avoid leakage** of information to people who are not entitled to know, it may be necessary to communicate information on, say, special learning requirements by word of mouth only. Learners can be very sensitive about their weaknesses or difficulties and easily become embarrassed if their personal secrets become general knowledge. Teachers are entrusted with knowledge about their candidates' affairs and learners must be made to feel that they can be sure that their confidences are not broken.

## Self-assessment questions

### Identifying available learning and support opportunities

1 List the range of qualification and non-certificated programmes you are concerned with.

2 For each programme specify the:

- entry requirements
- costs: tuition fees, registration and certification fees
- location: time, place
- attendance requirements/flexible learning opportunities
- modes of delivery
- training methods used
- facilities and resources available to teachers
- facilities and resources available to learners

3 What is meant by learner entitlement?

4 Can you recite your employer's mission? Obtain a copy of the training provider's mission statement and establish whether or not there is a commitment to its fulfilment.

5 What is meant by an 'open access policy'?

6 Explain what is meant by operating an 'equal opportunities' policy.

7 Where can your learners obtain more information about the following:

- advice on courses offered
- skills assessment and aptitude testing
- careers and higher education advice
- information on grants and welfare rights
- confidential guidance and counselling
- guidance support and advice for learners with special needs
- educational guidance for adults.

8 What is meant by the term 'referral'?

### Identification of learning needs

9 Identify the benefits that teachers and learners can derive from the ITN process.

10 Suggest methods of identifying learning requirements.

11 Explain how to put candidates at ease during an ITN interview.

12 List the range of interviewing and questioning techniques that could be used during an ITN session.

13  Explain the importance of using appropriate language when interacting with candidates.

14  Explain how candidates can be provided with clear and accurate information on the principles and implementation of the identification of training needs.

15  Explain how carrying out an ITN could help teachers and learners clarify learning needs and create achievable action plans. Examine your learners' action plans and check that the plan content and learning sequence give the best match between learners' needs and learning opportunities available.

16  Describe the system for recording, categorising and prioritising individual and/or organisational needs that is operating in your department.

17  How could ongoing analysis of learners' needs be implemented in your own workplace?

18  Describe how positive action can be taken to ensure that both sexes are treated fairly in terms of equal opportunity and avoidance of sex discrimination when identifying and allocating available learning opportunities.

19  How is feedback obtained about the suitability of learning programme content, activities offered and methods used to present the programme?

20  What is the value of keeping records of ITN outcomes and why is it necessary to store the records securely?

## Preparing for assessment: sample activities

### Activity 2.1 Identifying training and development opportunities

Survey the range of training and development programmes that are available for candidates seeking learning opportunities in your occupational area. Consider organisational requirements associated with the programmes and characteristics applying to the programmes. Write a summary of your findings and include information about:

● entry conditions
● enrolment procedures and fees
● registration, assessment and certification procedures and associated fees
● facilities and equipment available within the provider's premises
● resources and materials supplied by the training provider
● resources to be provided by the candidate
● time, place and location of course and/or work experience opportunities
● duration of programme
● facilitator inputs, methods used and learning opportunities
● support services provided.

Present your report as supplementary evidence for assessment against Unit A22 criteria.

### Activity 2.2 Identifying and agreeing individual training needs

A **training (learning) needs analysis** is carried out in order to obtain up-to-date information about a candidate's current competency and to establish their personal learning needs. Using data collected the training gap can be identified and suitable personal development opportunities provided, backed by effective training. Define and discuss each of the steps that should be taken in order to identify the training needs of individuals. Suggested steps are listed below but please add any others you consider necessary.

**Suggested steps**
- Identify the individual or candidate group concerned.
- Explain the ITN procedure to candidates.
- Clarify expectations and aspirations.
- Using established procedures (or by writing your own), carry out the ITN based on priorities and current and anticipated demands relating to the learner's role.
- Collect the necessary data.
- Analyse findings.
- Identify the 'training gap'.
- Identify suitable training and development opportunities and establish their conditions and characteristics.
- Identify suitable alternative providers if facilities are not available in-house.
- Write a report or prepare and agree with learners individual action plans.

Prepare a report covering each step. Add any points raised and comments made during the discussion. Include in your report a description of how you carried out the training needs analyses and how the activity was or could be integrated with other teaching roles. Add conclusions and recommendations about how current ITN arrangements could be improved.

Note: An effective training strategy could then be created that would enable initial training, top-up training or updating to be provided taking account of the individual's personal development objectives or group needs and priorities. Progress would be monitored and outcomes evaluated.

## Activity 2.3 Identifying group learning needs
Time is a valuable resource and sometimes providing individual reviews for all is not a feasible proposition. Identifying whole-group learning needs is a more cost-effective method of establishing principal learning requirements although individual reviews may reveal additional special requirements. Teacher-advisors will need to manage both individual and group ITN sessions effectively.

Prepare and present a plan for reviewing learning needs for a new group that you expect to teach. Include in your plan details of:

- a briefing session
- how candidates' role descriptions and curriculum vitae (CVs) can be used
- a variety of self-assessment activities
- how special requirements will be established
- a review of results
- a question and answer session
- a portfolio-building and assessment workshop.

Include in your evidence portfolio a briefing sheet that you have used or intend to use when introducing group ITN sessions and an information handout for your candidates to take away with them after the briefing. Gather samples of self-assessment instruments, written or computer-based tests and samples of any other evidence you have used or collected from candidates during group ITN reviews.

Write a report outlining any other methods of identifying learning needs and how training and development opportunities can be matched with learning needs taking account of the need to maintain non-discriminatory practices.

## Activity 2.4 Initial self-assessment
Read the performance criteria, range statements and evidence requirements for Unit D32 or another unit of your choice, consider what is involved and reflect upon what you already know about each element. Consider what you think you can do and what you will need to do to meet requirements.

List the evidence you already have and the evidence you will need to gather, and specify your training/learning needs. Discuss with your tutor, advisor or supervisor a strategy for collecting the evidence and preparing yourself for assessment.

## Notes

1  *Labour Market and Skill Trends 1992/93 (SEN 32)*, Employment Department Group, Sheffield 1991, pp. 3–6.

2  City and Guilds *7306 Further and Adult Education Teachers Certificate (NVQ) Centre Pack*, September 1993, p. 10. The Centre Pack and Candidate Packs are available from the City and Guilds of London Institute, 1 Giltspur Street, London EC1A 9DD.

# Key Role B
## Organising and resourcing learning opportunities

# 3

## Designing training and development sessions

The importance of careful planning lies in the benefits to be derived from providing training and development sessions that fulfil the needs and expectations of the individuals, sponsors and awarding bodies concerned. The aim of the planning process is to decide on a strategy that will enable vocational and developmental needs to be met. Information about the knowledge, skills and procedures involved in the tasks to be performed, together with a range of possible options for delivering the training, is absolutely essential when designing training and development sessions.

Identifying effective options for training and development sessions requires skill in matching opportunities with candidates' preferred learning styles. An approach to learning has been proposed by David Kolb, who described a model of learning which suggests that learning, change and growth are facilitated by an integrated process. His work on **experiential learning**[1] suggests that all prior learning is brought to bear on new experiences, and the Kolb Circle represents a **cyclical learning process** comprising four stages: **concrete experience, reflective observation, abstract conceptualisation** and **active experimentation**. Learners can enter the process at any stage. For example, learners could commence with the phase of concrete experience during which learning takes place by actual involvement in some kind of activity. This is followed by thinking about what happened, clarifying outcomes and examining products or processes involved. Then follows an analysis of the learning experience which leads to the formation of conclusions and understanding of the concepts involved. In turn these concepts and conclusions can be used to change existing behaviour or to devise new experiences which will lead to the fourth stage, that of active experimentation aimed at testing the theory or ideas formed and evaluating a new direct experience.

Kolb's theory suggests that as learners develop they learn by all the stages described above, but are likely to develop a preference for learning by one of the methods involved and thus a preferred learning style is developed. With this in mind teachers will need to select methods that will allow all phases of the learning cycle to take place. It is well known that we all have preferred learning styles and that a training method welcomed by one person may not suit another. However, it is likely that learning styles relating to the stages proposed by Kolb will accommodate all preferences. Teachers when planning their programmes must therefore be aware of the ways learners may choose to learn. This could mean providing new experiences, encouraging reflection on the concrete experiences provided, presenting theoretical inputs, arranging 'learning by doing' activities that will promote further experimentation, or a mix of all. At this point it would be useful for readers to turn to Activity 3.7 and consider how different teaching methods could be used for the different sections of Kolb's cycle and how the methods suggested might be applied when developing their own teaching strategies.

The implications of using available delivery methods must be understood and the best option selected. Training and development sessions can be based on lesson plans which specify aims and objectives, take account of needs and wants and include a variety of methods and resources. The plans should maximise opportunities for individual and group activities.

Teachers will need to utilise resources effectively when implementing the programme, monitoring progress, using checks of learning to assess achievement, evaluating outcomes and feeding back necessary changes to curriculum designers.

# Identifying options for training and development sessions

*The requirements of the training and development session are clearly and accurately identified*

Before creating a scheme of work or an individual learning programme teachers need to sort out exactly what has to be done. If teachers are not sure of where they are leading learners at the outset, outcomes will be variable and learners will become confused and demotivated. A suitable starting point is identifying learner requirements. Once these are known relevant session aims can be defined.

## Aims and objectives

An **aim** is a broad statement of intent and is the first step in planning a session programme. It is a non-specific guideline that relates to overall strategy rather than to detailed specifications. Once programme aims are known, **teaching objectives** can be established and **learning objectives** can be written outlining what the learner is expected to be able to do in order to demonstrate learning or particular competences. Aims and objectives can be derived from sources such as syllabuses or qualification criteria, task analyses, ITN reviews, business training briefs or candidates' job specifications and job descriptions. Alternatively NVQ/SVQ-type performance criteria that are written in purely behavioural terms can be consulted. Having established what needs to be covered teachers can give consideration to session design. Choosing the best option for presenting the session requires a knowledge of the learners' preferred learning styles.

## Learning styles

Widely ranging methods for delivering training sessions are available to teachers but skill in selecting the method best suited to a group of learners will have a considerable effect on the quality of learning they derive from the experience. Choosing the best method involves knowledge of group composition, learning characteristics and individual learning styles. Learning styles are the ways in which people process new concepts and acquire new skills, and **preferred learning styles** could be satisfied by plans that include one or more of the activities shown in Figure 3.1. Activities should be identified that are relevant to learners' perceived needs and that will promote enjoyable and effective learning. Presentations should allow for learner behaviour ranging from making **impulsive** snap decisions to abstract thinking and **reflective** measured consideration of tasks set.

Many learners prefer to tackle learning that involves hands-on activity. For them 'seeing is believing', and using their senses, handling items, smelling, making things work and doing things will best suit their way of learning. With this in mind teachers could arrange suitable **concrete experiences** that will enable learners to recall and repeat the activity later.

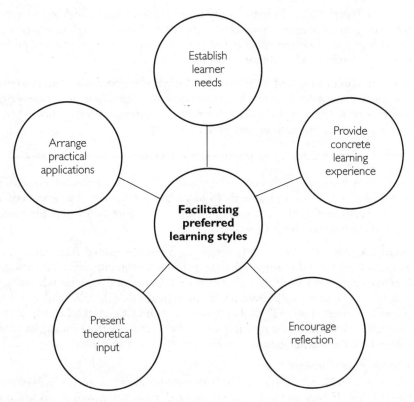

**Figure 3.1** *Devising a training and development strategy*

Some learners enjoy learning by **reflection.** They will relish the prospect of reviewing abstract problems and considering what has happened during a case study, demonstration or experiment. Using the processes of analysis, synthesis and evaluation they will try to make sense of results, and the benefit obtained from sharing feedback on outcomes with others will reinforce learning and help satisfy their needs. Academically inclined learners will probably prefer intellectual work based mainly on **theoretical inputs** concerned with laws, rules, principles and pure science rather than applied vocational studies.

**Practical applications** of languages, theories and simulations could be just what is needed by learners who share some or all of the other options mentioned above. Alternatively, **problem solving** calling for a mix of cognitive, affective and psychomotor skills could present the best means of suiting the majority of learner preferences while allowing positive attitudes, interpersonal communication skills, physical skills and powers of reasoning to be developed.

*A range of options for delivering the training and development session are accurately identified*

Teaching and learning options fall under two main headings: **teacher-centred** methods based on exposition, direction and control of activities, and **learner-centred** methods whereby individuals are involved in a personalised system of learning and are expected to take a fair degree of responsibility for identifying and agreeing targets, planning and implementing their learning activities and reviewing accomplishment with the programme facilitator.

Individuals may use resource-based learning techniques including computer programmes, discovery learning or distance learning. They may be working on assignments or 'off-college' on work experience, field trips, study tours or visits. **Teamworking** may be employed during seminars and human relations case study workshops. There are many methods available to choose from and teachers must either select the method themselves or preferably enlist the aid of group members when making the choice.

A mix of **student-centred activities** and formal classroom teaching is used by many teachers. The most widely used methods include action-centred learning, brainstorming, case studies and role-play, lecturing and skills instruction, demonstrations followed by practice and one-to-one coaching, simulations and exercises.

*Options are matched against all relevant factors and the most appropriate ones selected*

Differences between groups of learners and their learning characteristics will affect the choice of teaching and learning methods to be employed. Group size, unit content or syllabus and learning context are other important factors to consider when matching teaching and learning methods to programme requirements.

Adult learners will have widely ranging experience gained from informal learning activities or periods of formal study, and their prior achievements may be considerable or minimal. **Teacher-dependent** learners will at first tend to become anxious when asked to share responsibility for planning their own route through the NVQ maze and gathering their evidence. Given the chance they will probably opt for a **didactic** method of teaching where the teacher instructs, gives directions and passes on facts and information rather than for a **facilitative** style where the teacher acts as a catalyst, supporter and helper.

### Teaching large groups
When teaching large groups the **lecture method** might be the only feasible way of presenting information. If this method is contemplated motivation and attention must be maintained throughout. Because of the limitations of short-term memory only the bare essentials should be presented, in a logical sequence backed up with a handout, linkage with prior learning and other activities and a follow-up assignment or task. Changes in presentational method including the use of audio-visual resources, energisers and frequent short breaks should be planned. For effective learning, reinforcement and opportunities for transferring information to long-term memory must be implemented.

### Teaching small groups
Small groups, pairs and tutorials encourage the development of interpersonal relationships, active participation, cooperation and teamworking when tackling tasks set. Face-to-face contact enhances the effectiveness of communication and quality of discussion. The teaching role is supportive rather than didactic, taking the form of **facilitator** and group manager. This option is suitable for many learning activities but particularly for case studies, role-plays, problem solving, brainstorming and other **learner-centred group tasks** involving discussions, preparing reports and giving feedback during a plenary session.

### Teaching practical work
Training for vocational occupations and NVQs/SVQs can involve much **practical work**, often requiring observed **live performances** during related assessments. Wherever possible practical work should include elements of discovery learning, self-instruction or experiential learning. Work should be **learner-controlled** allowing activities, material and resources to be utilised at a rate to suit each learner. Learning opportunities should be negotiable and flexible, with plenty of 'hands-on' experience using facilities provided but with teacher demonstrations, coaching, feedback and guidance available when called for. Options for practical training sessions include negotiating projects that involve specific occupational area skills and writing up a final report.

### Teaching in workshops and laboratories

Conducting experiments and working in laboratories forms an integral part of engineering, science and craft-related occupational training programmes. The object of these activities is to encourage learning through **practical experience** by carrying out investigations, pursuing scientific inquiry, discovering relationships, confirming theories, promoting inventiveness and gathering data about innovations.

Options for training sessions include using equipment and developing new skills in handling apparatus in a safe environment so as to understand its purpose and functions and become competent in its usage; using experiments to develop an understanding of underlying principles by applying theory to practice and evaluating results; and carrying out experimental investigations or research projects. Activities should include selecting the methods to be used, planning work schedules, obtaining results and presenting conclusions and recommendations.

*Selected options are suitable to the needs of learners*

Learners' needs will vary considerably as will their innate intelligence, ability and motivation to learn. With this in mind teachers when selecting training options should take account of the degree of relevance of the chosen method to the needs of those concerned. Quite apart from deciding how best to help learners acquire the vocational skills to be learned teachers could consider learner characteristics that may affect the choice of method.

The **capacity to learn** will depend to some extent on the degree of common sense displayed, level of abstract thinking and all-round mental ability, the learning environment and everything and everyone that the learner comes in contact with. A learner's ability to **identify** with other group members, to fit in and to adopt their standards of behaviour will be affected by the **methods employed**. People have different attention spans, and using an unsuitable training option could easily lead to day-dreaming and complete loss of interest.

The learning activity selected can itself serve as a powerful **incentive** to achieve or it can result in feelings of unworthiness. The training option selected and learning process adopted should therefore take account of learner characteristics, the range of learners' needs identified and the learning outcomes desired.

*Resources needed for the different options are accurately specified*

When selecting resources for use in a training session it is necessary to consider how their use could benefit the learners. Once the aid best suited to the particular learning objective has been chosen it is necessary to look at the environment in which the aid will be presented and consider the desirability and feasibility of using the aid in that location. Key resources that may be needed include people, materials, equipment and other facilities. (See Figure 3.2.)

### People

Probably the most important resources within a training organisation are the people who work there. They provide the know-how, creativity and skills, commitment and energy to make training opportunities a successful and rewarding experience for learners. People who could be consulted when choosing training options include course team-leaders, other teachers, assessors, technicians, support staff and the learners themselves.

### Materials and equipment

The training programme is delivered by teachers, trainers and non-teaching staff who will need resources to support their inputs. Training aids can supplement other forms of presenta-

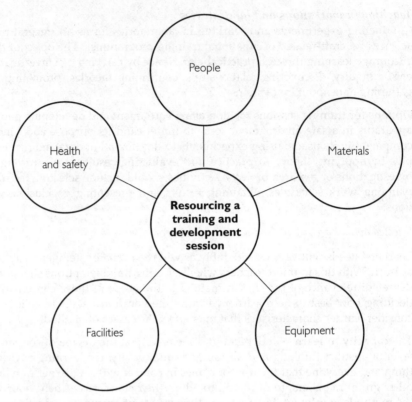

**Figure 3.2** *Resourcing a training and development session*

tion and enhance the process of perception and retention. Planned usage of teaching and learning resources increases the scope and coverage of learning opportunities.

Resources and materials used by teachers when presenting inputs or facilitating learning are known as **teaching aids**. Aids include various types of boards, overhead projectors and transparencies, computers, video, film and slide projectors, teaching packs and other commercially produced printed materials.

Any aids used by learners to help them learn or enhance the quality of their learning experiences and achievements are known as **learning resources.** Distance-learning packages, correspondence course materials, textbooks, computer programs, assignments, project specifications and handouts are examples of commonly used learning materials.

### Facilities
Facilities supporting a learning environment include labour, money, materials, accommodation and equipment; and systems for maintaining training programmes, information flows, skills assessment, learning resources and work placements. Student services, counsellors and administrative staff can be called upon for help when needed.

### Health and safety
A **safe workplace** is a place that is free from danger and that affords security and protection from harm. Teachers will need to identify potential **hazards** in the environment where they and their learners will be working and **eliminate** or **control** any hazard found.

Fire, accident and emergency procedures should be reviewed and all facilities checked for serviceability. **Protective clothing** and equipment must be provided and should be worn whenever necessary. The maintenance of **good housekeeping** and occupational **hygiene** is also important in order to avoid diseases such as skin complaints.

It is the **duty of teachers** and their learners while at work or in other learning places to cooperate with employers to enable any duty placed on those employers by the provisions in the **Health and Safety at Work Act** to be complied with.

### Resource implications for different delivery modes

Today's **resource constraints** mean that training budgets will be subjected to close scrutiny and that there is not now available, for example, an unlimited supply of textbooks, photocopies or consumables. Resource consumption must be controlled and if possible reduced. Such is the effect of the one-line budget that many providers are now working to.

This scenario suggests that teachers when specifying resources for a given option could usefully bear in mind the following requirements:

- The effectiveness of teaching or learning must be improved by using the resources specified.
- The use of a particular aid must be justified.
- The chosen resource must be relevant to learners' needs and programme objectives.
- The resource must be of a suitable standard.
- Sufficient resources in terms of people, money and time should be available to all learners.
- The planned resource should result in a cost-effective solution to the learner's need that it is intended to satisfy.
- The resources employed should meet health and safety regulations.
- All resources should be fit for the intended purpose.

*Selected options are confirmed with the appropriate people*

Contact must be maintained with programme managers and other course team members, and an agreed range of feasible options offered. Support staff are busy people and they too must plan their workload, so supervisors controlling resource centres and support services will need to be consulted in good time. Specialist rooms, workshops, laboratories, studios, teaching resources and technician help must be booked well in advance and caretakers advised of any special requirements or non-standard access to buildings. If a portfolio workshop is contemplated the availability of vocational assessors should be confirmed. The aim should be to look ahead and to have **contingency plans** if things do not go according to expectations.

## Designing training and development sessions for learners

Planning and organising suitable training and assessment can be crucial to outcomes in the form of learner attainment. Teachers should therefore be able to plan training programmes and produce lesson plans for given situations, adapting the plans as necessary to suit prevailing circumstances. Training plans for learning sessions will be designed to meet specific purposes whether they serve organisational or individual learner needs. Course teams will collectively have sufficient expertise to fulfil identified needs, and once these are known plans can be developed. At the planning stage the key design features shown in Figure 3.3 must be considered when deciding on the choice of method to be employed and also whether a single facilitator or a team-teaching approach could be used.

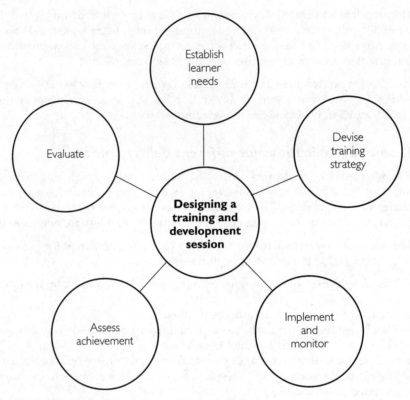

**Figure 3.3** *Designing a training and development session for learners*

## Session planning system

Before a learning programme can be produced it is advisable to consider a strategy that will be adopted for the training as a whole. This is where a design system can be helpful. A layout that could be used as a basis for programme design is given in Figure 3.4.

Planning may involve making decisions about some or all of the following:

- programme content and performance criteria
- methods and activities
- duration of training and length of lessons
- timetable of activities
- briefing of learners
- availability and preparation of resources
- assessment criteria and methods
- monitoring and evaluation of training outcomes.

*Aims and objectives of the training and development are clearly specified*

Starting points for learning programmes are training specifications, syllabuses or award performance criteria. Having an extensive knowledge of the required behaviour, conditions and standards implied will enable the teacher to derive lists of **relevant competences, aims** and **objectives.** Whatever training is proposed, there will be a need to work toward the achievement of **performance criteria** or specified learning aims and objectives. Once these have been

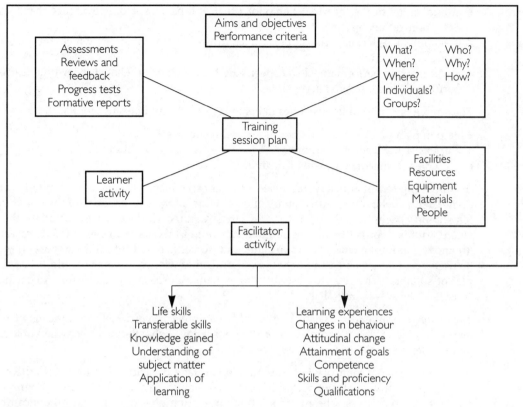

**Figure 3.4** *Session planning system*

identified and negotiated, the training programme can be planned and a scheme of work written. Learning methods, lesson plans, assessments, profiling and learner support can then be developed. The effectiveness of the training and learning programme can be measured against criteria by assessing the learner's ability to meet programme aims, perform behaviour described by learning objectives and demonstrate competences.

## *Writing aims and objectives*

Aims and objectives should be stated simply and concisely and should sum up what is the **intended outcome** in terms of **benefit to the learner.** Many teachers do not realise that the purpose of learner-centred objectives is to move the focus away from what the teacher will do to what the students will learn, and so they undervalue them.

The negotiated curriculum methodology now in place would seem to confirm the need for early and comprehensive discussion with learners when jointly establishing objectives for a particular training programme. Objectives should undoubtedly reflect the learners' identified needs and should be valid in terms of desired outcomes of the learning programme for which they are written.

### *Objectives*

An **objective** describes precisely what the **learner** is expected to be able to do, in order to demonstrate learning. Behavioural objectives may contain up to three component parts:

- an indication of the **terminal behaviour** that will be accepted as evidence that the learner has attained the objective
- a statement describing the important **conditions** (if any) under which the behaviour is expected to occur
- the acceptable performance level specifying how well or to what **standard** the learner must perform to be considered acceptable.

The advantages of stating objectives in behavioural or activity terms are that they:

- help in planning delivery, methodology and resources
- emphasise the learners' activities
- provide a means of evaluating learning.

In expressing terminal behaviour when writing objectives, teachers should avoid words that do not define behaviour clearly, or are open to wide interpretation. Each of the objectives written should specify exactly what the learner is required to do in order to satisfy the aim or award criteria. Words that do not define behaviour clearly should be avoided. Phrases such as 'to know', 'to understand', 'to appreciate' and 'to believe' fall into this category; they cannot be used accurately to measure behavioural outcomes. Concrete verbs should be used. Examples of suitable terms are: 'to describe', 'to explain', 'to select', 'to compare', 'to calculate', 'to construct', 'to solve', or 'to list'.

These are recommended because terminal behaviour can be measured in terms of what the learner is able to do on completion of the instruction. Behaviour will be observable and will **validate** learners' claims to skill ownership.

From the learners' point of view, the main advantage of strict behavioural objectives is that they know exactly what is expected of them and they can evaluate their own progress against the specified objectives. The main point about writing objectives is that others can obtain a clear picture of what the outcome of learning is to be. Unnecessary detail should be excluded from the objective. Only those elements that are required to describe all intended outcomes should be written into the statement.

*Examples of correctly stated objectives*
The following examples relating to driving training contain some or all of the three component parts that may constitute an objective:

- The instructor will be able to supervise and direct a learner driver in the safe and correct execution of: starting the engine, operating the clutch and using appropriate gear to move off and drive forward, giving appropriate signals and making all-round observation.
- The learner will be able to bring the vehicle to rest from a speed of 50 mph within a stopping distance of not more than 53 metres.
- The learner will be able to specify the current national speed limits applying to all roads unless signs show otherwise when driving a car in:
  a) built-up areas
  b) single carriageways
  c) dual carriageways
  d) motorways.
- The learner will be able to describe two main dangers at a road accident.
- The instructor will be able to demonstrate how to deal effectively with a front-wheel skid when driving an unladen 12-metre coach on the skid pan.

*Opportunities for meeting learning needs are clearly specified*

In a business context, **training specifications** are prepared after jobs have been studied. Careful consideration is given to the content and skills needed to carry out the work. Skills involved are listed and the work is broken down into mini-tasks. A sequence of activity is then drawn up. Key break points and areas of possible difficulty are noted, together with details of standards, resources to be used, safety factors, checks and quality assurance requirements. A **task analysis**, which may be as detailed as necessary, is then produced. It itemises the knowledge and practical 'doing' skills involved in carrying out the task effectively and at the right standard. From the data recorded, a training specification is written and an efficient learning programme is then designed. The procedure described above can also be applied to analysing any task and identifying the knowledge and skills elements involved. (See Figures 8.1, p. 106, and 9.1, in the *Documents Pack*.)

## Scheme of work

A **scheme of work** is a planning document that gives information about the syllabus and programme of lessons. Sometimes teachers add broad aims and performance criteria but these are often written into individual lesson plans. Other factors that may be included in the document are:

- **organisational details** such as location, appointments, lesson duration, programme information, training content, sequence, availability of resources, aids and equipment, and the staff and learners involved
- **methods of facilitating** and making the best use of learning opportunities
- **assessment** and evaluation methods, assessment documentation and feedback methods.

Teachers should be able to design a scheme of work that outlines in a logical sequence the way in which they and their learners working together may best cover the work that is to be learned and the skills that must be demonstrated. When drawing up the outline plan teachers will need to bear in mind the nature of the learner or group of learners, training content, performance criteria, timing and duration of lessons, reviews, guidance sessions and assessment procedures. Teachers will need to integrate their individual topic areas with those of other course team members.

It is not easy to think of a topic that will be known to all readers, but as many will be familiar with the Highway Code it will used as the subject for a lesson plan. The sample scheme of work and lesson plan shown in Figures 3.5 and 3.6 (see *Documents Pack*) will hopefully serve as useful examples when readers are writing planning documents for their own specialism.

The scheme of work specifies tasks and procedures to be accomplished by learners. Writing sets of these documents can help teachers plan and organise adequately resourced and logically sequenced learning opportunities for individuals or groups. However, when planning lessons it is advisable to start by analysing learner group needs and requirements and then to select content and strategies designed to promote effective learning.

## Writing lesson plans

Each step should follow a logical sequence. The starting point is the writing of performance criteria or objectives that state in behavioural terms what the learner is expected to be able to do as an outcome of the training. Then, detailed **lesson plans** are laid out similar in form to the example shown in Figure 3.6. The plan has been written to cover a **classroom** session on the Highway Code with particular reference to **motorway driving.** The steps follow conventional teaching and learning practice. Content should be structured in a logical sequence and details of methods, activities, training aids, timings and checks of learning should be included. Once the plan is complete the facilitator can set about selecting, collecting and preparing relevant subject matter, organising material and methods to be used and following up by checking facilities and rehearsing.

*Methods of evaluating the effectiveness of the training session are clearly identified*

The quality of **programme delivery** and the quality of **learning outcomes** are two important features that should be reviewed when judging the effectiveness of a training session. The process of ongoing **self-evaluation** and **self-criticism** is an essential feature of a quality-assured operation. With this in mind, teachers have found it useful to list all the instructional methods they use and then note the advantages and disadvantages of each. By identifying the main features of the methods most frequently employed it is possible to consider why these methods seem most applicable to your work. In doing this you will have reviewed and evaluated your methods, introduced improvements and probably justified their continued use.

Lesson plans should include frequent **checks of learning**. It is important to involve the learners in the evaluation process and they should be provided with means to self-assess their progress and learning outcomes. Feedback is an important motivator and learners will appreciate **early knowledge of results**.

Teachers will need to refer frequently to their scheme of work when planning individual learning sessions, to monitor its suitability week by week and subsequently to evaluate its effectiveness. After the **programme review** has been carried out, necessary changes can be implemented taking into account observations, ideas for improvement and suggestions made by colleagues and learners.

Processes and instruments relating to evaluating training and development sessions and the teacher's own practice are discussed at length in Chapters 17 and 18.

*Resources required to deliver the training and development session are clearly identified and secured*

Media used to support training programmes, for example audio, video and film, are important aids that can reinforce learning and add variety and interest. The value of resources and the deployment of the people, materials, equipment and facilities needed when delivering training sessions has been discussed earlier in this chapter, but there are a few important matters to consider before any learner group assembles. Rooms, technicians and facilities should be booked well in advance and the room laid out to suit the teaching method before students arrive. Before the training session, demonstration aids, audio-visual equipment and other resources needed should be inspected for serviceability and completeness using the lesson plan as a checklist. Lesson notes and OHP slides should be sorted into correct order and handouts counted out into sets that can be split in several packs and issued from several start points. This can speed up the 'passing around' process and avoid loss of concentration.

It has been found helpful to involve learners in identifying aids that they feel would make learning more enjoyable or otherwise improve the learning programme. The range of audio-visual skills available within the group can pleasantly surprise teachers. There are often video editors, sound experts, drama and performing arts people among the learner group. They will be keen to help, and if the practical experience of people is utilised when planning and presenting course material, lessons will be seen to be more relevant to their needs.

*Training and development sessions effectively promote equality of opportunity*

Teachers will need to consider developing provision for people with **special learning requirements** and providing **equal opportunities** with respect to social and religious background, ethnic or national origin, marital status, intellectual or physical capacity, age and gender. Care must be taken to avoid harassment, sex discrimination and stereotyping. In some cases there has been a lack of adequate provision for learners with disabilities, and insufficient thought has been given to compensating for serious and minor handicaps and temporary indispositions.

*Training and development sessions utilise a range of techniques and activities*

It is sometimes difficult to convey new ideas and unfamiliar information by words alone. We hear words but often have little understanding of the ideas and concepts behind them. For words to have meaning they must be related either to personal experiences or to real objects that people have come to know about. Aids serve to open up several channels for the communication of information and can create a variety of sensory impressions which enhance the process of perception and efficiency of learning.

People collect information using the five senses: sight, hearing, touch, taste and smell. How this information is perceived and the speed at which people interpret the signals reaching them varies from one person to the next. Learners' attention can be lost if the teacher displays visual information for too long or too short a period, talks too quickly or keeps up a tedious monologue. In order to reduce this possibility a mix of aural, visual and written resources and practical options should be employed throughout the session, and teacher input/learner activity balanced to suit the group.

# Self-assessment questions

1 Why is it necessary to identify a range of possible options for training and development sessions before creating a training programme?

2 Identify a range of options that could be used in your own training programmes.

3 Suggest other people with whom selected options could usefully be discussed and agreed.

4 Explain why factors such as learner characteristics, group size, training content and context must be considered when planning learning opportunities.

5 Explain what meant by a candidate's 'preferred learning style'.

6 Describe what is meant by the expression 'a concrete learning experience' and give examples.

7 List four key resources that you may use when resourcing a training and development session.

8 Describe the different constraints that you may meet when seeking resources for a given programme.

9 How can the use of a particular aid be justified?

10 Why should the resources selected be relevant to the learner's needs and programme objectives?

11 How is the effectiveness of teaching or learning improved by the use of resources?

12 Why must the resources used be of a suitable quality?

13 Why should training aids be designed to serve a specific purpose and back up what the instructor is saying?

14 How can teachers maximise the benefit derived from using people, money and time as resources?

15 What is meant by 'the cost-effective use of resources'?

16 Explain the value of preparing a scheme of work that gives information about:
   a) programme aims and objectives
   b) organisational factors
   c) methods of facilitating training
   d) assessment and evaluation methods and related documentation.

17 Describe each stage of the four-stage cycle used to assist lesson planning:
   a) identifying learner needs
   b) designing lesson components
   c) creating a suitable learning environment, providing resources and carrying out the training
   d) monitoring and evaluating lessons and programme outcomes and making improvements.

18 Why is lesson planning an important element of course provision and programme design?

19 How can a well-designed lesson plan help to enhance the quality of presentation and effectiveness of learning?

20 Why is it important for teachers to consider lesson content, learner ability and methods to be employed before starting work on the lesson plan?

21 Why are training specifications and task analyses helpful to teachers when identifying knowledge and skills elements involved in the topic to be taught?

22 Explain the importance of the three main phases in lesson preparation:
   a) collecting, selecting and preparing relevant subject matter
   b) preparing material and planning methods to be used
   c) checking and rehearsing.

23 Name the three main stages of delivery that should be indicated in a lesson plan.

24 At what stage of a lesson should:
   a) the task be set into context, lesson aims and objectives be presented and incentives be offered?
   b) basic principles be introduced, new work be linked to existing knowledge, and skills be progressively built up?
   c) recapitulation and consolidation take place and learner doubts be clarified?

25 Why are lesson plans built around specific performance criteria?

26 Why should a lesson structure include a variety of activities such as short question and answer sessions and frequent brief reviews?

27 Why should time be allowed for giving feedback and reviewing progress when planning lessons?

28 Lesson plans should be revised, updated and improved in the light of experience gained while actually presenting relevant lessons. Why is this necessary?

29 Describe how checklists can be used by teachers when self-assessing the effectiveness of their lesson plan and lesson outcomes.

30 Why must training and development sessions effectively promote equality of opportunity?

# *Preparing for assessment: sample activities* _____

### *Activity 3.1 Promoting equality of opportunity*
Examine your attitude towards current non-discriminatory legislation and check whether your training provision effectively promotes equality of opportunity.

Consider how bias and discrimination may operate during selection and enrolment and with respect to learner entitlement, and describe the steps you have taken to ensure that you are providing equal opportunities within your training sessions.

Analyse your teaching and learning resources and explain the measures you have taken to ensure that teaching materials (books, handouts, film and video) are free of bias and do not contain sexist or racist stereotyping or any other form of discriminatory material or references.

### *Activity 3.2 Choosing training options*
For any one of your classes consider the learning characteristics of the learners and review your main strategies for teaching the group.

Compile a list of learners and against each name note their preferred learning styles and any special characteristic observed.

Analyse your observations and try to establish a teaching style that best matches overall group needs.

### *Activity 3.3 Carrying out a task analysis*
Specify the benefits of preparing a task analysis before writing a lesson plan or giving a demonstration. Using the layout shown in Figure 9.1 (See *Documents Pack*) or one of your own design prepare a step-by-step analysis of a task that you will need to demonstrate during a training session. Your task analysis should contain a logical sequence showing function, underpinning knowledge and skills.

### *Activity 3.4 Identifying resources needed to deliver training*
Carry out a review of the teaching and learning resources available for your subject specialism. Produce a schedule of aids needed to deliver training matched to lesson or week number. Note the objectives facilitated by using the aid specified, how the aid will be used, and an alternative should the aid not be available for use when needed.

### *Activity 3.5 Writing a lesson plan*
Write a set of lesson plans for a training programme that you will need to present in the near future. Define the objectives, identify content and specify checks of learning. Include provisional timings, details of stages and main points, methods and resources employed. Allow for changes of activity such as inputs by facilitator, practice for learners, frequent assessment, guidance, review, feedback and recapitulation, summary and conclusion.

### *Activity 3.6 Identifying a range of options for training and development sessions*
Design a **scheme of work** that outlines in a logical sequence the way in which you in partnership with your learners may best cover NVQ/SVQ unit content or the topics in a syllabus. When drawing up the outline scheme consider learner characteristics; syllabus or unit content and programme aims, objectives and performance criteria; timing and duration of sessions; methods and resources needed; and opportunities for reviews, guidance and assessment.

Identify methods of evaluating the effectiveness of the sessions presented and use the methods to monitor the suitability of the scheme of work. Regularly update the scheme incorporating ideas for improvements that you have collected.

### Activity 3.7 Relating the Kolb circle to teaching strategies

The sequence and pacing of instruction should be organised and facilitated so as to accommodate (as far as possible) group and individual learning preferences. In the teaching of 'traditional' learning programmes 'theoretical topics' and 'practical work' may be separately taught and tested; whereas with competence-based programmes candidates will demonstrate a mix of skills, knowledge and contextual understanding and attainment that will be judged by teacher-assessors.

A number of teaching and learning methods that could be used to meet different learner requirements are shown in Figure 3.7. Consider how you might apply these methods and produce checklists that could be used when preparing and implementing your chosen strategies.

# The Kolb Circle and teaching methods

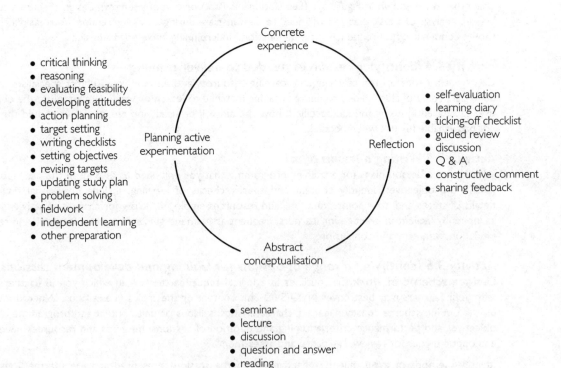

- simulation
- work experience
- task, exercise or assignment
- practical work
- laboratory work
- experimental investigations
- research projects
- case study
- demonstration
- computer work

- critical thinking
- reasoning
- evaluating feasibility
- developing attitudes
- action planning
- target setting
- writing checklists
- setting objectives
- revising targets
- updating study plan
- problem solving
- fieldwork
- independent learning
- other preparation

Concrete experience

Planning active experimentation

Reflection

- self-evaluation
- learning diary
- ticking-off checklist
- guided review
- discussion
- Q & A
- constructive comment
- sharing feedback

Abstract conceptualisation

- seminar
- lecture
- discussion
- question and answer
- reading
- literature search

**Figure 3.7** *The Kolb circle applied to teaching methods*

**Note**

1 See D.A. Kolb, *Experiential Learning: Experience as the Source of Learning and Development*, Prentice-Hall, Englewood Cliffs, New Jersey 1984.

# 4

# Preparing and developing resources to support learning

Teaching and learning resources are essential features of any learning opportunity. They are used to gain and maintain learner attention, to enhance presentations and to emphasise or illustrate key points. Aids cannot entirely replace the teacher but they can serve to open up more channels of communication and add interest by creating a variety of sensory impressions. Sound and vision are used to supplement word-only inputs, to brighten up presentations and to promote discussion. In many cases aids are used instead of the real thing which may itself be unavailable or too large to bring into the learning environment.

Given that learning at work or in a vocational training placement, workshop or laboratory may involve the use of all senses and provide the best experience, well-designed simulations and aids can often act as effective substitutes. When real-work learning opportunities are not available, teachers will need to make flawless presentations in contrived learning environments such as classrooms and workshops. High-quality delivery can be sustained by reviewing performance criteria, researching the topic well, developing a varied programme and using carefully prepared aids to support teacher talk. Only essential and relevant aids that attract interest, emphasise key concepts, stimulate imagination and help overcome problems of ambiguity and false perception should be used.

A flow chart can be produced showing the network of aids to be used during a session referenced to guide notes and cues. Overhead projector (OHP) transparencies and prepared flip charts can serve as a series of mini-teaching plans which can be followed as the session develops. Transparencies are widely used as a means of presenting factual information, and key notes and lessons can be structured so that suitable chunks of information can be projected in logical sequence. Successive slides are used to link subject matter. By using the technique of **revelation** teachers can see what comes next on the transparency before unmasking the line beneath and are able to present a smoothly flowing input. However, care should be taken not to overuse the OHP and cause what is referred to as 'death by viewfoil'.

Designers when preparing resources to support learning should take account of the characteristics of the learner group, the type of subject matter to be communicated and the media best suited to display the information to be represented.

## Preparing materials and facilities to support learning

*Learning materials are identified and selected which are suitable for learners, the learning environment and learning objectives to be achieved*

Teachers will need to survey the range of materials, resources and facilities available in the classroom or at the training place and find out what is available and, if it is a machine, whether it works. Learning materials fall into three main categories: **written, visual** and **audio-visual**, with learning packages, interactive video and other computer-driven presentations supplementing increased **learner-controlled activity** as higher student/staff ratios force the pace of change.

Learning materials are employed to get the best out of learning opportunities. They can be used effectively to illustrate relationships, to give an accurate impression of a concept, to demonstrate principles, to show how a machine works, to display the general arrangement of an assembly drawing, or to establish linkages between elements of the lesson.

Aids form a focal point and **attract attention**. They can be used to stimulate the exchange of ideas and opinions or to reinforce and consolidate important information presented earlier in the session. Models of delicate mechanisms can be enlarged for all to see and ponder over. Short quotations, phrases or passages can be displayed on flip charts in order to gain attention and interest or to support a point made. Projected material gives rise to curiosity and the desire to explore possibilities. When new aids are introduced there is often an increase in the learners' span of attention, and linkages with earlier work are created.

Aids reduce the need for lengthy explanation, thereby **saving time** when teachers are providing information, and promoting retention and memorising. They supplement description and help people understand better the spoken word. When transparencies are used to display information care must be exercised and only a limited amount of detail should be projected at one time. The OHP should not be used as a substitute for dictation or handouts. Learners may end up with a fine set of notes but they are unlikely to learn much from merely copying masses of data from transparencies.

Teachers can enhance programme effectiveness, content coverage and quality of learning by providing suitable materials and learning resources. In order for people to attain learning objectives or meet performance criteria the syllabus must be adequately covered. This implies supplementing teacher inputs with a mix of learner-centred techniques backed by facilities and equipment designed to add value and make learning easier.

Teachers can improve their effectiveness by using affordable and **cost-effective resources** that will meet group needs, increase learner motivation, gain attention, maintain interest and save on the time taken by learners to absorb the information presented and gain the skills concerned. While changes in activity may be desirable the availability and cost of resources needed to support the activity must be justified. Before investing time in making aids or purchasing expensive resources teachers should be satisfied that the items will provide learning experiences that otherwise could not be provided.

*Learning materials that are not suitable are adapted to meet the learning objectives*

Besides being able to generate a wide range of teaching and learning materials teachers will on occasions need to **modify** or **adapt materials** as a result of self-evaluation or comment from colleagues or learners. If the material originates from in-house sources it will be possible to contact the visual aids technician or originator and agree proposed changes with them. If, however, the item is commercially produced it would probably be better to contact the supplier's customer service department and discuss proposed adaptations before going ahead with changes. The learners themselves may well be the best people to advise on adapting independent learning materials to suit their needs.

Some learners are highly literate while others are not, and materials issued to them may not be suitable for all. However, reviewing learner progress against performance criteria enables difficulties to be highlighted. Associated learning materials can then be examined and account taken of learner comment and reactions. It may be that the level of language used creates a barrier to understanding or that task instructions are ambiguous or unclear. Technical terminology used may be inconsistent thereby causing confusion. Diagrams may be cluttered with redundant detail. Students with English as a second language may require a translation from English to their mother tongue. Problems of literacy and numeracy may call for more diagrams or tape-recorded instructions or even video representations. By regularly evaluating available aids, teachers can anticipate difficulties and make adaptations to suit learner groups.

*Written and visual support materials are accurate and in a style and format appropriate to the needs and capabilities of the learners*

It is important for teachers to ensure that equal opportunities policy is observed when they are **identifying learning opportunities** and providing resources to support the achievement of individual goals. Learners may experience **difficulties** when handling materials or with reading, writing, maths or study skills. No two learners are alike, and differences between individuals and their learning styles will affect the **choice of resources** to be employed. Teachers will need to be familiar with the many different types of learning materials and be able to select the resource that will yield the best outcome for a particular learner. If suitable material is not available teachers may need to adapt the content and style of 'off-the-shelf' programmes to suit individual needs.

Materials and tasks may be structured for active participation with differing levels of task difficulty within one main framework. This would provide opportunities for all to contribute in a way that is commensurate with their background and prior experience, educational level and learning preferences. Differences in intellectual ability and temperament could mean preparing a variety of materials that would support a practical 'hands-on' approach for some and a theoretical or academic style for others in either a teamworking or an individualised context.

*Simulation and exercise materials selected are sufficiently realistic to be credible to learners*

A **simulation** is used to reproduce the conditions of a given situation. Although there is no complete substitute for the real thing, simulations are sometimes used to model particular processes. Some real work activities and experiments are difficult to implement or indeed impossible to carry out at an acceptable cost or level of risk. Fortunately, nowadays the computer can be used to overcome many of these difficulties by simulation. Thousands of transactions can be effected in very little time and economic models can be tested to the extremes of bankruptcy or immense wealth using simulation techniques. The effects experienced under water, in the tropics or in arctic conditions can be reproduced with the learner seated comfortably and safely in the simulator under the watchful eye of the trainer.

A **simulator** is a device or system that can reproduce specific conditions or characteristics of the real thing for the purposes of **experimentation** or **operator training**. Using simulators in a training programme can save a great deal of money and downtime brought about by misuse, damage or incompetent handling. Their usage can also avoid the risk of inexperienced learners being injured when training in potentially hazardous environments.

Simulation exercises, role-plays and videotaped case studies should be credible and as **realistic** as possible. Activities should be **relevant** to the needs of people preparing for work or seeking to change their roles. Vocational simulations should provide practical **concrete experiences** while abstract teaching and too much teacher talk should be limited.

*Materials from external sources are adapted and used within the constraints of copyright law*

The rights of a person to be identified as the author of works such as books, articles or any other published work can be asserted by them in accordance with the Copyright, Designs and Patents Act 1988. This means that all rights are reserved and that no part of the publication concerned may be reproduced or transmitted in any form or by any means, electronic or mechanical, including photocopy, recording or any information or retrieval system, without permission in writing from the publisher or under licence from the Copyright Licensing Agency. Further details for such licences (for reprographic reproduction) may be obtained from the Copyright Licensing Agency Ltd, 90 Tottenham Court Road, London W1F 9HE. If in doubt about what to do about copying or adapting copyright material teachers should consult either their team leader or administration officer, or contact the publisher or the Copyright Licensing Agency.

*Materials selected promote equality of opportunity*

All teachers must be aware of current **equal opportunities legislation** and practice. This is not negotiable since it is legally mandatory. They should make it known to each learner and other course team members that they will not allow discriminatory practices or comments to go unchallenged either during their teaching programmes or elsewhere on the training provider's premises.

**Sexism** is prejudice or discrimination against a person on the grounds of their sex, and all new teaching and learning materials must conform to best practice. The principles of using **non-sexist and non-racist language** must be understood and implemented, and teachers must encourage their learners to challenge unfair references to gender, cultural stereotypes and sexist language. Existing material must be **gender neutral** – it must be free of sexist references. By the use of plurals such as 'learners', 'candidates' or 'they', gender-biased words such as 'he' or 'she' can be avoided. The words 'his' or 'her' can be replaced by 'their'. For example: 'The teacher can help by relating *her* teaching of principles to situations which the learner will meet in *his* daily work' could be replaced with: '*Teachers* can help by relating *the* teaching of principles to situations which the *learners* will meet in *their* daily work.' Handouts and assignments must be vetted and cleared of prejudicial, discriminatory, sex-stereotyped, offensive and racial references. Use of the suffix '-person' in place of man or woman produces **sexual neutralisation**, but when I tried to explain the usage to a neighbour who is the head cowman at a local farm he burst into uncontrollable laughter. I must admit that I had difficulty in keeping a straight face while I introduced him to the term 'head cow-person', and this leads me to suggest that care must be taken to avoid ridicule when introducing the concept of **politically correct** language.

People who have regard for the sensitivities of others will tend to use politically correct (PC) language in preference to expressions such as old (ageism), race (ethnic minorities), deaf (people with hearing difficulties), blind or partially sighted (personal seeing difficulties) or mentally handicapped (differing abilities). Well-intentioned teachers will attempt to set good examples to their learners by using accepted PC terminology and avoiding emotive, thoughtless or hurtful words such as failures, blind, stone deaf, cripples, backward or retarded, coloured, white, the poor and the unemployed. They will come to understand that students should not be referred to as 'the handicapped' even though they may have an impairment which results in a lack of certain functions that in turn may limit their ability to perform a given activity.

While the positive and sensible aspects of political correctness are to be applauded, extremists seeking to impose their will on others have promoted a backlash from the unconverted.

Opponents have responded by suggesting derisive phrases such as 'metabolically challenged' (dead) and 'trichologically challenged' (bald) in an attempt to ridicule those seeking to enforce PC. Perhaps the following extract from Nigel Rees's introduction to his *Politically Correct Phrasebook*[1] reflects the reality for many teachers: 'Another trouble with PC, however, is that it tends to encourage what is best described using the old phrase "lip service". The speaker who has been made aware of PC attitudes may say words that are ideologically sound, knowing that they are what is expected, but may still be thinking wrong thoughts.'

*Training facilities are appropriate and available for use when required*

In colleges and elsewhere printed and non-printed materials and resources are held in a storage, maintenance and retrieval system operated by support staff. The **learning resources centre** is usually headed by a librarian who acquires resources and maintains services at the required level. Teachers can book tutorial rooms and hire learning resources including video and hardware. Many centres are open-access and learners are encouraged to make good use of the service which is an essential feature of flexible and distance-learning strategies.

## Effective use of different resources

Costs of training materials provided must be kept within budget and should satisfy programme content, methods and learner preferences. Capital items can be expensive and it is unlikely that budget-holders will readily agree to purchasing new resources unless they can be justified. This means that teachers will need to make the best use of resources currently available. The range of resources accessible to teachers should be known when they are planning learning programmes so that suitable equipment and materials can be linked to content and method. Resulting **lesson plans** should list a **variety** of material to be included so as to break up long sessions, the aim being to obtain the best fit consistent with performance criteria. Only the most **suitable aids** should be selected and all equipment should be in **good working order.**

The type of accommodation provided will affect the classroom layout chosen, and before lessons commence the room should be inspected in order to identify any **restrictions** when using resources. The 'it will be all right on the day' attitude can be dangerous if you are planning to use aids but not inclined to check out rooms beforehand. Try to show a film in a room without a screen, blackout or blinds on a bright sunny day, or use an OHP without a screen or suitable wall or socket nearby, or attach magnetic aids without a metal board or cabinet and you will quickly find out why!

## Typical resources

### Overhead projectors (OHPs)
The OHP is probably the most widely used (and misused) resource in classrooms today. It is easily transported and can project words, diagrams, mobiles and the outline of real objects. Transparencies can be quickly prepared by hand, by printing direct from computer systems or by photocopying. Several overlays can be hinged onto a base transparency and flipped over to superimpose new information on existing. Sheets can be written on at will as points are made or solutions revealed. But overuse can bore an audience and attention soon lapses.

Care must be taken to present transparencies in the correct order and avoid presenting too much detail on a single sheet. Writing should be clear, legible and large enough for all to see. The screen should be angled correctly to avoid a keystone effect and the lens correctly focused. Teacher talk should stop while learners make sense of the projected image, and the

OHP should be switched off immediately a point has been made in order to avoid unnecessary distraction when exposition resumes.

When making OHP transparencies by hand:

- Plan your layout.
- Draft your design in pencil on squared paper having first marked on the maximum usable boundaries.
- Using masking tape fix your transparency over your draft; this stops the transparency from sliding.
- Using coloured pens trace the outline from your draft.
- Add colour and lettering as necessary.
- Secure to the cardboard frame with masking tape.
- Fix overlays or masks to the frame with masking tape or self-adhesive flexible hinges.
- Label the frame clearly for filing and write notes on the frame edge.

Computer-generated originals avoid the need for some of the operations described above.

### Boards and flip charts

**Whiteboards** and **chalkboards** are still widely used and are cheap to maintain. They can be used to record temporary information presented by the teacher or responses from learners as the lesson progresses. In order to avoid delays during the presentation, panels on roller boards can be written up before the lesson begins and revealed when needed.

Board work should be kept legible. The upper part of the board should be used wherever possible, and when writing on the board the teacher should talk to the group – not the board. Outlines of complex drawings should be prepared in advance. Faint lines should be drawn in pencil or chalk which may be seen by the teacher but not by learners. Diagrams or mathematical solutions should be built up step by step in a logical sequence. Technical words, key words and definitions should be highlighted in colour. Summaries should be developed as the lesson progresses and used later to recap and reinforce lesson content. Worked examples and unwanted material should be erased as soon as learners have finished taking it down. White boards are cleaner to work with and can also be used as projection screens.

**Magnetic boards** are made of steel. The boards attract magnets stuck to the back of cardboard cutouts representing real items. The cutouts can be moved around on the board and added to or removed at will.

When preparing magnetic aids:

- Select the textbook diagram from which the aid will be developed (or invent your own layout).
- Identify the number of cutouts needed and the shape of each.
- Decide on the magnification factor needed to ensure that the aid will be large enough to be seen by all.
- Scale each component from your diagram.
- Multiply each dimension by the magnification factor (or use a photocopier to increase size uniformly).
- Using white paper draw each shape to the magnified dimension and stick it to the back of coloured card.
- Cut out cardboard shapes and glue magnets to the back of each.
- Assemble cards on the magnetic board in the correct sequence to try out the design, and number each card with the correct sequence of application.

- Practise assembly several times ensuring that the magnets are strong enough to hold the cards without slipping when overlaid.

Flip charts may be prepared at home before lessons or seminars begin. Sheets are ordered in lesson sequence and flipped over one at a time during the presentation. A second chart and stand can be very helpful when teachers are recording feedback responses from the group. Summary sheets can be torn off and displayed around the room using Blu-tack to fix them temporarily to the wall.

When preparing low-cost flip charts it is sometimes necessary to leave a blank sheet between written-up sheets, as otherwise writing on the following page could be seen by participants. Caps of spirit-based pens should be replaced immediately after use in order to prevent them drying out and producing poor-quality writing.

### Audio-visual

Audio-visual resources include simple low-cost aids such as record players and cassette players that are often used by keep fit, music, drama, dance and language teachers; and more expensive aids such as films, video, computers linked to modems, databases and interactive video that people now take for granted as the modern sophisticated media industry expands. There is little doubt that interactive video will become a major form of student-centred learning which allows students to learn at their own rate and continuously assess their own progress.

When using video as a teaching resource:

- Preview the video and ensure it meets your objectives.
- Read the video notes and prepare a summary for review after showing.
- Make sure you are familiar with the video-playing equipment.
- Test the equipment and adjust volume and contrast before the class arrives.
- Ensure that direct sunlight does not affect the learners' viewing.
- Wind the tape to the start of the section you wish to play ready for instant replay.
- Increase learner interest and attention before running the video by giving the class a set of key questions that they will need to answer afterwards.

Large-screen computer presentations are being replaced by LCD (liquid crystal display) projection devices that operate directly from PCs and other computers. The device is placed on the OHP and the projected image is focused onto the screen or whiteboard. Data such as spreadsheets may be instantly presented to the whole group and input from CAD and CAM programmes easily reproduced for all to see.

### Reading lists

Learners are now being actively encouraged to find out things for themselves. As the scale and scope of project work, assignments and investigations increases, and learner-centred study techniques develop, there is a growing need for better direction and guidance in study skills and researching. All too often learners are allocated self-study periods with little or no briefing, negotiation or discussion of ways and means. Prepared reading lists and references have in the past served learners well in focusing their efforts without being prescriptive, and similar support material should be provided to learners at the onset of study.

### Handouts and worksheets

Handouts may be used either as **worksheets** or to **provide information** for learners to take away with them after the lesson. The problem with handouts is that they are likely to be neatly filed and forgotten unless the designer includes something for the learners to do concerning the material presented.

The **gapped handout** forming the basis of Activity 4.1 is intended to encourage readers to consider a range of resources that they might use when preparing to teach or otherwise support learning opportunities. The layout suggests a logical approach that readers may wish to adopt since it follows the sequence of the textbook chapter[2] in which basic information may be found. By completing the work specified in the handout readers will learn new things about the purposes and use of aids or they will at least have an opportunity to review their current knowledge.

The syndicate **discussion brief** given in Figure 4.1 (see *Documents Pack*) shows how contextual information may be presented in a short introduction, followed by task instructions and a note of key features that should be included in the syndicate reports.

*Training facilities conform to health and safety legislation*

**Environmental factors** such as noise levels, ventilation, lighting and atmosphere are matters that teachers will need to monitor when working with learners in any location. **Human factors** such as horseplay, inexperience, distractions, lack of attention and carelessness must be controlled by adequately supervising learner behaviour. **Accident prevention** should be at the top of the teacher's list, particularly when planning or supervising practical work.

The **Health and Safety at Work Act 1974** provides a framework for health and safety regulations and makes it clear that everyone has a **duty** to play a part in preventing people from coming to harm at work. Teachers as employees have a duty to take care of themselves and their students who may be affected by what they do in a learning environment. Health and safety regulations are designed **to protect** the individual at work.

Teachers could usefully carry out a **risk assessment** before using a classroom or workshop by identifying all **hazards**, assessing the risk and taking steps to eliminate or reduce risks of accidents and injuries to themselves and their students. Students should be properly **trained** and **supervised** when **using machines**, tools and plant or when **manually handling** equipment or materials. Display screen equipment should be checked for reflections, glare and flicker, and controls adjusted to suit the learner. Suitable **personal protective clothing** and equipment must be provided and used by learners to protect them from hazards in their learning environment.

If a substance has the potential to harm a person it is a **hazardous substance**. A learner's health can be damaged by touching, breathing in or swallowing the substance, or by allowing it to enter the body through cuts or open wounds. **The Control of Substances Hazardous to Health (COSHH) Regulations** apply to all workplaces, and employers are required to carry out risk assessments on all hazardous substances.

**Electric shocks** and electrical **fires** are the two main risks with electricity. Teachers will need to monitor the workplace for hazards such as water, overloaded sockets, damaged cables, and learners adjusting or cleaning machines without switching off power and unplugging the appliance.

Six new sets of health and safety regulations which will in some way affect many teachers came into force during 1993. The regulations cover:

● health and safety management
● work equipment safety
● manual handling of loads
● workplace conditions

- personal protective clothing
- display screen equipment.

Teachers will need to comply with those laws affecting their teaching duties.

*Materials and facilities selected are within agreed budgets*

**Budgets** are devices for establishing control limits for the resources we consume. They provide best estimates of the financial effects of curriculum plans and serve as guides to expenditure. Budgets may be based on prior usage in similar programmes or on pure guesswork. However, calculation of short-term resource requirements is necessary when any learning programme is planned. **Flexible budgeting** allows for contingencies since activities may not accurately mirror planned usage because of an increase or decrease in student numbers, curriculum changes or unexpectedly high or low student/staffing ratios calling for corresponding changes in method.

Budgets are monitoring devices for guiding management action, and use of resources is limited by budget allocation. Costs are controlled by means of cost centres which are allocated to courses or teams, and monetary values are applied to resource consumption. This information is then used to compare **actual consumption** in physical terms with **planned usage**. Cost consciousness is now an imperative among teachers who are encouraged to conduct a **cost benefit analysis** before implementing learning programmes. This is achieved by comparing proposed training methods and investment in equipment and consumable resources with the quality of learning experience and performance-related payments received by the training provider. Teachers will therefore need to make an inventory of available resources and make the best use of them while working within their budget allocations.

*Problems with materials and facilities are identified promptly and appropriate action taken to overcome them*

When things do not meet specified requirements action must be taken to ensure that non-conformance of any aspect of training provision is readily identified and rectified. The main sources of problems in education and training are:

- programme design and delivery
- physical and material resources
- teaching and training staff
- support staff
- the learners themselves.

Problems with materials and facilities must be dealt with quickly and concessions or corrective action taken. Such action must include the prevention of recurrence. The incident should be documented and the documentation made available for review later. Technicians should be called upon for help, and on no account should resources be returned to stores in an unserviceable condition without notifying the responsible person.

An audit of training resources would include testing the applicability of learning resources in relation to a specified learning objective.

# Developing materials to support learning

*The requirements of the materials are clearly identified*

Teachers will be able to recognise feasible learning opportunities and assess the methods best suited to the learner group's requirements. Then, depending on the method selected, materials needed should be identified and prepared for use. A few commonly used methods together with an outline of suitable materials are set out below.

**Lessons and lectures** are used to develop underpinning knowledge, factual information and reasoning skills. Materials needed for theory and practice could include computers, calculators, textbooks, handouts, worksheets, test papers, and stationery such as sketch pads and graph paper. Practical exercises would also need to be prepared.

**Demonstrations** are used to illustrate motor skills and processes. Checklists of resources needed would result from a study of the task analysis carried out before planning the demonstration.

**Discovery-based learning** is used to develop creative and divergent thinking and active experimentation. Material requirements for guided discovery learning would include programmed learning materials or, in the case of learning by **'undoing'**, assemblies made up of several component parts to be stripped, examined and their function determined.

**Fault-finding** materials for auto engineers, TV technicians and process workers would need to include flow diagrams, wiring diagrams and technical drawings as well as real equipment or simulators.

**Laboratory work** is used for developing cognitive and motor skills and confirming theory by experimentation. Materials needed could include laboratory sheets, protective clothing, hardware, apparatus, equipment and chemicals.

Materials for **small group activity** would need to include written materials such as briefs or case studies, role-plays, simulations and games in audio-visual or interactive formats.

**Project work** is independent work undertaken by the learner or small team supported by a facilitator. Work-based projects use all workplace facilities but college-based projects could require access to libraries and resources centres, questionnaires, sample materials and use of a word processor.

*A range of options for meeting the requirements of the materials are reviewed and a preferred option selected*

The basic choice to be made is whether to use existing materials which may not be ideally suited to the learners' needs or whether to originate new materials. Teachers must consider costs, production time available and how important and urgent the topic is when making the decision. Experience has shown that it is sometimes unwise to borrow resources from a colleague and present them without careful study and rehearsal. It appears that regardless of how comprehensive borrowed notes may be, they just don't seem to match the presenter's style. The same applies to resources and materials that are designed by a team which does not include the teacher who will be using them. Perhaps a middle course would be to modify the existing resources and develop new ones as and when deemed necessary, the aim being to choose the option that will best match learner needs and programme objectives.

*Possible types of material, media and delivery methods suitable to the subject matter, learning context and duration are selected*

Resource-based learning is a requirement for both practical and theoretical training and the integration of theory with practical experimentation whether in college laboratories or in workplaces. Teachers will satisfy the criterion relating to this topic if they are able to demonstrate understanding of the following concepts and apply underlying ideas to their teaching role.

**Paper-based materials** ranging from surveys using questionnaires to student notes are fundamental resources that are widely used in every aspect of teaching and training. Handouts, briefing documents, test papers and self-assessment instruments are all essential features of curriculum implementation.

As well as owning fundamental skills such as using an OHP or video recorder, teachers will need to demonstrate the ability to select and use **computer and audio-visual** instructional media that support learning. Typical resources would include TV, video, films, viewdata and teletext, computers, and aids for developing keyboard skills.

Fred S. Keller created a **personalised system of instruction** (PSI) called the **Keller Plan**, which comprises set reading, questions, exercises, vocational tasks and experiments backed by the occasional lecture. The plan allows learners to tackle material at their own speed until they achieve agreed objectives. This idea of self-paced and self-directed study enables the full potential of independent learning and project work to be realised. The quality of learning outcomes will depend largely on the facilitator providing learners with objectively focused study-support materials, clearly defined references to other sources of information, meaningful work experience and related assignments.

As with any learning proposition, assessment is an essential feature of the process and some kind of end test or review should be undertaken. Assessment checklists can be used to confirm achievement and to identify the need for remedial work.

**Syndicate work** involving case studies can be used to promote principle learning as well as the acquisition of interactive and interpersonal skills. Buzz groups, brainstorming and small-group activities such as role-playing and business games are thought to be effective means of developing creative thinking, adaptability and decision-making ability. The technique of discussion involves group dynamics, and teachers will need to have some knowledge of the psychology of small-group behaviour when facilitating this method of learning. Successful management of group work entails understanding the ways in which learners interact when participating in discussion. Teachers should also consider aspects of classroom management such as seating arrangements, leadership roles and aspects of sociometry when planning group work.

Teachers may prepare suitable teaching and learning materials after first carefully previewing unit content and then predicting learners' needs and setting objectives. Getting learners started quickly is a must, and this can be promoted by suggesting possible ways of tackling the task but leaving it to the group to decide how it will be accomplished.

**Vocational training** is designed to build on prior achievement and to promote competency in work roles. While the means by which learners can meet **psychomotor objectives** may be foremost in the minds of teachers when planning training sessions the importance of related **underpinning knowledge** cannot be overlooked. Vocational aspects of education and training often involve 'hands-on' operator training and behavioural instruction designed to perfect manipulative skills. **Projects** are widely used in colleges to encourage personal development and to promote competency in practical work. This is achieved by providing opportunities to learn a mix of **process skills** involving planning, problem solving and communication; and **product skills** demonstrated by precisely describable behaviour that is assessed by written and practical tests. Training in procedures and conducting laboratory or workshop-based commercial simulations can also serve to prepare learners for their chosen employment.

When selecting methods and preparing materials, teachers will need to consider the context within which training will take place as well as group and individual needs. Plans for theoretical sessions would be based upon a preview of **topic content,** while training in physical skills could entail **probing workplace needs** and producing **task analysis** sheets similar to those given in Figures 8.1 (p. 106) and 9.1 (see *Documents Pack*).

*Materials assist the structuring of learning*

The **effectiveness of learning** and the quality and **speed of perception** can often be improved by the use of aids. Information can be readily shared, demonstration time is reduced and improvements in transfer of training, reinforcement and retention are obtained. Teachers will frequently need to include learning materials in their lesson structure because aids are normally cheaper than the real thing and may eliminate hazards involved when using actual equipment. The form and content of aids may be adjusted to support learning in a variety of contexts depending upon the teacher's perception of the benefits to be derived from using them. Teachers can use resources most effectively by previewing and rehearsing the presentation in advance.

Teachers need to be constantly seeking new ways of structuring materials to support learning and improve methods used. The availability of reference materials or detailed instruction sheets can help to reduce errors that might result from word-only instructions or vague written procedures. Videod demonstrations and comprehensively written support materials can form a lifeline for learners who wish to check that the action they contemplate is right before going ahead with a task. Good back-up materials will help promote a 'right first time every time' attitude and probably reduce the time needed to attain specified objectives.

Teachers will need to be able to structure sessions using one or more of the following resource materials:

- simulations for problem solving and decision making
- computer-managed learning systems and computer-generated materials
- briefs for participative group discussion
- instructional texts, manuals and lecture handouts
- slide/tape programmes
- audio-visual
- videod demonstration followed by practice in operating equipment
- student projects
- Open University texts
- distance learning
- programmed texts
- NVQ/SVQ units, elements and performance criteria (pcs) – range statements and evidence lists.

*Materials clearly state their aims and objectives and their use in the development and recognition of learners' achievements*

When specifying resources to support learning, teachers should **start with the aims** and objectives or references to unit performance criteria. By specifying aims and objectives on materials issued they will enable learners to establish the programme designer's intentions and understand more clearly why they are undertaking the work involved in completing the activity; in this way learners will probably be better motivated to complete the task. Frequent self-testing can then be employed using valid **quality checks** or assessment instruments (test papers and other resources) with subsequent rapid access to solutions or knowledge of results. Some resources linked with computers enable learners to evaluate their own progress by quickly calling up an analysis of their responses. It is beneficial for teachers and learners if they can monitor progress and judge achievement against target criteria and range statements.

Aids should encourage learners to participate fully in the learning activity presented. For example, if an objective requires a person to demonstrate the operation of a piece of equipment then a model which is designed to promote this behaviour would be appropriate, otherwise there would be no requirement for the aid.

*The language, style and format of the materials are appropriate to the needs of learners and are designed to promote equality of opportunity*

Using poorly designed learning materials can serve as a potential **barrier to learning**. Teachers should be aware of this possibility and consider the effect that their aids may have on the learners. The aids must be meaningful to all and consideration must be given to those with **learning difficulties**. For example, computer aids may call for skills that go beyond programme criteria, and some mature learners could be disadvantaged. Some learners may not be able to read quickly while others will struggle to take notes from the OHP. If barriers are encountered, methods should be changed or extra training and support must be programmed into the course. Account must be taken of the learners' ability to overcome problems encountered.

If there is only one aid that will be shared by several learners, classroom activity must be carefully planned and controlled. Sufficient time should be allowed for *all* to use the aid, and tasks must be planned for students awaiting their turn so as to keep them busy with relevant and productive work.

The suitability of aids should be evaluated as they are being used. Teachers can estimate the effectiveness of an aid by observing the learners' responses when it is first presented. If questioning relating to the objective reveals understanding then the aid will have worked. Equally a sea of puzzled expressions or bemused faces will signal difficulties, and it may be better to dispense with the aid and try another approach.

As previously stated, measures must be taken to ensure that teaching materials, books, handouts, film and video do not contain examples of **sexist stereotyping** and that writers of learning support materials do not unconsciously prejudice any learner's opportunity to achieve satisfaction from using the resources.

The means of communication selected must be appropriate to the learning situation and learning group. Learning new vocabulary that appears in written material is thought by some to be more effective if learners first listen to new words, then read the words from the board or OHP before writing down the list. Others will argue that new words should be set in context rather than learned as an extension of the learners' vocabulary. The point is that vocabularies vary with age and social, cultural and ethnic background, and the level of written and spoken language employed by teachers should match the language abilities of the learners.

*Materials from external sources are adapted and used within the constraints of copyright law*

Key features of the copyright law that are relevant to the preparation and development of materials to support learning are summarised on p. 50 under the heading 'Materials from external sources are adapted and used within the constraints of copyright law'.

*Materials are produced within specified timescales and resources*

In order to keep up to date with lesson preparation teachers must **plan ahead**. They should already have noted resources needed on a scheme of work when planning the programme. By referring to the 'resources' column, they can find the dates when materials will be needed. Photocopying requests can be submitted allowing a few days' extra lead time before the date they are required, and films, videos and equipment can be ordered well in advance.

In order to continually improve our training provision we are asking you to tell us whether or not the training aids we used helped you to learn.

All information given will be treated as confidential and we value your help.

Lesson topic _____

Training aid _____

*Please circle the number which you think most nearly reflects your opinion*

|                                                          | NO              | YES |
|----------------------------------------------------------|-----------------|-----|
| 1  Was the aid relevant to the topic?                    | 1 2 3 4 5 6 7 8 |     |
| 2  Did the aid help you to understand the topic?         | 1 2 3 4 5 6 7 8 |     |
| 3  Was the aid presented and used effectively?           | 1 2 3 4 5 6 7 8 |     |
| 4  Did the aid save you time in learning?                | 1 2 3 4 5 6 7 8 |     |
| 5  Was the aid really necessary?                         | 1 2 3 4 5 6 7 8 |     |
| 6  Was the aid large enough?                             | 1 2 3 4 5 6 7 8 |     |
| 7  Could you clearly see the aid as it was being used?   | 1 2 3 4 5 6 7 8 |     |
| 8  Could the aid be heard?                               | 1 2 3 4 5 6 7 8 |     |
| 9  Was the aid too complicated?                          | 1 2 3 4 5 6 7 8 |     |
| 10  Was the language used clear?                         | 1 2 3 4 5 6 7 8 |     |
| 11  Is the aid correct and up to date?                   | 1 2 3 4 5 6 7 8 |     |
| 12  Is the layout effective?                             | 1 2 3 4 5 6 7 8 |     |

Please list the best and worst features of the aid overleaf:

**Figure 4.2** *Teaching aid evaluation rating sheet*

The need to **keep within budget** was discussed earlier under the heading 'Materials and facilities selected are within agreed budgets', and constraints on time and expenditure are recognised.

If new materials have to be produced the work must be **prioritised** depending on **urgency** and **importance** as it may not always be possible to fit in everything by the deadlines. Lesson plans should allow for such contingencies and also for emergencies such as breakdown of the photocopier.

Learners can be key players when it comes to designing, making and evaluating aids. It is likely that within every group there will be computer buffs, sound and vision experts and people with good design skills. Learner groups can be asked if they will participate in the design of suitable learning materials that will help them meet programme criteria. They will probably agree and will seldom refuse to lend a hand. If learners are actively involved in producing their own learning resources they will value them and the learning process will be reinforced. Learner evaluation of teaching aids should be encouraged and a form that might be used is given in Figure 4.2.

*Materials are stored in a suitable manner and in a way which assists their use by learners*

Materials should be stored in a suitable place which is **secure** but **accessible to learners**. If a store room is used the key must be available to users and some means of recording transactions provided. Book loans are normally controlled by library staff but sometimes book collections are held by departments or programme teachers. Learners could be asked to sign out books as these are items that quite often go astray if uncontrolled. But resources should be freely available on loan. If too many obstacles are encountered resources will be left in store gathering dust. Reserves of handouts should be maintained with some kept in hand for late starters and people who miss classes.

**Sufficient quantities** of materials of **suitable quality** should be available to learners. Resources should be regularly replenished and conserved by carefully putting them away after use. Fragile equipment must be protected before stowage. Instruction manuals, briefings, training and advice on safety aspects should be available to all users, and resources should be fit for immediate use.

Teacher candidates should maintain a **teaching file** and learners should be encouraged to build a **portfolio of evidence** as their programme develops. Learners should be asked to add material to their files as it is issued. With this in mind it would be helpful if handouts and learning materials could be coded to aid recognition and filing. All too often learners stuff paperwork into their files intending to sort it out later but inevitably fail to do so. This results in a jumble which causes confusion when they are revising or presenting evidence for assessment.

*Users are provided with clear and accurate information on how to access the materials*

Teachers should share with the team leader and their learners information on how to **access** programme materials required for their sessions. Listings showing resources and materials available to the group and how they can be obtained could be printed and issued early in the programme. Training must be given on the **handling of hazardous substances** and the **safe operation** of any equipment provided.

Quiet study areas are provided in many libraries, and equipment is installed that will enable learners to locate resources that will help them learn. The first step in finding material in a learning resource centre is to consult their **catalogue**. Books may be traced by subject number, author and title, and systems such as the Dewey decimal classification may be used to classify stock. Should learners be unable to find what they are looking for there are professional librarians available to help with the search.

**Microfiche** catalogues give details of books, slides, records and laser discs, cassettes, videos, microcomputer programmes and other resources held. There will normally be a **reference section** that holds encyclopaedias, dictionaries, bibliographies, abstracts, indexes, expensive reference works, trade catalogues, industrial directories and very comprehensive sources of information of all kinds. British Standards, study and information packs and archive materials including old newspapers are normally held. Constantly updated computerised data is available from **electronic information services** such as Prestel, Ceefax, Oracle, Reuters and on-line searching.

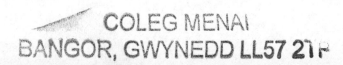

# Activity 4.1   Purpose and use of aids

*Complete ALL questions.*[2]

1   Describe how **learning resources** can help to gain and maintain attention.

2   List 12 advantages of **using aids**.

| | |
|---|---|
| (a) | (g) |
| (b) | (h) |
| (c) | (i) |
| (d) | (j) |
| (e) | (k) |
| (f) | (l) |

3   Describe some key features of using **pictures and photographs** as teaching and learning aids.

4   Sketch **three diagrams** (pie charts, bar charts, etc.) that may be used to **represent proportions** or **relationships**.

5   Observe a process and prepare a **block diagram** to represent each stage. If you do not have access to a process show how any finished item of your choice is produced from raw materials. Adapt the diagram for use as a teaching aid that shows basic details while avoiding **information overload**.

6   Describe why **behavioural objectives** and **performance criteria** should be considered before designing, specifying or selecting a resource to be used during a learning opportunity.

7   Describe how **magnetic aids** are produced and how they may be used effectively.

8   Describe how to produce a **paste-up original** that could be used to reproduce handouts or OHP transparencies.

9   List the types of **projected aids** available. State a practical example where each of these could be used to best effect.

10   Give examples of training situations where **video** can be used most effectively.

All the detail listed above could be considered when preparing to teach using resources to support the learning opportunity.

**Figure 4.3** *Activity 4.1: Purpose and use of aids*

# Preparing for assessment: sample activities

### Activity 4.1 Reviewing the purpose and use of aids

Typical range statements require teacher candidates to be able to identify, select, prepare, modify and use learning materials and teaching facilities. Evidence of underpinning knowledge could be confirmed by completing the outline survey sheet reproduced in Figure 4.3 and preparing to answer questions on the topics covered.

### Activity 4.2 Selecting, assembling and using learning resources for a specific programme

An activity that would generate evidence for assessment against Unit B33 criteria is described below. A written account of how the work was undertaken supported by materials produced and presented together with an evaluation report should meet evidence requirements.

**Method**

- Identify desired learning outcomes for a specific programme.
- Prepare session plans which show the resources needed to support your presentation matched to the performance criteria.
- Select the aids and handouts specified, check for completeness and serviceability and adapt as necessary. Include the use of information technology (IT) in the range of resources to be presented and show an awareness of equal opportunities when selecting or designing the resources.
- Arrange materials in the correct sequence ready for presentation.
- Maximise learning opportunities by demonstrating principles of visual communication when using the materials.
- Take account of identified constraints in terms of cost and environmental factors. Design a learner feedback questionnaire that can be used to evaluate the effectiveness of the aids presented or use the form shown in Figure 4.1 (see *Documents Pack*).
- Carry out the evaluation and using feedback obtained modify the resources as suggested.

### Activity 4.3 Creating materials for a participative learning programme

Write a carefully structured case study or role-play and set of briefs for syndicate groups or role-players. Include a set of instructions for the activity facilitator, observers and any other participants.

### Activity 4.4 Describing major aids designed for a programme

Describe one of the major aids you have designed for a learning programme. Justify its use and evaluate its effectiveness. Suggest how the aid or your presentation skills could be improved.

**Notes**

1  N. Rees, *The Politically Correct Phrasebook*, Bloomsbury Publishing, London 1993, p. xviii. This book is recommended reading for those who would like to read more about politically correct issues.

2  See L. Walklin, *Instructional Techniques and Practice*, Stanley Thornes, Cheltenham 1982 (reprinted 1994). Readers will find Chapter 9 helpful when reinforcing their knowledge about making and using aids and researching responses to the questions.

# Self-assessment questions

1  Why are audio-visual aids often used in learning situations?

2  Describe the sources that you use to identify relevant teaching and learning activity that will be included in your training programmes.

3 Choose a programme objective and select the type of aid which could best be used to help learners attain the objective selected. Justify your choice.

4 Explain the purpose of carrying out a task analysis.

5 How can the process of analysing a process or task be used to identify the need for learning resources?

6 What is meant by the expression 'an open and flexible learning format'?

7 Suggest sources of support materials, information and advice from which/whom learners might get help when working with 'flexible learning packs'.

8 Examine a variety of instructional manual formats and explain the reasons why these formats have been adopted. Describe the essential features of an instruction manual.

9 Describe six or more examples of written or display materials that you could use to support teaching and learning.

10 Observe a process and produce a block diagram representing each stage of the process. Explain how the observation was carried out and relevant information recorded.

11 Explain how using aids can help to overcome problems of boredom in class.

12 Why should videos and films be previewed by teachers before they show them?

13 Why should the use of a particular aid be validated and its impact evaluated before subsequent use?

14 Explain the benefits to be derived from having your aids evaluated by learners and other teachers.

15 What is meant by 'information overload' and how can this be avoided when presenting aids?

16 Explain what is meant by a 'simulation'. Suggest advantages and disadvantages of using simulation methods and materials.

17 Explain how 'health and safety legislation' affects teachers and learners in class or at work.

18 Outline the key features of current equal opportunities legislation and good practice.

19 What is meant by avoiding the use of 'sexist and racist language'?

20 Explain how copyright requirements are met in your workplace and how you personally avoid infringing copyright.

21 What action would you take if a teaching resource, machine or facility became defective while you were using it?

22 How can the language used, and style and format of learning materials cause 'barriers to learning'?

23 What is meant by 'producing materials within specified timescales and resources'?

24 Describe how resource files containing aids and instructional materials can be maintained for each session taught. Explain how learners may access the files or relevant learner support materials.

25 Explain what is meant by the statement 'Using aids can open up more channels for the communication of information.'

# Key Role C
## Facilitating and enabling learning

# 5

# Creating a climate conducive to learning

Promoting a favourable attitude to learning is one of the key duties of any teacher. It is particularly important for teachers to establish a desire to learn and to employ strategies which both maintain and develop the motivation of their learners. The hierarchy of needs put forward by A.H. Maslow is significant in enabling teachers to understand the importance of ensuring that learners' basic needs are satisfied in order for them to proceed to higher level needs such as accomplishing complex learning tasks. This highlights the necessity for teachers to ensure that the learning environment feels 'safe' for the learners to work in and is therefore conducive to learning. Particular attention would be needed in situations where, for example, a new member was introduced to a long-established group. In such cases strategies may incorporate a more learner-centred approach using small groups to facilitate interaction. In H.A. Murray's list of 'psychogenic needs' higher level or secondary drives are categorised into a framework embracing needs expressing ambition, desire for accomplishment and prestige. These models identify the importance of creating an environment which is mutually supportive, with balanced input from all learners. It is a scenario where realistic goals are set for the group, where support and encouragement is offered and where achievement is appropriately recognised.

Teachers seeking to support their learners and improve each individual's performance need to create a productive learning climate and promote learner satisfaction by creating a cohesive team committed to common goals. Team-building behaviour is exemplified by agreeing team standards, objectives and tasks and identifying aspects of personality and roles that will affect success. This procedure applies in a learning situation where, besides establishing the technical competence and needs of individuals, considerable effort must be invested in building strong morale, motivation and ownership of outcomes in teams of learners.

Promoting fair and suitable access to learning and achievement is another key role that implies legal duties under the anti-discrimination legislation and Health and Safety at Work Act 1974. This gives rise to a constantly changing role for teachers in terms of their responsibilities for supporting learners and promoting anti-discriminatory practice and for dealing effectively with equal opportunities and other matters, such as:

- identifying types of discrimination
- recognising sources of discrimination
- applying organisational anti-discriminatory policy and observing codes of practice
- preserving the dignity of women and men while working in the learning environment
- fulfilling their duties to people with disabilities
- recognising the rights of part-time staff working with them
- preventing racial and sexual harassment

- dealing with age and disability discrimination
- avoiding the use of disabling environments
- having open-minded attitudes towards differences in sexual orientation
- supporting the rehabilitation of offenders
- allowing for entitlement and differences in lifestyle between learners and other staff
- maintaining a correct level of confidentiality and data protection
- facilitating complaints and appeals from learners.

Learners like to be made to feel welcome at the start of any learning programme, and as their teacher you need to quickly establish a healthy working rapport. Arriving early at the venue and going to meet new arrivals at reception helps to meet these complementary requirements. Having gathered your flock leave someone standing by to gather up the stragglers while you return to the meeting place ready to greet people who subsequently make their way there. When the learners assemble for the first time give them a good reception and initiation. Break the ice with a cordial welcome and friendly greeting. Be pleasant and show respect. Be sociable and agreeable and above all demonstrate a polite regard for their values and feelings.

# Establishing rapport with learners

*Learners are made to feel welcome and are given appropriate time and attention*

First impressions are important. How learners feel about you when you first meet them will influence their attitude towards you later. Learners are entitled to expect a friendly and enthusiastic reception, and a positive attitude will result if time is spent welcoming people and giving them a chance to settle down. Setting the right tone and atmosphere is a key communication skill aimed at promoting a secure environment for newcomers.

Creating a climate that is conducive to establishing rapport is the joint responsibility of the facilitator and learners. Engendering a collaborative team spirit must begin on day one of the programme, and learning to work together begins when the class first assembles. Right from the start every effort should be made to ensure that learners are **put at ease** and encouraged to get to know one another. It is useful to open with an icebreaker or a 'Why are we here?' type brainstorm and discussion which provides an opportunity for people to get involved, ask questions or clarify initial doubts.

**Rapport** is an essential aspect of effective communication. When interacting with learners, factors that can affect the establishment of rapport include the facilitator's ability to establish trust, to maintain eye contact when learners are talking, to listen carefully to what they are saying, and on an individual basis to mirror various positive aspects of their behaviour.

*The manner of interaction demonstrates a non-judgmental acceptance of the learner*

It is important to show your enthusiasm for the subject being taught, to be knowledgeable about its content, and to establish a warm and friendly atmosphere. Early efforts should be made to establish rapport. Let every learner see that you are on their side trying to help them. Never talk down to them. Being too familiar can sometimes breed contempt and disrespect, while a severe, dominant manner can quickly alienate the group. A friendly democratic style usually produces more work and positive attitudes towards the teacher and the subject too.

Issues of equality of opportunity and non-discriminatory practice should always be in the mind of teachers when interacting with learners. Learning sessions should take account as far as possible of each individual's felt needs and should encourage all learners to express their opinions openly. The aim should be to maintain an atmosphere of mutual respect and to ensure strict avoidance of belittling statements and behaviour designed to discredit, defame or stigmatise students that you do not particularly like or feel alienated towards. The tendency for some learners to harshly criticise others and pick holes in their work or what they have to say should likewise be discouraged.

*Responses to the learner are based on both their verbal and non-verbal communication*

At first one might think that communication on a face-to-face basis is purely a verbal exchange, but on closer examination it can be seen that there are more subtle ways of communicating one's meaning. These include head nods, bodily posture, facial expressions, laughing, touching, and many others. During an interaction learners will signal their feelings by continually moving in various ways. Facial expressions and body language go with speech to make a total communication. Some movements called mannerisms may be unplanned and repetitive and will subsequently be associated with the person concerned. Care must be taken to prevent the others from mimicking them.

As well as being active listeners, teachers need to be good at interpreting their learners' non-verbal signals. Non-verbal cues play an important part in regulating and maintaining conversations. During a meeting speech is backed up by an intricate network of gestures which affect the meaning of what is said. Body postures adopted by a person provide a means by which their attitude toward the teacher may be judged and act as a pointer to their mood during the interaction.

*Learners are actively listened to*

Hearing what is said is not **active listening**. Listening implies giving your full attention to what the learner is saying. If you do this you demonstrate that you are taking an interest in what they are saying. Persuading and influencing learners and assessing how well your proposals are being received is an ongoing requirement of teaching today. Anticipating and handling objections raised whilst at the same time respecting learners' rights is an important part of the process which can only be achieved if teachers are prepared to listen intently and actively to what their learners are saying. Using the technique of active listening results in effective information gathering which should be followed up by emphasising and responding effectively to the points learners make. Focused questions can then be asked to elicit more information, and the answers provided used when reflecting on the learner's personal views. Teachers should try to reduce anxiety and encourage learners to make known their concerns. The value and importance of learners' comments and suggestions to the success of any learning opportunity should be stressed, and by carefully explaining the benefits of doing this learners will be encouraged to talk to you. It will also indicate that you think that what they are saying is important and by implication that they are too.

*Learners are encouraged to feel comfortable to express concerns, make comments or ask questions at their own pace*

Teaching in the late 1990s is centred around the need to give learners more flexibility to make decisions and freedom to act independently. This approach leads to empowerment of the learners and a willingness to take on delegated tasks. But before this happy state can be achieved learners must feel free to participate fully in any discussions and to express concerns and make comments without the fear of being put down or deliberately embarrassed in any way. Teachers should strive to reduce the learners' anxiety and make every effort to ensure that they are put at ease during meetings. Learners should be encouraged to ask questions and clarify doubts whenever they feel a need to do so.

*Learners are encouraged to express their personal beliefs, wishes and views, except where these adversely affect the rights of others*

How many teachers know what learners really think of them personally or their teaching style? Feedback on what they think can be very enlightening and if taken seriously can lead to improvements all round. If learners are encouraged to speak out, their felt needs and wants will be revealed, and if these are subsequently met all will be well. But if instead learners remain dissatisfied with the opportunities provided or are otherwise displeased, they will bear a grudge and go about complaining and breeding further discontent. If genuine complaints are left unheeded resentment will quickly replace commitment and the class will become a collection of quarrelsome malcontents. This would lead to a disastrous scenario, although it is not unheard of.

Learners should therefore be encouraged to express their personal beliefs, wishes and views, sympathetically and in a spirit of cooperation. Working together as a team should be the theme, and the teacher should be willing to work hard to secure consensus and reach an amicable outcome. Individual assertiveness and the right to challenge the status quo is to be encouraged except where this would adversely affect the rights of others.

*The manner, level and pace of communication with the learner is appropriate to their abilities, personal beliefs and preferences*

Good communication is crucial to the effectiveness of teacher/learner relationships. With this in mind, teachers will need to develop their skills of communicating formally and informally, orally or in writing, with both individuals and groups. Effective communication will depend upon teachers being able to:

- effectively control meetings with learners
- interpret and use non-verbal communications
- develop listening and questioning skills
- pace exposition to suit the learners' ability to make sense of the information being imparted
- use appropriate language effectively
- write clear and concise letters and learning materials.

Not all people are able to absorb information at the same rate. Furthermore, the learners' perception of how the task or information will impact on their life will also affect the way in which the communication is received. When sharing information the learners' abilities, personal beliefs and preferences should be taken into account.

The way in which a message is perceived could be influenced by factors such as:

- expectation about what will be said and its utility to the learners concerned
- the learners' readiness to receive the information
- the degree of anxiety felt by learners
- the degree of interest in the information given
- the importance and relevance of the message to the learners' felt needs
- the learners' prior knowledge and experience of the subject to which the information refers
- the learners' intellectual ability
- the learners' level of motivation and need
- the level of threat imposed – estimate of the 'need to know' factor.

*Constraints on communication with learners are identified and minimised*

Constraints on communication will be either intrinsic or extrinsic or a mixture of both, and if learners are to contribute to a discussion they must be convinced that what they have to say will not lead to recriminations. Otherwise, the main constraints on effective communication will probably be an individual's language skills and their social, cultural and environmental circumstances. Their ability to respond will be affected by the suitability of language used by the teacher and their perception of the message being communicated. Perception will be affected by excessive detail and the complexity of the communication, and the meaning clouded or distorted by previous knowledge and experience.

When receiving feedback, learners should be encouraged by hearing some good news as well as the downside. Teachers should avoid negative emphasis and concentrate on giving constructive comment. Furthermore, learners will feel constrained to speak out if they perceive a lack of confidentiality. Learners need to believe that what they say in confidence will not be made known in the public domain before they will confide in a teacher.

# Supporting learners' needs

*Learners' rights and choices are promoted in ways which are consistent with the practitioner's role and relevant legislation and policies*

Students have rights that are set out in 'student agreements' which give details of their entitlement and their responsibilities. For example, they are entitled to join in suitable learning opportunities provided in a safe and healthy environment. To be given credit for relevant prior achievement. To be taught by competent teachers and provided with adequate guidance and support throughout their studies. And to be treated courteously and in accordance with relevant legislation.

Most people want to succeed in life and in specific areas of challenge such as a learning programme which they take on. Learners come to the classroom with certain needs and expectations they hope to fulfil. These expectations include social needs, such as taking part in group activities and competing with others, and intrinsic needs, such as the need to make progress, to satisfy curiosity and to perform a task well. The teacher should be aware of these needs and should consider how these may be facilitated during the time available.

*The effect of own competence, values and beliefs is recognised and addressed in the way in which learners are supported*

Each teacher has a set of values or predispositions to behave in ways that can affect their relationship with students and consequently influence the judgements they make. Affective reactions to their perception of equal opportunities will probably result in their determination to be fair-minded and even-handed when dealing with learners. However, teachers holding conflicting values and beliefs will tend to make unsound decisions and act in a manner that could be unlawful. The anti-discrimination legislation requires that people are treated impartially, equally without distinction and fairly without favouritism. It is therefore the practitioner's duty to see fair play and ensure fair treatment so as to honour the learners' rights and entitlements. When there is a dispute they must be prepared to hear both sides of the story and consider suggestions and requests on the merits of the argument put forward by learners. Wherever possible individual needs should be met and account taken of the person's preferred learning style. Problems in accessing learning opportunities or support facilities should be rectified, and disadvantaged learners treated with respect and understanding.

*Guidance is sought from an appropriate person where there are difficulties in supporting learners*

People with particular learning difficulties or problems that cannot readily be resolved with the teacher during the initial assessment or as the course progresses, and those needing help with organising themselves, may be referred to qualified people in the special needs unit, educational guidance and counselling unit, student support services or specialist training providers as appropriate.

Typically the need for support may derive from:

- learning-related difficulties
- difficulty in gaining access to special learning materials
- the learning environment
- the social setting: domestic problems and lack of self-study opportunities
- problems with social relationships within the group.

Clients with learning difficulties or problems that cannot readily be resolved and those needing help with career choice would be referred to qualified staff based in support units. The support available might include a counsellor or an adult guidance coordinator; a numeracy or literacy tutor; a student union liaison person; a nurse or a religious leader; a vocational assessor or an internal verifier.

*Limits of support available are recognised and, where appropriate, explained to learners*

Some providers' mission statements and organisational objectives express high ideals and sincere intentions that may or may not be realistically achieved. There will inevitably be a limit to the amount of support available to learners, and the level of support that can be offered will be dictated by the availability of competent people and resources. It is no good making promises that cannot be fulfilled, and so it is imperative that the learners are made aware of what help they can expect to receive. Shortcomings in formal provision can sometimes be alleviated by promoting an ethos of self-help. By the use of collaborative styles of learning a powerful group self-support system can be created. People begin to trust one another and a climate of respect for one another develops. It soon becomes quite logical and natural for anyone with a problem to draw on the strength of the group for support in times of difficulty.

*Accurate sources of referral for additional support which learners may need are maintained*

Referral is the act of directing a student to a practitioner who is specially trained or equipped to meet the student's special needs. Alternatively a special programme of support could be made available to the student supported by a mentor. Records should be maintained of the sources of support available locally and care taken to find out about associated processes and procedures for referral. Learners seeking advice will expect teachers to respond quickly to requests for information about where to seek it and who to contact at referral agencies.

*Learners are given clear, relevant and timely information on sources of additional support in a manner which enables them to make informed decisions*

Steps should be taken to involve learners in decisions about their learning. The need for joint negotiation throughout the programme should be agreed from the start. Study guidance would include help for students when deciding on learning methods and resources to be used, the level of teacher support needed, the rate of learning and how this will be regulated. Guidance and review opportunities should be available to all learners. Giving guidance is a very responsible and demanding duty. The services of someone who is able to support them and help them identify sources of problems and feasible solutions is an essential requirement of any training provision.

Where specialist advice on how to make further progress is not available in-house it is advisable to refer learners to external agencies who may be better placed to handle the setback. A rationale outlining the procedure for giving information and advice to learners would include reference to action plans or personal training programmes that have been written, reviews of progress and achievement against unit criteria, opportunities for progression and transfer of training. Discussions with learners will bring into focus any difficulties that are holding up their progress and will serve to trigger remedial action.

*Referral is conducted in a constructive and sensitive manner which is supportive of the learner and their learning objectives*

Promoting learners' rights and choices and ensuring a commitment to equal opportunities should always be foremost in the minds of teachers. This is of utmost importance when teachers are called upon to adopt a guidance role and particularly when they are working with learners who will need to be referred to a remedial unit or remedial programme. The teacher should show sensitivity to the learner's feelings and respond to any signs of distress. The aim should be to build confidence and to act as an advocate who is interceding on the learner's behalf to help gain access to extra resources needed to support their progress. Confidentiality of learner data should be protected and care taken to ensure that loss of face as a result of actions taken is minimised. If a learner agrees and supports the referral suggested an amicable solution will be assured, but if the move is resisted there could be repercussions, in which case the learner concerned should be actively assisted to register an appeal.

# Promoting access to learning and achievement

*Barriers to access to learning opportunities are identified and minimised*

Blockages are not entirely restricted to barriers and contextual factors that must be overcome when learners are gaining physical access to learning opportunities. Adult learners also collect psychological baggage throughout life which can hold them back. **Physical barriers** to be overcome may include difficult access to buildings, poor signposting, an unwelcoming reception desk, complex information sheets, unhelpful staff, high course fees, travel to study costs, costs of study materials and books, need for crèche facilities – the list is endless.

A learner's own personality can adversely affect their attitude and determination to meet self-development goals, as can limited study skills, lack of confidence and feelings of inadequacy, self-doubt and fear of exposure or humiliation. Perceptions of earlier experiences of education and unpleasant memories of schooldays can also serve as tough barriers to be overcome, as can any negative attitudes of family and friends towards the learner returning to study. Mature learners may secretly feel that they are getting too old to learn, and fear that they may be made to appear dense in comparison with others. They may feel that they have been out of the game for too long and out of touch with modern training methods. There are countless reasons for fears and individual learning differences among people. Whether a real problem exists or not, if the learner thinks a problem exists then that person has a problem.

Individually teachers can do very little about structural and physical resourcing, for such power rests with the provider's senior management team, but they can do a lot to overcome or minimise many of the **personal barriers** suggested above by offering sympathetic support and encouragement and providing ongoing personal counselling and career guidance. Suggested ways of overcoming barriers and building learner confidence are given in Chapter 8 under the heading 'Identifying factors inhibiting learning' (p. 115).

*Barriers to opportunities for the demonstration and assessment of achievement are identified and minimised*

Opportunities to demonstrate achievement should be selected which provide access to fair and reliable assessment. This is equally applicable for the able-bodied and those with impairments or any other special requirements. Assessment requirements are **specific to the individual** and assessors must recognise the rights of adults as individuals and not as categories of people with disabilities or special needs. **Special assessment requirements** may for example arise as a result of physical or sensory disabilities, learning difficulties or emotional and behavioural difficulties.

Candidates with special requirements may have significant difficulties in mobility or communication that prevent them from participating in the regular assessment provision without additional help. The philosophy of equal opportunities requires the elimination of unfair discrimination, and teachers will need to support candidates by arranging access to fair assessment opportunities matched to their specific needs. This could involve enlisting the aid of specialist staffing, or in some cases by arranging for the use of special equipment in the assessment environment. The City and Guilds policy statement *'Access to assessment – candidates with special needs'* shown in Figure 15.4 (see *Documents Pack*) gives advice on making special assessment arrangements.

*Accurate and timely information and advice is given to learners to enable them to make informed decisions about their learning programme and possible qualification route*

In adult education, participation is often voluntary and people join classes simply because they wish to, but this is not always the case. Some are 'invited' to attend seminars; others seek information because redundancy or the need for retraining creates an urgent need to participate. In any event, there should be a strategy for assessing a learner's suitability for the training opportunity on offer. In particular the following factors might be considered:

● relevance of qualification sought to the learner's needs
● existing levels of knowledge, skills and experience
● perceived impact on employability and progression
● existing qualifications and profiles of competence
● recency of qualifications and prior experience
● relevance, scope and transferability of earlier training to the proposed programme.

Once the value of the training programme to the target learner group has been established it will be necessary to disseminate relevant information on good practice to course teams and other learners, and subsequently to embed the system within the total training provision. Typical enabling objectives for embedding good practice would be:

● to specify systems for giving information and advice to learners about learning programmes and qualification route
● to provide examples of good practice when informing, guiding and giving advice in order to assist staff training and development
● to identify ways of matching learner requirements to learning opportunities and awards
● to devise a strategy for embedding procedures in your own operations.

*Information and advice given to learners is based on an accurate recognition of opportunities available, constraints, learning context, and individual preferences*

People can make educational choices only if they are aware of the learning opportunities available that might meet their individual preferences. Pre-course guidance interviews can be used to provide learners with information and advice about learning opportunities offered and to demonstrate a commitment to equal opportunities. The prospectus or course information leaflets will give details of particular courses, but the teacher conducting the interview will need to explain the curriculum content, teaching materials, learning resources and assessment available. Information provided should be readily assimilated by all clients including people of different cultural and racial backgrounds.

Teachers will need to provide learners with information about:

- learning opportunities
- programme formats, including modular, roll-on-roll-off, part-time, full-time, open learning or drop-in workshops
- other providers, including local community based trainers and voluntary sector organisations
- timetables of learning opportunities – start dates, timing and location, starting and finishing times
- avoidance of discrimination
- arrangements for facilitating their progress.

*Information and advice given to learners avoids bias*

Teachers must not allow personal feelings and subjectivity to interfere with their relationships with learners. A **positive bias** towards an individual is exemplified by the 'halo effect' and influenced by someone creating a good initial impression. There may be a tendency to provide better quality information to a person who is evaluated highly on personal traits or where the teacher perceives a strong similarity between the learner and themselves or their offspring. A **negative bias** can be illustrated by stereotyping where judgements about a learner are based on an image or conception held by the teacher of the person concerned. In this instance the quality of information given could be adversely affected and the amount of time devoted to offering advice limited.

*Access to learning and achievement promotes equality of opportunity*

Learners have the right to participate in appropriate education and personal development programmes offered by providers, and clients with special learning requirements should be given adequate help in gaining access. Steps must be taken to ensure that educational establishments are providing equal opportunities for people to join in suitable learning opportunities.

When gathering evidence for this unit it could be helpful to survey the arrangements for gaining access within your employing institution and answer the following questions:

- Are both sexes treated fairly during selection and recruitment processes for training programmes?
- Is the advice given to all clients honest and free of bias?
- Is the provision offered available to all suitable applicants?
- Are you providing equal opportunities to those with whom you are involved?
- Are you free of bias when counselling, giving advice and enrolling learners?

*Access to learning and achievement takes account of previous experiences in order to provide a relevant and coherent learning programme with clear progression routes*

Account could usefully be taken of their prior experience at work and educational record when providers are enrolling learners on available courses or planning new training programmes. Things to consider might include part-time and full-time employment and work experience; school achievement, further education and workplace training; hobbies and leisure activity; and unpaid work such as helping out in the local community. Earlier practical experience gained while completing do-it-yourself projects, repairing the car, word-processing at home and the like can be utilised when learners are gaining new **vocational skills**. Experience gained while managing family matters and controlling budgets can yield evidence of **organisational skills**. **Intellectual skills** can be enhanced by reading and managing clubs and groups.

In order to provide a relevant and coherent learning programme with clear progression routes a matching exercise should be conducted. This would involve correlating existing skills distilled from sources such as the ones described above with target award criteria.

## Promoting anti-discriminatory practice

*Anti-discriminatory practice is promoted in ways which are consistent with the practitioner's role, organisational policy and legislation*

Under the **Race Relations Act 1976**, direct and indirect discrimination are unlawful. Teachers must therefore actively and overtly promote anti-discriminatory practices and encourage equal opportunities in every aspect of their work. Action should be taken to discourage any person who is heard using discriminatory language or promoting sex-role stereotyping. Teachers should themselves ensure that their **non-verbal behaviour** does not transmit discriminatory messages to their students. **Equal opportunity** issues may arise in matters concerning learners in relation to their race, gender, age, religion, class, background, culture, mental or physical ability, political beliefs or sexual orientation.

Under the **Sex Discrimination Act 1975** it is unlawful for employers (and teachers) to discriminate on grounds of sex or marriage. There are three types of discrimination: direct, indirect and victimisation. **Direct** sex discrimination is where a male learner is treated less favourably than a female learner or where a single person is treated less favourably than a married person or vice versa. **Indirect** discrimination is where a learner cannot comply with an unjustifiable requirement which appears to apply equally to men and women (or to married and single people) but in practice can only be met by a smaller proportion of people of one sex or marital status. **Victimisation** occurs when the teacher subsequently unfairly treats someone who has made a complaint to the training provider's responsible representative.

**Sexual harassment** is any unwanted sexual advance made verbally, physically or by gesture which causes a learner to feel threatened or humiliated. Obviously teachers must be very careful not to harass their learners, inadvertently or directly, for example by unwanted touching or other physical contact when giving praise or when offering study guidance or support. Even well-intentioned actions can be misinterpreted and may actually cause learner discomfort.

**Age discrimination** can occur when an attempt is made to exclude older people who wish to enhance their employability or otherwise further their personal development. Care must be taken by teachers to avoid discriminating when referring to their age or presumed intellectual status or ability to learn new things.

Equal opportunities are thought by some to apply only to race and gender but the same principles apply to discrimination against **disabled** learners. Care must be taken to ensure that the disabilities and needs of individual learners are addressed fully. Teachers should recognise that special needs are individual and cannot be collated into some kind of disability category that can be addressed by separation or grouping – even if well-intentioned and lavishly resourced.

In order to ensure that all candidates for assessment are treated fairly and on an equal basis I issue each client with a copy of the equal opportunities policy statement given in Figure 5.1

(see *Documents Pack*), and I and my colleagues are fully committed to satisfying these principles in all our activities and published materials.

*The way in which individuals are treated demonstrates recognised good anti-discriminatory practice*

A teacher's attitudes and behaviour regarding gender or racial issues will have a significant effect on the way their learners interact with the opposite sex, people from minority groups and those with special learning requirements. Teachers have a responsibility to take such steps as are reasonably practicable to prevent unlawful discrimination. This is true whether the individuals concerned are being recruited or selected for a given programme or are actually being taught in a group. The training provider's written equal opportunities policy should be reviewed from time to time and a commitment to its values overtly demonstrated. Teachers and learners alike should adopt a 'person-centred approach to training' by treating all learners equally and controlling any feelings of dislike or contempt for other groups. Entrenched attitudes held may be revealed by a person's belief in, for example, the intrinsic superiority of their nation, culture or social grouping. Teachers can reduce the incidence of prejudice by raising awareness of discriminatory practices operating and ensuring that curriculum materials are free of race and gender bias.

Sources of discrimination may be other learners, staff of the training organisation, or people in partner providers, and efforts should be made to maintain effective liaison with a view to encouraging those concerned to adopt an anti-racist perspective and actively challenge incidents involving prejudice and stereotyping.

*Relationships with learners are not exploitative or a misuse of the practitioner's role and power*

Ethics deals with moral duty and obligation. A teacher's **ethical responsibilities** govern their conduct and relationships with learners and require them to adhere to professional and legal standards. Interactions with learners should be honestly conducted and beneficial to them. Their privacy must be protected and confidentiality of individual data assured. Personal codes of conduct should deter teachers from abusing their authority by, for example, attempting to mislead, misinform, corrupt or manipulate learners, or make pawns of them or play off one against the other.

Social psychology is concerned with the ways in which a person's thinking and behaviour can be influenced by others, while **social influence processes** involve the attempts by another person or group to cause individuals to change their minds. Compliance has been studied by Asch,[1] Milgram[2] and many others, and their studies show how differently people behave when placed in situations controlled by others, particularly if those who direct activities do so from a position of power or authority. Learners can be caused to inwardly accept information delivered by credible sources which is aimed at attitudinal change; teachers are therefore in a position to control learners by persuasion, coercion or brainwashing, or by inducing them to behave in certain ways. This practice would be unethical and could lead to traumatic experiences for the learners concerned.

Teachers are now widely regarded as being 'managers of learning opportunities' rather than autocratic practitioners. As 'facilitators of change and learning' they will still need to provide a measure of direction, and to strike a balance between taking total control of learner activity and allowing them freedom to decide for themselves what they will do. A teacher's behaviour towards a particular student can have a powerful influence on the perception of the other learners towards that person. If this is true then teachers can play a major part in shaping behaviour and attitudes towards cooperative learning in multiracial groups or with people with learning difficulties.

*Guidance is sought from an appropriate person where the practitioner is unsure of appropriate non-discriminatory practice, or has discriminatory feelings towards an individual*

Some of us may have fixed opinions about people of a specific race or religion and actively dislike them. This will affect the way we feel toward such people and the manner adopted when we deal with individuals. It is no good saying that stereotyping and bias do not exist, denying our real feelings and blaming ourselves for holding these views. What we need to do is to confront our prejudices and take steps to seek out information on which to base a programme of reasoning and questioning of our preconceived opinions. Once we have come to terms with the reality it will be possible to question existing attitudes and counter our promotion of inequalities in the classroom. Many establishments now have people specifically assigned to issues of discrimination, and advice can be sought from the responsible person if we cannot manage the transition alone.

*Appropriate and consistent action is taken when learners use discriminatory behaviour, remarks or language, and the effects or consequences of their behaviour are clearly explained to them*

**Discriminatory behaviour** such as spoken abuse, insulting comments or jokes, and written abuse such as graffiti, offensive pictures and other materials should be banned from your classroom. Learners should not be permitted to engage in banter or deliberate attempts to humiliate or in any other way ridicule or undermine the confidence of any other group member. Any instance of this form of harassment must be **challenged** positively and directly by the teacher who is facilitating the session. If necessary a reprimand or verbal warning in line with the provider's harassment policy should be delivered to the harasser. The equal opportunities unit should be consulted if the practice persists.

*Appropriate action is taken in the event of a colleague using discriminatory behaviour, remarks or language*

While the thought of taking a colleague to task about breaches of equal opportunities legislation that you have noticed may be quite off-putting, it will have to be done. Informing a colleague about the consequences of unethical or illegal practices should not be seen as whistle-blowing but merely as a public-spirited duty intended to help a friend avoid setting a poor example to other teachers and learners. And you have a responsibility to the unfortunate victims to help stamp out discriminatory behaviour of any kind.

*Individuals wishing to make a complaint about discriminatory practice are appropriately supported in doing so*

Many training providers have now published student handbooks, codes of practice and policy documents detailing the rights of a student to be 'treated equally and with respect regardless of age, ability/disability, gender, ethnicity, sexual orientation, religious persuasion, marital status or any other relevant factor'. If a student considers that they are being unfairly treated and they cannot resolve the problem with the person concerned they can seek informal advice from someone they trust – a friend or teacher. If this is not acceptable then the complainant should be helped to lodge a formal complaint with the equal opportunities coordinator and activate the complaints procedure operated by the training provider concerned.

## Self-assessment questions

1 List factors that affect the establishment of rapport.

2 Describe how learners may be welcomed and put at ease.

3 Describe what is meant by the phrase 'non-judgemental acceptance of the learner'.

4 Describe ways of creating an atmosphere that is conducive to establishing rapport.

5 Describe methods that may be used to elicit a learner's personal views.

6 Describe some of the non-verbal signals that may be given by learners during an interaction and explain how these may be interpreted.

7 Describe the technique known as 'active listening'.

8 Explain the importance of encouraging learners to express their concerns, make comments and ask questions.

9 How does the pace of communication affect the way it is perceived?

10 Describe what is meant by 'learner entitlement' and explain how you promote learners' rights and choices.

11 List the anti-discrimination legislation in force today.

12 Give instances of 'direct' and 'indirect discrimination' and 'victimisation'. Explain how instances of these could be handled. .

13 Describe how health and safety legislation and good practice affects your teaching role.

14 List the referral agencies that exist to support learners with learning difficulties and special requirements.

15 Identify potential barriers to learning, describe their effects and suggest how they can be overcome.

16 What procedure is there in your workplace for helping candidates to cope with a return to learning?

17 What actions will need to be taken in anticipation that some or all of your learners may need help with aspects of learning?

18 In what ways will adult learners seeking places on programmes differ from young people in their previous experience and attitudes?

19 Define the terms 'bias' and 'stereotyping'.

20 Describe the significance of using 'non-stereotypical language'.

## *Preparing for assessment: sample activities*

### *Activity 5.1 Establishing rapport*
Provide evidence of how you established a healthy rapport with at least two learners. Submit a written report from an observer who witnessed the interaction. Write up your reactions and response to the observer's report and produce an action plan for the continuous improvement of your ability to create a team spirit and good relations during learning activities.

### *Activity 5.2 Learner support*
Obtain a copy of your employer's mission statement, organisational objectives, candidate's charter and statement of learner rights and entitlement. Produce your own versions if there are none available in-house.

Identify and list the range of learner support available and relevant referral agencies that you or your learners could currently call upon for help, and also note the constraints operating.

Explain how learners' rights and choices are promoted, and describe how you have recently provided or arranged support for two of your learners. Outline the benefits they derived from the help given.

### Activity 5.3 Barriers to learning

Identify possible barriers that might be encountered by people wishing to gain access to learning and achievement in any context that you wish to consider. Explain what needs to be done to overcome the barriers and list the steps that will need to be taken to eliminate the problems.

Explain how you have helped at least two learners avoid or overcome barriers to access to two different types of learning opportunities in your own college or learning environment.

### Activity 5.4 Researching personal development guidance facilities

The promotion of students' participation in their professional and personal development calls for teamworking since in general more than one teacher is responsible for this aspect of staff/student interaction.

Investigate the organisation of personal guidance provision in your workplace and produce a chart showing the individual role-holders and referral agents that you will need to work with to ensure that you are able to carry out your role effectively in this important work.

### Activity 5.5 Upholding anti-discriminatory practice

Prepare a list of appropriate 'non-stereotypical terms' applying to the particular groups and individuals that you are working with today and will probably encounter in the future.

Explain the significance of using non-discriminatory language and applying anti-discriminatory practice when facilitating learner groups.

Describe two different incidents where you took action to uphold the principles of anti-discriminatory practice.

### Notes

1 S.E. Asch, *Social Psychology*, Prentice-Hall, New York 1952.

2 S. Milgram, 'Behavioural Study of Obedience', *Journal of Abnormal and Social Psychology* 1963, vol. 67, pp. 171–8.

# 6

# Agreeing learning programmes with learners

People seeking access to education and training opportunities are entitled to an initial assessment designed to help them plan their future personal development programme. Initial assessment helps both training provider and learner sort out what it is that they wish to achieve. Action plans can be negotiated, credit for prior learning and achievement can be given and relevant training arranged to meet identified needs and the ability of individuals. Matching needs and expectations within the education and training provision is the key to success in the attainment of learners' goals relating to vocational competency or achievement in academic subjects.

Access to suitable learning opportunities has in the past not always been easy, and at best a compromise between what the candidate was seeking and whatever course or training was already 'on the shelf'. Today there exists demand for a wider range of training provision. This is needed to fulfil the expectations of employers seeking to provide quality products and services backed by a well-trained and competent workforce. In order to meet this challenge, providers will need to set up or improve access and initial assessment and teachers will need to be able to design programmes that are matched to the learners' requirements.

There is also a need to review and assess progress continuously against targets written into action plans, and to update the plans taking account of information gathered, options available and strategies agreed during the current review. Relevant learning opportunities can then be arranged to meet needs as far as is possible bearing in mind available resources and the ability of individuals to meet their achievement targets or occupational aims.

Reflection and review are of prime importance in any modern learning programme, and this technique should be practised by teachers. Aspects of planning learning programmes that could usefully be reviewed and assessed include:

- adequacy of preparation
- performance criteria and objectives specified
- inclusion of sufficient motivational factors
- context and relevance of the lessons to stated objectives and to the age and experience of the learners
- suitability of learning activities and matching of methods selected with learners' requirements
- choice of teaching and learning resources used
- compensation for physical and psychological handicaps or other special learner requirements where applicable

- means of establishing teacher/learner communication links and relieving learner anxiety
- relevance of programme content to learners' needs
- logical structure of lessons: development of fundamental manipulation and perceptual skills, core skills and occupational area knowledge and techniques
- use of planned progressive steps from known to unknown, basic to complex and concrete to abstract
- evaluation of outcomes: checks of learning, test results, efficiency and effectiveness of planning in terms of learning achieved
- relevance and suitability of teaching strategies employed.

# Negotiating learning programmes with learners

*The learning programme negotiated with learners is based on an accurate assessment of their learning needs, capabilities, aspirations and learning context*

When negotiating learning programmes teachers need to tune in quickly to the learner's requirements so that no time is wasted getting to know what they are thinking and what they hope to achieve. In order to do this teachers will need to create an attitude of genuine caring and establish rapport quickly. This requires that they act and look enthusiastic and demonstrate active listening skills so as to really understand what the learners are trying to say.

There will be a need to compare the amount of time allocated for learning a given task with the time the learner needs to accomplish it. Obviously the time needed will depend upon the learner's aptitude for the task, the degree of perseverance of the learner, the quality of teaching and the learning opportunities provided. The assessment specification, the level of testing against standards set and the assessment techniques employed will also affect outcomes. The allocation of study time for specific topics within the standard programme should also be considered when individual learning programmes are negotiated, and more or less time should be given to topics where learners exhibit strengths or weaknesses. This technique should serve to promote a better overall success rate, although facilitating a model negotiated programme for each learner could present considerable practical difficulties.

It is thought that learning is most effective when learners are actively engaged in doing things, and especially when learning opportunities and tasks negotiated relate closely to the learners' prior experiences. The way in which programme content is covered during instruction will also affect what is learned. For example, learners could find abstract concepts too difficult to absorb and prefer the greater use of concrete experiences and representational approaches in order to learn. For the learning programme to be most effective, account should therefore be taken of current capabilities and the need to provide new sensory experiences that learners can relate to earlier concrete experiences.

Some teachers like to start their programmes with essential topics that they know from experience will reflect typical learner requirements. This gives them a chance to observe and form initial impressions (which can admittedly on occasion go well beyond the facts) of their learner group before negotiating individual learning programmes. Nikki Glendening, an experienced training officer, likes to write notes about each of her trainees and thereby gain an insight into their characteristics, needs and personalities. She finds this very helpful when forming a relationship with the learners that is based on mutual respect and trust. An example is given in Figure 6.1.

Ways and means of establishing learner needs and training opportunities are discussed

## Reflections on a formative assessment and review

Claire is the eldest in the group and is in her early fifties. She is currently employed as a senior staff nurse on a medical ward in a community hospital where she has worked for the last 10 years since her children left home. Her husband is supportive of her desire to return to formal learning if not somewhat quizzical that she should wish to at 'such a late stage in her career'. He wishes her well but hopes that her study will not interfere with their social life and her role as a partner and wife.

Claire's own expressed motivation is that she has recently recognised an unexpected opportunity to fulfil a lifelong ambition for promotion to ward sister – a dream she has harboured for many years but believed to be both unrealistic and unreachable due to an earlier career break and move to part-time work. Claire views this course as a stepping stone to entering a university diploma programme and as a way to update knowledge and skills for the role of sister; and as a barometer of how she might deal with the 'conflicts of academic study and home demands'.

She is highly motivated to succeed and does not hesitate to clarify her understanding of relevant concepts by interrupting and asking questions. However, when Claire wishes to interrupt she puts her hand up in the air rather than call out her question straight away. This gesture usually results in a peal of laughter, although not unkindly, from other group members who find this action both old fashioned and amusing. It is this laughter that catches my attention if, at first, I do not notice Claire's hand in the air.

Interestingly, following a formative review Claire said that although she is aware of this reaction she isn't worried about it and finds it hard to change the way she was brought up. She positively enjoys the role of mother figure....

Source: Nikki Glendening

**Figure 6.1** *Reflections on a formative assessment and review*

at some length in Chapter 2, and a sample action plan is given in Figure 2.4 (see *Documents Pack*). Action planning is also discussed in Chapter 12, and relevant processes are shown in Figures 12.1, 12.14 and 12.15.

*Types of learning opportunities and methods available are clearly and accurately explained to learners*

The types of training and development opportunity available to learners should be outlined during the initial assessment session or during induction to the programme. Proposals that describe clearly and accurately how the learner's requirements could be met can be presented, and there should be plenty of opportunity for learners to ask questions and seek clarification. The opportunities outlined should be matched as far as possible with learner aspirations and abilities, but it will probably not be feasible to provide an exact match because in some instances there will be a very limited range of options to choose from. Bearing this in mind, suitable contexts through which the learner's expressed and felt needs and goals may be achieved can be identified and a scheme of work with relevant aims and objectives can be discussed. Account should be taken of any special learner requirements and the need to make adjustments to standard programmes to suit learners with differing abilities or special learning difficulties. Responsibility for making the choice must remain with the learner. All that the teacher can reasonably do is provide factual information and advice, and recommend options which in their opinion will best meet the learner's declared needs. Once the learner has indicated their preferred programme option the teacher can point out the advantages and disadvantages of following that route.

*Resources available are clearly and accurately explained to learners*

No one can deny that it is important to explain clearly and comprehensively the facilities and resources that are available to learners. But the timing and amount of information imparted at one time is very important. A broad-brush approach could be adopted when initially explaining to learners the range and scope of facilities and resources available. Giving a blow-by-blow account of the people, facilities and equipment involved in the programme would probably serve to confuse and adversely affect the newcomer's motivation and confidence. All that can be done initially is to give the broadest outline of what is available and perhaps issue learners with a guide to the resource centre or listing of what is available and how to access it. The learners can be introduced to learning resource centres and equipment stores during the programme after they have had time to settle in and cope with the flood of paperwork, instructions and form-filling. They will also need time to recover from the shock that often accompanies the first sight of unit criteria and associated terminology. Making sense of criteria, range statements and evidence requirements tends to overwhelm beginners in the early days of many programmes.

*Boundaries of negotiation and constraints on options available are identified and clarified with learners*

Learners like to know where they stand when it comes to making complaints or negotiating their action plan content. All too often, teachers resort to 'top down' **broadcasting,** by either oral or written means, decisions they have taken without consulting those who will be most affected by the consequences. A better way might be to encourage learner **empowerment** by establishing a partnership and working together to understand and accept programme constraints and jointly make decisions. Learner empowerment would promote open behaviour and 'bottom-up' or **upward feedback** would result in people listening to one another's points of view.

Relevant **roles and responsibilities** should be laid down and each party should play their part in working for an understanding. Both sides should demonstrate a willingness to cooperate when taking unavoidable actions to meet programme constraints. Where there is little or no choice of option open to learners a spirit of give and take and a willingness to meet halfway should be promoted, rather than attempting to impose a decision. By all means be businesslike, but try to limit the impact of appearing as an authority figure and ensure that suggestions from learners who show initiative are taken seriously. Their views must be respected and valued.

*Possible progression from the learning programme is accurately identified and clarified with learners*

Routes to progression should be explained to learners who should be encouraged to be forward-looking. Teachers can help learners seeking favourable opportunities by pointing out possibilities and openings such as bridging courses and stepping stones to higher level courses that will permit career advancement. Learner reviews provide an excellent opportunity to negotiate individual and group action plans that will pave the way towards greater achievement and the chance to succeed in one's aim to get ahead and make progress.

At classroom level, **progression** means moving forward according to individual needs and differences in learning styles. The Dalton Plan developed by Helen Parkhurst in the 1920s exemplifies the method whereby the learning programme was covered by learning contracts that were agreed by individual learners. The learners accepted the tasks assigned for each month, signed their contracts, organised their workload and progressed through the work at their own rate. Teamworking was encouraged, the contracts were returned to the teacher with completed work and progress was regularly reviewed and recorded. Today, this method is reflected in the importance teachers attach to negotiating and agreeing action plans with their learners.

At award level, the learner will need to decide which course or training programme to tackle next, and progression will depend upon having the required qualifications or work experience to meet entry requirements. However, with NVQ/SVQs there are not normally any prerequisites since they are competence-based vocational qualifications.

Long-term career pressures and well-established institutional structures, gatekeeping and available opportunities to satisfy aspirations will all influence progression from the learning programme and may present barriers that will not be easy to overcome. It might therefore be necessary to consider all options before making the choice that will give the best match. The **SWOT analysis** is a useful device that may be completed by learners wishing to identify potential courses of action that may be open to them. The analysis identifies personal strengths and weaknesses and highlights the threats and opportunities presented by external factors or the environment in which the learners operate. The object of the exercise is to establish how to **utilise strengths**, to **overcome weaknesses** or enlist support, to neutralise or **counteract threats** and to **seize opportunities** identified. A sample SWOT analysis is given in Figure 6.2.

**SWOT analysis**

| Strengths | Weaknesses |
|---|---|
| Good team member | Poor at maths |
| Willing to try anything | Lack IT skills – no home computer |
| Not afraid of hard work | Poor spelling – written work untidy |
| Can generate lots of ideas/suggestions | Very short attention span – get bored easily if pace slows down, easily distracted |
| Good communicator (orally) | Tendency to give up if I cannot get quick results – or maintain progress |
| Have prior experience of some topics comprising the target qualification | Find it hard to take adverse criticism from authority figures |
| Work-based experience available | |

| Opportunities | Threats |
|---|---|
| Can count on friends for support | Accident prone |
| Success could lead to upgrading at work and extra pay | Competition with others for a place on the programme |
| Three training providers nearby | Limited availability of sponsors' funding |
| Improved employability – skills to be learned are transferable to other jobs | Disruption to my home and social life |
| Flexible study programme – would fit in with domestic life | Knowledge is tested by written examination |
| | Would expose limitations in my study skills |
| | Strapped for cash – tight budget |

**Figure 6.2** SWOT analysis

*Expected ways of working are clarified and discussed with learners*

**Rules** and **norms** give direction concerning methods of working and procedures to be adopted in the learning environment. Control can only be maintained if the teacher and students know the routines and recommended modes of working. In order to clarify expected ways of working, teachers must themselves have a thorough knowledge of course materials, methods and context and be able to illustrate the purpose of a particular training programme. This will entail sharing with prospective learners the aims, objectives and content of the programme.

Learners are entitled to receive a reasonably detailed plan or scheme of work which focuses attention on the process and progress to be undergone during the programme. The plan is subject to negotiation but should be approved by the internal verifier or examining board moderator. The processes by which course purposes, content, assessment and resourcing may be the subject of modification and agreement between parties concerned should be laid down. **Appeals procedures** similar to the example used for D32, D33, D34 and D36 candidates which is given in Figure 6.3 (see *Documents Pack*) could be issued to students to whom the arrangements apply. More detailed information on procedures should be available on demand.

Time-honoured traditional professional values should be recognised. Fair play and correctness of behaviour in the classroom should be maintained, and when it becomes necessary to apply sanctions each case should be considered on its merits. The observance of **health and safety** and **equal opportunities** regulations and the spirit of anti-discriminatory legislation should be promoted.

*Information and advice is given to learners in a manner which enables them to make informed decisions and is sufficient to meet their requirements*

Adequate information and advice about the options and choices open to the learners should be given factually and clearly whether this be orally or in written form. Accurate information supplied in written format is preferred by some learners provided that the content is unambiguous and a balanced approach is used. Meditators like to mull over information given, reflect in private and take their time in making decisions. Written information giving details of realistic and achievable criteria for changes would probably suit this group. Debaters like to talk things over together before making decisions and may dislike too much paper-based data. Opposers might prefer to confront the need for change directly, and perhaps challenge the information provided and adapt the proposed programme to suit the revisions agreed among themselves. Conformists might prefer to follow the crowd or take the teacher's word for it. An alternative approach might be to set small groups a number of related problem-solving tasks highlighted in programme reviews and put their proposals to the whole group and the course team.

The key to success lies in the teacher's ability to produce for the group a comprehensive summary of information, facts and comments derived from the programme review together with an indication of those matters needing priority attention.

*Learners are encouraged to feel comfortable to express their wishes and concerns, and to ask questions*

Learners must feel free to participate fully in any discussions, to express concerns and to make comments without being subjected to any form of embarrassment. Teachers should strive to reduce the learners' anxiety and make every effort to ensure that they are put at ease when agreeing their learning programmes. Learners should be encouraged to make suggestions, ask questions and clarify doubts at any time during the negotiation. They are entitled to play an active part in the planning process and by doing so will be better motivated to reach the targets agreed in the resulting action plan.

*The learning programme clearly identifies all relevant information*

Planning and organising a suitable training programme can be crucial to outcomes in the form of learner attainment. The learning programme will inevitably contain information about some or all of the following:

- programme content and performance criteria
- methods and activities
- duration of training and length of lessons
- timetabling of activities
- briefing of learners
- availability and preparation of resources
- assessment criteria and methods
- monitoring and evaluation of outcomes.

When compiling training programmes and assessment plans for learners, the teacher must take account of the skills, complementary and underpinning knowledge, attitudes and standards relating to the content to be learned. Schemes of work relating to the resulting learning programme must clearly identify each of these aspects, and the teacher will need to take account of features such as these when reviewing progress against achievement targets.

From time to time teachers may need to review the scheme of work with colleagues and learners and if necessary modify the scheme, taking account of any observations or suggestions made, and subsequently evaluate its effectiveness.

*Points of disagreement about the learning programme are identified, explored and resolved in a manner which maintains an effective learning relationship*

Teachers should be prepared to revise and modify schemes of work, incorporating ideas for improvement that are collected during the monitoring and evaluation stages; and most importantly, take good account of learners' criticisms and suggestions. But trying to please every learner all the time can be stressful. It is not easy to maintain a helpful, attentive and caring attitude all day long every day, especially if you are feeling that other pressures of work are about to overwhelm you. Nevertheless, overcoming learners' objections and handling difficult situations is becoming a routine part of a modern teacher's role. The resolution of points of disagreement takes assiduity and drive on the part of the teacher and a willingness to face up to the issue in order to bring matters to a head. Changing things for the better can take a lot of time, willpower and determination, and it may at first appear easier to defer action to a later date or just let the matter drop rather than expend a lot of energy overcoming obstinacy and sticking points.

Where learners disagree with features of the learning programme, summaries relating to the points of disagreement should be produced and used to provide group feedback and to resolve any conflict. Learners have the right to make constructive suggestions and see changes implemented. They will be more likely to cooperate willingly in reviews and programme changes if they are empowered to take decisions that will be taken up in earnest by the supervising teacher. This could mean negotiating and agreeing roles within the group, delegating responsibilities and intervening personally when facilitating the programme. However, it is sometimes necessary to take the bull by the horns and dedicate oneself to implementing changes where a consensus cannot be reached, although negotiated settlements are to be preferred. The key consideration must be to maintain rapport and effective working relationships within the group.

# Reviewing learning programmes and agreeing modifications with learners

*The use of information resulting from the review is clarified and agreed with learners*

Information collected from individuals and groups during reviews may be qualitative or quantitative or a mix of both. A **qualitative analysis** of information gathered is carried out by drawing distinctions between the learners' perceptions of the processes and the kind of things that happened during the learning programme. The degree to which teacher **expectations** and learner **aspirations** have been met can be estimated by examining **teacher generated narratives** such as records of work, mark sheets, verifiers' reports and the like, together with **learner accounts** of events and experiences. **Cause and effect** relationships might then be identified, and action taken to correct perceived imbalances or deficiencies in programme resourcing, content or method. Programmes are presented by teachers and therefore the programme review and analysis could be used to assess the impact that teacher behaviour demonstrated while teaching and supporting learners has on learner attitudes and achievement. For example, teachers may be characterised on the basis of their personal qualities, attributes or traits, and the analysis could signal a need for a change in their attitude or teaching style. The learning behaviour and experiences of students resulting from the menu of opportunities programmed will also be affected by the teacher's choice of content and method.

The **outcomes** of teaching and learning can be evaluated by **quantitative analysis**. This is a scientific method whereby the amount of each process input or output is quantified or measured. In the case of a learning programme the features to be measured might include performance indicators such as attendance patterns, ratio of starters to completers, grades and marks gained by learners, certificates awarded, and other measurable criteria. Information derived from this type of analysis could indicate a need to modify the programme in terms of its content, methods, resources, instructional processes and amount of learner support.

The use of information resulting from the review should be clarified and agreed with learners. But the effect of the learners' own behaviour on outcomes could legitimately be raised when discussing the effectiveness of learning programmes and opportunities provided. Low achievers tend to shape classroom conditions and the interaction pattern to suit their personal agendas, which may differ considerably from the teacher's original intentions thereby affecting the nature of the learning outcomes. Some of the purposes of reviews are set out in Figure 6.4.

*The agreed methods of reviewing the learning programme are used within the agreed timescale*

Regular learner evaluations and reviews of classroom teaching and learning outcomes are now seen to be important features of programme evaluation and continuous improvement of the training provision. However, the methods used to collect information and carry out reviews can sometimes affect results. Methods of reviewing and timescales for completion should be agreed with the learners beforehand. Frequent monitoring will enable the group to make constructive suggestions that can be acted upon while the programme is running – before it is too late to do something about problems encountered. Summative reviews are very useful for updating new programmes but the reviews are unlikely to benefit the current cohort. The frequency and timescales for implementing reviews will therefore be an important consideration for teachers.

The **administrative conditions** will affect the way learners complete their evaluation forms and decide their programme ratings. Sufficient time should be allowed for the learners to con-

---

**Purposes of reviews**

- To help learners to clarify learning needs and to create an action plan
- To encourage candidates to see how seizing the opportunity to accredit existing skills and planning to gain new skills can help them meet their personal development target and enhance career opportunities
- To prioritise the importance of action plan content and to derive an effective sequence of learning, bearing in mind costs and benefits of decisions taken
- To monitor and record progress against earlier action plans; to clarify confusion or lack of understanding; to adjust current plan accordingly
- To write sets of aims and objectives designed to enable sought-after skills to be defined and understood
- To identify college-based tasks and workplace activities that will enable new skills to be learned and practised and existing skills to be accredited
- To agree the settings and context in which knowledge gained or the achievement of competence may be demonstrated and recorded
- To analyse and reflect upon the relevance of the learner's experiences in the workplace to the achievement of personal development targets and qualifications sought
- To review progress and to allow for study guidance, counselling and monitoring of the learning process and outcomes of any assessments
- To carry out accreditation processes for prior learning and achievement and to discuss how best to integrate new learning into occupational work

---

**Figure 6.4** *Purposes of reviews*

sider carefully each item on the form; this means that the evaluation form should not be administered a few minutes before the class ends, otherwise students will be busy packing up and will pay scant attention to filling it in. And **unreliable feedback** could be obtained if, for example, the teacher walks around the room while learners are ticking the boxes and adding comments or if respondents are asked to write their names on the forms!

*Learners are encouraged to feel comfortable to comment on the learning programme*

The results of learner evaluations of the learning programme will provide useful information about teacher effectiveness and also yield general comment on facilities and methods. Learner feedback will probably be the most useful source of suggestions about how teaching effectiveness can be improved, and so it is absolutely essential to obtain honest and descriptive feedback from the learner group. Learners should be invited to make frank comment and their outspokenness should be promoted. They should be allowed, or preferably actively encouraged, to say what they think without fear of repercussions. In order to do this learners must feel safe. This openness will depend on there existing a sense of mutual trust, both with one another and with the teachers involved in the learning programme.

*Information and views about the learning programme are interpreted in a way that can be justified*

The information collected from reviews must be clarified and agreed with the learners concerned before action is taken or changes are made. People's perceptions of events can be notoriously fallible and open to many interpretations, so that when reviewing learning experiences and the use of associated resources we must carefully analyse information gathered in terms of the learning programme objectives and what has actually been achieved by the learners. When undertaking reviews and responding to learners', colleagues' and external assessors' comments we must always test the applicability of the information gathered against the stated programme standards or assessment specifications. This is the only way we shall be able to make valid and reliable judgements and justify action taken as a result.

*Review results are recorded, passed on and used as agreed*

A training record card such as the one shown in Figure 6.5 (see *Documents Pack*) could be used to summarise training outcomes. The example given relates to the job of a sales assistant in a large store. The card contains essential information relating to job responsibilities and training factors. Three main job responsibilities are defined (see Codes A1–A3) and key training factors have been listed against each code. The training programme will be planned and learner performance will be assessed against factors listed. Checklists similar to that given in Figure 6.6 (see *Documents Pack*) can be used when assessing and recording performance.

Simply maintaining records and transferring results to archive files may be of little value to anyone concerned with the training programme. Something needs to be done with the results recorded. Assessments of competence can be used as a basis for certification of single units and application to the award body for a 'unit credit', or the unit may be added to the candidate's record of achievement while they are building up sufficient units for the target NVQ/SVQ award. Results of internally held written examinations and/or the candidate's responses to externally set scripts can be forwarded to examination bodies for the award of the relevant certificate. Formative records can be built up by making entries in the learner's log book or diary, or by compiling reports and review sheets, or by adding to the learner's profile. Results will normally be passed on to the next stage in the recording system and used as evidence of attainment when the learner is applying for certification, or will serve as feedback of achievement to responsible stakeholders.

*The learning programme is suitably modified and agreed with learners and others involved in its delivery*

Once teachers have reviewed with learners the outcomes of a given learning programme it may be necessary to make changes. This is where a collaborative approach to deciding how the changes will be made can often yield more acceptable ways and means of going about things than making a hasty solitary decision. It has been suggested that an effective way to agree learning strategies to meet necessary programme changes is to conduct and conclude amicable negotiations with the learners and others concerned with programme resourcing and delivery. The decision makers should then be able to reach agreement in a manner that preserves mutual goodwill and trust. This joint decision-making approach normally results in enhanced motivation and a collective determination to meet redefined targets. The important requirement is to provide ample opportunities for the learners and other team members to ask questions and seek clarification. This strategy will often have the desired effect. The available options will be openly discussed and joint recommendations will be adopted, thereby having greater potential for success.

*Auditing the learners' entitlement*

Learners are entitled to gain access to certain aspects of a training provider's service when entering the system. The provider will need to have in place documented procedures that will enable them to do so. When negotiating and agreeing learning programmes with learners an effective process would logically lead the candidate from awareness raising through stages to an appropriate induction programme.

Learner entitlement may include:

- recognition of previous learning and experience
- accreditation of prior achievement
- opportunities for progression and personal development

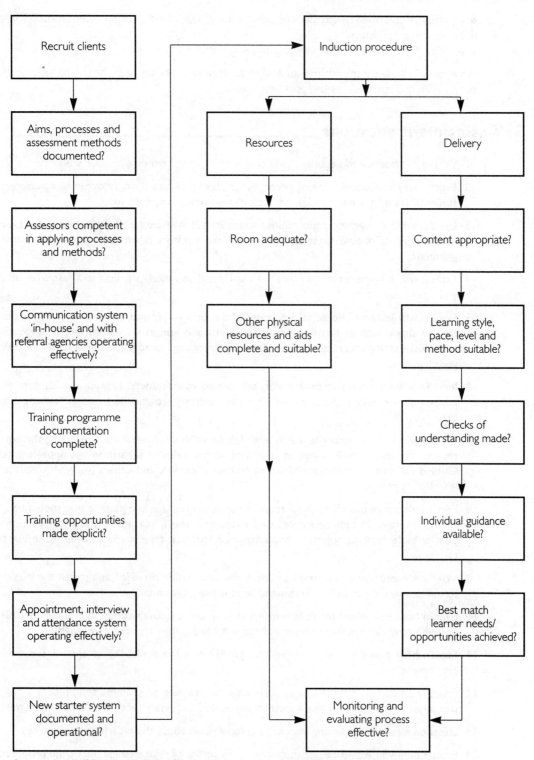

Source: L. Walklin, *Putting Quality into Practice*, Stanley Thornes 1992, p. 248.
**Figure 6.7** *Audit: learner entitlement and induction procedures*

- equality of treatment regardless of gender, race, age, ability, sexual orientation or religion
- an effective induction
- information, guidance, counselling and support.

An audit of the learner entitlement and induction process could be based on asking the questions given in Figure 6.7 on the previous page.

## Self-assessment questions

1  Why is it important to negotiate individual learning programmes with your students?

2  Explain why negotiated learning programmes should be based on an accurate assessment of the students' learning needs, capabilities, aspirations and learning context.

3  List the types of learning opportunities and methods available to your learners and explain why it is necessary to explain these accurately to your students when negotiating their learning programmes.

4  Explain why it is important to point out clearly and accurately the essential resources available to your students.

5  Explain why learners should take account of the boundaries and constraints of the options available to them, such as qualification requirements and budget limitations, when negotiating their individual learning programmes. Describe how you would identify and clarify such constraints with your learners.

6  Identify possible routes to progression available to your learners. Explain why learners should be advised of how they might progress from their existing programme to other learning opportunities.

7  Explain why it is necessary to clarify with learners the expected ways of working throughout the programme. Include references to rules and norms, relevant legislation and appeals procedures. Outline the roles and responsibilities of teachers, learners and others involved in facilitating the learning programme.

8  Prepare details of the relevant information about the learning programme that should be provided to your learners. Include references to the learners' needs, aspirations and priorities; learner support available; learning objectives and associated activities; assessment procedures, review and certification.

9  Why is it important to sequence and pace the information provided and match the language used to the learners' capability to understand what is being presented?

10  Explain how you would set your learners at ease and encourage them to feel comfortable to ask questions and express their wishes and concerns about their learning programme.

11  Explain how group size and composition could affect the availability of options for the learning programme.

12  Produce a rationale for the design of an individual learning programme and prepare a programme that takes account of all relevant matters negotiated and agreed with the learner concerned.

13  Describe methods of eliciting learners' personal views about their learning programmes.

14  Explain how you would set about resolving any points of disagreement about the proposed learning programme so as to maintain an effective and friendly learning relationship.

15 Explain what is meant by 'qualitative' and 'quantitative' information and give examples of each.

16 Explain the benefits of maintaining formative records of progress and competences attained.

17 Why is it important to review and update personal programmes to take account of the learner's progress and achievement? How would you identify gaps in achievement that will need attention?

18 Detail the ways in which bias could affect the interpretation of information during reviews and evaluations.

19 Produce a flow chart showing how the results from learner reviews are recorded, passed on and used.

20 How can feedback obtained from learners during reviews be used to improve the quality of your service to the learner group as a whole?

## Preparing for assessment: sample activities

### Activity 6.1 Devising a group learning programme

Devise a negotiable learning programme covering organisational requirements and anticipated learner needs and using available resources. Produce a rationale for use when interpreting the programme review. Carry out a review of the programme with learners and record outcomes. Justify any changes made and modify the programme accordingly. Circulate the revised document to others involved in delivering the learning programme and gain their support.

### Activity 6.2 Negotiating individual learning programmes and agreeing action plans

**Part A**

Negotiate a learning programme with an individual learner, agree with them an action plan and provide evidence of how you negotiated the programme. Your evidence should include the following:

● how you put the learner at ease
● how you gained the learner's commitment and interest
● how you outlined the learning opportunities available taking account of equal opportunities legislation and best practice
● the questioning techniques you used and a checklist of the questions asked together with the learner's responses
● how you matched the proposed programme with learner needs, role requirements and preferred learning style.

**Part B**

Describe how the programme was implemented and provide evidence of how you reviewed progress with the learner(s) concerned. Your evidence should include details of the following:

● how you avoided personal bias and discriminatory practices throughout the procedure
● how you recorded the information gathered and updated the action plan
● how you maintained confidentiality of recorded information
● how you passed on the information and how the data was used.

### Activity 6.3 Group characteristics and programme options

Evaluate the effects of group size and composition on the options for a proposed learning programme and its implementation. You may need to consider factors such as:

● group characteristics: differences in age, sex, nationality and personality
● shared aims: cohesiveness, consensus and decision making

- sociometry: group dynamics and social climate
- size effects: communication and participation
- sub-groups, cliques and individuals
- recognition of behaviour patterns: norms and codes of conduct
- rules, roles and sanctions
- proposed teaching and learning activities
- effect of physical learning environment: location, facilities, layout and seating arrangements
- group activities: tasks and monitoring strategies
- evaluation of group work.

### *Activity 6.4 Resources and support available for learners*

Write an account describing the various resources and support that could be accessed when you are negotiating learning programmes or making modifications to existing learning programmes available to your learners. Include in your report information about the following:

- the library and learning resources centre: give details of distance-learning materials and open-access learning and computing facilities available
- pre-entry and initial assessment guidance services
- sources of additional in-course study guidance, information and advice available to referrals
- careers guidance and information about opportunities for progression.

# 7

# Facilitating learning in groups through presentations and activities

Successful teaching depends on two key conditions. First, teachers must be prepared to consider carefully **learner requirements** and expectations and must take good account of the needs identified when defining the purpose and goal of any activity designed to fulfil those requirements. Second, teachers must effectively communicate their intentions, plans and ideas to the groups concerned and find the correct actions towards that goal. This is why the ownership of well-developed **presentation skills** will determine how much benefit may be derived by learners in both formal and informal learning settings.

The ability to perform the **presenter role** effectively will be demonstrated by the quality of facilitation, sequencing, pacing and intervention skills and the leadership style adopted. Presenters will need to keep things going and continuously monitor and review progress made throughout the presentation; they will also need to conduct an end-of-session review, evaluation and conclusion before looking forward to the next session.

Consideration of our practical teaching experience will help us to recognise that people are all different and therefore prefer to learn in different ways. It is clear that no one approach is right for any given situation or subject area and that it is important for teachers to have a broad understanding of the different **conditions of learning**[1] proposed by R.M. Gagné, in order that they may be better able to design, adapt and modify their strategies and to evaluate the effectiveness of those strategies. Gagné's eight classes of learning, ranging from simple **recall** to **problem solving**, serve as a useful checklist for the teacher to consider together with the subject matter, student group and other relevant factors when identifying which strategy would be the most effective. For example, where an explanation of new theories is necessary, **concept learning** and **verbal association**, **chaining** and **multiple discrimination** are important in helping learners name something in order to recognise it in the future and describe its characteristics. As a further example, **stimulus response learning** is useful in areas such as computer-based training where practical skills are developed through correct 'responses' on the keyboard, and **signal learning** applies when keying errors are identified by a bleep and the user is required to try again. **Trial and error learning** and **Gestalt** theory or insight learning would be considered by teachers when preparing guided discovery, experimentation and problem-solving activities.

Presentations should be developed around the needs of the group. Barriers to learning are encountered when individual learners have had earlier bad educational experiences. Learner ages are also significant when deciding on overall presentational strategy. Younger learners may be used to and prefer a more **directive** teaching style similar to the lecturing style adopted by some training providers. Older learners may prefer **facilitation** styles and methods which encourage the group to share experiences and learn from each other. Mismatching method with learner experience and expectations could lead to confusion and dissatisfaction, as in the case of a group of personnel managers, each with over twenty years' practical experience, who felt affronted when an inexperienced teacher chose to 'lecture' them on 'The basic principles of personnel management'.

Teachers may serve as situational leaders when presenting group activity. If this is so, they will need to provide a secure environment with adequate support for their learners and thus avoid introducing feelings of anxiety and unease. When acting as facilitators they will need to anticipate learners' reactions to the proposed activity, and may encounter people with prior knowledge of the topic and fairly entrenched ideas about what they think should be happening based upon past experiences. Their learners may have ingrained attitudes towards the task, topic, teacher or other learners. They may have preconceived expectations of the current or impending activity. These factors can affect the facilitator's choice of presentational methods.

In order to 'keep it simple' and readily understandable, material should be presented in a clear and logical way and at a pace appropriate to the learners' ability to absorb and clarify what is said. The use of aids to support verbal input will enhance the probability that information presented will be more readily perceived, and back-up handouts should be issued to reinforce instructions and key points made. Procedures for group activities should be reviewed during initial briefings, and written briefs issued for reference purposes. Facilitators should listen carefully to any comments made during the briefing, and should use check questions to ensure that the learners understand what they have heard and what is required of them before launching into the activity.

# Giving presentations to groups

*The manner of the presentation takes into account the size and composition of the group*

The type of training envisaged, group size, physical environment and the aims and tasks to be accomplished will probably be the main determinants when selecting the method of presentation to be used. With problem-solving and task-based work **large groups** of adults will comprise people with diverse ability and aptitude for solving problems or sharing out work, but there will probably be less opportunity for each and every learner to contribute much of substance. A few key players may emerge to dominate activities allowing the others to fade into the background and offer little. The obvious answer for group activity is to split the large group into smaller sub-groups of say two or three learners. However, with more **formal** controlled discussions, and theory and principle sessions where **limited learner interaction** is planned, the teacher will take the leadership role and the larger group could be beneficial since the greater will be the range of knowledge, skills and experience available to draw upon.

Splitting the whole group into several **smaller sub-groups** may be possible providing that the learning area can be rearranged to suit group activity. Wider scope for teacher/learner and learner/learner interaction will be possible within **informal** sub-groups, where intimate relationships will quickly form and all members will be required to work productively in order to complete the task set.

The composition of groups will vary from class to class, and membership may be all male, all female or a mix of male and female of varying age, race and character. The structure of small groups may lead to internal competition and battles for power and control or for the attention of a single male or female member. With larger groups there can be greater differences in behaviour and a tendency for members to create rules and share out work.

*Information is clear and accurate and presented in a tone, manner, pace and style appropriate to the needs and capabilities of the learners*

The type of information to be shared with the learners will govern the way in which it is presented to the group. Teachers should present group work clearly, giving only **essential instructions** and allocating tasks in a calm and orderly manner. Adequate time should be spent when reviewing oral or written task instructions with group leaders so that they can obtain a clear picture of what needs to be done. This is essential in order to avoid confusion when they brief their teams.

Where subject-specific **principles** and **factual information** are to be learned, the teacher could effectively control the discussion while encouraging learners to clarify points made by asking questions and commenting on offerings. The teacher might facilitate logical progression through a topic by first introducing the aims and objectives and then making a short formal input, followed by issuing a handout or questionnaire for group discussion and feedback. Another input would follow and the cycle would be repeated, progressing at a rate suited to the learners' needs. The teacher would determine **pace** by evaluating checks of learning introduced during the group feedback sessions.

When a discussion is controlled by the learner group the teacher acts as a **facilitator,** intervening only if it appears obvious that help and guidance is needed or when group leaders call for adjudication or decisions to be taken that they do not feel competent to make themselves.

*Visual aids are legible, accurate and used in a manner which enhances the clarity of the information presented*

Facilitators need to develop personal presentation styles and methods that are suitable for use with group learning activities. They can only achieve this by preparing carefully and rehearsing a forthcoming presentation. When facilitators are addressing small groups the selective use of **visual aids** can help to ensure that effective, persuasive, systematic and memorable presentations are made. Aids that are properly used can help to retain the attention of the group, especially when reinforced by the facilitator's own **non-verbal communication** skills.

Aids should only be used to **enhance** or to **clarify information** presented to learner groups. Video is widely used to provide **impact** when presenting scenarios for simulations, case study and role-play, and also to capture subsequent group activity. Learner perception of the event portrayed is enhanced because two senses are used when learners are watching and listening to a video during briefings. Sections of the video can be replayed when learners need to review or clarify what they have achieved, and also to provide evidence for FAETC candidates or to facilitate objective criticism of their presentational skills. Video facilities can be beneficial to group members during evening **syndicate work.** Access to information presented and events recorded earlier in the day forms a vital part of this kind of group work since it encourages ongoing review, feedback and interaction among participants.

*Learners are encouraged to feel comfortable to ask questions and make comments at appropriate stages in the presentation*

When learners are **empowered** they become proactive and more outgoing and tend to allow their natural curiosity free reign. Confidence grows when power and responsibility for decisions is properly delegated to them. They take more interest in activities and become involved. Perceptive teachers must encourage this sense of confidence and be ready to observe the difference in quality of contributions made to group work by people who are well supported, highly motivated and feel that their inputs will be valued.

Considerable benefit derives when learners are encouraged to:

- express their views, worries and doubts
- make comments and suggestions without fear of rejection
- ask questions without being made to feel foolish
- clarify misunderstandings and participate actively in discussions
- give and receive criticism
- be decisive and confident while respecting the rights of others
- recognise the importance of their contribution
- get the most out of good news when it comes their way.

Nowadays, it is rare for learners to raise their hands when they wish to interrupt. They prefer to wait until they can catch the eye of the facilitator. This makes it very important for the facilitator to monitor the group constantly, watching for raised eyebrows, frowns, head-nodding and other signs of confusion which signal the learners' need for clarification or desire to intervene.

*Clear and accurate supplementary and summary information is provided on request and where appropriate to reinforce key learning points*

Confusion, lack of direction and inadequate support materials are common reasons for the failure of learner-centred exercises, role-plays and other group-working activities. The facilitator neglects to prepare adequate supplementary information needed to support the individuals or group throughout the session and spends too little time introducing the activity. This can cause problems for the learner group, and to avoid such problems the facilitator should:

- carefully explain the purpose of the activity
- gain the commitment of the group
- describe the context and situation
- define and allocate roles
- provide paper-based supplementary materials and physical resources needed
- appoint observers and reporters
- outline timescales
- schedule a plenary (report-back) session
- evaluate outcomes in terms of processes, procedures and learning outcomes.

Paper-based supplementary materials will include **briefing sheets** describing the context:

> You are a consultant who has been asked to solve a human relations problem at Charlton House Enterprises Ltd, a small firm producing well-designed, high-quality educational products. Recently a large number of complaints have been received about the unhelpful attitudes of the certain sales representatives who lose interest in the customer's needs once an order is confirmed, who appear to be interested mainly in the amount of commission they will receive as a result of orders gained, who are not available when needed or slow in responding to subsequent customer enquiries about delivery and quality of service…

A **'what to do'** sheet is also provided:

> Your task is to examine the causes of unsatisfactory performance of the sales staff concerned and deteriorating customer relations and recommend ways in which sales force motivation and attitudes can be improved...

Scripts defining the **roles and responsibilities** for each character are issued together with case-study materials. **Summary information** issued after the session could include 'model solutions', references for additional reading and self-study, briefs for written reports, evidence required for assessment purposes and exit questionnaires.

*Adjustments are made to the presentation in response to learners' needs*

The effective use of available time is a fundamental classroom management skill that must be demonstrated by teachers when making presentations. Your **personal effectiveness** as a presenter will be measured by observing the degree to which you are achieving your **training objectives** and your learners are achieving their **learning objectives** – which hopefully will coincide. But sometimes things do not go as planned and you feel that learners are not responding as you had expected, or your learners complain that what is on offer is neither meeting their requirements nor up to their expectations. In this instance adjustments should be made and action taken to restore their interest and attention. You will probably need to:

● realise that what you have in mind might not suit all your learner group
● react when learners signal the need for a change of direction, a change of activity or a slowing down or speeding up
● be confident, maintain your composure and avoid getting into arguments
● handle complaints, objections and other difficult situations in an appropriate and empathetic way
● transmit to the learners involved a feeling that you are interested in their problem and will attend to it immediately or at the earliest opportunity, bearing in mind the needs of the whole group and their demands on your time
● regain rapport quickly with the learners
● establish consensus by using questioning techniques to identify the learners' actual requirements.

*Distractions and interruptions are minimised wherever possible*

To secure effective learning outcomes, learners need to maintain attention by concentrating on the matters at hand and listening intently to teacher presentations. This can be achieved by shutting out competing stimuli in the form of **distractions** and **interruptions** which interfere with the learning process.

Learner-originated disruptions, turmoil caused by fire practices and noise from external sources can interrupt and hinder the otherwise smooth progress of a lesson. Responding to the fire alarm is a must and cannot be avoided, but something can be done about other distracting influences. Possible techniques include:

● gaining insight and awareness of learners' motivation for causing disruption – 'hidden agendas'
● avoiding confrontations with learners and maximising possibilities for agreement
● keeping control of conversations with demanding learners

- handling discontentment, difficult situations that crop up and complaints from disgruntled learners
- handling objections quickly and gaining commitment to proceed with the allotted task
- discouraging other teachers from dropping in for a quick word
- dealing assertively with technicians and contractors who burst into your classroom to carry out repair work or remove equipment
- dealing with interruptions such as 'urgent' unscheduled meetings
- diverting telephone calls
- avoiding marking and completing paperwork in the classroom
- being available to support your learners.

## Facilitating exercises and activities to promote learning in groups

*Exercises and activities are based on an accurate identification of group members' needs*

Activities should be designed not only to teach learners new skills but also to get them to develop their approaches to innovation and methods of thinking. The facilitator can identify needs by conducting an **informal appraisal interview** designed to motivate individuals and identify their needs for training. Processes such as those described in Chapters 2 and 12 could be used to gather the necessary information and agree relevant action plans. If training can be related to learners' needs this will lead to improved performance.

Goals agreed should be neither too hard nor too easy to achieve. When **targeting activities** group members should be encouraged to identify their own requirements and negotiate and agree realistic, achievable and measurable objectives. The facilitator will have already set standards and communicated them in a clear and constructive way having first referred to award criteria. How the learners meet the required standards is a matter for them to address. Facilitators can create an environment favourable to the achievement of criteria but they cannot learn for their learners. The ultimate responsibility for maintaining a commitment to achieve outcomes and review targets and progress towards them must remain with the group.

*Group members are given clear information about rules, norms and ways of working in the group*

Modern management thinking suggests that **self-managed teams** that maximise individual contributions and recognise the strengths and differences of team members are the basis of 'dream teams'. With self-managed teams, members are allowed to choose **team structures** and create suitable frameworks for operation. This approach enables the teacher as group-work facilitator to operate as a logistics person and observer, thereby avoiding an imposed hierarchy of 'power'. Furthermore, if group members are invited to define the **rules** they will be more likely to keep to them.

A **norm** is a shared pattern of perceiving and thinking involving shared communication, interaction, common attitudes and beliefs and shared ways of doing whatever the group is required to do. Group norms will dictate the method and rate of working, quality standards and outcomes, and also the interaction, rewards and sanctions operating within the group. The teacher will, however, be responsible for the prompt and appropriate handling of disruptive or unhelpful behaviour.

**Working methods** will (hopefully) be based on a teamwork approach whereby teams are encouraged to take responsibility for group behaviour and sense of direction. Individual members can be encouraged to trust each other and overcome cultural barriers by building joint commitment and encouraging an open and free exchange of information and ideas.

A written **code of practice** defining the rules and how the group should operate will be needed if the teacher intends to adopt a **supervisor-led approach** to groupwork. However, this method implies a **policing** attitude that may not be well received by mature learners. Perhaps more thought could be given to changing the autocratic teacher's attitude from that of managing by **controlling** to one of gaining the respect and trust of the group by developing an **open style** of group management. This can be achieved by **coaching** individuals and contributing to the achievement of group goals by developing learner skills and responsible behaviours while at the same time maintaining a low profile.

*Group members are given clear information about the aims and expected outcomes of the exercise or activity*

A **clear picture** of what must be achieved while completing an exercise or participating in a group activity can be obtained only if learners are given the necessary information in the form of a briefing that includes broad aims and clearly defined objectives describing intended outcomes. **Redundant information** can confuse learners, so unnecessary detail should be avoided. Only key information should be provided and words kept to a minimum. Details of specific roles, activity objectives, summaries of case studies and form of reporting to be adopted are helpful to sub-group leaders. **Block diagrams** and **flow charts** giving an overall picture of the system or process to be discussed can serve as useful aids during briefings.

*Group members are given clear and sufficient instructions in order to enable them to perform the exercise or activity*

Improved learner involvement in group activities can be promoted by **alerting**[2] the group to what they will be asked to do, starting with a statement such as: 'Let's all think about what this activity involves and what's in it for you.' This should get the learners **actively involved** from the start and gain their attention, but the initiative will be quickly lost if teachers then follow up by spending too much time reciting chapter and verse on how to tackle the task or giving their detailed interpretation of material provided.

Written instructions should be provided for learners, but teachers should recall that there are many learners with very limited reading skills who would find written instructions difficult to understand. **Passive input resources** such as reading and writing materials, study guides and handouts giving details of the purpose and tasks relating to the assignment, case study or role-play should be backed by audio/video resources and clear oral explanations to enable learners to clarify doubts and to overcome reading deficiencies.

*The manner, level and pace of communication are appropriate to group members*

Sense experience followed by **perception** and the **analysis** of experiences and facts are thought to be very important aspects in the science of teaching and learning. By interpreting things that are seen, heard or otherwise encountered learners can develop reasoning and understanding. However, activities and written learning material should not be imposed on learners until they are ready for it. This implies that the **level**, **pace** and **method** of communication and teaching should be matched with the learner's stage of **intellectual development** or level of **psychomotor skills**.

Action-centred and experiential learning stimulate interest and could effectively precede contrived skills training or the teaching of related subject matter during theory sessions. Learners should in any event be afforded opportunities to test out theories and be encouraged to experiment, examine products, clarify factual information and discover new things for themselves.

The content of your communication is as important as the way you put it across. High-level and specialised language can easily confuse learners, especially when the rate of presentation is inappropriate for the learner group. Effective communication will depend upon **perceptual speed** as measured by the learners' ability to take in and interpret information presented. Some are very quick on the uptake. They tend to get it right the first time and switch off. They will not listen to every word but will be impatient to get going. Others will be slow to catch on and will need considerable support. In this case tell them what you are going to tell them, tell them and repeat what you have just told them. It is probably the only way that you will encourage them to make a start.

*Group members are encouraged to feel comfortable in order to participate effectively*

Learners feel the need to get on with the teacher and other learners and to enjoy friendly social interaction in any learning situation. Over a period of time good working relationships can be built, but when classes form learners may feel ill at ease and have feelings of anxiety which must be allayed. A.H. Maslow proposed a hierarchy of **basic human needs** which included the need for safety and security. This is also true of any learning environment where the need to feel safe and secure is of paramount importance to learners.

Teachers when contemplating group work will need to allow for the various processes of social interaction that occur whenever small ad hoc groups are formed to undertake a task. There will be groups containing **incompatible** members who are unable to get on with the others and there will be **cohesive** groups where everyone gets along well. There will be groups with **shared norms** and accepted behaviour patterns and there will be those lacking in agreement where **dissonance** predominates; there will be those with a **flat** structure and there will be those with **hierarchies** of power and control or pecking orders. **Role conflict** may be evident and some members will be under pressure to behave in ways that for them are unnatural and hence withdraw from planned activities. These possibilities must be allowed for, and teachers should be ready to make necessary adjustments to group composition or activities if progress is impeded or learners are being deliberately excluded from the proceedings. Problems of procedure and resourcing may need to be addressed to meet special learning requirements of one or more group members.

*Exercises and activities are appropriately structured in order to maximise learning*

A written plan showing the what, when, why, how and where for the proposed activity will be needed in order to structure a session in the most effective way. Time must be allocated for each part of the event and slots will be needed for such things as:

- domestics
- initial briefing
- documentation issued
- sub-groups formed
- leaders appointed
- small/large group activity:
  - allocation of individual briefs or tasks
  - data sort
  - discussion
  - clarification
  - monitoring (details of the observer's role should be included)

- summarising
- reporting back
- whole-group comment
- summary
- conclusion.

*Excluding or discriminatory behaviour or language is challenged appropriately*

**Equal opportunities** policy stems from **legislation** such as the Race Relations Act 1976, the Sex Discrimination Act 1975, the Disabled Persons (Employment) Acts 1944 and 1958 and the Chronically Sick and Disabled Persons Act 1970. **Policy statements** contain details of the training provider's intention to implement equal opportunities for education and employment within the organisation regardless of race, ethnic group, gender, marital status, religion, physical or learning disability, sexual orientation or age. A **code of practice** is normally available to teachers, setting out practical advice for promoting good relations. In general the code is not a set of rules to be obeyed; however, evidence about whether or not the code was followed may be important in a dispute.

**Discriminatory behaviour** such as spoken abuse, insulting comments or jokes, and written abuse such as graffiti, offensive pictures and other materials should be banned from your classroom. Learners should not be permitted to engage in banter or deliberate attempts to humiliate or in any other way ridicule or undermine the confidence of any other group member. Any instance of this form of harassment must be **challenged** positively and directly by the teacher who is facilitating the session. If necessary a reprimand or verbal warning in line with the provider's harassment policy should be delivered to the harasser. The equal opportunities unit should be consulted if the practice persists.

*Adaptations and interventions which are likely to improve the effectiveness of the learning process are effectively made*

**Facilitation skills** involve designing activities that allow for individual learner differences and enable learners to go at their own rate. As a **facilitator** you will need to give clear outlines of the proposed activity, link it with existing skills and knowledge, and set targets and related timescales for achievement of each stage of the task. The **sequencing, pace** and **leadership style** may be frequently changing in order to allow you to react quickly to changes in individual and group demands. A **reserve** of material must be available for both slower and faster learners so that all can be actively involved all the time. As long as learners are made aware of what they are required to be doing and what are their target outcomes they will be inclined to respond positively to **interventions** from the 'teacher' and requests to **evaluate** their progress against standards for the agreed task.

The leadership style adopted will decide whether the teacher or one or more of the learner group will control the activities and take responsibility for:

- monitoring progress – taking the observer role
- keeping things going
- reviewing and evaluating outcomes
- concluding the session.

**Adaptations** should reflect difficulties experienced by individual learners, feedback from the group and evaluations of relevant activities measured against programme criteria and personal targets. **Interventions** which are likely to improve the effectiveness of the learning process can be effectively made but only after learners have been encouraged to **review** their work, **identify** their errors and shortcomings and **sort out** their difficulties. They will know only too well what they have done well and where improvements are needed. But they may not know how best to overcome their problems, and this is where the facilitator will need to 'intervene' by asking **probing questions** such as 'What do you think went wrong?' or 'How can you put this right?', and giving the necessary information only when there is a need to **clarify** important principles or correct serious errors and misconceptions.

*Timely feedback is given to learners in a positive and encouraging manner on the process of learning and progress towards learning outcomes*

Feedback resulting from various methods of review and assessment gives information about a learner's progress. Teachers must be able to give feedback which will enable learners to take positive action to enhance their current achievement. However, feedback should not be perceived as being a 'one-way' or 'top down' process with the teacher at the top passing comments down the line or making only critical and subjective observations.

Constructive feedback serves to **reinforce learning** and permits early correction of errors, provided it is received **soon after an event.** It should be **objective** and **descriptive** and must be soundly based upon the observation of performance. The **core process** of giving learners **timely feedback** on their progress and performance in a positive and encouraging manner is discussed in more detail in Chapter 11.

## Self-assessment questions

1 Explain why it is necessary to negotiate and agree with learners the aims of a group activity.

2 Why should teachers consider the session aims when deciding group size for a particular activity?

3 Explain the importance of room size when teachers are choosing the method of presentation.

4 Explain how limitations of eye contact could affect the method of facilitating group learning.

5 Sketch and describe three commonly used layouts of classroom furniture, and comment on the advantages and disadvantages of each when teachers are facilitating group activities.

6 How can rooms be arranged so as to promote effective communication?

7 Describe how interruptions and noise can disrupt your learners' concentration and how these unwanted factors can be minimised when you are teaching the group.

8 How do you decide on whether you or one or more of the learners will take the leadership role during group presentations?

9 List the advantages and disadvantages of small-group and large-group presentations.

10 How can teachers avoid total dominance of the learning group when making presentations?

11 Suggest ways in which you could elicit active learner participation during learning opportunities.

12 Explain how sequencing and pacing can affect learners' perception of the information presented.

13 List the various ways in which teachers can usefully 'intervene' in the learning process during class-work and learner-centred group activities.

14 Define the terms 'closed questions' and 'open questions' and explain how the questioning technique can be effectively used during presentations to groups.

15 Describe the circumstances that would require you to adapt learning materials needed to support learning.

16 Describe the critical factors pertaining to small-group presentations.

17 Describe methods of putting learners at ease during one-to-one interactions.

18 List the various signals coming from the group which might indicate confusion, unsuitable pace and an unsuitable language level.

19 Outline the type of interventions that you could use when facilitating group learning and describe when and how you would use each method.

20 Describe how you could elicit participation when learner motivation and energy level seems to be flagging.

## Preparing for assessment: sample activities

### Activity 7.1 Planning, preparing and giving a presentation

Plan and prepare a lesson during which information will be presented to learners. Produce a session plan that includes an introduction, main body and conclusion. Specify on the plan the resources to be used, the methods of presentation, learner activity, and how progress and evaluation of learning will be judged. Include in your plan a short introductory period that will enable the learners to settle down and feel at ease and a summary that will enable you to reinforce key learning points.

Use the plan as an aid when facilitating the session and presenting information to your group. Be prepared to provide supplementary and summary information if requested to do so.

### Activity 7.2 Functions of learning materials

A list giving the various functions of learning materials is given below. Explain the purpose of each function and describe when, why and how you would use the materials to promote learning.

- to provide information
- to exemplify
- to provide work experience
- to simulate
- to evaluate achievement
- to give instructions
- to stimulate the exchange of ideas and opinions
- to facilitate group working
- to evaluate progress.

### Activity 7.3 Preparing learning materials

Explain how written texts, graphics, audio-visual materials, games and simulations can be used to support learning. Prepare two or more different sets of learning support materials that your learners will require in order to meet unit performance criteria and the group's collective needs.

### Activity 7.4 Facilitating group activities

Assess the needs of a small group of not more than six learners. Plan an activity and write a session plan giving details of presentational techniques you intend to employ and audio-visual support materials to enhance your presentation. Back up your input with supplementary and summary information to reinforce key learning objectives.

Include in your lesson an action-centred learning opportunity that will encourage learner participation. Give clear instructions during your initial briefing. Ensure that the activity leader and all actors are provided with relevant written briefs. Plan your interventions and allow sufficient time for feedback and review.

**Notes**

1 See R.M. Gagné, *The Conditions of Learning*, Holt, Rinehart and Winston, New York 1965. This topic is discussed in L. Walklin, *Teaching and Learning in Further and Adult Education*, Stanley Thornes, Cheltenham 1990 (reprinted 1995).

2 See J.S. Kounin, *Discipline and Group Management in Classrooms*, Holt, Rinehart and Winston, New York 1970.

# 8

# Facilitating learning through demonstrations and instruction

The **traditional** method of job instructional training involves the seven main stages set out in Figure 8.2. A whole task or a particular skill is demonstrated, supported with a commentary by a teacher while the learner observes. The learner then tries to emulate the teacher and endeavours to meet associated performance criteria. Learning hold-ups are sometimes encountered which delay progress, but after a while the learner overcomes the difficulties and reaches the required standard. Nowadays, a systematic approach to training based upon **task analyses** and national criteria is often used. This leads to an efficient, validated programme that relates instruction and assessment to properly identified, relevant, realistic and achievable performance criteria.

In a commercial situation, the job is studied and broken down into skills elements which may be demonstrated separately. Key learning points, essential underpinning knowledge and performance skills may be identified, together with specific aspects of a particular technique. As a result, the teacher is able to plan a training programme that allows identified skills criteria to be fully integrated and matched with teaching phases and sequences. Performance criteria will define what the learner must be able to do and will also serve as standards against which to carry out accurate assessments. Past experience will also help the teacher when arranging for the learners to practise and master each element. Learners are then required to combine individual skills into what is a demonstration of skilled performance under assessment conditions.

Time to reach assessment standards by this **analytical method** is thought to be shorter and more effective than by the so-called **traditional method**. Learners benefit from experiencing less frustration, and learning hold-ups are reduced or eliminated, consequently leading to savings in training time.

## Demonstrating skills and methods to learners

*Demonstrations of skills are based on an accurate analysis of the components of the skill and the sequence in which they need to be learned*

Before the teacher prepares a plan for the proposed demonstration, the task itself should be analysed and the following questions asked:

- What is done?

- Why is it done?
- When is it done?
- Where is it done?
- How is it done?
- Who does it?

Once answers to these questions have been established a task analysis is carried out.

## Task analysis

A **skill** is the ability a person has that allows them to perform a task expertly. It is either instinctive and not formally learned, or it can be acquired by practice. A **task analysis** is carried out in order to separate procedures into their component parts, so that a learning programme and demonstration can be devised and used to enable people to learn quickly and perform their work effectively.

| Turning in a road by using forward and reverse gears | | |
| --- | --- | --- |
| **Function** | **Knowledge** | **Skills** |
| Choose turning place. | Good visibility. Plenty of room. No obstruction. | Observation. |
| Stop on left side of road. | Position relative to kerb. | Judging position. Using mirror. |
| Check way is clear front and rear. | Check front, rear and side. Give way to passing vehicles. | Observation and using mirrors. |
| Drive slowly forward to bring car across road. | Turn steering wheel to right. Get car at right angles across road. | Briskly turning wheel. Positioning. Clutch and gas control. |
| Change lock to left while moving. | One metre from kerb. Still moving. | Estimating distances. Manipulating wheel. |
| Declutch, stop and apply handbrake. | Declutching and use of footbrake. Effect of road camber or gradient. How to apply handbrake. | Progressive application of footbrake. Synchronising clutch and brake pedal movement. |
| Select reverse gear. | Location of gear. | Engaging gear. |
| Check way is clear. | Clear road condition. | Observation. |
| Back slowly across road with lock hard left. | Positioning and steering routine. | Handbrake, clutch and gas pedal operation. |
| Change lock to right when nearing kerb. | Risk of overhanging kerb. | Full lock quickly. Gas and clutch control. |
| Declutch, stop and apply handbrake. Select first gear. | Location of gear. Other factors as above. | As above. |
| Check way is clear. | Clear road condition. | Observation. |
| Drive forward and regain left of road. | Moving off and regaining near side. | Adjusting to camber. Straightening up. Accelerating away. |

**Figure 8.1** *Task analysis*

Each task is analysed under three headings:

- function
- underpinning knowledge required
- performance skills involved.

The example in the analysis given in Figure 8.1 is the procedure for 'Turning in the road by using forward and reverse gears'. It involves the learner in carrying out a sequence of well-defined actions. In order to do this correctly, the driver must learn the sequence and gain the knowledge and skills needed to perform the manoeuvre competently. Careful coordination of hand and eye movements ensures that the task is skilfully carried out.

## Task analysis: benefits

The benefit derived from carrying out a task analysis is that the following are identified:

- key elements of the task
- logical sequence
- suitable break points in instruction
- level of manual dexterity and hand skills
- sensorimotor skills involved
- necessary coordination of movement
- kinaesthetic senses involved
- need for learning aids
- need for special exercises, drills and practice
- estimate of knowledge aspects of task
- degree of concentration involved
- estimate of training time.

*Demonstrations of skills and methods are an accurate reflection of real practice and are paced and sequenced to maximise learning*

Having completed a task analysis to identify the knowledge required and skills involved in performing a **real work task**, the teacher can set about planning the necessary **demonstration**, **explanation** and **practice** in detail. Ways and means are then developed whereby the learner may practise the individual skills elements making up the task.

Some teachers like to give several demonstrations with explanation of a complete task. This gives the learner a clear picture of what they should be able to do by the end of the training session. A task is demonstrated while the learner watches. The learner then practises each element until all skills elements have been accomplished. Finally, all elements are combined into a completed task. Practice follows which ensures that all the elements of safe and competent performance are integrated until the learner reaches assessment standard.

The **traditional** method of instructional training involves the seven main stages set out in Figure 8.2. A whole task or a particular skill is demonstrated, supported with a commentary by a teacher while the learner observes. The learner then tries to emulate the teacher and endeavours to meet associated performance criteria. Learning hold-ups are sometimes encountered which delay progress, but after a while the learner overcomes the difficulties and reaches the required standard.

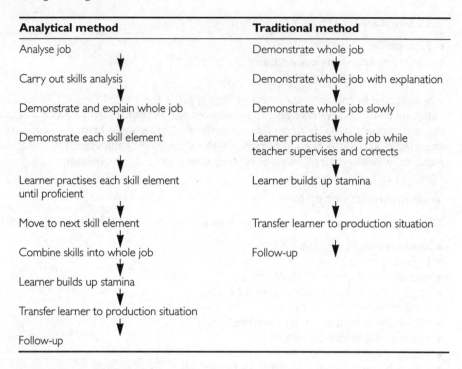

| Analytical method | Traditional method |
|---|---|
| Analyse job | Demonstrate whole job |
| Carry out skills analysis | Demonstrate whole job with explanation |
| Demonstrate and explain whole job | Demonstrate whole job slowly |
| Demonstrate each skill element | Learner practises whole job while teacher supervises and corrects |
| Learner practises each skill element until proficient | Learner builds up stamina |
| Move to next skill element | Transfer learner to production situation |
| Combine skills into whole job | Follow-up |
| Learner builds up stamina | |
| Transfer learner to production situation | |
| Follow-up | |

**Figure 8.2** *Comparison of job instruction methods*

## Demonstration features

A suggested sequence that can be used when instructing by demonstration is given in Figure 8.3. Whether demonstrating to individuals or groups it is important to set the learners at ease, adopt a logical sequence and pace the activity to suit their needs. If the initial demonstration goes well the learners will nod their heads and your credibility will have been established. If there is a series of blunders or too much hesitation they will not appreciate your reasons for underperforming. It therefore pays to rehearse and ensure that everything needed is on hand and in serviceable condition. Throughout the demonstration you should encourage learners to ask questions and clarify misunderstandings, and you should ask them plenty of confirmation-type questions. The demonstration should be followed by a practice session to gain new skills and reinforce skills already owned.

*Demonstration equipment is as realistic as possible and any significant differences between the demonstration and 'real life' practice are highlighted*

Learning opportunities involving the use of **simulations** do not always convey the urgency, interruptions, stresses and frequent decision making normally experienced in the workplace, so that a measure of **reality** will inevitably be lost if this method is substituted for the real thing. **Learning from experience** is a method that is now highly valued and relevant to modern practice in further and adult education. Manual skills gained by repetition and practising 'doing' skills that go beyond the level of minimum competency are thought to be more permanent than knowledge-based activities that depend simply on recall or the manipulation of information. If this is true then demonstration and practice should where possible relate to **real work**, supported by on-the-job training using actual equipment rather than role-play or simulations. However, the ownership of general principles and concepts will enable learners to transfer the knowledge gained to a number of new and different situations.

| Sequence | Remarks |
|---|---|
| *Preparation* | |
| Plan demonstration | Include key factors<br>Logical sequence |
| Obtain apparatus | Do not leave anything to chance |
| Rehearse demonstration | Perfect sequence and delivery |
| *Delivery* | |
| Lay out apparatus | Each element in correct order |
| Establish rapport | Create suitable atmosphere for learning |
| State aims | What you intend the learners to achieve by the end of the session |
| Show end-product | Establish in learner's mind the need to participate |
| Demonstrate silently at normal speed | Repeat several times<br>Allows learner to focus attention on process and arouses curiosity |
| Demonstrate at slow speed | Describe hand or body movements and senses involved |
| Ask learners to explain process | Learners think for themselves and are actively involved |
| Discuss safety aspects | Forewarns and creates awareness of inherent dangers |
| Ask for volunteer to attempt demonstration | Encourages competition<br>Other learners asked to spot mistakes |
| Each learner attempts demonstration | Remainder watch and comment<br>Instructor corrects faults |

Once learners have mastered a technique it presents no further challenge. They must be moved on to another stage. By all means watch for signs of boredom, but do not confuse boredom with fatigue. Do not flog flagging horses. Instead, think of some way of reviving them.

**Figure 8.3**  *Instructing by demonstration*

**Demonstration and practice** is an **interactive method** of teaching that can be used to promote a mix of natural learning brought about by learner-centred activities, practical applications of ideas and planned interventions by the demonstrator.

*Learners are encouraged to feel comfortable to ask questions and make comments at appropriate stages in the demonstration*

The benefits of inviting learners to ask questions and make comments at any stage during the demonstration and to evaluate their progress and performance are discussed in Chapters 7 and 11.

*Learners are supported in practising the skills and given further demonstrations as appropriate*

A practice session immediately following a demonstration is essential in order to **reinforce** procedures. Learners learn best by doing. There is no substitute for **repetition and practice** when learning processes and procedures or acquiring a skill. Learners must learn to cope when things go wrong but they should not be abandoned and left entirely to their own resources. They should be encouraged to sort mistakes out for themselves, and while **unlearning** can be difficult, learners must be taught to learn from their mistakes. While early **intervention** should be avoided there should be someone on hand to help the learner identify their errors and recognise where they are going wrong. As a last resort the teacher should nudge their learners towards a solution. If that fails they should show and explain the correct approach and tell the learners how errors can be avoided. Further demonstrations should be given to **clarify** skills and procedures involved. It is said that practice makes perfect, but in order to maintain the currency of skills owned there is always something new to learn or improvements to make.

Health and safety legislation must be enforced and **good practice** should be encouraged. Immediate individual attention must be provided to help correct unsafe practices, errors and omissions. Overconfidence, lack of attention and poor attitudes can quickly develop but **bad habits** are difficult to unlearn once established.

After confidence has been built up, **higher order skills** such as accuracy, style, rhythm, optimum speed and quality can be concentrated on. But any achievement target set should be within each learner's mental and physical capacity. **Reward** with praise wherever possible. Praise acts as a reinforcer. Never blame a learner. No good can come of this. Aim to stimulate, not to distress. No one deliberately sets out to make mistakes. Be positive. It could be your fault so look at your instructional method and try a new way. Once learners have acquired a technique it presents no further challenge. They must be moved on to another stage. By all means watch for signs of boredom, but do not confuse boredom with fatigue.

*Sites and locations for demonstrations allow for optimum visibility and conform to health and safety legislation*

A safe learning environment affords security and protection from harm – somewhere that is virtually free from danger. But it is well known that no workplace is completely safe. Familiarity can breed contempt and this can increase the vulnerability of learners to the risk of injury. Accident prevention is an essential part of the teacher-demonstrator's role. Accidents occur unintentionally or by chance but can result in injury or death. Learners must know to whom an accident must be reported, and details of all incidents where injury, no matter how trivial, is caused must be reported and recorded in an accident book kept in the workplace.

Before contemplating training activities it is necessary to carry out a thorough safety inspection of the classroom, laboratory or workshop in which demonstrations and practice will take place. Checks should be made to ensure that fire, accident and emergency procedures are up to date, complete and clearly displayed, and that the demonstrator and learners have been instructed on procedures and know:

- the way to the fire exit
- the location of first-aid boxes
- how to use fire extinguishers
- what to do in an emergency.

The **hazard** presented by a substance or situation is its **potential to cause harm**. Some substances can cause harm if they are breathed in or swallowed, or come into contact with the skin. Potential hazards should be identified and the risk of any learner in your charge being harmed must be **controlled** but preferably **eliminated**. In a training situation teachers will need to question learners to check awareness of the hazard presented by the substances they are handling. They will also need to check that learners have sufficient knowledge of rules and procedures relating to other dangerous substances, machinery, lifting heavy or awkward objects, hygiene and housekeeping.

Properly fitted **protective clothing** and well-maintained equipment must be provided for learners, and this must be used in accordance with regulations. Watches, rings and jewellery should not normally be worn when working. Loose clothing and ties must not be worn when there is a chance of their being caught up in rotating machinery.

During a demonstration and practice session the teacher assumes responsibility for providing an inherently safe working environment. When learners are on the register the teacher is in charge and must accept responsibility for all aspects of safety and control of the environment in which learning is taking place. If a situation arises where any aspect of the work is judged to be hazardous to the health or welfare of the learners, the work must be stopped immediately and a report made in writing to the management.

Since the teacher is ultimately in charge of the demonstration, instruction and practice session, other support staff, whilst being helpful, can only offer advice to the teacher. The teacher is responsible for ensuring that all parts of the demonstration can be seen and that learners are properly instructed, supervised and observed while operating machinery and processes. Technicians and other support staff are not normally authorised to do so.

Teachers should be familiar with legislation such as the:

- Health and Safety at Work Act 1974
- Electricity at Work Regulations 1989
- Protection of Eyes Regulations 1974
- Control of Substances Hazardous to Health Regulations 1988 (COSHH).[1]

Where a teacher's knowledge of health and safety matters is inadequate, the organisation and the teacher must recognise this and obtain expert advice from a qualified health and safety practitioner in-house, or seek such advice externally.

*Distractions and interruptions are minimised*

In order to make the best possible use of available time, learners need to maintain attention and concentrate on watching the demonstration and listening to supporting commentary. In order to do this distractions and interruptions should be minimised. Techniques for reducing the probability of disruption are discussed in Chapter 7.

# Instructing learners

*Instruction is based on an accurate identification of learners' learning needs*

A job **training needs analysis** is carried out to establish and checklist the basic core skills needed to carry out a particular activity. The job content is examined and analysed and a specification of what the learner needs to be able to do is prepared. Then each learner's **training needs** are identified by matching the current level of competency against the specification. The identified needs may comprise a mix of cognitive or knowledge-based skills, interpersonal skills and manual skills. Alternatively, the needs could be referred to as **task-related skills** and **task management skills** needed to rectify faults, complete manual tasks or otherwise carry out the activity analysed. Symptoms of learner needs will also be revealed during performance reviews and during feedback sessions following learner activities. Learning support or further instruction will then be geared to the solution of any problems identified and to meeting sensitively other learner requirements.

A fairly new method of developing criteria for training and updating learners is called **job modelling.** This involves asking job holders in occupational areas where the learners will seek employment for details of what they are **doing today** and what they expect to be **doing in the future** that is different from today's criteria. This practice allows the teacher to keep up to date; it also encourages forward planning and ongoing curriculum revision.

The principles and practice of establishing learners' learning needs and training opportunities are considered in more detail in Chapter 2.

*Instruction is based on an accurate identification of agreed learning outcomes*

Perhaps the first consideration should be the purpose of the proposed demonstration. The strategy to be adopted will depend on whether the instruction or demonstration is intended to:

- arouse interest in a topic
- raise awareness of what a process or procedure can do
- show an application of general principles, essential theory and subject knowledge
- reinforce theory sessions (seeing is believing)
- evaluate designs, projects and inventions
- promote discussion
- apply problem-solving and fault-finding techniques
- promote the learning of specific practical skills
- illustrate the transferability of skills
- give opportunities for 'hands-on' experience rather than skills training
- facilitate discovery learning.

The objectives written will reflect the intended purpose and will define the boundaries and limitations within which behaviour is to be demonstrated. They will also provide standards against which to evaluate outcomes. When planning a demonstration there is a need first to negotiate and **agree learning objectives** and then find the **best method** of demonstrating the required process or skills. The teaching objectives will reflect the need to build up the demonstration in small stages which can if necessary be practised by learners in chunks. By writing a series of objectives covering knowledge inputs and related skills a logical approach can be devised that will set the scene and enable learners to be told and shown what to do followed by supervised practice.

An objective may contain up to three parts:

- a description of what is to be demonstrated as evidence that the learner is competent to undertake the task
- a statement describing the important conditions (if any) under which the behaviour is expected to occur
- the acceptable performance level specifying how well or to what standard the learner must perform to be considered competent.

The chief advantages of using objectives are that they:

- help in planning and delivering training
- let all concerned know what is expected of them
- emphasise what it is that must be learned and demonstrated
- help candidates to judge their own progress
- provide a basis for the assessor's judgement of performance.

The following examples contain some or all of the three component parts that may constitute an objective. The candidate will be able to:

- prepare, cook and present for service a four-egg plain omelette
- fit correctly a 13-amp plug to an electric fire
- without referring to any books or notes write in legible handwriting with not more than four spelling mistakes a 200-word description of the role of a beauty therapy salon receptionist.

*The manner, level and pace of instruction is appropriate to learners*

Teachers will from time to time need to vary instruction and learning methods to suit individual learners, local conditions and the training environment. For example, some learners need more encouragement and support than others. Some like to work in small groups and frequently seek help from the facilitator while others prefer to sort things out for themselves and are best left alone to get on with the task. In the case of a learner with very limited experience it may be sensible to give the initial demonstration in a quiet corner using a one-to-one method. Sensitive teachers will know that it is not uncommon for learners to become **distressed** at the very thought of having to perform in front of others. For some, the first practice session can be a very uncomfortable experience. Where there is a **risk of damage** to sensitive or expensive equipment it is sometimes necessary to use a **simulation** or an area laid out for the purpose of training and assessing attainment of a particular technique or competence. What must always be borne in mind is that learners should not be allowed to practise **unsupervised** unless the teacher is satisfied that they will do so safely without creating a hazard to themselves or other people.

People learn at different rates, and teachers must bear this factor in mind when counselling learners on meeting their own attainment goals and instructor-set targets. When planning lessons a key factor will be deciding how quickly to move through the stages of a lesson. How much time should be spent on factual inputs and how much time on relevant learner activity? What about the methods to be used and the sequencing of various activities? The age-old dilemma will be encountered: how can the mass of syllabus subject matter be covered in the time allocated whilst allowing sufficient time and practice for learner-centred activity? If too much time is spent on **formal input** and too much material is thrown at the learners there will be a risk of very little being accomplished without sufficient practice to reinforce learning. If too much time is spent on **practising specific tasks** and meeting relatively few criteria then the possibility of getting the big picture will be forgone. This is where learning packages and computer-based programmed learning can be employed to transfer pacing decisions from the teacher to the **individual learner**. But **whole-group** target pacing rates will have to be decided by the teacher in consultation with the learner group concerned, and lesson-by-lesson time allocation decided on the spot as the teacher estimates the mean rate of group progress. If the teacher has norm-referenced attainment targets in mind it will be obvious that some learners will be left behind and others will be held back. However, the possibility of waiting until all learners have grasped the material before moving on is probably not an option.

*Learners' understanding is checked regularly and instruction modified as appropriate*

Learner performance must be monitored and **checks of understanding** made throughout the demonstration and practice session. This can be done by watching learners working on the task and asking a selection of confirmation questions. Learners are expected to be able to show that they are in complete control of the task under conditions described in range statements. Learners will need to self-assess their progress against criteria and teachers will need to satisfy themselves that learners can use facilities and handle equipment safely at the requisite **level of competence** wherever they are working.

Competency is demonstrated when learners provide under all conditions an effective and safe performance of the task set. This is not achieved without exercising a lot of care. Learners should not be criticised for making mistakes while practising a given skill provided that they have exercised due and **reasonable care** and avoided inappropriate behaviour. Instead, they should be encouraged to **review** their work and **discover** where they went wrong and **correct** the mistakes during the next attempt. Learners build up an acceptable level of performance by accomplishing individual elements of competence and integrating these into a whole skilful demonstration that is judged by the assessor to meet unit **standards**.

During a practice session following the demonstration teachers will need to **monitor** continuously the learner's performance on each of the elements that make up the skill. It is too late to put things right at the end of a training programme. Performance should be evaluated by the teacher and learner at regular intervals so that a smooth progression to higher level skills may occur. Routine assessment of learner achievement is essential to logical progression and success, but as in all learning situations, learners are individuals, each developing a **style** and **rate of learning** that suits them.

*Timely feedback is given to learners in a positive and encouraging manner on the process of learning and progress towards learning outcomes*

The **core process** of giving learners **timely feedback** on their progress and performance in a positive and encouraging manner is discussed in Chapters 7 and 11.

*Factors which are inhibiting learning are accurately identified and explored with individual learners*

Some teachers feel that having expertise in crystal-ball gazing would be very useful when trying to identify what is hindering a learner's progress. Some students are quick to make their difficulties known but there will be a number who will prefer to remain silent. Do you know how many of your learners are **experiencing problems**? How many **complain** to you? How many do you think are really happy with the way you deal with them? How many will complete the coaching programme reasonably painlessly? How many will feel dissatisfied and **leave** and how many others will they **tell** on their way out?

Teachers must quickly respond to complaints or danger signals, and they can achieve this by **ongoing appraisal,** tracking progress and collecting and using data obtained. Checks of training outcomes will confirm achievements but will also generate **deficiency lists** which may be used to negotiate ways of overcoming problems revealed. Detailed **assessment checklists** based upon systematic **task analyses** can be used to pinpoint items for attention as well as to confirm satisfactory performance against criteria.

**Motivational factors** can also affect progress. Goals established by others without involving the learner concerned will tend to reduce effort and enthusiasm. **Adverse criticism** of past underperformance can affect a learner's attitude towards the current learning opportunity. Fear of yet another 'failure' can inhibit progress and reduce the effort put in to accomplish the tasks set.

When considering in what ways individuals differ in their approaches to learning it is useful to think about their:

- level of motivation and expectations
- retention capacity, long-term and short-term memory
- existing knowledge, skills, practical ability and experience
- access to facilities, resources, time and support for study when away from the study centre
- powers of concentration and problem-solving skills
- confidence level and capacity for learning new things.

## Identifying factors inhibiting learning

Barriers to learning can be teacher-inflicted, self-imposed or related to non-study causes such as overwork, fear of redundancy, demanding social and domestic commitments, addiction to watching television or engaging in more pleasurable pursuits. Some people set themselves unrealistic goals: their targets are too difficult to achieve or they find that there is too much work involved in meeting their expectations. Learners need to gain personal satisfaction from activities and setting undemanding targets results in lack of commitment. Some mature adults may feel that they have been out of the game for too long and are lacking in confidence. So in order to overcome such barriers learners must want to win and they must be encouraged to approach their learning programmes with enthusiasm. Reluctant learners tend to become underachievers and there will be an underlying reason for this failure to meet expectations.

Barriers to learning take many forms. Self-perceived inferiority results in feelings of unworthiness, fear of failure and withdrawal. There could be clashes with peers leading to disagreement and controversy that needs to be resolved. There may be causes of tension that must be discovered and removed. Learners may prefer to work alone and will avoid the company of others and not get involved in teamworking. Others may appear to be busily working at the task set but when monitored will be revealed to have been busy doing the wrong things or using unsuitable techniques and getting nowhere. Disorganised learners will be seen shuffling piles of notes, frantically searching for what they need and getting into more of a mess. They will be constantly looking over the shoulder of their peers or latching on to friends, copying and trying to catch up with the others.

You may overcome or reduce barriers by:

- negotiating learning objectives and agendas for action with individual learners (if possible)
- developing your own listening skills and hearing what the learners have to say
- making learners feel at home in class
- teaching in small digestible chunks, giving plenty of practice and reinforcement
- explaining things carefully, moving from the known to the unknown
- identifying transferable skills and building on learners' existing skills
- delivering your input in a logical sequence, hooking each new piece of information to the last piece
- taking your time when instructing and avoiding rushing and panicking the learners
- excluding jargon and avoiding being too theoretical
- avoiding becoming impatient when learners are slow to grasp the point
- inviting questions and rewarding learners who volunteer answers
- encouraging learners to express an opinion on any topic discussed
- encouraging self-evaluation and quality assurance practices
- using frequent checks of learning and operating a continuous assessment policy
- monitoring and frequently checking learner progress
- using multiple-choice questions rather than lengthy written tests to evaluate learning
- turning learners' mistakes into valuable learning experiences
- offering constructive feedback
- praising and rewarding so as to maintain attention and motivation
- pointing out advice available and help and support on hand
- giving advice on improving study skills and learning out of class
- encouraging learners to develop self-confidence.

*Clear and accurate supplementary information is provided where appropriate to reinforce key learning points*

Giving supplementary information to learners is discussed in Chapter 7.

## Self-assessment questions _____

1 Describe how a demonstration can be used to show fundamental principles and actions.

2 Explain the analytical method of job instruction training.

3 What is the point of carrying out a task analysis before demonstrating skills?

4 Why should demonstrations as far as possible accurately reflect real practice?

5 Why are simulations often used in place of the real thing during demonstration and practice sessions?

6 Why should learners be invited to ask questions and make comments during demonstrations?

7 Why is there no effective substitute for repetition and practice when learning skills?

8 Why must learning environments conform to health and safety legislation?

9 Explain what is meant by the term 'hazard'.

10 Why should protective clothing be worn by teachers when giving demonstrations, and by students during practice sessions? Give examples of the type of clothing and equipment that should be worn by learners to protect them from specific hazards.

11 Why should distractions and interruptions be minimised during demonstrations?

12 Explain the importance of identifying the learners' training needs before instructing them in a particular skill.

13 Why is it necessary to involve learners in negotiating and agreeing learning objectives for a particular learning session?

14 Explain the importance of presenting a demonstration at a level and pace suited to the learners' abilities.

15 Why should frequent checks of understanding be carried out during a demonstration and practice session?

16 Explain the importance of giving learners timely, constructive and objective feedback on their progress and achievement.

17 Describe some of the factors that inhibit learning.

18 Explain how display and demonstration can be used in the teaching of concepts.

19 Explain how you would incorporate a demonstration in the teaching of a psychomotor skill.

20 Prepare a demonstration involving the use of an apparatus.

## Preparing for assessment: sample activities _____

### Activity 8.1 Using task analysis techniques
Use the following methods to carry out job training analyses. Record your task analyses and collect relevant evidence for your portfolio.

**Observational technique**
● Identify the job or NVQ/SVQ unit evidence requirements to be analysed.
● Establish the tasks and responsibilities involved.

- For each task establish:
  - what is done
  - why it is done
  - how it is done
  - what skills and knowledge are required to complete the task.

### Experienced worker analysis
- Ask a job-holder to record his or her own task-related activities and also those of any helpers. Choose your own data categories but include also details of:
  - operations performed
  - quality assurance preparations and inspection checks
  - transports – any movement of materials and resources
  - storage of work.

  Note the source of any delays and establish the causes.

  Note any difficulties experienced in performing work-related activities.
- Analyse records and identify key functions.
- Highlight task-related knowledge, skills and attitudinal requirements.

### Job analysis interview
- Design and issue a pre-interview questionnaire to be completed by the job-holder well before the meeting.
- Prepare an interview checklist listing questions concerning underpinning knowledge and processes relating to the task to be analysed.
- Make notes of comments made and answers to questions given by the job-holder during the interview.
- Use the information gathered when writing up the task analysis.

### Analysis based on own experience
- Identify the task and key performance criteria to be demonstrated.
- Write a description of how you managed to accomplish the tasks involved.
- Identify the essential knowledge, understanding and methods needed to tackle the task.
- Look at the tasks from your learners' point of view.
- Consider what the learners will already know.
- Identify suitable break points and split the task into manageable chunks.
- Adopt a demonstration sequence using only short inputs such as:
  - getting ready
  - doing the work
  - checking and inspecting – evaluating outcomes
  - clearing up.

## Activity 8.2 Preparing a task analysis
Select a task and, using the format shown in Figure 8.1, prepare an analysis of the skills and underpinning knowledge involved. Write a session plan for your demonstration using the task analysis as a guide.

## Activity 8.3 Instructing learners
### Giving instruction
- Explain the importance of using suitable language when giving instruction.
- Describe what is meant by sequencing and pacing a learning session.

### Identifying factors inhibiting learning
- Describe what is meant by blockages to learning
- List any bad experiences you have had as a learner and note things that have in the past prevented you from learning.

- Identify the causes of blockages and factors that have inhibited your achievement.
- Identify occasions when your teaching style has caused problems and discomfort for your learners and how you overcame these difficulties.

### Giving supplementary information
- Describe what is meant by giving learners supplementary information.
- Present supplementary material that you have handed out when facilitating a learning session and justify your reason for doing so.

### Monitoring progress
- Describe how you have monitored the progress of several learners, judged their achievement and given constructive feedback.

## Activity 8.4 Demonstrating process and manual skills to learners
- Having prepared the skills analysis and session plan during Activity 8.2 choose a suitable location to demonstrate the process involved.
- Explain the reasons for your choice of equipment and facilities to be employed during the demonstration.
- Demonstrate the processes and safe use of relevant equipment.
- Allow the candidates to do the work under your supervision.
- Judge the candidates' performance and give constructive feedback and advice.
- Evaluate the quality of your instruction and learner achievement and consider how improvements can be made.

### Note
1  A booklet containing a list of Health and Safety Commission/Executive publications is available from the Health and Safety Executive Library and Information Services Unit, Broad Lane, Sheffield, S3 7HQ. The booklet gives details of publications produced by the Health and Safety Commission and the Health and Safety Executive since 1974. HMSO also produces a number of leaflets and titles catalogues on selected titles and themes.

Teachers will find the information invaluable when monitoring the learning environment in the context of health and safety. By conforming with regulations and making use of the advice outlined in the publications teachers will be able to demonstrate competence in this important area of responsibility.

# 9

# Facilitating individual learning through coaching

'What is coaching?' This question cropped up during one of my FAETC classes when Stephen Carey, our City and Guilds moderator, was monitoring the session. The group offered many explanations but the consensus was that 'coaching is an essential teaching skill that aims to maximise everyone's abilities and identify and utilise strengths and talents that may have been lying dormant. The strategy being to counsel, guide or otherwise support learners and set them on the road to success.' I subsequently asked Stephen to suggest a definition and he kindly responded with the statement: 'I define coaching as the setting, supporting, monitoring and reviewing of performance targets that encourage, stretch and improve the candidate.' Another well-known definition of coaching is: 'One-to-one instruction aimed at helping individuals to perform a task to standard'.

Coaching is, then, a method of **communicating** with learners, identifying individual **learning styles**, **motivating** and providing incentives for action, **making judgements** and **giving feedback** about progress to date with a view to enhancing subsequent performance. It is a means by which a student or a small learner group can receive **personalised support** designed to meet their special individual learning requirements. Coaching is often based upon **identified learning needs** or **barriers** that are holding up progress. Sessions may be negotiated in order to supplement a standard learning programme or to facilitate remedial activity. The method is widely used and is suitable whether for high achievers or for slower learners.

**Teacher aides** appointed from the learner group and supervised by the programme facilitator (who is preferably a qualified teacher) can be used very effectively to coach and support their peers. The beneficial effects of people working in teams can be further enhanced if members are encouraged to help slower learners maintain progress and to take some responsibility for coaching their less confident peers and supporting those with special learning requirements.

With **team teaching**, members of the course team take it in turns to teach or facilitate a session. The **lead teacher** presents the learning material while the other teachers observe or are busy in a workshop or laboratory setting up for **coaching sessions** with smaller groups or preparing for **individualised practical work** that will follow the presentation.

**Specialist teachers** can be employed to coach talented learners or those with learning difficulties. They may also advise the course team on how best to meet particular learner needs or entitlement. In some instances voluntary workers and **members of the community** may be called upon to offer coaching for learners in specific academic, arts or vocational topics.

# Coaching individual learners

*Coaching is based on an accurate identification of individual learning needs and learning style*

In order to maximise everyone's abilities and to identify and utilise their strengths and talents, some form of performance **appraisal** or **learning needs identification** must be undertaken. But people tend not to like being formally appraised against a checklist of factors which the interviewer briskly runs through either ticking off or marking with crosses. Negative effects can, however, be reduced or eliminated by empowering learners to take responsibility for pointing out difficulties they are having and expressing an opinion as to the sources of their problems. Teachers can help to avoid anxiety by emphasising each learner's known strengths and inviting **self-appraisal** in order to pinpoint areas for improvement. An important aspect of coaching is to help underachievers realise their full potential and overcome barriers to progress.

Sources from which coaching needs originate include:

- employment practices and work methods
- new equipment or technology
- the need to work more efficiently and effectively
- training surveys
- changes in the nature of the service to be provided
- the need to update knowledge and skills
- personal requirements.

*Coaching is based on an accurate identification of agreed learning objectives*

Implementation plans for proposed coaching sessions must be finalised with those concerned within agreed timescales. Learners should be quite clear about the aims, objectives and processes of the coaching session and the benefits to themselves before starting work. This means that they must be involved in negotiating purpose, content and context so that intended outcomes can be clearly described and agreed. When asked for suggestions, learners may sometimes appear reticent and unwilling to speak up, and the teacher will need to propose a course of action. In this case learners should be encouraged to express their views or seek clarification. However, when invited to ask questions some will probably say nothing and the teacher will need to prompt by asking a few questions in order to get them started. Adjustments to the original aims can then be made in order to achieve the best match.

With NVQs, the performance criteria, range statements and evidence requirements are clearly specified leaving little room for negotiation; however, this does not preclude the candidate's right to individualised coaching and access to fair and reliable assessment.

*Coaching in skills is based on an accurate analysis of the components of the skill and the sequence in which they need to be learnt*

To be **competent** a person needs to have sufficient and suitable **skill**, **knowledge** and **experience** to perform consistently to specified **standards** the work related to role or occupation. With this in mind it is necessary when coaching to **pinpoint** the necessary skills for working effectively to award standards. In order to obtain a clear picture of the components of the skill requirement a **task analysis** is carried out. This analysis will reveal the **practical skills** and essential **underpinning knowledge** that needs to be learned. Sample task analyses are given in Figures 8.1 and 9.1 (see *Documents Pack*).

*Coaching is given in a manner and pace appropriate to the learners*

Coaching is not exclusively the preserve of remedial work, slow learners and those with special learning requirements. The method is equally suited to the needs of exceptional students. The skills and techniques that coaches use to create winners in the field of sport will also work in training and education. It is important therefore to recognise those with **high potential** and to motivate and challenge superstars and underachievers alike.

Most learners will respond to helpful **guidance** and will happily give of their best to reach their highest levels of accomplishment given adequate and ongoing support in the achievement of their objectives. But it is important to beware of the **halo effect** and the risks associated with giving too much praise and individual attention to one at the expense of **alienating** others. The aim is to negotiate **achievable tasks**, introduce a little healthy **competitive spirit** and maintain a **cohesive team**.

The coaching session may be planned either as a **task-centred** activity or as a **learner-centred** activity, depending on the identification of agreed learning objectives. Task-centred activities will relate to performance-based operations and products according to some training programme or learning schedule, whereas learner-centred activities will be designed to meet specific individual needs and may include revision or top-up training. In both instances maximum benefit can be obtained by first discussing and agreeing a course of action, thereby preparing the learners and putting them at ease.

## Coaching method

As when teaching by demonstration, a generally acceptable method of coaching in specific skills is that of **explanation**, **demonstration**, **practice** and **reinforcement**. Attention must be gained when starting the session, and coaching should demonstrate clarity of thinking and application of the teacher's knowledge and experience. Being able to give brief instructions in understandable language, explain and clarify key points, and use analogies from peer-group experiences to help candidates remember important features are essential prerequisites to a successful outcome. The coaching session concludes with a **summary** consolidating what has been achieved, a restatement of **underpinning knowledge** and opportunities for candidates to ask **questions**. Throughout the session pace is very important and inputs should be matched to individual learners' capacities. Information overload should be avoided and the pace of presentation slowed to stress important points, speeding up for less important material.

*Learners' progress is checked regularly and coaching modified as appropriate*

**Formative records** of achievement and progress towards their goals should be kept for all learners. Teachers can gather information on a micro scale by monitoring improvement against criteria during programmed coaching sessions and noting any individual coaching requirements that can be facilitated right away. Learners should be kept informed of how they are progressing during the coaching activity.

In order to assess progress over a longer term a **reviewing** and **recording system** could be established to suit the coaching method. The system would enable teachers and learners to check the suitability and quality of learning experiences against unit standards or session aims and objectives. Performance evidence gathered and comments recorded during the session would provide formative assessment data to be used during reviews and when giving feedback on progress and achievements.

Collecting feedback from multiple sources is a personal development technique that is known as the **360° approach**. The method is thought to maximise the benefit of feedback by encourag-

121

ing comment on learner achievements from other learners, customers, colleagues, teachers, support staff and supervisors, in fact from anyone who is able to offer constructive criticism and guidance. Deciding how often to meet to review progress and update progress reports will depend on the learners' needs and the recording system used. But in any event, coaching and review sessions should close on an upbeat and positive note.

Learners should be encouraged to accomplish each **chunk** of material or each **stage** of a practical task before moving on to the next challenge. They will need time to absorb their experiences and reinforce what has been learned in order to understand and retain the knowledge and skills involved. But learning does not always progress smoothly and a **skill acquisition curve** might show the rate of progress of the learner temporarily flattening out. This is a signal for the coach to look at their coaching style, **turn negatives into positives** and perhaps modify method or resources to help overcome the setback and restore improvement.

**Problem students** whose progress is held up should be helped to recognise and come to terms with the situation and series of events that led to their current difficulties. They should be encouraged to discover their own solutions, especially when their problems are self-inflicted. Counselling is not without risk and may be best left to expert counsellors.

*Timely feedback is given to learners in a positive and encouraging manner on the process of learning and progress towards learning objectives*

The **core process** of giving learners **timely feedback** on their progress and performance in a positive and encouraging manner is discussed in Chapters 7 and 11.

*Factors which are inhibiting learning are accurately identified and explored with learners*

Factors tending to inhibit learning are discussed in Chapter 8.

# Assisting individual learners to apply their learning

*A range of opportunities to enable learners to apply what they have learnt is identified*

The learners' approach to demonstrating and reinforcing new skills will probably reflect the strategy they used when learning the material in the first instance. Some will learn by **rote** while watching and mimicking the trainer. They will adopt a step-by-step approach to learning the skill and will commit to memory in a given sequence only the essential operations and relevant facts. They will not be concerned with gaining the whole picture. Others will feel the need to **understand** what they are doing, know why they are doing it that way and realise how practical activity, underpinning principles and related knowledge combine to enable them to perform work competently.

For example, inexperienced computer operators may have been trained on a particular screen but not on the whole menu. They will gain experience and improve their speed by **repetition**. If they meet with a problem or if in doubt they will be able to refer to **quick reference guides** or 'idiot cards' provided. If they are unable to overcome the problem they will seek help from a supervisor. Newly trained but more versatile supervisors might need to cover the whole menu, and their approach to applying new skills relating to the system will be different. If in doubt they will use **problem-solving** skills. Before consulting a senior person or technician they will try to overcome the problem by interpreting messages on the screen, calling up algorithms or fault-finding charts, consulting manuals or phoning the help line.

Teachers will need to identify potential contexts for learners to **apply new skills, progress** and

**transfer training** within training programmes, off-college and in the workplace. This will involve making decisions on **training locations** and **work experience opportunities.**

*Opportunities identified ensure that learners will have the opportunity of achieving agreed learning objectives*

Finding the **best match** between learner needs and expectations and available opportunities is no mean task. This is not a perfect world in which unlimited resources and ideal work placements can be provided. **Team planning** and programme preparation must therefore take account of the need to maximise learner participation directed towards gathering **valid evidence** in-house or elsewhere, either by simulation, demonstration and experimentation or by other acceptable means backed up with essential 'live performance'. Whether to **start afresh** or to build upon **existing techniques** is another decision that will need to be taken. It is sometimes difficult for people to **unlearn** material that could interfere with the current learning programme, but **prior achievement** must always be carefully assessed in order to avoid unnecessary repetition of work.

*Opportunities identified enable learners to practise skills, acquire knowledge and gain experience in a structured way*

A suitable starting point when planning a coaching session might be **agreeing objectives** and context for the proposed activity and then checking the **outline plan** against award criteria, range statements and evidence requirements. Then when planning how best to facilitate the learning opportunity teachers should give consideration to the cognitive, affective and psychomotor **skills involved** and possible **learning conditions** ranging from signal learning to problem solving as described by R.M. Gagné.

Two main methods spring to mind: the **conventional approach** – explanation followed by practice; and encouraging learners to find out things for themselves using methods such as **active experimentation** and discovery learning. A mix of the two is thought to be more effective than relying solely on either method. Alternatives include laboratory work and simulation, but with experimentation, outcomes should be analysed using the **Kolb Circle** (see Figure 9.2).

Structuring learning experiences to form a **logical development** is essential if learners are to carry out effectively any tasks involved. This is also important when building up **confidence** and promoting a **commitment** to reach **competent worker standard**, and when learning opportunities involve **work-based training** and assessment.

*Ways of integrating different learning opportunities are identified and agreed with learners*

The training programme for a particular course will be affected by the number and level of units making up the award, group size, ability and experience of learners, course team structure, number of contact hours available and many other factors. This will affect the scope of possible learning opportunities and coaching support.

Learners should be given time to discuss with the teacher and with one another what learning opportunities and methods are or will be made available to them during their training programme. The way people prefer to learn and the pace of learning varies from one person to another, and there is no set pattern of learning that suits everyone. For these reasons it is essential that method and content are negotiated and agreed as far as is possible during the induction period and from time to time as the need arises.

The programme **scheme of work** will show the planned strategy for **integrating learning opportunities.** Typically the document gives details of the learner group, organisational fac-

# The Kolb Circle

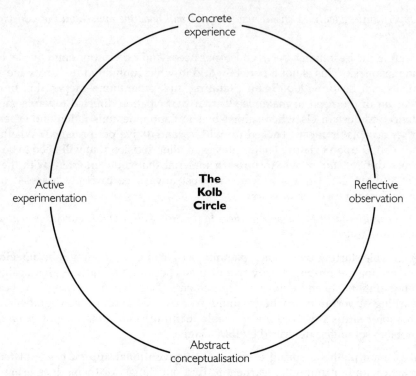

Learners can enter at any of the four stages but must follow the sequence clockwise around the circle until adequate understanding is achieved

- **Concrete experience**
  Does something tangible

- **Reflective observation**
  Carefully observes outcomes and considers what happened as a result of the activity

- **Abstract conceptualisation**
  Defines relationships and forms abstract ideas for improvements or changes from observations

- **Active exploration**
  Selects alternative approach, adapts existing method and defines new activity

## Conditions for coaching

Learning by doing and experimentation is a principle on which coaching practice is based. While learning takes place throughout life by trial and error it is desirable that practice in simulated situations should precede practising in real work situations. For teachers, coaching provides a means by which safe practice can precede assessment against performance criteria. Anxiety is one of the main barriers to progress, and anxious learners tend to erect protective barriers and avoid novel learning experiences. The ability to experiment, to try out, to explore and 'fail' without being penalised or harming anyone is one of the main justifications for using coaching as a learner support activity.

**Figure 9.2** *The Kolb Circle applied to coaching*

tors, programme content, sequence, methodology and resources. But this planning document is not set in concrete, and **training content** and the overall design of the programme must be adapted as necessary to suit an individual's requirements or in response to **suggestions** made by the learners and others. **Teamworking** is a way of integrating one's own teaching with that of others and freeing up time that can be used to support individual learners.

*Learners are given clear and accurate information about other people and resources involved in helping them to apply their learning*

The question of who does the initial training will require an early decision, but any of the following could be called upon to **help** learners apply what they have learned:

- teacher
- team leader
- learner group
- mentor
- other internal training resources
- workplace line manager
- external training agency.

The person responsible for providing **study guidance** would advise on:

- vocational choices
- deciding learning methods
- level of trainer support available
- rate of learning and how this will be regulated
- referral agents
- financial support available
- resources and materials available
- facilities, locations, tools, equipment and manuals
- protective equipment.

*Timely feedback is given to learners in a positive and encouraging manner on the progress towards learning objectives*

The **core process** of giving learners **timely feedback** on their progress and performance in a positive and encouraging manner is discussed in Chapters 7 and 11.

*Factors which are inhibiting learning are accurately identified and explored with learners*

Factors tending to inhibit learning are discussed in Chapter 8.

*Ongoing support available to learners is clearly explained to them*

For the learners' objectives to be supported there have to be locations where learning can take place, different types of learning opportunities to meet differing learners' needs, and people to give guidance and to help make decisions on behalf of the learner. These factors, the learners' attitudes and the desired outcomes all affect the decisions that have to be made in order to support the achievement of individual learners' objectives.

Learners may be reluctant to approach a teacher for advice and could turn to their peer group for help. **Peer-group support** could be provided in the shape of a small group of learners forming a **quality circle** meeting regularly to discuss problems encountered while learning and to suggest possible solutions. Peers can give good advice and offer sensible opinions because they are sharing the same learning experiences, and constructive criticism from one's peers is often more readily accepted than from other sources. But peer-group pressure can be unintentionally destructive and can cause problems.

Regular **monitoring** will reveal the need for specialist help, and learners should be made aware of the range of support services available to them. Referral can be seen as arranging for a learner with a problem to be advised by a person more qualified to deal with it than the teacher concerned. It is the learners' right to be allowed to refer themselves to the person that they deem the most suitably qualified to understand their problems. Extra tuition could be scheduled, during which a fresh approach and new perspective on their problem could be obtained.

It is a growing practice within the educational system for students to have a **mentor,** preferably someone who has previously completed the programme or a person with considerable relevant experience who can be called upon at any time for help and advice. But many providers now employ a qualified counsellor to deal with difficult personal problems.

In some instances subject teachers specialising in a given discipline may be called upon to support learners who are having difficulty in getting to grips with a problem, but whenever possible learners should be pointed in the direction of the **learning resources centre** and encouraged to accomplish the task themselves using **self-teaching** facilities.

## Self-assessment questions

1 Define 'coaching'.

2 What is meant by 'setting the learner at ease'?

3 Why is it important to establish relevant standards of performance before commencing a coaching session?

4 Describe how individual learning needs can be assessed.

5 Why is it important to involve the learners when identifying objectives for coaching sessions?

6 Explain how clear goals may be established and agreed with learners.

7 Why is it important to take account of individuals' preferred learner styles when planning a coaching session?

8 How can attention and motivation be maintained throughout a coaching session?

9 Why is it essential to establish existing skills and prioritise learner requirements before commencing a coaching session?

10 What are the benefits of analysing tasks and explaining performance standards to be achieved?

11 Explain each stage of a typical task analysis.

12 Explain the importance of carefully 'structuring' a learning experience.

13 What essential features should be considered when preparing a suitable environment for a coaching session?

14 Explain what is meant by 'resourcing a coaching session'.

15 Describe the monitoring process as applied to a coaching activity.

16 List factors that might inhibit learning during a coaching session.

17 Describe how the level of language and pace of delivery used when coaching could influence the effectiveness of learning.

18 Why is it important to encourage learners to discover and rectify their own errors rather than to promote a passive and dependent attitude on their part?

19 List the various methods that can be used by teachers when checking learners' progress during coaching sessions.

20 Explain how to give objective and constructive feedback.

21 Why is it important to involve learners in self-assessment of progress and achievement?

22 What are the benefits of guiding and supervising the learner, correcting errors and giving ongoing constructive feedback during coaching sessions?

23 Explain the benefits of keeping 'formative records' of learner progress.

24 Why is it important to provide a range of opportunities to enable learners to apply what they have learned?

25 Why should learners be given clear and accurate information about the people and resources involved in helping them to apply their learning?

## *Preparing for assessment: sample activities*

### *Activity 9.1 Coaching methods*
Define 'coaching' and explain key features of the coaching method of training listed below and any others that you consider to be important:

- setting the learner at ease
- establishing relevant standards of performance
- establishing existing skills and and prioritising learner requirements
- analysing tasks and explaining performance standards to be achieved
- preparing a suitable environment for the coaching session
- resourcing the session: facilities, materials and support
- guiding and supervising the learner, correcting errors and giving ongoing (formative) constructive feedback
- targeting and agreeing the learner's next goal.

### *Activity 9.2 Coaching learners*
Prepare for a 'live performance' of a coaching activity, gather material needed to support performance evidence and arrange for an assessor to judge your performance against unit standards. A possible approach is outlined below:

- Identify the learner's needs (ITN).
- Conduct a task analysis.
- Agree learning objectives.
- Use ITN and data gathered from the task analysis to prepare a coaching plan.
- Write a coaching activity checklist.
- Set the learner at ease.
- Brief the learner on the coaching activity.

- Provide inputs or otherwise support the achievement of the learner's objectives.
- Monitor the learner's progress.
- Identify and help to overcome barriers to learning.
- Judge the learner's progress and outcomes.
- Give feedback and record achievement.
- Provide opportunities for the learner to build up stamina.

### Activity 9.3 Assisting learners to apply new learning

Teachers and others involved in supporting learners will need to identify opportunities for learners to apply and reinforce new skills that they have acquired.

- Write a detailed account of how you have identified opportunities for learners to apply new knowledge and skills.
- Write a rationale for the resources employed.
- Provide a copy of the information supplied to learners.
- Describe how you made the arrangements to apply the knowledge and skills.
- Explain how you followed up by monitoring progress and evaluating the outcomes.

# 10

# Facilitating group learning

The term **group** defines a set of individuals who are interdependent. In training situations learners join together in achieving a particular purpose such as completing a preset task or group-determined activity. The object of a group presentation may be to give information, to complete a task set or to develop individuals within a supportive group setting. During group work an event that affects one individual also affects other group members, and they share the benefits of successfully accomplishing tasks and the disappointment when things go wrong.

Teachers may serve as situational leaders when presenting group activity. If this is so, they will need to provide a secure environment with adequate support for their learners and thus avoid introducing feelings of anxiety and unease. They will need to have some knowledge of **group dynamics** – the interaction between people's different motives, emotions and drives – if they are to appreciate what is happening when teaching learners in groups. Dependency on the group leader, scapegoating, dominating, withdrawal and passivity, conflict and confrontation are but a few examples.

Teachers when acting as facilitators will need to anticipate learners' reactions to the proposed group activity. When working with groups, they may encounter learners with prior knowledge of the topic and fairly entrenched ideas about what they think should be happening based upon past experiences. Their learners may have ingrained attitudes towards the task, topic, teacher or other learners. They may have preconceived expectations of the current or impending activity. They may be concerned about how their behaviour within the group or the result of group decisions could affect them in the foreseeable future. These factors can affect the facilitator's choice of group size and composition, activity, context and presentational methods.

The 'KISS' style should be adopted during briefings. In order to 'keep it simple' and readily understandable, the material should be presented in a clear and logical way and at a pace appropriate to the learners' ability to absorb and clarify what is said. The use of aids to support verbal input will enhance the probability that information presented will be more readily perceived, and back-up handouts should be issued to reinforce instructions and key points made. Procedures for group activities should be reviewed during initial briefings and written briefs issued for reference purposes. Facilitators should listen carefully to any comments made during the briefing and should use check questions to ensure that the learners understand what they have heard and what is required of them. Readers are recommended to find out more about group teaching by referring to D. Jaques' book: *Learning in Groups*.[1]

# Managing group dynamics

*A range of facilitating, managing and intervening skills is used appropriately to maintain learning within the group*

A group may be defined as:

> a set of individuals who are interdependent; they perceive themselves as 'belonging together' and they interact in achieving a particular purpose. They share a common fate so that an event that affects one individual also affects other group members (i.e. they may jointly share rewards or suffer punishment.[2]

F.E. Fiedler and J.E. Garcia suggest that the term 'leader' refers to:

> the person who is elected or appointed or who has emerged from the group to direct and coordinate the group members' efforts toward some given goal. The leader generally plans, organizes, directs and supervises the activities of group members and develops and maintains sufficient cohesiveness and motivation among group members to keep them together as a functioning unit.[3]

Having defined the terms 'group' and 'leader' we can now consider what is meant by 'facilitating, managing and intervening skills' in regard to the maintenance of learning within a group.

A **facilitator** is a learning resource – an enabler who helps self-directed learners and also individuals working in groups to realise their ambitions. **Management skills** are used by teachers when supervising group activities and when people are learning in larger groups; planning, controlling, organising, resourcing, directing, liaising and using information technology are but a few of the skills demonstrated by modern teachers. **Facilitation skills** can be used by teachers when tutoring, mentoring, counselling, negotiating learning agendas or otherwise supporting learners in the achievement of their goals. Three important attributes of an influential facilitator are: flexibility, responsiveness, and the ability to teach learners how to learn effectively in any learning situation.

Jaques says that 'A competent tutor should be versatile, able to use all the interventions (listed below), and to judge when to make them.' He quotes the following six categories of verbal and non-verbal intervention for group leaders:

| Authoritative mode | Facilitative mode |
| --- | --- |
| prescribing | releasing tension |
| informing | eliciting (suggestions and responses) |
| confronting | supporting[4] |

A group of FAETC students was asked to discuss facilitation and intervention skills. The text given below summarises the recommendations made during the discussion:

> The following suggestions were made by a members of a group of FAETC students during a discussion covering facilitation and intervention skills:
>
> ● Having been set a problem or task, sub-groups should be given sufficient time to discuss their own ideas, views and opinions before any intervention is contemplated.
> ● The facilitator should initially act as an observer to determine whether or not the discussions are on the right track.

- If the facilitator considers that an intervention is necessary, this should be unobtrusive using open-ended questions to allow group members to formulate their own ideas and responses to get discussions back on track.
- The facilitator should be available to mediate or to answer specific questions asked by individuals or groups.
- The facilitator should make all participants aware of the time remaining for discussion to enable groups to formulate opinions and agree summaries.
- Each sub-group should be encouraged to report their findings to the whole group. Again facilitation is the key concept – with the teacher maintaining a low profile.
- After such presentations the facilitator may summarise certain key points for reinforcement.
- Praise should be given where appropriate in order to boost confidence and self-esteem.

Gary Miller
Evidence reference Element C271 (pc 'A')

*A balance is established between tasks to be accomplished and the group process*

A group needs a leader or coordinator for it to function effectively. The leader role may not be permanent since leadership can change in response to the needs of a developing situation. Typically, group-work leaders tend to open proceedings with descriptions of the task on hand and then encourage group members to participate. They act as referees throughout the ensuing discussions and monitor and summarise progress at various stages. Group work takes time, sometimes far longer than anticipated, thus it is necessary to share the learning objectives with the group and agree timescales for completion of the tasks.

The function of the team leader will be to negotiate group objectives, plan, brief and control members, inform, review progress and evaluate outcomes. **Action-centred leadership** theory suggests three sets of needs that overlap and interact in any teamwork activity:

- needs relating to the task
- individual team members' needs
- overall team maintenance needs.

The need to accomplish the task set will clearly affect each of the other two sets of needs. Each individual's needs must somehow be satisfied, and supportive leadership is essential to success. The leader will reinforce team maintenance by making good progress with the task and keeping up team morale. A delicate balance between the three sets of needs must be maintained in order to get the task completed without losing group cohesion and individual support.

In order to promote group cohesiveness and consensus when initially establishing sub-groups or task forces the maintenance of the group process becomes all important. The formation of cliques and the promotion of exclusive groups within the main group can adversely affect subsequent relations and team spirit and should be avoided. As far as possible all decisions should be arrived at by mutual agreement. However, a balance must be established between tasks to be accomplished and the group process, and this could call for a group composed of people with special skills appropriate to the task objectives.

The following incident described by Gary Miller shows how group consensus was ensured when task forces were being formed.

The NEBSM course with whom I carried out my teaching practice relied heavily on group work activities. The formation of 'task force' teams was carried out on the first day. The whole group was given the option to organise and formulate their own task forces with four people in each team. The only conditions imposed were that there should be an appropriate gender mix and that each team had at least one member who was computer literate who could assist the team in preparing word processed reports and evidence for their portfolios. There were four photographers in the group and they requested to form their own task force as they had common interests. This suggestion was challenged by one member of the group who considered this undemocratic. The implications of this request were discussed by the whole group, i.e. the proposed formation of a clique containing individuals with less diverse vocational backgrounds with which to form group opinions and promote new ideas. After some discussion about the advantages of a heterogeneous mix of team members the group as a whole decided to allow the photographers to work together. The argument being that the photographers would hopefully identify with each other and derive mutual support from compatibility of their vocational interests.

Gary Miller
Evidence reference Element C271 (pc 'E')

*Group members are encouraged to feel comfortable to participate effectively*

By becoming actively involved together in a group task learners will learn more and probably retain more information about the task set than by working in isolation. Previous experiences can be shared and used to move learners forward to understanding new concepts. Teamworking can promote a build-up in confidence and help people to learn effectively by actively doing things, with the teacher acting as a facilitator reinforcing new learning.

Learners should be encouraged to listen to each other and to seize on opportunities to inject worthwhile comment and express agreement or disagreement with what is heard. Active involvement does not come easily to all learners and so the participation of quieter members must be nurtured. Reticent members should be gently led towards being more open in order to enhance the benefit they can derive from group working.

The group learning process becomes more rewarding for learners since they own their ideas and inputs rather than the teacher. However, the teacher can help by being available as a human resource and by ensuring that disruptive influences are kept to a minimum; otherwise group working could become less effective. It is the teacher's duty to provide a climate that promotes the physical and emotional well-being of all group members.

This topic is also discussed in Chapter 7 (see p. 100).

*The manner, level and pace of communication are appropriate to group members*

The manner, level and pace of communication should match the group's ability to keep up and concentrate on what is being said. The pace should reflect the complexity of the information to be shared with the group. Short, weighty sentences should be used, and written briefing instructions will be needed to reinforce the message. The brief will serve as reference material during subsequent group activity. Simply 'telling' or 'giving instructions' will not ensure that learners comprehend the meaning of what is being said. The teacher will need to check understanding by asking a few questions and also obtain feedback by observing their body language.

Knowing how to interpret body language is important in group-work activities. Verbal messages are often contradicted by body language subconsciously exhibited by learners, which should be noted since it could signal a need for a change of tactics.

Typical indicators include:

- facial expressions which reveal doubt or lack of understanding or the need for more thinking time
- lack of eye contact (possibly downturned) or a glazed expression, which may indicate that the individual is bored
- fully raised eyebrows, which may signal disbelief
- rubbing the back of the neck, which is a sign of frustration
- looking at a watch or rubbing the wrist, which indicates that the person is aware of the time and may even wish to be elsewhere
- leaning forward whilst someone else is speaking, which demonstrates active listening.

This criterion is also discussed under the same heading in Chapter 7 (pp. 99–100).

*Stereotyping of individual roles and behaviour in the group is challenged constructively and used to enhance learning*

**Stereotyping** is the act of attaching labels to individuals based upon a standardised image or conception of the characteristics of learners representing a particular social group. Teachers' and other learners' judgements about individuals can be negatively influenced by their attitude towards the clique or group to which the stereotype belongs. On the other hand positive views can result when learners present favourable first impressions, or when teachers perceive group members as being like themselves or extremely hard-working.

People can be categorised in terms of their **behaviour** as well as by unfair stereotyping. For example, learners might exhibit deviant behaviour by reacting adversely to authority. They might adopt a resentful manner when legitimate requests are made for their cooperation during a group task. Aggressive personality behaviours including stubbornness and refusal to cooperate might be witnessed, together with unhelpful group working behaviours such as being inattentive and lazy, or resorting to inappropriate coping responses such as opting out or withdrawing from group activities. In order to maintain a cohesive group these unhelpful behaviours should be **challenged** and attempts made to channel negative energy into constructive and supportive effort.

Typical group roles that might be exhibited include those suggested by Margerison-McCann. Their Team Management Wheel[5] model outlines four main categories embracing eight important roles that could be adopted by people working in groups, plus a 'linker'. The roles are:

- explorer/promoter
- thruster/organiser
- controller/inspector
- reporter/advisor
- assessor/developer
- concluder/producer
- upholder/maintainer
- creator/innovator.

R.M. Belbin (1981) observed many groups in industry to establish what is a 'good' team and found that ideal team roles might include those of:

- **chairperson** (coordinates team effort, is disciplined and has good judgement)

- **plant** (observer, source of original ideas, careless of detail, may resent criticism, can switch off at times)
- **resource investigator** (salesperson, sociable extrovert, draws contributions from others)
- **teamworker** (supportive of others, holds whole process together, listens, encourages and understands others)
- **shaper** (has drive, is energetic thinker, outgoing, dominant, irritable and impatient)
- **monitor/evaluator** (intelligent team member, analyst, dissector of ideas, weakness seeker, can be aloof, tactless and cold)
- **company worker** (practical organiser and administrator)
- **finisher** (rounds up situations and adheres to schedules).

Ideally groups should be made up of an equitable gender and ethnic mix and people from various social and vocational backgrounds. Efforts should be made to avoid the formation of cliques or groups that are likely to dominate the learning opportunity. However, the formation of 'task forces' can result in cohesive and supportive frameworks for individual and team development and the successful completion of tasks undertaken.

*Excluding or discriminatory behaviour or language is challenged appropriately*

Excluding or discriminatory behaviour and language speaks volumes about underlying prejudices held. Deep-seated prejudice is revealed by unfair behaviour towards disabled people, older people and gay people. Similarly, racist feelings or sexist attitudes, stereotyping and negative assumptions formed about people that one cannot easily relate to can lead to racial harassment and unlawful discriminatory behaviour. People have rights that must be honoured, therefore professional codes of practice should be adhered to whether one is working with learner groups or interacting with individuals. Rather than looking the other way teachers should challenge instances of overt discrimination witnessed.

This criterion is also discussed under the same heading in Chapter 7 (p. 101).

*Power, authority and influence in the group are used constructively to enhance learning*

Dr Fred Fiedler's 'Contingency Model of Leadership Effectiveness' is a widely cited leadership theory. The basic hypothesis is that leadership effectiveness depends on both the leader's personality and the situation. He suggests that a person might be highly successful in one set of conditions and ineffective in another, and that there is no one best leadership style or leader behaviour. It therefore follows that in order to make use of the talents and abilities of individuals, teachers must be placed in a position where they can effectively use their intellectual abilities, technical knowledge and experience to the best effect.

Issues of **power** and **authority** frequently arise when groups form. Power seeking can be recognised when certain learners exhibit the following types of behaviour:

- attempting to force their own opinions on the group
- monopolising the available talking time
- interrupting others while they are speaking
- making sarcastic remarks regarding the opinions of other group members
- aggressiveness and hostility in speech and body language.

It is the responsibility of the facilitator to monitor such behaviour and to ensure that control is maintained and that tension, friction and personal threats are not allowed to develop. Individuals who feel threatened 'switch off' and do not participate in the proceedings. Suitable intervention must be carried out to diffuse any possible conflict and the risk of damaging group cohesion.

*Conflict within the group is dealt with in a way which maintains the ability of group members to continue learning*

People forming groups often start with fairly fixed ideas about a topic or method of accomplishing a task set, and the statements they make will accurately reflect their opinions. Unfortunately things do not always run smoothly, and a few careless comments may cause dissent. Members display feelings of hostility, anxiety, resentment and self-pity. Some experience feelings of inadequacy, some are afraid to speak, some ridicule statements made by others and some make sarcastic remarks. Emotions such as anger or fear result from oversensitivity to remarks made. These are the factors which prompt various kinds of responses in a group situation.

Instances of aggressive competition, confrontation and lack of harmony lead to lack of agreement and disruption. The group as a whole will probably signal its disapproval if rules are broken or norms ignored. But serious breakdowns cannot be tolerated because an otherwise productive and happy climate can quickly be destroyed. The clear aim of group working is to allow people to re-examine and modify their attitudes in an atmosphere free of threat and to promote desirable outcomes. Conflict must be resolved and the facilitator must gain control so that tension, friction and personal threats are not allowed to develop. They must however avoid becoming the central figure through whom all points made are channelled. In a well-organised group the facilitator should remain silent for much of the time, allowing group members to explore the task in their own way.

## Facilitating collaborative learning

*The purpose, process and intended outcomes of group activity are agreed with the group*

In order to maximise team performance and derive the greatest benefit from collaborative learning, the team formed should be suited to the **purpose** for which it has been assembled. A **predetermined behavioural objectives** approach could be used when a programme or group session is planned. In this case the intended **outcomes** of group activity are agreed prior to the group activity and clear, **highly specified team objectives** and performance standards are set leaving little opportunity for negotiation. Alternatively, the **intended purposes** could be outlined, leaving plenty of room for exploration and widening of the scope of group activities. This method allows for **ongoing renegotiation** of the team's goals to suit the changing situation.

The potential of the team acting collectively will probably far exceed the potential of individual team members acting alone, therefore the **methods** adopted for teamworking should give participants plenty of **practice** in unlocking team potential while problem solving and coping with challenging tasks.

*Group activities are adapted to the size and composition of the group*

There will be an optimum group size for each activity contemplated. The task should be designed to keep all members fully occupied, but it must not be too complex nor must it overload small teams. When considering the effect of group composition on interaction and achievement of task Jaques says:

> As a general rule, a heterogeneous mix of students in each group provides the best chemistry for interaction and achievement of task. Such qualities as age, sex, nationality and personality may be taken into account, though one can never be sure what mixture might lead to good participation.[7]

He goes on to discuss group tasks and says:

> Tasks will vary in quality and quantity. Some are too difficult and too lengthy to be tackled in a given time; others are best done individually rather than by the group. There are tasks which demand no more than a 'surface' approach of students while others require a 'deep' or 'holistic' style of argument. It is the tutor's job to select tasks accordingly.[8]

*Adaptations and interventions are made effectively to improve the learning process*

Having a policy of fostering an empowerment culture within the group is desirable. Supporting one another in the accomplishment of group tasks must be the prime mover in any teamworking situation, and this can be promoted by encouraging teams to accept accountability for innovation and practices adopted. This is the approach now being widely used by market leaders in the business world to develop, motivate and incite people to give of their best, the idea being to encourage people to fulfil their potential. The driving force behind motivated achievement now appears to be challenge, responsibility and the ownership of outcomes.

A degree of teacher direction is necessary in any learning situation. It is no good standing back and allowing silence and confusion to reign. The style of leadership best suited to the needs of an empowerment strategy would probably be that of a facilitator who is able to enthuse the learners and promote genuine teamworking by providing close support and intervening only when absolutely essential. However, learning experiences provided need to be carefully planned, as the thought invested in sequencing and structuring group-work activities will affect the degree of intervention needed later to keep things going smoothly. Adaptations might include taking a critical look at the methods currently in use when things are not going well and introducing new, challenging and creative tasks. The facilitator should arouse curiosity and a sense of excitement by introducing more discovery-learning and problem-solving features into the group activity. This might mean rearranging the sequence of activities or providing additional resources.

*Factors which contribute to individual group members' ability to learn are explored with the group*

Happy and motivated teams of learners can make a big contribution to the learning process and to the success of group activities. The secret of making learners work hard is to treat them as equals and take care to delegate responsibility while providing adequate support, feedback and encouragement. In this way they will be able to get the most out of group work. Feeling empowered is the key to success, but this must be backed by becoming actively involved in group tasks and having the ability to communicate effectively with others. An inability to get the message across would inevitably inhibit the rate of progress.

A key aspect of the group's role in contributing to an individual learner's ability to learn is its ability to help them accept that continuing personal development is their own responsibility. No one can learn for them. This is why learners with special educational requirements should be encouraged to draw support from the group whenever they feel the need. There will almost certainly be someone in the group who will be able to offer advice or one-to-one coaching.

Adult learners will have had a number of post-school learning experiences. Some will have been formally taught while others will have learned almost entirely by maturation and experience. Thus the learning styles adopted will reflect their preferences. For example, a person who was previously used to formal presentations may initially feel uncomfortable with group work. Conversely, a student familiar with controlling their own learning outcomes may feel stifled if formal presentations predominate. Group work helps to alleviate these difficulties since it encourages learners to learn by giving them freedom to apply prior experience to new situations within the safety of the group. They can learn at their own pace and can learn effectively by becoming involved with others in collective activity.

*Group members are encouraged to reflect on the way in which they have been learning and participating in the group*

The practice of reviewing experiences gives learners an opportunity to think about what they have accomplished, related events and the degree of success or failure of the group effort. Commenting on the evaluation of group teaching, Jaques says:

> The most effective kind of evaluation for group teaching is, therefore, one which develops the students' awareness of the way groups work, and increases their sense of responsibility for each other and for the quality of work they do together. In this way the evaluation itself can become a vehicle for the students to learn many of the valued social aims of group work.[9]

He gives the following list of fairly simple methods of evaluating participation in groups by eliciting personal views:

- **Process questionnaires:** completed by group members and tutor. Results are discussed and ways of effecting improvements are decided.
- **Do-it-yourself checklist:** each student writes down three statements about the group activity. The statements are collated and rated in turn by everyone.
- **Reporting back:** the first five minutes of each meeting are devoted to a critique of the previous meeting.
- **Diaries:** notes on group dynamics, processes and outcomes are recorded at the end of each meeting. The notes are used as the basis of subsequent reviews.
- **Fishbowl:** Students from another group are invited to observe the target group at work. Their observations are discussed afterwards.
- **Self-made evaluation:** Two or more sub-groups devise an evaluation technique to use on the other sub-groups, and then administer it.
- **Video or audio playback:** the recording can be played back and members can contemplate their own and others' behaviour.

*Progress of individual group members is monitored sensitively*

In order to operate effectively, teachers require excellent **process management skills** and knowledge of facilitating techniques. They will need to develop their powers of **observation and analysis** and continuously improve skills used while monitoring group processes. Aspects to be monitored will include the level of participation and the emotional and physical well-being of the group. The aim should be to build individual and group commitment to accomplishing the task set by maximising involvement and harnessing creative energy. Signals picked up while monitoring progress will reveal the need for interventions which can help keep the group process, content and structure on the right track. Thoughtful interventions produce positive results whereas inaction allows confusion and loss of motivation to replace effectiveness and enthusiasm.

Successful team building depends on facilitators responding sensitively to the needs of individuals. This involves gaining insight into various aspects of individual learners' personalities and roles. Misreading the causes of learning difficulties or hold-ups in progress and their impact on the learner's emotions could result in conflict or distress and this could be difficult to resolve. This is why individuals should be invited to comment on their progress first, with the teacher adopting a supportive mentor/good-listener role. The way is then open for development of learner comment on features of their progress or the difficulties they are experiencing.

If an individual seeks advice, you must take care to avoid putting your personal views forward. The use of open-ended questions may assist the learner in clarifying matters or identifying possible solutions to their problem.

Care should be taken to avoid disrupting the remainder of the group or influencing their line of thinking by your own preconceived ideas or by unwittingly giving the solution to the problem set. You will have to judge whether to redirect the question to the group and risk an unwelcome intervention, direct the inquirer to relevant reading so that they can find the answer themselves, or take the individual to one side for a private discussion. The individual should be steered in the right direction using Socratic questioning techniques.[10] Only as a last resort should you give the answer directly. It would probably be beneficial to all concerned if you could agree to meet privately after the session in order to clarify any remaining doubts.

*Timely feedback is given on progress made and the process of learning to the group and to individual members in a positive and encouraging manner*

The **core process** of giving learners **timely feedback** on their progress and performance in a positive and encouraging manner is discussed in detail in Chapter 11.

*Timing and pace of group activities is managed effectively*

When managing group activities timing and pacing is all important. There is nothing worse than running out of time before groups have completed their tasks. People like to get things clear in their minds before starting an activity, so it is important to explain and summarise relevant instructions clearly before setting the groups to work. Confirm what is required. Ask the learners whether there are points needing clarification. Specify time limits for each activity or task element. Be prepared for the task to take longer than you anticipated. Allow time for deliberation and practice if applicable. Be reasonable and allocate sufficient time. Watch the clock, monitor progress against the planned timetable. Sticking to a timetable is essential if the task is to be completed on time. Check understanding and application by visiting groups soon after they get started. Carry out frequent progress checks. Allow time for randomly helping those who need advice. Be prepared for groups that finish early and be ready to allocate relevant bolt-on tasks or otherwise extend the activity. Reserve time for the plenary and allow sufficient time for members to reflect on the processes involved and group accomplishments. Identify important learning points, sum up and comment on the effectiveness of the activity.

*Group dynamics are managed effectively*

**Group dynamics** is a study of the behaviour of groups of people and of the interaction of individuals as members of a group. It is concerned particularly with the development of common perceptions through the sharing of emotions and experience. When managing group dynamics six key factors should be considered:

- **Group size:** small groups of between five and eight may be most effective and can result in greater satisfaction with a higher rate of participation per group member. Group processes may take up more available time when larger groups are operating, thereby leaving less time for task-related activity.
- **Group composition:** see above under the criterion 'Group activities are adapted to the size and composition of the group' (pp. 135–6).
- **Group cohesiveness:** the affiliation and partnership of group members leading to closeness, heightened self-esteem and consensus among group members.
- **Group communication patterns:** the network of communication linkages and channels through which messages can be passed or non-verbal signals picked up. The effectiveness

of communication can be affected by the degree of eye contact and gaze possible and the seating arrangements employed.

- **Group leadership:** appropriateness of leadership style adopted: autocratic, democratic or laissez-faire; or action-centred, situational or charismatic leadership style.
- **Group norms:** codes of conduct, acceptable behaviour, willingness to respond reasonably to propositions made by others, acceptance of rules of procedure, honest dealings, openness and freedom of speech, equal opportunities and avoidance of any form of discrimination or repression, respect for each other.[11]

The teacher will be readily accepted by learners as the person who is in charge of the group and has the authority to assign tasks, set goals and specify procedures and learning methods. They will support that view as long as their teacher remains within the bounds of expected behaviour. That is, the teacher must follow a professional code of practice and never overstep their authority. But with group-work activities leaders either emerge or are elected by the team. It has been suggested that, when given a specific task or placed in problem-solving situations, intelligent and competent team leaders drawn from the group will devote more energy to a task that is intellectually demanding and this effort will be reflected by group performance.

## Self-assessment questions

1 Explain what is meant by 'group dynamics'.

2 List the facilitating, managing and intervening skills that are used by teachers when maintaining group learning.

3 Describe how a balance between getting the task done and maintaining a healthy group process can be established.

4 Explain how individuals can be encouraged to feel comfortable and able to participate effectively in group activity.

5 Explain the importance of maintaining a suitable level and pace of communication when working with groups.

6 Prepare a list of typical indicators of boredom, confusion, frustration, lack of interest and poor motivation. Why is it important to monitor constantly the learners' body language?

7 What is meant by 'active listening'?

8 Explain what is meant by 'stereotyping' and how this can affect a teacher's view of individual students.

9 What is meant by the expression 'categorising people in terms of their behaviour'?

10 Outline key theoretical models of group work and typical group roles. Identify the different roles exhibited by your own learners when they are working in groups.

11 Describe instances of 'excluding and discriminating behaviour' that you have witnessed in learner groups and explain how you have challenged this behaviour. Summarise the outcomes.

12 Comment on the following statement: 'Intelligent and competent leaders make more effective plans, decisions and action strategies than do less able leaders.'

13 Give your views on the following statement: 'If the leader is put under interpersonal stress by group members her or his intellectual abilities will be diverted from the task to counterproductive matters.'

14 Discuss the following statement: 'Unless the group complies with the leader's directions, the leader's plans and decisions will not be implemented; to be effective the group must support the leader.'

15 Identify possible causes of conflict within groups. Give examples of how you have in the past dealt with conflict among members of your own groups.

16 Explain the terms 'dependence', 'pairing' and 'fight and flight'.

17 Explain why it is important to agree with your groups the purpose, process and intended outcomes of the proposed learning activity.

18 Describe how you have adapted group activities to suit the needs of a particular learner group.

19 Outline the circumstances in which you would intervene in a group activity. Describe typical intervention strategies.

20 Explain the benefits of reviewing experiences and reflecting on group processes and accomplishments.

21 Explain the importance of monitoring the progress of individuals working in groups. Give details of instances where you have responded to an individual's request for help.

22 Explain the need to give positive and encouraging feedback to group members when monitoring their progress and evaluating outcomes.

23 Outline the ways in which the timing and pacing of group activities can be managed effectively.

24 Define the following terms: 'group size', 'group composition', 'group cohesiveness', 'group communication patterns', 'group leadership' and 'group norms'.

25 Explain how the issues of equality of opportunity and non-discriminatory practice can be related to group work.

# Preparing for assessment: sample activities _____

### Activity 10.1 Identifying different types of group activities
Research the various types of group activities used in education and personal development contexts. Evaluate the advantages and disadvantages of each type of activity. Include a consideration of the following in your report:

- brainstorming
- buzz groups
- competitions
- debates
- games
- quizzes
- peer tutoring
- role-play
- seminar work
- simulations
- single specified tasks.

List the benefits to teachers and learners of using each type.

| Socio-emotional area: A positive reactions | | | Task area: B attempted answers | | | Task area: C questions | | | Socio-emotional area: D negative reactions | | |
|---|---|---|---|---|---|---|---|---|---|---|---|
| 1 | 2 | 3 | 4 | 5 | 6 | 7 | 8 | 9 | 10 | 11 | 12 |
| | | | | | | | | | | | |
| | | | | | | | | | | | |
| | | | | | | | | | | | |
| | | | | | | | | | | | |
| | | | | | | | | | | | |
| | | | | | | | | | | | |
| | | | | | | | | | | | |
| | | | | | | | | | | | |
| | | | | | | | | | | | |
| | | | | | | | | | | | |
| | | | | | | | | | | | |
| | | | | | | | | | | | |
| | | | | | | | | | | | |
| | | | | | | | | | | | |
| 1 | 2 | 3 | 4 | 5 | 6 | 7 | 8 | 9 | 10 | 11 | 12 |
| shows solidarity; raises other's status; gives help; reward | shows tension release; jokes; laughs; shows satisfaction | agrees; shows passive acceptance; understands; concurs; complies | gives suggestion, direction; implying autonomy for other | gives opinion, evaluation, analysis; expresses feeling; wish | gives orientation, information; repeats; clarifies; confirms | asks for orientation, information repetition, confirmation | asks for opinion, evaluation, analysis; expression of feeling | asks for suggestion, direction; possible ways of action | disagrees; shows passive rejection, formality; withholds help | shows tension; asks for help; withdraws out of field | shows antagonism; deflates other's status; defends or asserts self |

*Instructions*

Use the chart to observe the group behaviour. Try scoring each occurrence of the twelve categories of interactions in the columns on the chart. You will find it near impossible to score all the participants so first pick one person and score his or her responses. There are likely to be more responses in the 'TASK' area if you ask the group to discuss some problem, such as how unemployment could be reduced. Alternatively, you could try doing this exercise when observing a discussion going on in a TV programme.

Instructions source: J. Greene, *Communication*, Social Psychology Course D305 Block 11, Open University, Milton Keynes, p. 50.

Adapted from W.P. Robinson, *Language and Social Behaviour*, Penguin 1972. Figure 1, p. 44. Copyright © W.P. Robinson, 1972. Reprinted by permission of Penguin Books Ltd.

**Figure 10.1** *Chart for Bales's interaction process analysis*

### Activity 10.2 Forming a cohesive group

Identify the key purposes of groups. Explain what is meant by a 'cohesive' group.

Describe how you set about forming sub-groups or task forces during one or more of your teaching programmes.

Explain how the concepts 'self-selection', 'mission', 'corporate identity', 'logo', 'motto', 'morale' and 'motivation' can be helpful to students wishing to promote positive images of their group or task force.

### Activity 10.3 Managing a group

Describe how you have constructively used your power and authority as a teacher, firstly when managing relationships between members of your group and secondly when demonstrating the use between yourself and the group as a whole and with individual members.

### Activity 10.4 Running different types of groups

Explain your techniques for handling the group dynamics operating within two different types of groups that you work with. Your report should also describe how you manage large and small groups of mixed ability, mixed status and members employed in different occupational areas.

Include an account of how you explain group activities to learners, allocate roles, interpret non-verbal group communication and meet individual needs within a group setting.

Append a relevant observer's report or an assessor's checklist.

### Activity 10.5 Bale's interaction analysis

A comprehensive study of group behaviour during a group-working activity can be made by completing a 'Bales interaction process analysis chart' (see Figure 10.1).

Select a group to study. Then score each occurrence of the twelve categories of interaction on the chart. When completed, the chart gives an overall picture of the behaviour witnessed while members of the group are working. As it is near impossible for a single person to score the whole group, only one person at a time should be reported on unless you wish to enlist the help of other observers.

Analyse the group behaviour and present the resulting report as evidence for Unit C27.

When the group activity has been completed and the chart updated results could be discussed with the group.

### Notes

1 D. Jaques, *Learning in Groups*, Croom Helm, London 1985.

2 F.E. Fiedler and J.E. Garcia, *New Approaches to Effective Leadership*, John Wiley, New York 1987, p. 3.

3 Ibid., p. 2.

4 J. Heron, *Six Category Intervention Analysis*, Human Potential Research Project, University of Surrey, Guildford 1975. See D. Jaques, *Group Teaching*, in *The International Encyclopedia of Teaching and Teacher Education*, ed.M. J. Dunkin, Pergamon Press, Oxford 1987, p. 295.

5 See Margerison-McCann, *Team Management Systems*, marketed by TMS Development International Ltd (1995), 128 Holgate Road, York, YO2 4DL.

6 R.M. Belbin, *Management Teams: Why They Suceed or Fail*, Butterworth-Heinemann, Oxford 1981.

7 D. Jaques, *Group Teaching*, in *The International Encyclopedia of Teaching and Teacher Education* (ed. M.J. Dunkin), Pergamon Press, Oxford 1987, p. 291.

8 Ibid., p. 294.

9 Ibid., p. 297.

10 A series of carefully thought out questions is asked with the intention of leading learners towards the solution of a problem, using step-by-step questioning.

11 See M.D. Gail, *Discussion Methods*, in *The International Encyclopedia of Teaching and Teacher Education* (ed. M.J. Dunkin), Pergamon Press, Oxford 1987, pp. 234–5.

# Key Role D
## Assessing achievement

# Giving feedback

Teachers must be able to give feedback which will benefit the learners and enable them to take positive action to enhance their current achievement. However, feedback should not be perceived as being a 'one-way' or 'top down' process with the teacher at the top passing comments down the line or making only critical and subjective observations. Feedback shared with others should be constructive. It should be **objective** and **descriptive** and be soundly based upon the observation of performance. Criticism reflecting a subjective opinion or a whim and thunderbolt approach would be unhelpful. Teachers and assessors must display **openness** and be willing to receive feedback on the effectiveness of their planning, presentations and assessment judgements from peers and learners too.

In this chapter the **core process** of giving learners **timely feedback** on their progress and performance in a positive and encouraging manner is discussed. The content covers essential underpinning knowledge relating to performance criteria appearing in several of the earlier chapters on **facilitating** and **enabling learning** and the five chapters on aspects of **assessing achievement** that follow.

## Giving feedback

In industrial terms, the 'feedback' concept applies to linking a system's outputs to its inputs, thereby monitoring what is happening and keeping the system under control. In a training context, feedback provided by various methods of review and assessment gives information about the learner's progress. Being able to give and receive feedback is an important skill for learners, teachers and assessors.

Receiving **positive feedback** about learning outcomes and achievements is good for learners, but **negative feedback** given skilfully can also aid learning. The learner, teacher and assessor will need to be able to share their perceptions of the good and not so good aspects of the demonstration or learning activity.

Feedback may be obtained during **performance reviews** where learners are able to find out just how well they have done. In some cases feedback is more immediate, as in the case of a word-processor operator who loses several pages of work when the programme crashes. Here, the teacher would be able to use the incident to give constructive comment on the process that led to the problem and to offer advice on how to take positive action to avoid a repetition in the future.

Giving feedback can be valuable, even when an assessment confirms that all performance criteria have been met and standards achieved. Objective reviews and helpful criticism encourage the development of a healthy rapport and reinforce confidence. **Self-referenced** feedback is recognised as being of great value to learners, for it is what they say and think about their 'achievements' and 'failures' that really counts.

When learners fail to meet performance standards because of lack of concentration, dangerous actions or other shortcomings it will be necessary to offer corrective feedback. If this is the case, unsatisfactory behaviour should be identified but shown to be capable of being corrected. Judgements should be avoided, as should statements likely to cause a defensive stance and hostile responses. Ways of converting weaknesses to strengths should be suggested to learners so that they may overcome their problems.

Teachers should avoid telling learners that 'you will make a good receptionist' or 'you will never have an accident if you continue to perform as well as you did today'. These are judgements that can only represent an opinion and not indisputable fact. Comments made should be factually correct and based on actual instances observed. Teachers should 'own their feedback' and accept responsibility for what they say to learners. They should ensure that their comments are understood and that what is said is an honest and objective personal judgement that is valid only at that time and made under the prevailing circumstances.

If when giving feedback the teacher can start by **recounting** some of the good aspects of the learner's performance, learners will be better able to appreciate comment that follows. There will be a greater probability that subsequent supportive and constructive criticism will be well received and will be acted upon.

The teacher will need to maintain with the learner a conversation link by promoting better listening. Good listeners are able to understand and reflect back what is being said to them, and a teacher should endeavour to become a competent listener.

Information shared should be clear-cut and detailed. Vague generalisations are not helpful when giving feedback. Comments, whether descriptive or evaluative, should be narrowly focused. Arguments should be avoided and defensive attitudes discouraged.

Learners will expect to be told or otherwise helped to discover just what it is that they need to do to put matters right when they go wrong. They will not appreciate a teacher's attempts to evade the truth or to introduce vagueness and ambiguity.

It has been suggested that learners prefer teachers to use **descriptive** rather than **evaluative** statements when commenting on their performance. Descriptive accounts of what the teacher saw or heard during the lesson provide tangible examples of good and bad practice that learners can readily understand. These accounts are of more use to the learner than bland statements that are open to many interpretations, such as 'That was OK', or 'You did that well', or 'I think you're capable of doing it better'.

**Open-ended questions** have a place in the review process, throughout learning and when assessing underpinning knowledge and skills, but feedback given must be specific. The teacher must be explicit when discussing aspects of learner performance, and reference should be made to particular incidents observed or to features of their work. Actual examples should be quoted. Feedback should be restricted to knowledge, skills and attitudes that can be changed.

*Feedback given should enable the learner to identify exactly where further action is needed to meet the standard demanded or to confirm competent performance.*

Where possible, feedback must be given immediately after an event. Delay allows thought and recollection to fade with the passage of time. Learners will seek early confirmation of their ability to overcome obstacles, to do things well and to meet performance criteria. But they will also need early recognition of their 'achievements' or 'failures'.

*Feedback serves to reinforce learning and permits early correction of errors, provided it is received soon after an event.*

# Changing behaviour

## Promoting change

The acquisition of new knowledge and skills provides the potential for **behavioural change.** The learner's ability to memorise facts, to understand concepts and to carry out tasks can be readily evaluated and fed back. While feedback about performance may not always greatly affect the pace of learning, it can result in learners changing their opinion and attitude towards the teacher or the learning programme itself.

A person's behaviour will be adjusted to the surroundings and their personality, and inborn potential will dictate how well they get on in the learning process. Some teachers have a tendency to operate outside their brief in that they attempt to promote change in a learner's approach to life as well as to their college studies or vocational work. If this is the case, care should be taken to avoid pushing learners beyond their capacity to change their pattern of behaviour. The temptation to take such actions that may be considered unethical should be resisted. Unfairly or unreasonably attempting to secure changes in behaviour that are beyond the control of the learners, or asking them to do things that they are incapable of doing, should be rigorously avoided.

*Feedback intended to promote change should be restricted to approved action that is feasible and likely to help learners achieve attainable objectives.*

When reviewing assessment outcomes, learners should be encouraged to take decisions about whether or not to make use of any feedback provided. They must choose the course of action to be taken. Any attempt to push them into remedial activity, imposed retraining or extra lessons will probably be met with considerable resistance. A negotiated approach which allows all concerned to examine the pros and cons of taking a certain decision is recommended.

*Telling, directing or insisting that people do it 'your' way will probably not result in the desired outcome.*

# Reinforcement

## Carrot or stick?

**Reinforcement** is often thought of as being a form of strengthening or support, and this may be true when applied to the learning process. But in the training sector, rewards are known as **positive reinforcers** and punishments as **negative reinforcers.** In other words, rewards can help while punishments tend to hinder.

Some psychologists believe that rewarding a person is much more effective than punishment when attempting to promote learning or when seeking cooperation. Punishing someone for doing things incorrectly may help to inhibit that behaviour pattern, but it will not necessarily wipe it out completely. Rewarding someone for doing what is required will, however, often reinforce good behaviour.

When assessing someone or being assessed ourselves, we must be careful not to arouse feelings of resentment, dislike or fear. A few careless words may destroy rapport and create strong, unhelpful emotional responses in others involved.

*When assessing others it is better to highlight good features and adopt a positive approach than to be destructive and concentrate mainly on the not-so-good elements.*

When reviewing the achievements of others, teachers will need to be able to:

● establish contact and a communication link
● reward candidates with compliments for doing good work
● welcome suggestions from candidates for improving their performance
● thank candidates when appropriate for efforts made in performing work carefully and correctly
● turn aspects of 'failure' into opportunities for candidates to accept the challenge of accomplishing whatever is holding up progress
● use their 'power' properly and sensitively
● avoid giving any indication of pleasure derived from 'failing' or otherwise 'putting down' the candidates
● arrange reviews so that the presence of others does not cause candidates any loss of status or self-image
● avoid abusing candidates by misjudging the severity and intensity of criticism offered or the effect of comments made to them
● ensure that adverse constructive criticism is not repeated to others nor used for the purpose of providing a lesson for the whole group unless the candidate concerned is in agreement
● realise that quiet 'soft' private remarks made during reviews are more effective and will be better received by candidates than 'loud' public pronouncements made to everyone
● avoid feelings that their image as an assessor will suffer if onlookers note that they can find no fault in a candidate's performance.

## Key aspects

### *Giving feedback*

Giving feedback is an important duty that teachers will be asked to carry out, and one that calls for a good deal of tact, imagination and understanding. Feedback can help candidates in their ongoing personal development, but when badly handled it can leave people confused, demoralised and disheartened. Fortunately, increased use of competence-based assessment over recent years has resulted in sensible suggestions about how best to go about sharing feedback with candidates. Some useful tips are outlined below.

● Encourage. Start with the good news. Give some positive aspects of the candidate's performance.
● Be explicit. Be definite and relate to particular instances, product evidence and tangible things (see Chapter 1, pp. 6–7). Make specific points and avoid generalities.
● Refer only to aspects of the candidate's performance that can be changed. Encourage candidates to turn constructive criticism and suggestions offered into positive intent followed by action.

- Tell candidates how criteria have or have not been achieved. Give praise where due. When criteria have not been met suggest achievable alternatives or ways forward.
- Be descriptive. Say what you saw or heard. Be objective and avoid making value judgements.
- Stand by your feedback. Admit ownership of what you say. Take the responsibility for saying 'No'. Don't blame others or use expressions such as 'I'm sorry but *they* wouldn't accept this as evidence.' Let what you say be honest and worth listening to.
- Offer factual feedback. Allow candidates to make decisions and select courses of future action. Leave candidates with facts to chew over and allow them to choose their way forward. Never attempt to impose your decision.
- End on a high note.

## Self-assessment questions

1 Explain why teachers should be active listeners during reviews.

2 Describe how sharing feedback can provide information about a learner's progress.

3 Why should feedback be shared as soon as possible after an event?

4 Why is receiving positive feedback about learning achievements good for learners?

5 How can discussions and performance reviews provide feedback on the effectiveness of teaching and learning?

6 What is meant by the expression: 'Learning involves behaviour change'? How can teachers promote further positive behaviour change when giving feedback?

7 Why should teachers share factual information rather than subjective opinion when giving feedback?

8 Why should feedback be descriptive, clear-cut and detailed?

9 Why is self-referenced or learner-generated feedback recognised as being of greater value to learners than purely formal assessments made solely by a teacher?

10 Why should arguments and defensive attitudes be discouraged?

11 Why must teachers avoid arousing feelings of resentment, dislike or fear when they are giving feedback?

12 Open-ended questions should be used except where factual information or 'Yes' or 'No' answers are needed. Why is this?

13 What benefits derive from starting and finishing feedback with good news? Why should teachers end the feedback session on a high note?

14 Why should teachers 'own' their feedback, accept responsibility for what they say and not blame others for having to tell the truth?

15 What are the disadvantages of telling, directing or insisting that people do things 'your way'? Why might this approach not have the desired effect? Describe a better way of encouraging improvements or corrections to be made.

# *Preparing for assessment: sample activity* _____

### *Activity 11.1 Assessing performance and giving feedback*

Negotiate and agree with a candidate an assessment plan for gathering evidence in the workplace so that you can judge their performance against unit standards. Make the necessary arrangements for the planned assessment to take place. Brief your candidate on the assessment process and observe them following the assessment specification when they are performing the assessment task.

The candidate should receive prompt and accurate feedback when they have completed the work. Review with them their performance, ensuring that you first encourage them to self-assess and to evaluate their own achievement before offering your feedback. Ensure that you discuss any comments that you noted on your observation checklists while they were completing the assessment tasks, and, if necessary, ask sufficient questions to probe for further evidence of their ability to perform competently.

Complete all relevant assessment documentation, and if the candidate has failed to demonstrate competence against all unit criteria a new assessment plan must be mutually agreed. Retain copies of the assessment documentation for your portfolio of evidence.

# 12

# Advising and supporting candidates when identifying prior achievement

**Prior learning** is learning that has occurred in the past. Prior learning leads to **prior achievement**, and it is the achievement aspect that is particularly relevant when a candidate is seeking admittance to a particular course or formal learning opportunity, and not the formal or informal learning process that led to the achievement. Evidence of prior achievement is used by assessors to give credits towards NVQ or SVQ units.

Unintentional learning deriving from everyday experiences, independent self-study out of college such as by correspondence courses and watching TV programmes, and experiential learning in the workplace, at home or on DIY projects are prime examples of the means by which prior learning and achievement may occur.

The candidate is now rightly seen by many providers as the central figure in the educational process. This was not always the case, and even today there is still much evidence of teachers adopting the role of authoritative central figures who attempt to direct and control every aspect of what is offered to learners. These 'pillars' or 'guardians' of institutional standards often held the key that could open the door to learning opportunities, and they could easily exclude anxious learners on the grounds that they 'did not meet the formal entry requirements for the qualification sought'.

Nowadays, giving credit for current competency, and the growth of formal accreditation of prior learning and achievement (widely known as APL), is changing matters for the better. Candidates are now encouraged to claim their entitlement to a place on a given course and exemptions or credits towards a particular qualification.

Initial assessments and APL sessions provide opportunities to collect and judge oral and written evidence brought forward from existing experience. Present levels of achievement can be established by asking a series of carefully framed questions or administering preset tests covering the performance criteria of the unit or element being assessed.

Being able to specify objectively just where the candidate stands enables the APL advisor to outline what is on offer and to negotiate the candidate's way forward. This chapter covers the means of identifying previously acquired competence and how to help candidates identify areas of current competence, agree assessment plans and prepare their portfolio of evidence for assessment. The content will also be of value to those seeking advisor qualifications such as the C&G 7281/23 (D36) Advising on Prior Achievement Award (previously known as the APL Advisors Award).

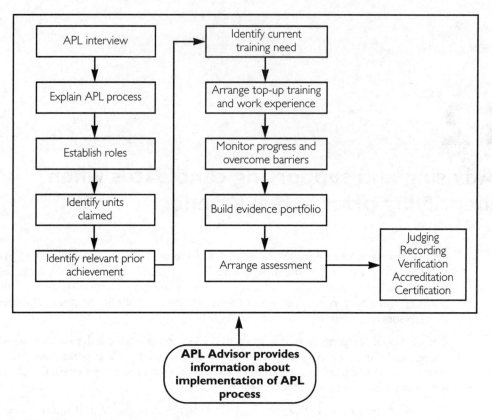

**Figure 12.1** *APL process flow chart*

## Helping the candidate to identify relevant achievements

*The candidate is given clear and accurate information about the principles and implementation of accreditation of prior learning*

Advisors will need to give their candidates clear and accurate information about what the identification of prior achievement is, how it applies to NVQ/SVQ candidates and how they can benefit from it. Candidates will wish to understand how procedures for the APL review process and the assessment of achievement are implemented. In order to do this candidates should be led through some or all of the stages listed in Figure 12.1 and be given a brief summary description of the principles of APL such as the example provided by Pete Jordan in Figure 12.2 (see *Documents Pack*). However, they will probably not appreciate a complex or lengthy briefing during which every aspect of the process is explained chapter and verse. People are easily confused when confronted with a mass of detail and particularly the terminology associated with NVQs and the like. It is better to present the basic important stages shown in the APL process flow chart during the first meeting and concentrate on understanding these rather than to waste time and effort on detailed explanations.

Suggested **fundamental roles** for a teacher-advisor who is operating a guidance and support service for candidates are given in Figure 12.3. Action verbs describe each part of the role, which if carried out will result in unit-specified performance that can be observed or otherwise assessed and achievement recorded.

# Candidate's charter

**Advisor's Mission**

My key purpose is to provide an excellent advisory, guidance and support service for candidates, covering a range of vocational schemes and educational programmes.

**Role of Advisor**

My role as advisor is to:

**Establish** a sympathetic relationship and create an atmosphere conducive to establishing rapport with candidates.

**Explain** the 'Assessment of Prior Learning and Achievement' (APL) and 'Identification of Learning Needs' processes to candidates.

**Support** the principles of equal opportunities and best non-discriminatory practice; make arrangements to meet candidates' special needs and requirements; and strive to break down personal and structural barriers obstructing access to learning opportunities.

**Establish** with candidates the target qualification with reference to the NCVQ database of NVQs, GNVQs, SVQs, College prospectus, Careers Service, Training Access Points (TAPS) and other sources of information.

**Arrange** an initial diagnostic and assessment session within a comfortable and friendly environment while maintaining candidates' confidence and self-esteem. Provide prompt, constructive and objective feedback on outcomes.

**Interview** candidates. Put them at ease and encourage them to self-assess prior accomplishments, review sources of achievement and complete a listing of experience.

**Assess** whether the individual candidate is likely to benefit from APL, and whether their previous learning experiences would be likely to generate evidence of achievements.

**Identify, prioritise and agree** learning needs with candidates.

**Advise** candidates on the conditions and characteristics of assessment, training and personal development opportunities available, and provide guidance on progression.

**Register** candidates for an award (where appropriate).

**Negotiate and create** with candidates learning programmes, action plans and assessment plans.

**Arrange** top-up training and where necessary facilitate individual or collaborative learning opportunities within a healthy and safe working environment.

**Provide** guidance on identifying, selecting and gathering evidence.

**Propose** a suitably structured folder or similar means of containing and presenting evidence, and guide portfolio composition and preparation.

**Make an appointment** – on the candidate's behalf – with a vocational or accredited assessor for the target qualification sought.

**Support** candidates at all stages of the process, from initial assessment to final accreditation.

**Maintain** the security, accuracy and confidentiality of candidates' records.

**Advisor** _____ **Candidate** _____

**Figure 12.3** *Candidate's charter*

Considerable benefit can derive from forming teams of teacher-advisors charged with:

- counselling individuals about qualifications and the requirements of relevant awarding bodies
- interviewing 'clients' (potential candidates) who are seeking help in identifying relevant achievements
- identifying candidates' prior achievements
- identifying target vocational qualifications
- identifying current learning needs and aspirations

- agreeing realistic goals
- establishing priorities for action for achieving qualifications sought
- agreeing and recording action plans for achieving target units with those concerned
- helping candidates to locate, gather, prepare and present evidence for assessment
- liaising with awarding bodies and vocational assessors.

The complete APL process can be **practised and perfected** using role-play with groups comprising the advisor-candidate (the FAETC student or D36 candidate concerned), the candidate (the substitute candidate seeking APL advice) and an observer. Other criteria such as facilitating collaborative learning and managing group dynamics could also be observed and assessed when this method is adopted. Evidence from role-plays is **not acceptable** as performance evidence when you present your own D36 evidence to the assessor. The assessor must judge performance evidence through **observation** of the advisor-candidate with candidates, either by witnessing the interviews and support sessions, or by means of a video or an audiotape or other approved methods.

A briefing document outlining the principles and methods of the accreditation of prior achievement should be discussed with candidates and copies given to them to take away after the meeting. People do not always get the message immediately and tend to avoid asking too many questions even when actively encouraged to do so. Further details are given in Activity 12.2 and Figures 12.2 (see *Documents Pack*) and 12.24.

*The candidate is encouraged to review all relevant experience*

Candidates seeking NVQ and other qualifications will need help in identifying the gap between what they can already do and what they need to be able to do in order to meet award criteria. They will expect to be provided with **unbiased** and sufficient **relevant** information about the APL or ITN process, and with **guidance** when completing listings of experience, self-assessment instruments and assessment tests and identifying previously acquired competence. Teams of teacher-candidates and others working towards the C&G 7306 and the Advising on Prior Achievement (APL Advisor's) Award have found documents similar to the ones reproduced in Figures 12.4 and 12.5 (see *Documents Pack*) helpful when gathering portfolio evidence. Role-plays and simulations enable group members to take their turn at adopting the role of advisor, candidate and observer, and hence to gain valuable experience while practising the APL reviewing procedure in a safe collaborative learning situation.

*National standards which the candidate may potentially be able to achieve currently are accurately identified from the review of experience*

Having set the candidate at ease, explained the APL process and provided award criteria, the advisor sets about gathering information about potential areas of relevant current experience. The candidate could be asked to complete forms similar to those given in Figures 12.4 and 12.5 (see *Documents Pack*). This activity is a fundamental part of the process as it encourages the candidate to think about and recall the many and varied sources of experience that have contributed to their present-day performance at work and in life outside the workplace. Time spent on this part of the review will be well rewarded since the review will reveal many transferable or core skills owned by the candidate that could otherwise be overlooked. Some people find it difficult to record relevant past experiences and prior achievement and write no more than a few lines. Others dislike writing down anything at all and tend to dismiss the task as unnecessary form-filling. This is when the advisor will need to provide considerable support and to coax the candidate patiently towards thinking hard about their current capabilities and earlier achievements and to identify evidence of prior achievement needed to gain credits sought.

*Occupational area question checklists*

Sometimes it will be necessary to apply written tests, questionnaires or computer-based assessments to establish the currency and sufficiency of the candidate's knowledge and understanding. In such instances it would be helpful if the advisor had lists of preset questions available to supplement other self-assessment information gleaned.

*Support and the way it is given encourage self-confidence and self-esteem in candidate*

Attending an APL interview will be a new experience for many people. Some will feel anxious, insecure and exposed in unfamiliar surroundings, and lack the confidence needed to get the best out of the opportunity. This possibility should be recognised by advisors, and care taken to avoid making matters worse by thoughtless or impatient behaviour.

Learners must always be encouraged to feel safe in any learning or assessment environment in which they find themselves. They are after all centre stage in the training and development world. Advisors should provide appropriate moral and emotional support, guidance and encouragement, and help their candidates recognise and value past achievement and what it means in terms of value today. Care must be taken to avoid brushing aside their offerings or degrading them by regarding earlier achievements as obsolete or of little value today. Something objective can be said of any learning experience and it is the positive aspects that should be stressed, not the downside.

Support offered should meet candidates' inherent need to avoid feelings of inadequacy and inferiority. Steps should be taken to avoid introducing the concept of failure with its attendant feelings of shame, humiliation and ridicule. Instead, achievements should be recognised and candidates should be praised for what they can do and encouraged to make progress and overcome obstacles (see Figure 12.7).

The advisor's role is to promote **self-confidence** and **self-esteem** in their candidates. When people are encouraged to act as **originators** they will readily accept responsibility for their actions and outcomes. They feel personally in control of events and this is good for morale. However, when others control events and make decisions for them people feel inferior – manipulated just like **pawns**. Confidence is lost and self-esteem suffers.

*Options open to the candidate are explained clearly and constructively, if the candidate expresses disagreement with the advice offered*

When helping candidates to identify relevant achievements, advisors will be called upon to offer different types of advice based upon their in-depth knowledge of the award body's **normative needs** (award criteria and assessment specification) that all candidates must fulfil in order to qualify for the target award, plus their perception of the candidate's requirements and the candidate's **expressed needs**. If the advice given is sound and relevant and clearly matches the candidate's expectations there is unlikely to be a problem. However, candidates will also have **felt needs** that only they are aware of, and if options open to the candidate do not meet these intrinsic needs there could be disagreement.

There are a number of ways of avoiding difficult situations and reducing the probability of aggressive or defensive behaviour on the part of candidates. For example, the advisor might be able to maintain constructive interaction by agreeing or disagreeing with comments candidates make and building on the positive aspects. Statements made could be **reframed or refocused** so that key objectives, relevant achievements highlighted and possible benefits more nearly match the candidate's target goals and job objectives. The causes of any underlying conflict of views and disagreement should be established in a friendly way, for it is no use causing resentment by leaving discontent to fester. Individual, interpersonal and

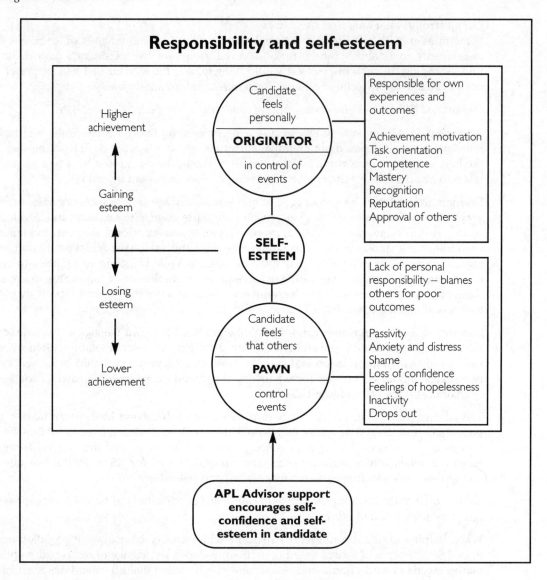

**Responsibility and self-esteem**

Higher achievement

Gaining esteem

Losing esteem

Lower achievement

Candidate feels personally **ORIGINATOR** in control of events

**SELF-ESTEEM**

Candidate feels that others **PAWN** control events

Responsible for own experiences and outcomes

Achievement motivation
Task orientation
Competence
Mastery
Recognition
Reputation
Approval of others

Lack of personal responsibility – blames others for poor outcomes

Passivity
Anxiety and distress
Shame
Loss of confidence
Feelings of hopelessness
Inactivity
Drops out

**APL Advisor support encourages self-confidence and self-esteem in candidate**

**Figure 12.7** *Locus of control*

organisational barriers to agreement should be explored and the means of overcoming obstacles jointly agreed.

Refusal to accept advice on the part of the candidate, or other forms of disagreement between the advisor-candidate (i.e. the teacher or advisor seeking to gain D36) and the candidate (i.e. the person seeking advice or support) may not arise when the authorised assessor is judging performance against the D36 criterion given in the heading above. When this does arise, City and Guilds recommend that assessors 'look for evidence that the candidate understands how to handle situations in which the candidate disagrees or declines to accept advice'.

# Agreeing and reviewing an action plan for achieving qualifications

*Candidates are given accurate advice and appropriate encouragement to enable them to form realistic expectations of the value and relevance of prior achievements*

In order to carry out a comprehensive and logically ordered review of current competency and to identify learning needs the advisor should prepare a list of topics to be raised and questions to be asked. The **checklist** given in Figure 12.8 could be complemented with **interview notes** recorded on forms such as those shown in Figures 12.9 and 12.10 (see *Documents Pack*).

Academic expectations can be influenced by successes or failures and the feedback associated with earlier learning experiences. People can become very concerned about what teachers, assessors and friends think about their competency at work and level of academic achievement. **Successes** can boost confidence leading to hopes and anticipation of further successes. But overconfidence often results in candidates setting themselves unrealistic achievement targets. Persistent underachievement in the past and consequent loss of esteem arising from **failure to achieve** their goals and reach their level of aspiration can lead candidates to underestimate their ability to achieve success in any learning proposition. But it can also lead people to overestimate their capabilities, which may be a core reason for their continuing failure (see Figure 12.11).

Taking a keen interest in unit content and its application to the real work environment tends to promote higher achievement, and success breeds success. People like working hard on things that they enjoy doing and where they receive positive and objective feedback on progress from others. On the other hand, if candidates programme themselves to expect the worst and look for the downside in everything they attempt, outcomes probably will match their expectation. A kind of self-fulfilling prophecy will then reinforce feelings of unworthiness, dent the self-image and impair progress.

The advisor can help candidates make judgements about the feasibility of their self-set goals and help control levels of anxiety by supporting them throughout the APL interviewing and planning session and injecting a measure of realism into the process.

*Target vocational qualifications identified are appropriate to candidate's prior achievements and future aspirations*

Before entering into any detailed discussion of a particular qualification it is necessary to identify and define exactly what to measure current skills and experience against. This requires that **target qualification criteria** are available and that the needs and expectations of the candidate are established in order to define a satisfactory match. This should be followed by agreeing and prioritising which criteria are key to achieving candidate satisfaction and meeting occupational or vocational objectives, rather than stipulating unachievable targets based on unrealistic aspirations. The best match can only be obtained when a clear picture is gained by taking account of listings of experience, interview notes and other data gathered from the APL review process. Obtaining reliable information from candidates who are not sure of what they want is sometimes not easy, and suggesting what you believe the candidate needs to do rather than ensuring that you are led by the candidate can easily result in conflict.

**Empowering** learners and candidates to accept responsibility for taking decisions based upon a clear understanding of unit standards with the support of an advisor will encourage them to take ownership of the results and the consequent effects of their choice.

# Interviewer's checklist

## TOPICS AND QUESTIONS

### Target qualification sought

What is your present occupation?
Have you any changes in mind?
Which qualification are you seeking?
Is your work creating a need for you to go for the award?
Will you get any support from your employer?
Generally speaking, do you know what is involved in working for the award?
Are you familiar with the units and performance criteria involved?

### Key prior achievements

Have you done anything like this before?
Do you have any formal qualifications that might be relevant to the award you are going for?
Have you done anything before that could be used to gain exemptions or credits for any part?
Have you done any part-time work that might be compatible with the award you are seeking?
Voluntary or other unpaid work?
Simulations?
Leisure activities?
Previous education and training?
TV, radio or reading assignments, projects or similar?
DIY?

### Units to be claimed

Have you identified any units you feel you can claim credit for right away?
Shall we now go through your listing of previous experience and sort out any potential areas of current competence that would apply to the new award?
Now that we have done this we shall need to make a note of what you think you can claim and create an assessment plan.

### Portfolio of evidence

*Identifying evidence*

Do you feel confident that the evidence you intend to present for assessment will cover all the unit requirements?
What do you understand by the term *direct evidence*?
Do you intend to provide any direct evidence for assessment?
What do you understand by the term *indirect evidence*?
Do you intend to provide any indirect evidence for assessment?
What do you understand by the term *performance evidence*?
Do you intend to provide any performance evidence for assessment?
What do you understand by the term *knowledge evidence*?
Do you intend to provide any knowledge evidence for assessment?

Let us make a note of the evidence you have identified for collection and presentation for assessment.

### Gathering evidence

Do you foresee any difficulties in collecting the evidence?
You will need to match your evidence against the elements and performance criteria. Will you need any help with this matching?
If you experience difficulties with interpreting performance criteria where could you get help?
I suggest that you file and index your evidence in a ring binder as soon as it becomes available. This will prevent a confusing build-up of paperwork that takes some sorting out if it gets out of hand. Remember that you need to produce only sufficient recent evidence related to the units being claimed. In some cases you may need to demonstrate competence where evidence from prior achievement is not available.

### Notes

### Advisor_____

**Figure 12.8** *Interviewer's checklist*

*Advice to the candidate accurately identifies unit(s) which might reasonably be claimed on the basis of prior achievement and evidence of continuing ability to achieve the element(s) within the unit(s)*

Detailed matching exercises are carried out by some awarding bodies, and tables are provided showing where earlier qualifications gained are likely to cover the requirements of a given element or whole unit. Using this information advisors can indicate where their candidates may gain exemptions. Examples provided by City and Guilds relating to the assessor and verifier units are shown in Figure 12.12, while Figure 12.13 shows how an APL advisor's recommendations were matched to the Institute of the Motor Industry element A7.1, 'Carry out scheduled examination of the vehicle systems' (see *Documents Pack*).

As can be seen, holders of the earlier C&G 9292 or C&G 9293 can claim exemption for six of

---

## Interview notes

**TARGET QUALIFICATIONS AND PREVIOUS ACHIEVEMENT**

**Target qualification identified**

**Key prior achievements**

**Units to be claimed**

**Evidence to be gathered**

**Top-up training needed**

**Referral agency to be consulted**

**Assessment plan created and agreed**          YES ☐    NO ☐

**Notes**

**Advisor** _____     **Candidate** _____

**Interview date** _____     **Date of next meeting** _____

**Figure 12.9** *Interview notes pro forma*

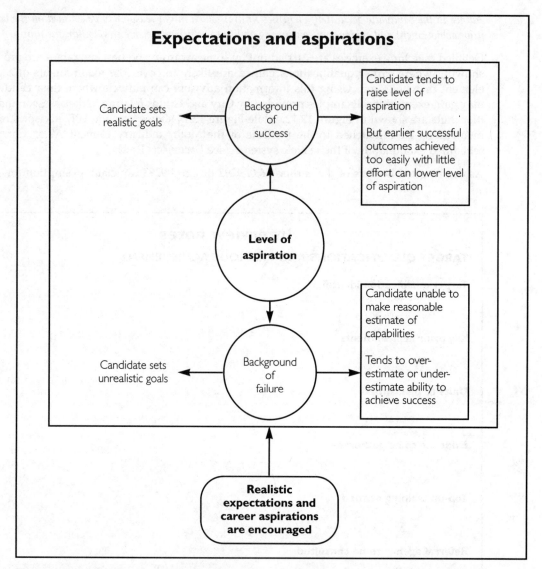

**Figure 12.11** *Effect of level of aspiration*

the seven elements comprising the current C&G 7281/22 award. However, holders of the C&G 7281/22 Vocational Assessor's Award (Units D32 and D33) gain no exemptions towards C&G7281/23 Advising on Prior Achievement (APL Advisor's) Award (Unit D36) but are likely to gain credit for the whole of Units D32 and D33 when going for the C&G 7281/24 Internal Verifier Award, leaving only D34 to do. Knowing what credits are available to candidates seeking particular awards is invaluable, and advisors must have a thorough knowledge of the NVQ/SVQs and other qualifications available, especially those pertaining to their occupational area specialism.

*Opportunities to use evidence from prior achievement are accurately analysed*

The unit performance criteria, range statements and assessment guidance provided by awarding bodies define the performance and supplementary evidence required. Guidelines provided describe required candidate behaviour, conditions under which it will be demonstrated and knowledge evidence concerning methods employed together with related information underpinning competent performance.

Teacher-advisors will help collate evidence provided by the candidate and cross-reference resulting APL claims with award criteria described above. They will carry out a **matching exercise** that will enable the candidate to gather supporting evidence needed to gain exemption from some or all elements and identify evidence to be generated or extra work needed to meet the requirements of whole units or the complete award.

*The plan agreed with the candidate identifies realistic actions to collect and present evidence of prior achievement efficiently*

Sources of evidence that could be listed in an assessment plan include full-time and part-time employment, unpaid work, leisure activities and earlier education and training. Advisors are expected to agree with their candidates an effective mix of evidence from prior achievements and current assessment that will be presented for assessment. Problems can arise where a candidate wishes to claim just a few performance criteria that fall well short of a whole unit or even a single element. Obviously, competency in a job suggests carrying out whole tasks or suitable chunks of work rather than unrelated bits of the task, and this possibility must be explained to the candidate so as to avoid misunderstandings and disappointment.

The vocational assessor will be looking for confirmation of **authenticity** or genuineness of evidence presented or proof of ownership; its **currency** or its present time value, its **validity** or relevance to units claimed today; its **consistency** or its typicality and conformity with previously demonstrated attitudes and behaviour rather than a 'one-off' performance for an assessor; and its **sufficiency** or adequacy of quantity and quality.

Before the session is concluded either an APL assessment plan or an action plan or both are agreed and recorded. The form and scope of the plans are a matter for negotiation, and the content and context will vary according to individual needs identified. The action-planning process is summarised in Figures 12.14 and 12.15, and sample plans are provided in Figures 12.16 and 12.17 (see *Documents Pack*).

The key purpose of planning is to ensure that all concerned obtain a clear picture of the way forward in terms of the candidate's gaining credit for current competency, arranging top-up training and preparing for related assessments. The outline strategy will be recorded in an action plan which will clearly specify the candidate's career goals and qualifications sought, the context for training and assessment, learner support and proposed dates for reviews and assessments.

*The candidate's motivation and self-confidence is encouraged throughout*

Earlier learning experiences may have caused candidates to lose faith in educational processes, and some become anxious, even fearful, when it comes to joining a training and assessment opportunity. But even so they will have a strong inherent need to achieve and to excel in whatever endeavour they choose to pursue. We are all ambitious to some extent, and **achievement motivation** is the force driving us to derive satisfaction from meeting challenges presented.

People have high level **self-realisation needs** requiring them to make the best of their abilities and respond to challenges. Most people experience psychological forces or **ego-enhancing factors** such as the need to achieve targets and gain status or recognition for accomplishment. Candidates will experience **cognitive drive**, the motivational need to demonstrate skills,

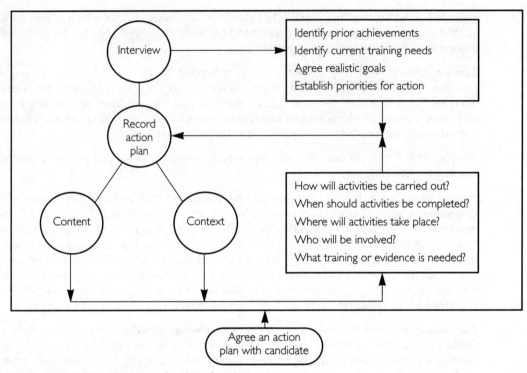

**Figure 12.14** *Interviewing and action planning*

knowledge and understanding: that is, to be seen to be competent and able to accomplish certain tasks thereby gaining the approval of others.

Regretfully, candidates are sometimes confronted by obstacles that are not easy to overcome. They become frustrated, tired and lacking in drive. Prestige is threatened and they look around for someone to blame for their difficulties. Learners experience this kind of frustration, giving rise to problems in the college or workplace.

In such circumstances the advisor, backed by members of the learner group, should be on hand to suggest ways forward and to help revive the motivation to succeed. Ensuring that teacher-advisor commitment is visible and active and fully communicated to the learners, and creating the 'right' culture by adopting the roles described in the provider's **mission statement** or Candidate Charter, will encourage and maintain learner motivation. But candidates must determine their own destiny and feel in control of events, otherwise a state of learned helplessness will creep in and passive behaviours or even complete withdrawal from the programme may occur.

Advisors could consider encouraging achievement motivation by:

● promoting the value of success as a way of improving candidates' self-image and self-esteem
● presenting the opportunity as a challenge and inviting candidates to rise to the occasion
● convincing candidates that they can or should succeed in their chosen task
● negotiating realistic and reasonable goals
● explaining and clarifying what it is that they (the candidates) hope (or intend) to achieve
● offering incentives, strengthening the desire to achieve and thereby increasing the effort made

- matching candidate intentions with related activity that may be demonstrated during day-to-day work or experience
- promoting candidate responsibility for directing their own behaviour towards the overall goal and using their abilities to best advantage
- recording progress towards the attainment of agreed targets
- praising accomplishments and showing appreciation of the candidates' efforts
- assuring support throughout the process and counselling overanxious candidates.

*If the candidate expresses disagreement with the advice offered, options open to the candidate are explained clearly and constructively*

Candidates should play a prominent part in the planning process. From the outset, they should be encouraged to put forward ideas as to how they might make the most of their prior achievements. Then, once the framework of the NVQ/SVQ and the means of access to the target award have been jointly reviewed, the action plan should be prepared. If all goes well, the candidate's self-confidence and motivation to succeed will be high and there will be no disagreement. If, however, the candidate has special assessment requirements that they feel are not being met, or considers that the advisor's proposals are blocking access to a fair assessment opportunity, there will be disagreement. Discrimination and bias of any kind must therefore be avoided at all costs.

If there is any disagreement which cannot be resolved on the spot, options which may be put to the candidate include: sleeping on it overnight, meeting again for further discussion, longer-term postponement, accessing advice from another advisor, reviewing which qualification to seek, and withdrawal from the assessment process.

---

# Action plan

**Candidate name:** _____

This plan created during the planning interview held today has been agreed by the undersigned.

**Career goals:**

**Qualifications sought:**

**Target date:**

**Review dates:**

**Context for activity:**
    Location:
    Performance criteria:
    Resources:

**Assessment arrangements:**

**Support required:**

**Other comments:**

**Advisor** _____     **Candidate** _____

**Date of planning interview** _____

---

**Figure 12.15** *Action plan format*

Refusal to accept advice on the part of the candidate, or other forms of disagreement between the advisor-candidate (i.e. the teacher or advisor seeking to gain D36) and the candidate (i.e. the person seeking advice or support) may not arise when the authorised assessor is judging performance against the D36 criterion given in the heading above. When this is the case, City and Guilds recommend that assessors 'check the advisor-candidate's knowledge and understanding of how to deal constructively with a candidate who disagrees or declines to take advice offered'.

*The plan is reviewed appropriately with the candidate*

Assessors will wish to examine action plans prepared by advisor-candidates for two of their candidates. The action plans should cover at least three elements and show how the candidates will achieve target vocational units or qualifications. The assessor will probably discuss with advisor-candidates the factors taken into consideration when negotiating and agreeing the plans with candidates. Questions will be asked in order to establish the advisor's underpinning knowledge relating to how the target qualifications were identified and how opportunities to use evidence from prior experience were analysed and matched to the units to be claimed by the candidate. The action-planning process is summarised in Figures 12.14 and 12.15, and sample plans are provided in Figures 12.16 and 12.17 (see *Documents Pack*).

## Helping the candidate to collect and present evidence for assessment

*The candidate is provided with suitable support to prepare a portfolio of evidence*

Candidates following NVQs, GNVQs, SVQs and GSVQs will need to demonstrate competences that will be assessed and judged against award criteria. Being able to meet unit requirements entails not only the ability to provide performance evidence at the right level but also the ownership of sufficient underpinning knowledge that supports such behaviour. A portfolio of other supporting evidence associated with the elements assessed can be built up and used to supplement performance and knowledge evidence demonstrated during assessments.

The preparation of a portfolio can become a daunting task. People register for awards and receive their candidate packs, but the contents, although comprehensive, may appear to be shrouded in mystery and difficult to read, let alone make sense of. Some candidates will put the pack to one side and give up while others are left scratching their heads wondering where to turn for help. There is no doubt that candidates need considerable support, especially when making the transition from 'traditional' courses to competence-based programmes, and will find it hard to get going unless help is available in the early stages. Candidates will probably welcome advice about selecting, gathering and filing evidence while building their portfolio right up to the time of its presentation.

*Guidance provided to the candidate during portfolio preparation encourages the efficient development of clear, structured evidence relevant to the units being claimed*

While it is recognised that each and every candidate will have different needs and varied levels of confidence, experience and clerical ability, many will appreciate guidance when preparing their portfolio. It is, however, necessary to avoid a rigid or prescriptive approach concerning what should and what should not be included. But certain pieces of evidence will be common to all candidate portfolios. With this in mind the advisor might propose an **outline format** for a particular unit or award. This could be just what the candidate needs to overcome inertia which may be preventing progress.

A **personalised presentation binder** containing numbered plastic pockets would be suitable for holding evidence. When assembling the portfolio a **contents list** similar to that shown in Activity 12.3 should be filed near the front. Evidence which must be **cross-referenced** to criteria can then be inserted in the relevant pockets. The same piece of evidence can sometimes relate to several elements, and if so this must be clearly specified to avoid confusion. Candidates are generally very familiar with the location of documents filed. They know just where to find a piece of evidence but their assessors may not, especially when files containing a mass of irrelevant material are hastily thrown together. The inclusion of **summary sheets** listing evidence filed with each unit or element performance criterion helps to overcome this problem.

*Liaison with assessors establishes mutually convenient arrangements for review of portfolio and maintains the candidate's confidence*

Advisors will need to maintain a list of **contacts** that includes vocational assessors, internal and external verifiers and award body liaison persons (see Figure 12.18). Candidates for assessment often ask advisors to make appointments with assessors so that they may present their evidence portfolios for assessment. Mutually acceptable dates for reviews should be agreed with those concerned.

A **diary of key interactions** (Figure 12.19) and **candidate guidance records** (Figure 12.20) of appointments could be maintained for each candidate, together with a **summary sheet** similar to that shown in Figure 12.21 (see *Documents Pack*).

*Opportunities are identified for the candidate to demonstrate achievement where evidence from prior experience is not available*

Advisors will need to make decisions as to the **sufficiency** of evidence gathered by their candidates. If the evidence appears to meet target qualification criteria the vocational assessor can be contacted and a meeting fixed so that evidence may be judged and accreditation arranged.

If the APL evidence is substantial but inconclusive, top-up training, skills testing, projects and assignments or knowledge-based tests can be arranged so that deficiencies can be corrected. The process is shown in Figure 12.22.

It may not be possible for the advisor-candidate (i.e. the teacher or advisor seeking to gain D36) to identify opportunities for the candidate (i.e. the person seeking advice or support) to demonstrate achievement where evidence from prior experience is not available when the authorised assessor is judging performance against the D36 criterion given in the heading above. When this is the case, City and Guilds recommend that assessors 'look for evidence from other sources' that the advisor-candidate can meet this criterion and understands how to identify opportunities for the candidate to demonstrate relevant achievement.

*Awarding body documentation, recording and procedural requirements are met*

Each lead body has its own procedures for assessing candidates and **recording outcomes** prior to certification, and awarding body documentation, recording and procedural requirements must be met. Documentation must be complete and up to date. Verifiers and moderators operating awarding body systems must ensure that the quality of assessment meets requirements before certificates of achievement can be issued. Advisors must be aware of these procedures and keep themselves up to date by establishing links with external verifiers and participating in the internal verification process in-house. Disputes and appeals that cannot be reconciled locally should be referred to the appropriate authority, and close liaison maintained throughout with the candidate, assessor and centre concerned.

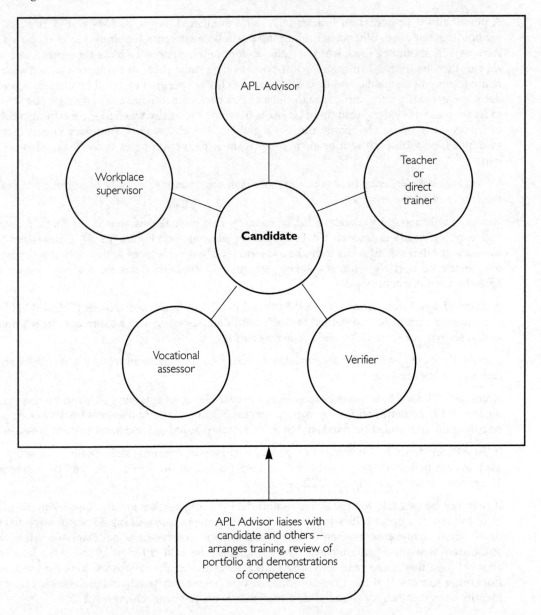

**Figure 12.18** *People involved in training, review and assessment*

The City and Guilds flow chart showing suggested **routes to certification** for APL candidates is given in Figure 12.23.

*If there is disagreement with the advice given, options available to the candidate are explained clearly and constructively*

Any disagreement must be handled constructively. An advisor's temperament is revealed in the way they behave towards their candidates. Some people are easily upset or irritated and their volatile nature can lead to sudden outbursts that are later regretted. This is a two-way

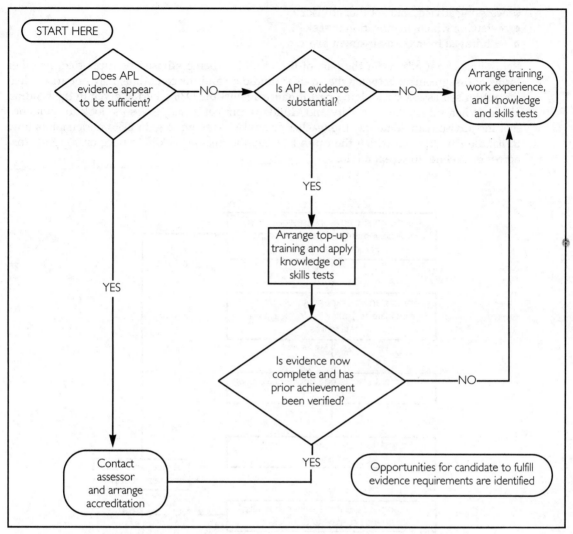

**Figure 12.22** *APL evidence assessment flow chart*

phenomenon and advisors must keep their temper under sometimes trying circumstances. Quick decisions taken on an intuitive basis should be avoided, and advisors should take care not to be seen to be impatient listeners who are not really interested in the candidate's development needs. Time should be found to review the candidate's experiences and value any feedback that they may offer to questions asked or suggestions made.

Preparing the facts before reviewing the candidate's evidence portfolio, anticipating barriers you think you will face and identifying ways of overcoming these barriers, concentrating on strategies for success and using sympathetic interviewing techniques will go a long way towards avoiding disagreement in the first instance. However, if in spite of this positive climate the candidate still registers disagreement, options suggested by City and Guilds include:

- further discussion
- postponement

- accessing advice from another advisor
- reviewing which qualification to seek
- withdrawal from the assessment process.

Refusal to accept advice on the part of the candidate being advised or supported, or other forms of disagreement between the advisor-candidate and the candidate, may not arise when the authorised assessor is judging performance against the D36 criterion given in the heading above. When this is the case, City and Guilds recommend that assessors 'look for evidence that the advisor-candidate (i.e. the teacher or advisor seeking to gain D36) understands how to handle situations in which the candidate (i.e. the person seeking advice or support) disagrees or declines to accept advice'.

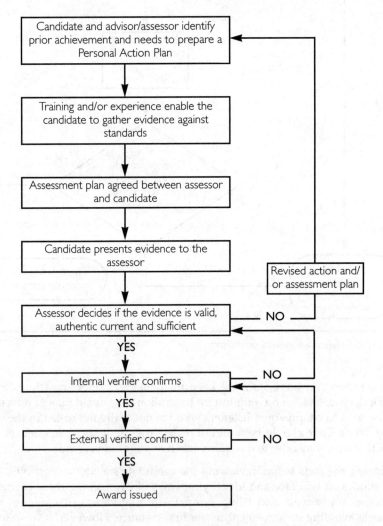

Source: C&G 7281/23 *Advising on Prior Achievement Candidate Pack* TD-23-7281 (1995) p.7. Published by City and Guilds of London Institute, 1 Giltspur Street, London EC1A 9DD.

**Figure 12.23** *Routes to certification*

# Self-assessment questions

## Helping candidates to identify areas of current competence

1 Explain how the candidate is provided with clear and accurate information on the principles and implementation of accreditation of prior learning and achievement.

2 Describe how you personally encourage your candidates to carry out a broad review of all relevant experience.

3 Explain how the following five sources of experience could provide material that might be included in a Listing of Experience:

- full-time employment
- part-time employment
- unpaid work
- leisure activities
- education and training.

Can you suggest any other potential sources of experience?

4 Describe how a Listing of Experience could be used to help you and the candidate accurately identify and analyse potential areas of their current competence.

5 Explain how your style of support encourages self-confidence and promotes self-esteem in your candidates.

6 Describe other relevant means of support that you know of which could be helpful to your candidates.

7 Describe how your approach changes (if at all) when helping people who:

- are young adults as opposed to mature adults
- are employed/unemployed
- are confident/non-confident
- have special needs, including physical or intellectual impairment.

## Agreeing APL assessment plans with candidates

8 How can realistic candidate expectations and attainable career aspirations be encouraged?

9 Explain what is meant by NVQ/SVQ Levels 1–5

10 Describe where information about a wide range of occupational areas can be obtained.

11 When advising candidates why is it necessary to identify accurately units which they might claim?

12 Describe how appropriate target vocational qualifications can be identified and matched to a candidate's current competence and future aspirations.

13 With reference to the APL assessment plans which you have prepared with your candidates, explain how you have provided an effective mix of evidence from prior achievements and current assessment.

Describe how your approach changes (if at all) when helping people who:

- are young adults as opposed to older adults
- are employed/unemployed
- are confident/non-confident
- have special needs, including physical or intellectual impairment.

14 Explain how you maintain records of interactions with your candidates.

### Helping candidates to prepare and present evidence for assessment

15 Describe how you can help your candidates prepare and present their portfolio of evidence for assessment.

16 Describe and give examples of portfolio content that you may be called upon to handle.

What are the following?

- direct evidence
- indirect evidence
- performance evidence
- knowledge evidence.

17 Explain the means by which you liaise with your candidates' assessors. Describe some purposes and outcomes of relevant liaison activities.

18 Explain how you help your candidates maintain their confidence and motivation to succeed.

19 In what ways would you adjust your approach when giving support in the case of the following?

- one-to-one coaching
- group tutorial
- supported self-study.

20 How can you ensure that awarding body documentation, recording and procedural requirements are consistently met?

## Preparing for assessment: sample activities

### Activity 12.1 Discussion brief: Conducting an APL assessment interview

An APL assessment interview is carried out in order to obtain up-to-date information about a candidate's current competency and to establish personal training or assessment needs. Once the data has been collected the training gap can be identified and suitable personal development opportunities provided, backed by effective training. Define and discuss each of the steps that should be taken when you are conducting an APL assessment interview in order to identify prior achievement and future training needs of individuals. Suggested steps are listed below but you may add any others you consider necessary.

Working with others in a small group prepare a report covering each step. Add any points raised and comments made during the discussion. Include in your report conclusions and recommendations about how carrying out APL assessments could be integrated with other teacher roles.

**Suggested steps**

Identify the individual or candidate group concerned.

- Explain the APL procedure to candidates.
- Clarify expectations and aspirations.
- Carry out the APL assessment using established procedures (or write your own).
- Collect data.
- Analyse findings.
- Identify additional training requirements.
- Write a report or prepare individual APL assessment plans.

Note: An effective strategy would then be created that would enable prior achievement to be accredited and initial training, top-up training or updating to be provided, taking account of the individual's personal development objectives or group needs and priorities. Progress would be monitored by the APL advisor and achievement evaluated by a qualified vocational assessor.

### Activity 12.2 Writing an APL information sheet

Design and produce an information sheet covering the range outlined in Figure 12.24. Consult with others about their perceived needs for sources of easily understandable information that will help overcome obstacles and break down barriers blocking access to learning or assessment opportunities. Ensure that your information sheet covers any particular requirements of candidates from your own catchment area, the needs of the unwaged and people of differing cultural and racial backgrounds. The information sheet produced would be suitable for evidence reference 06 in the contents list for Activity 12.3 below.

---

## Information sheet

### PRINCIPLES AND IMPLEMENTATION OF THE ACCREDITATION OF PRIOR LEARNING PROCEDURES

**Write up a draft form ready for use with your candidates**

Teacher candidates should add information here that they consider necessary for their candidates (candidates, customers, students or trainees) to know about the APL process. Copies of the briefing document produced would be discussed, handed to or posted to candidates seeking learning opportunities or assessment of prior achievement when or soon after the first contact is made. Being observed while administering the information sheet could serve as evidence towards units A22 'Identify individual learning needs', C21 'Create a climate conducive to learning' and D36 'Advise and support candidate to identify prior achievement'.

**Content could include:**

● Statement of principles, philosophy and operation of APL

● Methods of identifying prior learning and achievement

● Methods of identifying learning needs or top-up training required

● Commitment to equal opportunities and non-discriminatory practice

● Types of information that could be supplied by candidates for reviews

● Types of candidate support that you/the employer/the training provider can offer

● Potential sources of experience that could be discussed during the review or considered for APL assessment

● How the review and identification of candidate current status will be conducted

● Where detailed information about learning programmes and assessment opportunities may be obtained

● Notes on resources available and organisational requirements.


**Date information provided** _____

**Advisor** _____     **Candidate** _____

---

**Figure 12.24** *Information sheet*

### Activity 12.3 Building an APL advisor's portfolio

Gather the evidence specified in the contents list given below ready for presentation to your assessor.

## Contents list

**D361 Performance evidence**

01  Initial self-assessment documents: compiled by candidates

02  Listing of experience documents: compiled by candidates

**D361 Supplementary evidence**

03  Correspondence: letters of validation

04  Candidate's Charter/Advisor's Mission

05  'Role of APL guide': self-assessment

06  Principles and implementation of APL: information sheet (own interpretation)

07  Information skills checklist

08  Interpersonal skills checklist

09  Initial assessment and review: purpose of

10  Reviewing evidence: key questions

11  Maintaining candidate self-esteem: responsibility for

12  Action planning: flow chart

13  'Equal opportunities': City and Guilds statement

14  *Access to assessment: candidates with special needs*: City and Guilds statement

**D362 Performance evidence**

15  APL advisor's interview checklist: topics and questions

16  APL advisor's planning interview notes: records of several interviews

17  Elements of competence and performance criteria used when creating and negotiating candidates' assessment programmes

18  'Occupational area' checklisted questions: samples

19  Candidate assessment plans created during planning interviews

**D362 Supplementary evidence**

20  Competence in guidance and counselling: self-assessment

**D363 Performance evidence**

21  Individual records for candidates advised

22  Group records: compiled during candidate support sessions

23  Diary of key interactions with candidates

# 13

# Monitoring and reviewing progress with learners

**Formative records** of achievement and progress towards their goals should be maintained for all learners. Information can be gathered on a micro scale by monitoring improvement against criteria during programmed coaching sessions and noting any individual coaching requirements that can be facilitated right away. Learners should be kept informed of how they are progressing during the coaching activity.

In order to assess progress over a longer term a **reviewing** and **recording system** could be established to suit the training method. The system would enable teachers and learners to check the suitability and quality of learning experiences against unit standards or programme/session aims and objectives. Performance evidence gathered and comments recorded would provide formative assessment data to be used during reviews and when giving feedback on progress and achievements.

Collecting feedback from multiple sources is a personal development technique that is known as the **360° approach**. The method is thought to maximise the benefit of feedback by encouraging comment on learner achievements from other learners, customers, colleagues, teachers, support staff and supervisors, in fact from anyone who is able to offer constructive criticism and guidance. How often meetings should be held to review progress and update progress reports will depend on the learners' needs and the recording system used. But in any event, coaching and review sessions should close on an upbeat and positive note.

Learners should be encouraged to demonstrate understanding of each **chunk** of learning material and accomplish each **stage** of a practical task before moving on to the next challenge. They will need time to absorb their experiences and reinforce what has been learned in order to understand and retain the knowledge and skills involved. But learning does not always progress smoothly and a **skill acquisition curve** might show the rate of progress of the learner temporarily flattening out. This is a signal for the teacher to evaluate methods used and the coach to look at their coaching style, **turn negatives into positives** and perhaps modify method or resources to help overcome the setback and restore improvement.

Students encountering problems that are delaying progress should be helped to recognise and come to terms with the situation and series of events that led to their current difficulties. They should be encouraged to discover their own solutions especially when their problems are self-inflicted. Counselling is not without risk and may be best left to expert counsellors.

# Collecting information on learners' progress

*Valid, reliable and relevant information on learners' progress is obtained from a range of sources*

Sufficient valid and reliable information will be forthcoming only when learners perceive the teacher gathering the information as being an honest broker with an open and approachable manner. A suitable starting point when collecting information on your learners' progress might be to explain to those concerned the principles and purposes of the monitoring and reviewing process. Having done so, there is a need to promote a relaxed and safe atmosphere that will permit the learners and others providing information to do so openly and without fear of unpleasant repercussions. In order to obtain a clear overview of progress against targets sufficient objective information should be gathered using a variety of methods of collection.

When gathering information that will support a useful review, teachers will need to have in-depth knowledge of the range of programmes on offer and detailed background knowledge of the learners' chosen subjects. The information collected will need to be **valid** and **reliable** and **relevant** to the learning programme criteria. The **validity** of information collected can be assured by ensuring that the evidence gathered properly matches what is being monitored. This means that evidence presented and knowledge assessed covers what is to be achieved in terms of the performance criteria or assessment specification. Information gathered must also be reliable. The extent to which information provided by third parties and assessments carried out by different assessors **consistently** define the learner's accomplishments is a measure of the **reliability** of evidence of achievement gathered. General factors that may affect reliability include the form and content of the review and the environment in which it takes place. Reviewer-related factors include the spoken or written language used, cultural bias and

---

## Review process

Introduce the review and explain its purposes.
Assess the impact of training to date.
Identify what is already known and accomplished.
Identify benefits derived so far and record achievement.
Establish new goals.
Clarify and obtain commitment about what is to be learned.
Establish best method of learning new skills.
Agree key facilitating objectives.
Establish timescales.
Update action plan.
Encourage learner participation.
................

### Ongoing

Monitor progress: gather information from a range of sources.
Give feedback.
Record progress.

---

**Figure 13.1** *Review process*

supervision style. Candidate-related factors include an individual's mental, physical and emotional state, their degree of motivation and their relationship with the reviewer.

Only justifiable sources should be used when gathering information for reviews. Tittle-tattle and staffroom gossip can sometime provide helpful comment concerning other teachers' experiences of a learner's performance but care should be taken to avoid listening to malicious chatter or unfounded rumours about a person. It is far better to rely on the evidence of formal assessments, authentic third-party testimony and reports from other practitioners, mentors, and assessors. By all means consult with other people concerned in delivering the learning programme, but do so on an honest and open basis and try to take an unbiased account of their views. Your own informal discussions with learners before, during and after classes can be very helpful in building trusting relationships and estimating a learner's progress. A suggested approach to the review process is given in Figure 13.1.

*Methods for collecting information are appropriate to the organisation and capable of producing the required information*

Information is collected primarily by the teacher concerned although other staff members, assessors and third parties may be in a position to offer supplementary evidence of progress and achievement. The methods of collecting evidence will probably include:

- audits and questionnaires
- 'identification of needs' analyses
- learner self-assessments
- the observation of live performance while carrying out tasks on or off the job
- the examination of products
- simulations
- conducting periodic phase tests and skills tests
- seeking third-party reports, references and testimonials
- circulating an assessment report form to other teachers and departments
- examination of records of achievement
- earlier formative assessments and archive records
- setting essays, assignments, homework and written tests
- oral testing
- guided discussion and appraisals.

**Quantitative** information about learning outcomes can be obtained from the results of periodic tests and assessments, assignments, projects and homework. **Qualitative** information is obtained from narrative or non-numerical data. Some teachers tend to base judgements on intuition or their perception of attributes, events or behaviour, and as such, decisions taken may be value-laden, unreliable and open to bias or error.

*Information is collected in time to give effective feedback to learners and other people involved in delivering the learning programme*

Formative assessments are intended to give timely information about programme delivery and outcomes to the teachers, learners, managers and support staff involved in the learning opportunity. Assessments take place throughout the training programme and provide comment on the learners' progress and ways and means of achieving remaining learning objectives. The method of continuous formative assessment fulfils a number of purposes in that it:

- encourages learner involvement and helps to maintain their motivation
- provides for ongoing assessment of learner achievement throughout the course

- gives an overall picture of actual performance indicating what learners 'can do' or 'have done'
- monitors progress and provides feedback about the benefits and drawbacks of the programme
- identifies learning plateaus and singles out difficulties for remedial work
- highlights strengths, serves as a reward mechanism and promotes continuing effort
- reveals weaknesses and promotes the need to take corrective action
- helps shape the individual's future learning agenda
- informs the 'delivery system' of shortcomings and the need for additional inputs or resourcing.

Information concerning the learner's progress should be given during reviews held as soon as possible after an event. Reinforcing success by providing early **knowledge of results** relating to current outcomes will then probably have a positive, encouraging effect on future performance. But receiving unconstructive feedback about poor results can adversely affect later training. This is why it is so important to use the utmost tact when handling learner feedback concerning their underachievement.

Feedback to learners will be immediate when information is collected by asking them to complete self-assessments or from direct contact with the reviewer concerned. In some instances a report form will be circulated to a number of departments or the programme course team and it could take some time to collate the necessary progress report ready for the face-to-face review. With the current trend towards providing flexible learning opportunities, information needed to obtain a clear picture of development could also be collected from a number of sources such as past records, examination of artefacts and data supplied by third parties.

*Interpretation of information is justifiable and avoids bias*

Of necessity, because of constraints on time and facilities available and the need to apply cost-effective measures, many courses are 'delivered' at a uniform rate, topic by topic according to a prepared scheme of work. In such circumstances the teachers concerned will no doubt be hoping that their learners will still somehow derive maximum benefit from the learning experiences provided. However, not all people learn at the same rate or in the same way, so that the teacher or facilitator must accurately assess their potential and ensure that advice and support given during progress reviews will help them exploit their strengths and address any weaknesses.

In student-centred learning situations it is important that learners receive advice on their progress and are given information about the direction that their future learning experiences will be taking in order to meet agreed personal learning objectives. Formative assessments allow the reviewer to give guidance on how best to make use of the learning situations yet to be provided and build up the learner's confidence by letting them know that they are moving in the right direction. Self-assessments of work by the student, formative assessments made with the help of the teacher and coursework subject to continuous assessment all serve to confirm in the learner's mind what they have learned and which skills they now own. Assessment of information gathered may also suggest areas where learners will need further guidance and advice if they are to maintain progress.

During formal appraisals a **rationale** describing the reason why there is a requirement to collect the information should be provided. Where reviews are imposed on learners the need to monitor their progress regularly should be justified and their cooperation sought. Any assessment specification or list of criteria used to judge progress should be validated and used to check the **objectivity** of information and evidence collected. Feedback offered should be objective, descriptive and constructive.

*Information is suitably collated and summarised in order to give effective feedback to learners and other appropriate people*

A formative assessment document can be used to consolidate review findings. The teacher as a **collator** of information carries out a matching procedure by bringing together and **summarising** information from many sources and using it to identify learner accomplishment. Accomplishment can be confirmed by a comparison of learner performance against standards. Key findings are recorded and shared with the learner during reviews when their comments can be added to the document.

An initial sort might be used to classify the information gathered as either **current** or **outdated**. When the teacher is collating and analysing information suitable questions to ask might be: 'When was the competency last demonstrated?' and 'Are the standards used for the assessment still current?' The next classification might be its **relevance** and **applicability** to the target criteria: 'What was done?' 'Why was it done?' and 'Where was it done?' The teacher then **discriminates** between **experience** and **achievement** by comparing tangible performance or knowledge evidence with standards and looking for points of comparison. At the same time unfulfilled criteria will be discovered. This audit can be facilitated using award standards and checklisted criteria to validate judgements made about learning outcomes.

In order to give effective feedback to learners and other appropriate people it is necessary to prepare well for the review session. **Key issues** arising from the information-gathering operation will have to be addressed as will any **learning difficulties** or other critical points noted. In order to maintain credibility you will need to have satisfactory answers ready so that you can properly respond to anticipated learner questions on these matters. The feedback session will also allow both sides to **exchange views** and draw comparisons between observed or recorded behaviour and the evidence specified in the unit standards.

*Information is recorded and passed on to other appropriate people as agreed*

Teachers will need to be familiar with the process for completing and updating records that operates within their employer's organisation. They should be able to name the people responsible for completing each record and describe the security procedures for record keeping and storing candidate files. Records may be kept in archives or locked filing cabinets and the keyholder should know who is authorised to access the records.

Computers can be effectively used for record keeping, and computer systems have many advantages, such as:

- giving instant access to vast amounts of information stored
- providing easy editing, updating and cross referencing of records
- requiring less space than filing cabinets, folders and paper-based systems
- facilitating the networking of information and provision of printouts
- giving multiple access to essential users who may be dispersed over several sites
- compiling accurate statistics and number crunching.

The Data Protection Act 1984 grew out of public concern about personal privacy in the face of rapidly developing computer technology. Designed to protect people from misuse of computerised information, it gives rights to individuals and demands best practice in handling information about them. This is particularly relevant where information is computerised for the purpose of formative reviews, since the Act covers any personal data which is 'automatically processed'. Thus the Act works in two ways, giving learners certain rights whilst, in turn, requiring the teacher who records and uses this computerised personal information to be open about the use of that information and to follow sound and proper practices.

Non-computerised information is not covered by the Act. It is up to those responsible for keeping records to maintain confidentiality by ensuring that information stored is disclosed only to those who have a right to use the information.

# Conducting formative assessments with learners

*The purpose of the formative assessment and the use which will be made of information obtained is clearly explained to individual learners*

The purpose of formative assessment is to gain a clear picture of the learner's progress through the use of a wide range of valid and reliable information. The object is to carry out with learners an impartial examination of their progress against action plans or target qualifications by sharing and discussing the information collated. As well as reviewing progress towards the objective, the assessment will identify problem areas. Further help and support may be required and the review may result in renegotiation of targets. Review outcomes will also inform action planning for the next stage by indicating how well the learners' requirements are being met and identifying presentation and programme shortcomings so that changes may be made and improvements implemented. Modern training practice tends to be rather more candidate-centred than in the past, and assessments and reviews now take the form of inviting learners to reflect on their learning experiences and discuss training outcomes. Apart from feedback obtained during normal classroom discourse, formative assessments may place during subsequent counselling and guidance sessions, debriefings and regular programme reviews. Democratically agreed achievements are then recorded on learner profiles or competence checklists. **Formative assessment** is an ongoing process designed to improve training and learning by reviewing outcomes and progress. Feeding back to the training provider information from reviews or negotiations with learners enables any problems identified to be overcome.

The **NVQ assessment model** reproduced in Figure 13.2 allows for the assessment of **performance-related** evidence of competence as well as essential **underpinning knowledge**. It can be seen that the model embraces several different methods of collecting evidence that could be used for formative assessment purposes as well as for final assessments.

Using a combination of the methods outlined above together with supplementary evidence gathered from prior achievements and knowledge-based assessments, the reviewer and the learner together will be able to assess progress against the action plan or award criteria.

*Learners are provided with clear and accurate information about the learning objectives and assessment criteria which they are being assessed against*

Nothing much will be achieved during a review unless the learners' commitment is first secured. The reviewer should therefore explain the purposes to which information gathered during formative assessments will be used before commencing the review. The reviewer could encourage commitment by pointing out the benefits of using information provided by learners during reviews to improve the training provision by:

● modifying the training programme content or methods to better match learners' needs
● ensuring that lessons and other training opportunities are being presented correctly
● helping to make assessment procedures more effective and user-friendly

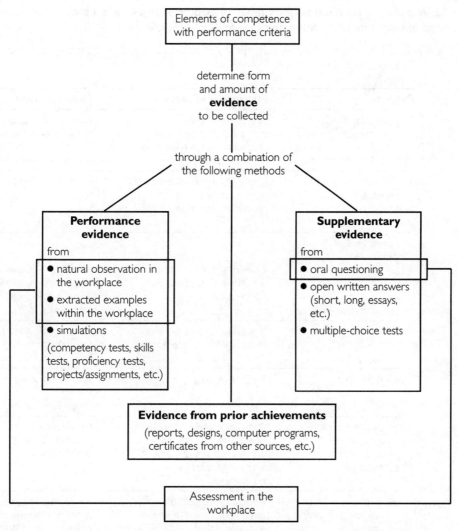

Assessment in the workplace should include live observation supported where necessary by guided discussion with the candidate and others. Examination of products and supportive documentation may also be needed.

**Figure 13.2** *Assessment in the workplace using NVQ assessment model*

● ensuring that learning objectives can be met and targets achieved.

Learners will be willing to cooperate if they are given sufficient information about why they are being assessed (or being asked to assess themselves) and how the assessment will operate. They should therefore be given clear details of the criteria against which their performance is to be measured (or compared) and know who will help them when reviewing their progress. The kind of information needed might take the form of national standards, organisational standards, house standards or learning objectives, the point being that it is not possible to assess oneself or any other person's progress unless there are relevant criteria against which behaviour can be compared. Alternatively, the assessment could be based on criteria generated from taxonomies of abilities that learners might demonstrate as a result of participating

179

in learning opportunities. A number of educationalists have produced suitable taxonomies and amongst these the following are well-known examples:

- knowledge, comprehension, application, analysis, synthesis and evaluation (B.S. Bloom's cognitive domain objectives)

| Purpose | Measures/indicates | Requirements |
|---|---|---|
| 1 Evaluation of instruction | Effectiveness of an instructional sequence or procedure when applied to a particular group | Pre-test/post-test systems to consider group achievements in terms of overall objectives and skill enhancement |
| 2 Comparison of instruction | Comparative effectiveness of instructional sequences or procedures, or instructors | Pre-test/post-test systems in terms of group achievements either cross-sequence or cross-group based |
| 3 Assessment of individuals (a) for awards | Level of graduation to be accorded, or suggested/pass fail decision | Sampling of all the individual's work considered relevant, using mainly content-standard test scores |
| (b) to determine transfer to higher grade | Suitability, or otherwise, of individual for transfer to the next (higher) part of a course | Sampling of all work at present grade using mainly content-standard tests |
| (c) to measure progress | Degree of mastery of specified objectives and skills | Specific objective-related tests (criterion-referenced) of a progressive nature |
| (d) to predict future achievement levels and success expectancy | A prognosis relating the level of achievement that may be anticipated to that required for success, i.e. pass/fail, graduation | Criterion-referenced tests that can be interpreted in probabilistic terms |
| (e) diagnosis of weaknesses and difficulties | Areas of weakness or misunderstanding in specific subjects; individual ability problems, e.g. language, reading difficulty | Structured and graded criterion-referenced tests in limited areas of study as part of feedback-correction procedures |
| (f) self-criticism reward by individual | To the individual, some of the aspects of 3(c), 3(d), 3(e) Provides a measure of reward either in terms of the score or in progress to the next item | Structured criterion-referenced tests with in-built success pattern, e.g programmed learning text |
| 4 Consolidation of learning | Usually very little except that those completing the test have made the effort and have therefore added to what had been previously taught | Exercises which extend individuals beyond the levels already achieved, usually with subjective assessment (e.g. essays) or short-scale content-standard tests |

Source: *Notes for Guidance*, R. Whitlow, Bristol Polytechnic

**Figure 13.3** *Tests: purposes, indications and requirements*

- understanding terms, understanding fact, principles and generalisations, ability to explain, ability to calculate, ability to predict, ability to recommend appropriate action and ability to evaluate (R.L. Ebel's measures of educational achievement).

Clear, accurate supplementary evidence and summary information should be provided as necessary. As when teaching classes it is important to summarise and reinforce key points of the interaction. This could involve asking the learners to write down the relevant information or to summarise entries to be made on their records, or giving them a full explanation of the importance of material discussed. Alternatively, handouts completed during the review or summaries giving information about important aspects and other sources of reference could serve as useful reinforcers.

*Suitable materials and facilities are provided to help learners to identify their achievements*

Formative assessments which cover knowledge gained, skills acquired and prior learning and achievement are carried out by the learner assisted by the teacher or advisor concerned. Information technology systems can be useful in providing data for the review, as can questionnaires to be completed by learners prior to the event. Various forms of testing can be also be used to help learners to identify their achievements, and Roy Whitlow's list of test purposes, indications and requirements given in Figure 13.3 provides an excellent guide to test constructors. For each category of test, a note is given of what the test will indicate and of any requirements for pretesting, sampling and the like.

*Assessments of current competence are valid, reliable and conform to any specified instructions*

It is not possible to make valid judgements purely on the strength of learners' claims that they 'know it', 'can do it' or ' have done it all before'. The learners' knowledge, understanding and skill relating to the competence being assessed cannot be taken for granted. Assessments must be judged against specified criteria and conform with any specified conditions under which the assessment will take place. If evidence does not occur naturally during the performance of work, preset tasks will need to be performed or other 'outcome' or 'process' evidence provided. It may therefore be necessary to arrange workshop activities including the demonstration of practical work, skills tests and simulations; or classroom work such as written tests, essays, multiple-choice papers or computer-based assessments.

Methods of formative assessment include learner self-assessments, observation, questioning and review of assignments. The assessment model given in Figure 13.4 shows how assessment of achievement against a set of performance criteria could be carried out. There is no one system that will meet every assessment requirement but many of the factors relating to the process and practice of assessing achievement are included in the model. Possible links between participants are shown.

It is well known that assessment is a collaborative activity. The candidate and assessor each have a different role and responsibility but depend on mutual cooperation in order to carry out an acceptable assessment. Throughout the whole formative assessment procedure there is a need to communicate, to negotiate and to give and receive feedback.

When preparing to conduct formative assessments a suggested approach is to:

- Present the learner with a 'Candidate's Charter' which outlines their entitlement, or otherwise brief the learner fully on the purpose of the assessment. Arrange a mutually convenient day, time and place. Issue any pre-review questionnaires and information sheets.
- On assessment day, greet the learner and set them at ease.
- Explain once again the purpose of the assessment and then seek the learner's views on how they are progressing.

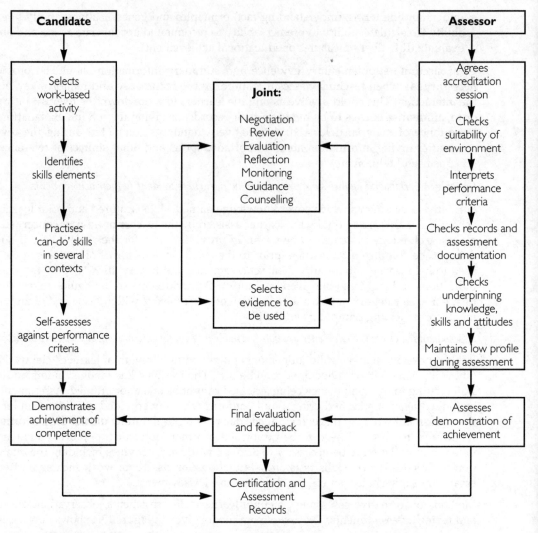

**Figure 13.4** *Assessment model*

- Go through the information gathered prior to the assessment with the learner, comment on their progress and agree achievement.
- Update assessment documentation and records of achievement.
- Update the learner's action plan showing how personal development needs will be met, how problems can be overcome and details of additional support requested.
- Summarise what has been agreed and set a date for the next review.

*Learners are encouraged to reflect on the way in which they have been learning*

When formative assessments are conducted learners should be encouraged to reflect on the way in which they have been learning. **Reflection** involves thinking about an event that has in some way affected them. In the case of a learning experience reflection will help them to form mental images of the practical aspects and to associate key words with actions performed. Learners will be able to organise patterns in their minds that will aid recall. Being able to form mental pictures can be helpful in many circumstances. For example, contestants in TV shows may be better able to recall the names of goods that pass before them on a conveyor belt and hence win more prizes.

If we have learned something from an experience we shall be able to recall at will some or all of what we did. If what we did involved practical activity we should be able to repeat the behaviour. If the learning experience was mainly academic we should be able to apply the principle or solve similar problems. But being able to hang on to the knowledge will depend on our ability to memorise the information and retain it. So in order to maximise the possibility of remembering the new knowledge we gained at the time, we shall need to go over the learning experience in our minds recollecting what we did, how things worked out and what obstacles we overcame. We need to hook the learning onto some part of the event in order to aid recognition and recollection later. By **reflecting** on a learning experience and talking it over with someone, we shall hopefully manage to link the new learning with prior learning and add to our network of knowledge of the topic or activity.

Learners can also gain from reflection by self-assessing and evaluating the benefits derived from their learning experiences. They should be encouraged to think through the event or their work to date and to measure the good and not so good aspects of their performance against programme objectives. Auditing the quality of their accomplishments, checking the effectiveness of their efforts, comparing their action-plan schedule with targets achieved and renegotiating timescales for completion of the next stage should become an everyday event. Reflection following a concrete experience is also an important stage in the Kolb learning cycle shown in Figures 3.7 and 9.2. The learner does something tangible and then carefully considers the outcomes. Then follows a period when the learner forms ideas for improvements, selects an alternative approach, tries a new way and reflects once again.

*Learners are encouraged to feel comfortable to ask questions and express their views*

It is important that learners should understand the review process and play an active part throughout. Simply telling learners the facts is an unsuitable technique for reviewing progress. Some direction from the reviewer is necessary, but two-way communication provides a better means of ensuring that sources of error and misunderstanding are reduced or eliminated. The reviewer's attitude must be seen to be positive throughout. Establishing a rapport with the learners is essential, as this will encourage them to interrupt in order to ask questions and clarify matters. Learners must feel free to participate fully in any discussions, to express concerns and to make comments without being subjected to any form of embarrassment. Teachers should strive to reduce the learners' anxiety and make every effort to ensure that they are put at ease when negotiating their learning programmes. Learners should be invited to clarify doubts at any time during the negotiation and should never be rebuked or belittled for making suggestions. Questions should be encouraged from either party during the review and clear explanations sought or given. Learners are entitled to play an active part in the progress review, and by doing so will be better motivated to contribute to the formative assessment process and to set new targets in their updated action plan.

*Learners are given feedback on their formative assessment in a positive and encouraging manner*

Giving formative feedback is an important duty that teachers will be asked to carry out, and one that calls for a good deal of tact, imagination and understanding. Positive and encouraging feedback will be well received by learners since it can help them in their ongoing personal development. But when badly handled it can leave people confused, demoralised and disheartened. Teachers must therefore be able to give feedback which will benefit the learners and enable them to take positive action to enhance their current achievement. However, feedback should not be perceived as being a 'one-way' or 'top down' process with the teacher at the top passing comments down the line or making only critical and subjective observations. Feedback shared with others should be constructive. It should be **objective** and **descriptive** and be soundly based upon the observation of performance. Criticism reflecting a subjective opinion would be unhelpful. Teachers and assessors must display **openness** and be willing to receive feedback on the effectiveness of their planning, presentations and assessment judgements from peers and learners too. Giving feedback is discussed in more depth in Chapter 11.

*The process of formative assessment promotes equality of opportunity and learners' ability to learn*

All learners should be treated equally and fairly. Treating one student more favourably than another should be avoided. Arrangements for formative assessments should maximise access to opportunities for every learner who wishes to review their progress on learning programmes. Resources to meet a learner's special requirements should be available so that every learner is able to make the best possible use of the training provider's facilities. In addition there should be 'Additional tuition, counselling, technical equipment and non-teaching assistance necessary to enable a student with special needs to participate in appropriate regular provision in a college or centre'.[1] The formative assessment process operated should promote equality of opportunity, and non-discriminatory practice should be adopted so that the individual learner's ability to learn is matched with provision. Reviewers should not take sides and must be seen by both learners and faculty head to remain unbiased in all that they say and do, treating each learner as an individual with equal rights.

*Assessment records are completed correctly, passed to the relevant people and stored appropriately*

Formative assessment records for individuals or groups should be completed preferably at the time of the review and countersigned by the reviewer and the learners concerned. Entries should be legible and accurate and the records should be stored securely. The appropriate level of confidentiality should be maintained and information gathered passed on only to the responsible persons entitled to access the data.

# Reviewing progress with learners

*Assessment of progress is based on accurate formative assessments and learners' views about their progress and learning programme*

Reviewing progress and conducting formative assessments is now becoming a day-to-day occurrence in continuing education. Reviews are of paramount importance to learners, whether they are acting alone or interacting with helpers such as their teachers, tutors, assessors or peers. Quite often learners are blissfully unaware that they are running behind their agreed schedule or spending a disproportionate amount of time on trivial matters and neglecting important issues. The list of problems that may crop up is endless, so opportunities for reviewing progress should be embraced by the teacher and learners alike. Reviews should therefore be built into all learning programmes.

Learners require their teacher or facilitator to provide them with advice and information continually so as to ensure that opportunities to achieve their learning objectives can be realised. Formative assessment is important and will involve regular reviewing so that advice can be offered when drawing up learning agendas and negotiating learning contracts and action plans. This is becoming more and more important as individual learners are now being encouraged to work at their own rate, often alone and away from the training provider's facilities. When managing learner-centred training methods, advice and information from the

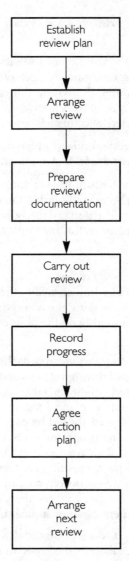

**Figure 13.5** *Learner review flow chart*

teacher must be constantly available in order to ensure that no learning opportunity is missed and its full potential realised.

Peers can also give sound advice and honest opinions, because they will probably be sharing the same learning experiences and facing the same difficulties. This type of constructive criticism is often more readily accepted than criticism from persons who are not part of their group. Nevertheless, any advice given should be monitored because it could unintentionally have a detrimental effect on the candidate seeking help. Similarly too much competition within groups caused by peer-group pressure could have either positive or negative effects.

A flow chart showing a typical reviewing system is given in Figure 13.5.

*Information gathered is interpreted in a way which is justifiable, avoids bias and is checked with learners*

Teachers should check out the validity and suitability of evidence gathered before attempting to evaluate a learner's progress against target awards. Spending time interpreting irrelevant material or working hard doing the wrong things cannot be justified and helps no one. The methods of collection and type of information gathered will also influence the teacher's consideration of material collected, and this will affect the quality of subsequent feedback given.

Being **biased** towards someone can lead to having an irrational predisposition towards them and being prejudiced about their work. Among other things, bias can also result in:

- prejudging learners on the basis of little factual information
- looking for evidence that is currently fashionable
- being obsessed about certain aspects of the syllabus that particularly interest the assessor
- being hypercritical and intent on finding fault (nit-picking)
- overvaluing trivia
- snobbishness
- unhealthy prejudice and covert racism
- showing favouritism and blinding oneself to the learner's shortcomings
- being unfair, one-sided and making unbalanced judgements
- rating all work and actions highly on the basis of good quality work submitted earlier in the programme.

By adopting a clear, honest and positive approach you can avoid **bias** when interpreting information that you have gathered during reviews and formative assessments. Your interpretation of evidence should be based solely on what you have observed and examined, and you should avoid adopting a subjective and judgemental approach based upon personal whims and fancies. Any feedback shared should be descriptive and objective and be matched to the relevant assessment criteria or programme objectives. The candidate should be invited to speak first and comment on their own performance rather than being subjected to a verbal onslaught during which all the things that are 'wrong' are recounted by the teacher. By starting and finishing with positive aspects you can help the candidate to value their positive achievements and to perceive areas where they are not yet competent as opportunities for potential new learning and personal development.

Feedback should be adjusted to meet candidates' differing levels of confidence and experience. Giving constructive feedback is discussed at some length in Chapter 11.

*Learners are encouraged to feel comfortable to express their views on their progress*

Individual **discussion** with learners is an excellent way of reinforcing their accomplishments and confirming the achievement of particular learning objectives. When conducting reviews it is absolutely essential to get people talking about what they did, how they did it, and the good and not so good aspects of the programme to date. You can help them to get started by asking open-ended questions such as:

- 'Overall how do you feel about the programme so far?'
- 'What parts of the course do you enjoy most?'
- 'Is there any part of the programme that you are finding particularly difficult to cope with?'
- 'Are the facilities and resources OK?'
- 'Is the balance between practical and classroom activity suitable?'

Learners should be actively encouraged to participate freely during reviews and should be commended for speaking out constructively whenever they feel a need to do so. The formative reviewing process becomes a valid and worthwhile experience when the learners are invited to take over the progress review. This can be promoted by splitting the main group into smaller sub-groups, allowing the learners to discuss matters of individual and group concern and exchange information on progress to date. The feedback from such deliberations can sometimes be very enlightening for the teacher concerned.

*Information is accurately matched against agreed learning objectives*

When teachers are reviewing achievement and progress with learners, information gathered must be correctly matched with relevant learning objectives. This will ensure that any assessment judgements are valid and reliable and that the behaviour, conditions and standards specified in the objectives are fully met. A matrix showing numbered objectives or criteria, cross-referenced with a folio number marked with the evidence reference number, and an 'evidence seen' signature box is a useful method of ensuring that each criterion is supported by evidence of achievement. Alternatively, a record card such as the one shown in Figure 13.6 could be used when identifying relative experience during the reflection and review session.

| What to assess | How learned | Evidence of learning | How assessed | Accredited by |
|---|---|---|---|---|
|  |  |  |  |  |

**Figure 13.6** *Record card*

*The achievement of learning objectives is correctly determined*

Sharing the outcomes of progress tests with learners provides a good opportunity for them to comment on how well they did and how satisfied they are with their results. The 'inquest' following examinations and assessment testing enables learners to compare their progress against programme objectives so that a constructive self-evaluation can take place. Similarly, self-assessments and discussions about course content and achievement after each module is completed can help to encourage reflection and reinforcement of what has been learned while highlighting areas for further attention. Frequent reviews enable all concerned in the programme to monitor progress and the effectiveness of their inputs, and to this end planners should build review sessions into the programme timetable.

Assessment specifications, marking schemes and mark allocations, vocational assessors' checklists, performance criteria and range statements, behavioural objectives or any other clear statement of required test performance can validly be used to determine a learner's achievement. Methods of interpreting information and determining individual attainment could also include the analysis of practical and written work produced by learners using assessment instruments such as those given in Figure 13.7

*Feedback on progress is given in a positive and encouraging manner*

Feedback resulting from various methods of review and assessment gives information about a learner's progress. Teachers must be able to give feedback which will enable learners to take positive action to enhance their current achievement. However, feedback should not be per-

| Type/description | Application |
|---|---|
| **Multiple-choice** Consisting entirely of Type M items | Mainly skill areas ICAF* (in order of decreasing suitability). Intermittent and short stage test, basic abilities grading tests, pre-/post-testing, formative testing, tests associated with programmed and/or packaged learning. |
| **Short answer** Consisting entirely of Type S items | All skill areas generally. Stage tests, terminal tests, both formative and summative, in-class testing, private-study testing. More useful than M for expressive and creative work. |
| **Long answer** Consisting of one or more Type L items | All skill areas generally. More useful than M or S for expressive and creative work, of limited use in terminal testing, well suited to private-study testing. |
| **Practical test** Consisting essentially of Type P items | Specifically to test psychomotor skills with or without associated intellectual skills. |
| **Coursework** Consisting of items integrated within coursework | That portion of coursework functioning as a test, whether formative or summative, that is to be incorporated in the overall assessment. |
| **Oral test** Test question and response given orally | May include written, visual, aural or tactile stimuli, but strictly oral question and response. Particularly useful for testing level and type of response. |
| **Terminal test** Test given at the end of the learning process related to a unit or part | Usually a timed, unseen examination demanding written and/or graphic response, with or without study aids (e.g. course notes, texts, information sheets, etc.). |

*Note: Skill areas

| I | = Invention | M | = Multiple choice |
|---|---|---|---|
| C | = Comprehension | S | = Short answer |
| A | = Application | L | = Long answer |
| F | = Factual recall | P | = Practical test |

Source: *Notes for Guidance*, R. Whitlow, Bristol Polytechnic

**Figure 13.7** *Applications of test items*

ceived as being a 'one-way' or 'top down' process with the teacher at the top passing comments down the line or making only critical and subjective observations.

Constructive feedback serves to **reinforce learning** and permits early correction of errors, provided it is received **soon after an event.** It should be **objective** and **descriptive** and must be soundly based upon the observation of performance. The **core process** of giving learners **timely feedback** on their progress and performance in a positive and encouraging manner is discussed in more detail in Chapter 11.

Alternative sources of advice can be obtained by eliciting the participation of peers. Learners may be reluctant to approach the teacher continually for advice, so the peer group can provide an alternative source as in the quality circles approach used in manufacturing and business contexts. A small group of learners meet during the programme to discuss problems encountered while learning, the aim being to obtain a fresh perspective on their problems and suggest possible solutions or improvements. Extra-curricular activity negotiated with the programme facilitator can often help learners seeking extra tuition or further learning support.

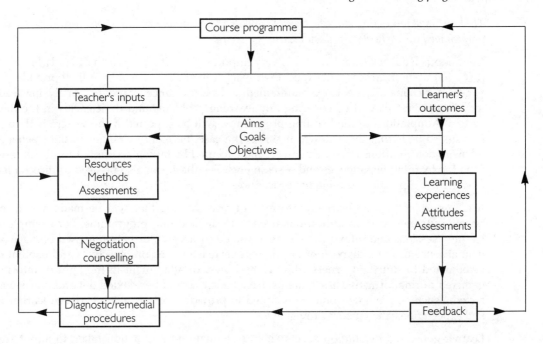

**Figure 13.8** *The feedback loop*

*New learning needs, aspirations and learning objectives are identified*

It will be necessary to identify shortcomings in both learner achievement and programme structure and facilities when considering any modifications needed to the learning programme. Feedback on performance obtained during reflection and review sessions will confirm learner successes and may also reveal the need to establish new objectives or negotiate further learning opportunities and support in order to meet existing criteria. The way that the feedback dimension fits into the course programme is shown in Figure 13.8

Methods of establishing new objectives will vary from simply starting a new unit and adopting prescribed NVQ/SVQ **performance criteria**, to carrying out a task analysis, finding out what is involved in performing the task and writing **enabling objectives** against which performance will be judged. In some instances, a learner's unsuccessful attempt to achieve something will cause an observer to suggest a parcel of mini-objectives that could lead to accomplishment of the task, or the learner will set their own targets, perhaps with the help of their trainer. Someone should be responsible for monitoring the ongoing relevance of programme objectives and the extent to which these are being achieved.

In some situations feedback is immediate, as when a weightlifter fails to lift a load. The reasons for the failure may be discussed with a trainer, who, having observed the attempt, would be able to give advice on an improved method that could be adopted by the lifter. New objectives would then be set. While feedback is unlikely to alter broad programme aims, it does bear heavily on the specific behavioural objectives that are written into the training and assessment brief. It may well be that expected behaviour, conditions and standards of performance will be revised as a direct result of comments fed back by learners and of performance indicators derived from assessments.

*The benefits of proceeding with the training and development and modifications needed to the learning programme are clearly identified with learners*

Continuous feedback from learners is very important, but its true worth can only be realised if it is acted upon. Learners will expect their teacher to act on the feedback they provide if motivation and cooperation is to be maintained and performance improved. Analysing feedback may be the best way of discovering any learning problems and deficiencies in the delivery system. Adaptations to the learning programme will be expected if the system is thought by learners to be letting them down. If this is the case, necessary changes in the teacher's and learner's contributions must be planned and executed by taking account of feedback resulting from the learning experiences and assessments. Feedback can also be used to direct a learner to suitable diagnostic and remedial procedures.

It is important to keep learners informed of any changes that will be made and to match review outcomes with modifications needed to the learning programme. For example, extra learning sessions and tutorials could be arranged to cover information missed because of student absence or the indisposition of the regular teacher. Lesson objectives and content could be adjusted to suit the learners' abilities and level of attainment in the light of information gathered during formative assessments. Irrelevancies could be weeded out and omissions corrected. Teaching methods could be adapted to provide a better match between learner needs and expectations and current provision.

Learner-generated evaluation sheets should be analysed and action taken to adopt suggestions and make necessary improvements in provision. It should be possible to implement minor changes although major structural changes based on wider course evaluation will probably take longer to effect. But again it is important to keep people informed of developments (or reasons for apparent inactivity).

*Records are completed correctly, passed to relevant people and stored appropriately*

This criterion has been discussed above.

## Self-assessment questions

1 Explain the principles and purposes of conducting formative assessments.

2 Why is it necessary to gather valid and reliable information about your learners' progress from a range of sources when you are preparing for a formative assessment session?

3 Explain what is meant by the terms 'qualitative' and 'quantitative' information. Give examples of each type of information.

4 Explain what is meant by the terms 'valid' and 'reliable' information.

5 Explain what is meant by 'witness testimonies'. Describe what a witness does and list the people who may witness and authenticate your learners' evidence.

6 Describe any legal constraints that apply when collecting and analysing data concerning learners that will be used by others.

7 Obtain a copy of your employer's policy on confidentiality as applied to methods of recording, storing and using information and file this in your portfolio of evidence.

8 List the sources that could provide suitable information for learner reviews.

9 Why is it necessary to gather information about current achievements, difficulties and other train-

ing-related issues when you are conducting learner reviews? Why is it also important to take account of prior achievement and the transferability of skills owned when you are reviewing progress and action planning?

10 Outline the methods used within your employer's organisation to collect required information about a learner's progress.

11 Why is the timing and content of formative assessments important to the learners concerned and to other people who are involved in delivering the learning programme?

12 Write a rationale that you could use when interpreting information collected about a learner's progress and achievements.

13 Explain how you can avoid bias when interpreting information about a learner's progress and achievements.

14 Why is it important to be well prepared when you are managing formative assessments? Produce examples of suitably collated and summarised information that you have used when giving feedback to learners, course tutors and sponsors.

15 Produce a flow chart and written procedures showing how information for/from formative reviews is recorded and passed on to responsible people concerned.

16 Explain how the use of information technology can facilitate the effectiveness and efficiency of record keeping and improve access to data for authorised users.

17 Explain why learners should be thoroughly briefed about formative assessment procedures and the use that will be made of information obtained. Highlight the possible benefits to the individual learner and to the training provider.

18 Explain why it is essential to provide learners with a clear indication of the learning objectives, performance criteria or other standards against which they are being assessed before discussing their progress and achievement.

19 Describe the materials and facilities that may be provided to help learners to identify their achievements. File copies of the resources that you provide in your portfolio of evidence.

20 Explain what is meant by 'reflecting on one's learning experiences'. Why is it important to encourage people to reflect on what they have learnt and the way that they have been learning?

21 When conducting formative assessments why is it necessary first to set the learner at ease and feel free to express their views, self-assess, comment, ask questions and clarify points?

22 Describe the ways in which reviewers can elicit learner participation during formative assessments.

23 Explain how you offer a formative assessment process that promotes equality of opportunity to learn and progress and avoidance of any form of discrimination.

24 Explain how feedback may be given in a positive and encouraging manner.

25 When assessing progress why is it important to take account of the learner's personally defined self-development objectives as well as achievement against the formally agreed programme criteria? Explain how your assessment records are correctly maintained and securely stored.

# Preparing for assessment: sample activities

### Activity 13.1 Collecting information on learners' progress

Discuss this assignment with colleagues and submit a report on the following objectives that concern collecting information on learners' progress.

a) Explain the principles and purpose of reviews.
b) Identify data-collection techniques and explain any legal constraints on their use.
c) Identify candidates and units concerned in your review.
d) Explain how information is collected and summarised (include obtaining information from other staff, records of achievement and formative assessments).
e) Explain how the validity and reliability of evidence appraised may be established.
f) Write a rationale for analysing and interpreting information gathered.
g) Describe how to prioritise and summarise information effectively when reviewing and evaluating findings.
h) Explain how information technology can be effectively used in recording and storing information and record keeping.

### Activity 13.2 Implementing formative assessments

Discuss this assignment with colleagues and submit a report on the following objectives that concern conducting formative assessment with learners:

a) List the information you would give to learners about the purpose and use to which information gathered during formative assessments would be put.
b) List the materials/techniques you would need to use for formative assessment.
c) Describe how you would conduct your learners' formative assessment.
d) Prepare for your learners suitable information sheets describing how the formative assessment would be conducted.
e) Design assessment documentation.
f) Explain the importance of giving feedback.
g) Conduct the formative assessment(s).
h) Throughout the review record learner comments and note matters for further clarification. Share your feedback with the learners concerned and ask them to check and confirm the correctness of any notes made.

### Activity 13.3 Reviewing progress with learners

Discuss this assignment with colleagues and submit a report on the following objectives that concern reviewing progress with learners:

a) Explain why it is important to encourage learners to participate in peer-group assessment opportunities and to self-assess their own progress against programme targets.
b) Describe how you would set about reviewing progress with learners.
c) Describe how you would elicit the participation of individuals and groups.
d) Explain how you would review progress and weigh up the evidence gathered with learners.
e) Produce documents that contain records you have made during reviews of learner progress.
f) Produce documents that you have used or could use to report on progress made by individual learners and groups.
g) Produce documentary evidence showing how you have confirmed your learners' achievements.

### Activity 13.4 Modifying learning programmes

Describe how you would match the results of formative assessments and reviews with modifications needed to the relevant learning programme.

Explain how you have taken account of new learning needs, learners' aspirations and additional learning objectives identified whilst reviewing progress and subsequently modifying a training programme. Show with the aid of a scheme of work for the learning programme how you have cross-referenced any necessary updating or modifications with relevant award criteria.

**Notes**

1 J. Fish, *Special Needs Occasional Paper*, Longman for the Further Education Unit, Longman Resources Unit, York 1989, p. 21.

# 14

# Conducting non-competence-based assessments

The three main reasons for conducting assessments are to assess individual progress and achievement, to evaluate the teacher's effectiveness and to evaluate the programme effectiveness as a whole. This chapter is concerned with the purposes of testing and assessment and the various approaches to assessment that could be adopted.

When designing assessment programmes a starting point might be to agree with those concerned what is to be assessed and what methods could be used to gather relevant evidence of achievement. Once the need for assessment has been identified the next stage will be the consideration of essential aspects of an effective assessment scheme and ways and means of testing topics and abilities that must be assessed. The methods of testing and assessing available should then be reviewed and their suitability for testing the types of knowledge and skills to be judged should be confirmed. Then follows the writing of implementation procedures and the production of examination papers, test construction and the design of practical skills tests. Those responsible for planning assessment arrangements must be aware of the need for valid and reliable testing processes, procedures and assessment instruments. Effective and efficient assessment techniques will need to operate once the test format and documentation has been established and the candidates have commenced their written papers or practicals.

The need to employ properly trained and accredited invigilators and assessors to implement the assessment programmes and to supervise candidates during examinations and testing sessions must be recognised. Qualified people will be needed to analyse evidence presented by candidates and to mark examination papers reliably against approved assessment criteria and marking schemes. Evidence of accomplishment will need to be impartially reviewed and individuals provided with clear, constructive and suitable feedback on their performance and achievements. Assessment outcomes will need to be recorded and achievement reported as required by examining bodies. Finally, there is an important need to identify the limitations of assessment methods used and to evaluate the effect of testing on your learners and other candidates who may be seeking an 'assessment only' service.

## Conducting non-competence-based assessments

*Assessment tasks and their requirements are clearly specified and agreed with all relevant parties*

The essential requirement when specifying assessment tasks, examinations or tests is that assessment task instructions, examination paper and test content are matched with the **test**

| Unit topic area | Topic as % of assessment | Motor skills | Intellectual skills | | | |
|---|---|---|---|---|---|---|
| | | | Information | Comprehension | Application | Invention |
| A | 45 | | 3 | 14 | 14 | 14 |
| B | 11 | | 1 | 10 | | |
| C | 8 | | 1 | 5 | | 2 |
| D | 6 | 2 | 1 | 1 | | 2 |
| E | 30 | 5 | | | 15 | 10 |
| | | | | | | |
| | | | | | | |
| | | | | | | |
| | | | | | | |
| | Percentage of assessment for entire unit | 7 | 6 | 30 | 29 | 28 |

The header spans: **% of total assessment** over Motor skills and Intellectual skills; **Intellectual skills** spans Information, Comprehension, Application, Invention.

**Figure 14.1** *Assessment specification*

**specification** and syllabus material. Tests should be **valid** and **reliable** and the selection of tasks or knowledge items to be assessed should cover the syllabus range.

The **breakdown** of a learning programme by topic and types of learning given in Figure 14.1 could be used as a key to the production of a detailed assessment specification. The topics expressed as a percentage of assessment for the programme should be weighted so as to reflect the relative importance of topic content and the number of hours devoted to each topic during the training programme.

The **test specification grid** given in Figure 14.2 shows how the number of questions and marks could be allocated for each topic of a particular programme. Notice how the calculations topic to be tested has been broken down into the four categories of intellectual skills given in the initial programme topic breakdown plus an allowance for testing related psychomotor skills. As can be seen, the number of questions asked will depend on the setter's perception of the relative importance of each aspect. In the example given, ten marks have been allocated for ten **information** type questions to be set whereas 45 marks are allocated for only six **application** questions. The grid when complete should cover each syllabus topic so that the finished test instrument covers all required candidate knowledge and abilities.

*Individuals are provided with clear and sufficient guidance on the assessment tasks*

Candidates are entitled to receive **adequate guidance** before undertaking an assessment task or sitting an examination. The instructions at the head of an examination paper (the rubric)

| Marks allocated / Topic item | Information | Comprehension | Application | Invention | Motor skills | Total marks |
|---|---|---|---|---|---|---|
| Calculations | | | | | | |
| Use of tables | 1 | 2 | 5 | 0 | 0 | 8 |
| Indices | 5 | 2 | 5 | 2 | 0 | 14 |
| Setting out of calculations | 1 | 1 | 5 | 1 | 1 | 9 |
| Quadratic equations: | | | | | | |
| Solution by factors | 1 | 4 | 10 | 8 | 0 | 23 |
| Solution by formula | 1 | 4 | 10 | 8 | 0 | 23 |
| Graphical solutions | 1 | 4 | 10 | 8 | 0 | 23 |
| Number of questions to be set | 10 | 8 | 6 | 5 | 1 | 100 / 30 |

**Figure 14.2** *Test specification grid – syllabus topic: 'calculations'*

could be read out clearly before candidates are allowed to start work and if necessary doubts clarified to meet the differing needs of individuals. There are many people with limited reading skills, and care should be taken to avoid discriminating on the basis of their poor command of language. While the assessor should neither aid nor hinder candidates by interfering with them while they are working on content, it is essential for the candidates to be clear in their minds about the **assessment strategy** and related matters such as:

- how progress and skills will be evaluated
- whether knowledge will be assessed using paper-based written tests, multiple-choice papers or oral questioning
- how problem solving, skills testing, observation and videotaped performance will be used to assess psychomotor skills
- how questionnaires and personality tests, videoed interaction with candidates or other methods will be used to assess affective domain skills such as interpersonal behaviour and attitude.

Well before test day, advice might reasonably be given about the examination procedures and test-paper format that will be used. A supply of past examination papers could be distributed for practice purposes in the weeks leading up to the examination. Practical hints could be given about interpreting the format and wording of questions and the need to identify key words and answer every part of the question. Mock examinations could be arranged. Practice could be given in correctly marking up response sheets for multiple-choice papers. The machine marking process could be explained and the need to record responses correctly stressed, so that subsequent scanning only picks up the intended choice and candidates do not lose marks because of spoilt papers.

*All relevant information and training related to assessment is identified and accessed to ensure own practice is up to date and meets all requirements*

Teachers who assess for target qualifications must be competent and qualified to current requirements. To meet this requirement teachers will need to review systematically their own development needs in order to keep up to date. Quite apart from meeting the essential basic conditions for carrying out assessments, teachers should be looking for ways and means of improving on current procedures and assessment practices. This requires an open-minded and willing approach to enhancing their assessment techniques when, for example, **examiners' reports** indicate the need for attention to particular points. The reports can also be used to inform the training programme since they often indicate typical errors made by candidates as well as misperceptions, ambiguity and key points missed.

*Factors which impact on assessment are identified and taken into account in assessment practice*

The assessment principles, processes and methods to be used should be clearly understood by assessors before they administer relevant assessments. A sample of the factors which could impact on the effectiveness and validity of assessment include:

- the clarity of test administration procedures and the quality of the invigilator's communication skills
- the effectiveness of pretesting in evaluating the quality of individual examination questions before the final version of the examination is compiled
- the weighting of marks allocated for different parts of the examination.
- the quality and relevance of the standard against which the suitability of the test instrument for a given purpose may be evaluated
- the extent to which the test or examination does what it is designed to do

- the degree to which an examination tests all programme content and objectives
- the consistency of examination results when used to assess similar groups of candidates on different occasions
- the value of the assessment as a diagnostic testing device and means of diagnosing learning difficulties
- the effect of self-assessments and self-evaluation
- the literacy and numeracy skills of candidates
- practical considerations such as:
  - stereotyping
  - adopting discriminatory practices
  - the 'halo effect'
  - using leading questions
  - judging progress rather than actual attainment measured against standards.

*Approval by the relevant organisation for acting as an assessor is obtained where necessary*

An **accredited assessor** is an individual with an appropriate qualification who has been nominated by an assessment centre or examining body to undertake the assessment of candidates. Examination bodies normally specify detailed criteria for approval as assessors and examiners, and when approval and licensing arrangements have been completed their verifiers will regularly check that centres and assessors are properly fulfilling their role. The eligibility of individuals to practise as assessors should be checked against awarding body criteria before they are authorised to assess candidates for the qualifications offered.

*Assessment tasks are carried out correctly*

Programme tutors and supervising teachers are normally held responsible for instigating proper procedures when conducting examinations and assessment tasks. They will also be expected to **monitor** the assessment practice and quality assurance arrangements by observing invigilators and assessors, and checking an adequate number of candidates' assessment records in order to confirm that they are meeting examination board requirements. Verifiers will probably need to check that **examination conditions** are fulfilled. This will involve observing candidates completing assessment tasks, checking that tasks are being carried out correctly and examining samples of assessed coursework and marked scripts so as to maintain the standard of assessment.

Task instruction sheets should be carefully worded so that candidates are able to interpret the examination questions or task instructions in the way intended. The reliability of tests would be adversely affected if the candidates' perception of the set task or available options were to differ considerably. Instructions should therefore be written so as to avoid the possibility of different interpretations by candidates.

*Evidence from assessment tasks is collected according to agreed timescales and resources*

Teachers must be able to gather, by means of efficient selection, valid and reliable performance and knowledge evidence from assessment tasks, and written and verbal evidence from examinations. This immediately raises several questions, such as:

- What is the timetabled schedule of assessments and examinations?
- Is there a list of assignment 'issue' and 'due' dates?
- Would it be preferable to use several objective tests and short-answer tests rather than a longer single test?

- Should coursework assessment be used for suitable chunks of the programme?
- Who will be involved in gathering the assessment evidence?

Time is a scarce resource nowadays, and questions about how to carry out assessments properly and about cost-effectiveness will be on many teachers' minds. In order to use assessment time productively, those concerned might choose to invest precious hours in testing key abilities, principles and invention skills, rather than less important factual recall knowledge. Assessors could use interviewing techniques and reviews to cover a lot of ground with a small number of candidates rather than seeking lengthy and time-consuming written answers. However, written papers would probably be used for assessing large numbers of candidates on knowledge aspects of a topic, although marking the papers could take a long time.

The amount of assessor time available, the physical resources and the efficiency of the evidence-gathering process will affect the method of evidence collection employed. But important questions to ask might be: Does the assessment process make the best use of available time? Does it take up a lot of study programme time? Is the balance of learning time and assessing time reasonable? Are all the assessment tasks absolutely necessary?

*Evidence is handled according to the specified rules of confidentiality and security*

The process for registering candidates and completing and updating records from registration through to certification should be understood. Teachers should be able to name the people responsible for completing each document and describe the security procedures for record keeping and storing candidate files. Records may be kept in archives or locked filing cabinets and the keyholder should know who is authorised to access the records. The Data Protection Act 1984 is designed to protect people from the misuse of computerised information, but non-computerised information is not covered by the Act. It is up to the teacher as record keeper to ensure that information stored is disclosed only to those who have a right to it.

# Analysing evidence to form an assessment decision

*Assessment criteria are clearly specified and made available to all the appropriate parties*

When designing tests, teachers must ensure that the test is **valid**: that is, that it covers relevant assessment criteria. Tests should be structured so as to satisfy criteria laid down in the programme in the form of **performance objectives** or, as is now the case in so many areas, **competence objectives**. The assessment instrument must contain questions that are based on the criteria, and practical test specifications must clearly define what must be done to achieve assessment criteria. Whether the tests are internally or externally set, markers and assessors must be given the assessment criteria, and must clearly understand marking schemes and assessment schedules, otherwise judging and scoring will be unreliable. Assessment criteria must be clearly specified and made available to all parties concerned with the assessment process.

Validity is inextricably linked with programme objectives, so that three important criteria must be fulfilled in order that the complete learning package may be validated. These are:

- programme content
- learning experiences
- testing.

*Evidence is correctly compared to the specified criteria*

When a candidate's 'live' **performance** is judged, their behaviour can be observed and assessed against lists of competences and features, or **prepared checklists** matched with

---

**Abilities to be assessed in projects**

- Logical working method
- Appropriate use of reference material
- Compliance with relevant regulations and codes of practice
- Technical accuracy
- Economy of materials and labour
- Problem solving ability; appropriateness of solution
- Organisation of material into a report
- Clarity of written expression
- Clarity and accuracy of drawings
- Accuracy of calculations

Source: C. Ward, *Designing a Scheme of Assessment*, Stanley Thornes 1980, p. 91

---

**Figure 14.3** *Abilities to be assessed in projects*

award criteria. The checklists should fully cover all relevant behavioural aspects of the assessment, thereby allowing the assessor to 'tick off' aspects observed and identify any shortcomings. While the **observation method** of assessment encourages objective judging, subjective opinions are still possible. **Knowledge evidence** can be judged against validated checklists of 'preset' assessors' questions or by completion of questionnaires and structured reviews.

**Assessing projects** against specific criteria can sometimes present difficulties, and Christine Ward makes the following comment:

> For a project, it is not usually possible to specify the syllabus topics which are to be covered, since coverage is likely to be small in any one project. The project is, however, mainly concerned with the higher abilities and communication skills, and not particularly with the recall or comprehension of particular facts, which are better tested in some other way. It is therefore sufficient, for most projects, to prepare a list of abilities to be assessed [as in the example in Figure 14.3]. Each project must be so devised as to require the student to give evidence of each of these abilities.[1]

*Scoring systems are correctly applied and the results accurately recorded*

Oral tests and impression-marking techniques can give some indication of a candidate's current level of achievement but better estimates can sometimes be obtained by the use of an **analytical scoring system**. If, however teachers intend to use analytical marking they will need to consider using either mark allocations or mark schemes. D.S. Frith and H.G. Macintosh distinguish between the two as follows:

> The **mark scheme** provides the comprehensive statement of the explicit criteria against which the relevant work/answers are to be assessed. The **mark allocation**, which may or may not be indicated to the respondents, assigns specific marks to specific questions or parts of questions, and it is the marker's task to allocate these accurately and appropriately.[2]

The example given in Figure 14.4 illustrates the form that an analytical **mark scheme** might take.

---

**Question 1**
*Explain the difference between 'fixed assets' and 'current assets'. Give three examples of each type of asset.*

| Mark scheme | Marks |
|---|---|
| **Fixed assets** are: | |
| non-trading business assets of a relatively permanent nature | 2 |
| which are used as the basis for generating business, | 2 |
| as opposed to **current assets** which are: | |
| operating assets used in the course of business | 2 |
| which are convertible into cash within a year | 2 |
| | |
| **Examples of fixed assets** are: | |
| property | 1 |
| plant | 1 |
| equipment | 1 |
| **Acceptable alternatives** include: goodwill, fixtures, premises | |
| | |
| **Examples of current assets** are: | |
| cash | 1 |
| stock | 1 |
| work in progress | 1 |
| **Acceptable alternatives** include: bank deposits, marketable securities, debtors, finished goods, accounts receivable, temporary investments | |

---

**Figure 14.4** *Marking scheme layout*

The example given in Figure 14.5 illustrates the form that a **mark allocation** might take.

---

**Question 1**
*Explain what is meant by the expression 'the net assets of a company' and define the term 'net asset value' (NAV).*

| Anticipated correct answer | Mark allocation |
|---|---|
| The **net assets** of a company for equity holders are the total assets of the company, minus all the liabilities in the balance sheet minus all the prior capital (including debentures, loan stocks and preference shares). | 6 |
| | |
| The **net asset value** (NAV) is calculated by dividing the net assets by the number of shares to give a figure per share. | 2 |

**Question 2**
*Explain the strategy of an investor who is described as a 'stag'.*

| Anticipated correct answer | |
|---|---|
| A **stag** is someone who subscribes to a new issue, not to keep the shares, but to make a quick profit when dealings in the shares begin | 1 |

---

**Figure 14.5** *Mark allocation*

When preparing mark schemes the criteria shown in Figure 14.6 could be used as a framework for constructing the schemes and for checking the completeness and quality of the finished instrument.

---

**Criteria for the preparation of mark schemes**

- Suggested answers are appropriate to the question.

- Suggested answers are technically and/or numerically correct.

- The mark scheme embraces every point required by the question.

- Marks are allocated for each point.

- The model answer in the mark scheme includes only points required by the question.

- Marks are allocated strictly according to the knowledge and abilities which the question requires the candidate to demonstrate.

- Sufficient acceptable alternative answers are provided.

- Marks are commensurate with the degree of difficulty of the question and the time which would be required to answer it.

- Time allowance is appropriate for the work required.

- The mark scheme is sufficiently broken down to allow the marking to be as objective as possible.

- The totalling of marks is correct.

- The mark scheme does not reflect undue bias towards one viewpoint at the expense of others.

Adapted from D.S. Frith and H.G. Macintosh, *A Teacher's Guide to Assessment*, Stanley Thornes 1985, p. 93

---

**Figure 14.6** *Criteria for the preparation of mark schemes*

*Evidence used in the analysis is clearly specified as being relevant to the assessment process*

Assessors should be issued with a listing showing the activities or material evidence that would be acceptable for assessment, together with a note of the examination conditions, the type and level of acceptable knowledge evidence and its relevance to the assessment process. An assessment specification might detail one or more of the following methods of collecting evidence of competence: essay writing, responding to question papers requiring closely defined short answers, oral testing, open-book tests, assignments and projects, skills testing or observed performance.

A part of the Royal Life Saving Society UK (RLSS) National Pool Lifeguard Qualification training programme is reproduced in Figure 14.7 (see *Documents Pack*) As can be seen, details of the Theory Assessment and Practical Pool Assessment are given. The evidence requirements are clearly stated and relevant to the training programme and subsequent assessment. Detailed performance criteria are also provided in units (such as H3) that are used by qualified and fully trained RLSS assessors when assessing candidates for appropriate qualifications.

*Evidence is analysed fairly and impartially*

Issues of equality of opportunity and non-discriminatory practice should be foremost in the minds of assessors who are called upon to judge evidence presented by candidates. All candidates are entitled to a fair and impartial assessment of their achievements. This means that assessors must ensure that unfair discrimination is eliminated and that evidence is judged against only those criteria, range statements and evidence requirements specified in the standards or in approved marking schemes. But even so, examination papers or other evidence presented must be checked carefully for authenticity, validity, currency and sufficiency. To be fair, assessors must be careful to avoid leading their candidates when questioning them, and their judgements must cover *all* the evidence requirements.

**In-course assessment**, like traditional final examinations, must yield consistent results, but a comment in the NATFHE publication *Assessment* points to serious difficulties that could be experienced with continuous or in-course assessment:

> Assessment may be based partly or even wholly on work not done under examination conditions – on laboratory work, essays and projects, and general class and homework exercises. In this case there can be two serious difficulties:
>
> (i)  It can be very difficult to decide what is due to 'syndicate' or other aided performance and what is due to the unaided effort of the student himself (or herself).
>
> (ii) The non-examination work may be subjective and hence more difficult to assess. Points raised in favour of objective testing as opposed to subjective assessments, e.g. essay examinations, may with equal logic be raised against in-course assessment based on essays etc.[3]

It is clear that in order for evidence to be analysed fairly and impartially decisions will have to be made in respect of the precise educational objectives of the training programme or award criteria.

*Assessment decision is made on the basis of all the available and relevant evidence*

When making assessment decisions, the assessor will need to consider all relevant evidence presented by candidates. Different types of evidence will be required for different assessment purposes, and sources of suitable evidence could include:

- continuous assessment records
- external assessments
- natural performance in the workplace
- simulations
- projects and assignments
- candidate and peer reports
- candidate's evidence of prior learning and achievement
- third-party evidence.

*A rationale for the assessment decision is provided to all the appropriate people*

A **rationale** is a logical explanation giving details of the why and wherefore of the decision-making process. It defines the fundamental reasons for the assessment judgement made. Rationales and associated **assessment checklists** based upon test standards should be provided to candidates, assessors who will be making the assessment decisions, internal verifiers and training standards supervisors. The choice of rationale format used would depend upon the examining body requirements or 'in-house' procedures. The rationale provides an explanation of how target criteria should be or were met, and enables the quality and reliability of judgements to be maintained.

A rationale that could be used when assessing assignments is given in Figure 14.8.

*Assessment decisions are verified according to the specified assessment procedures*

It is the responsibility of the verifier to ensure that assessors have followed the assessment guidance provided by the examination board or the awarding body concerned. The reason for

## Assessment by assignments

The assignments used must meet all the performance criteria. The candidate must achieve all parts of the assignment to the criteria and assessment guidelines contained in each Examinations Board unit.

If the candidate does not achieve all the performance criteria, an opportunity should be given to repeat the task. If the assignment is limited and only tests a few of the performance criteria the whole assignment should be repeated, for example: shorthand transcription. However, if the assignment is an integrated one that takes the candidate several hours to complete, the candidate should only repeat the part incorrectly completed. For example: if only one document of an integrated financial assignment which includes sales/purchases documentation, ledgers etc. is incorrect then only that document should be repeated.

Assignments which form part of the candidate's portfolio of evidence should not be written on by the assessor as moderators prefer to see clean examples of work. All assessments submitted by the candidates should have a front sheet and these may contain relevant assessor comments.

## Grading of assignments

Assignments completed on time and without error may be graded Distinction. If a small error occurs or there are a few spelling errors it may be graded Merit. All other assignments will be graded Pass or Resubmit. These gradings are to assist staff in motivating those candidates that are capable of achieving the performance criteria with the minimum of assistance, and are obviously achieving a good standard through their own efforts. The grading of Distinction and Merit will not appear on the final certificate but may be included in the candidate's Record of Achievement.

Source: Lynda S. Bourne
Assessment Centre Manager

**Figure 14.8** *Rationale for assessing assignments*

this is to ensure that all assessors engaged in similar assessment activities are consistent in their interpretation of approved assessment rationales. In some instances it will be necessary for verifiers to monitor the assessment process by observing an assessment session. Requirements for verification might also include the need to sample written work, products or services rendered in order to validate the candidates' attainment. The consistency of one assessor's judgements over a period of time and also different assessors judging the same criteria could be verified by course tutors or awarding body staff.

*Assessment decisions are accurately recorded using the specified documents*

**Formative records** contain information gained during ongoing assessments that are designed to improve training inputs and monitor learner progress and achievement. The records could be used to feed back to the training provider information from assessments or negotiations with candidates, thereby enabling learning difficulties to be overcome or progression to other units or more advanced work arranged.

**Summative assessment** is made at the end of a training programme in order to determine the overall effectiveness of training and quality of learning outcomes. A form of certification known as a **summative statement of achievement** is sometimes used to validate attainment. Evidence that is collected during examinations, tests and assessments is recorded during a process of continuous assessment, and this together with any final assessment combines to form the record.

A statement in the form of a **personal profile** may be used to summarise the assessment of achievement. It also gives an estimate of development potential at the end of a course of training. The statement derives from learner self-evaluation of all the experiences and outcomes obtained while learning backed by a final review with the trainer or assessor. The profile builds on earlier in-course developmental reviews and takes into account the process of continually monitoring, evaluating and recording learning achievements. **Profiling** is used for recording information such as a candidate's scores in single-subject assessments, terminal examinations, in-course assessment and end tests, other academic and practical skills attainment, and in some instances personal attributes. Profiles can take the form of grids or open-ended reports. Spaces are normally provided for learner responses and teacher comments under various headings. The reporting of both positive and negative aspects of performance will enable tutors, parents and prospective employers to save time reading between the lines and trying to spot breaks and omissions. But do not concentrate on reporting every single item that the candidates cannot do as this would demotivate them, and after all, employers will probably be more interested in what people can do than what they cannot do.

Summary statements may be used to support bids for final awards, and features indicated on the relevant personal profile include:

- details of the candidate
- prior learning and achievement
- details of the action plan
- essential details of the training programme completed
- experience gained during training
- work experience provider's comments
- attendance record
- performance criteria and competences attained
- qualifications achieved
- comments on reviews.

According to D. Garforth and H. Macintosh[4] the contents of profiles should contain the following three basic elements:

- A list of items forming the basis of the assessment. These may be called 'criteria' and may be in the form of a list of skills and qualities or may be embodied within a course description.
- A means of indicating the level and/or nature of performance reached for each item on the list. Almost any means can be used including marks, grades, percentages, histograms, bar graphs, statements and descriptive assessments.
- An indication of the evidence used to arrive at the description provided. This element is unfortunately often ignored but it is vital to indicate the context in which a particular skill is assessed if the nature of its performance is to be fully understood.

**Records of achievement** known as the National Record of Achievement (NRA) and the National Record of Vocational Achievement (NROVA) are used to store evidence of attainment such as certificates, training records, employers' letters and skills tests results. This information together with projects, assignments and reports stored in personal portfolios can be used to validate claims of prior achievements. Other examples of typical record-keeping documents, relating to Chapter 15, are given in the *Documents Pack*.

# Providing feedback to individuals on the assessment decision

*Feedback is provided in a suitable environment*

The environment and context in which feedback is shared will influence the candidate's behaviour and attitude towards receiving feedback and asking for clarifications. While it may be expedient to huddle in a corner of the workshop in which the candidate works it may not be conducive to good communication. Quite apart from the possible blocking effect of noisy conditions, the review could draw unwanted attention from colleagues and inhibit the candidate's contribution. The same would be true if individual feedback were broadcast to the whole group. It would therefore be sensible to find out what facilities are available when negotiating the assessment plan, and to agree a quiet nearby place in which to conduct the review.

*A rationale for the assessment decision is provided to the individual*

It is thought that to be most effective many small rewards may be better than a few large rewards; thus a rationale for the assessment decision supplied to the candidate concerned should focus on key features but contain specific reinforcements. The rationale could take the form of an **assessment checklist** with added comments completed by the assessor while the candidate is carrying out the assessment task; alternatively, a written **summary assessment report** form could be used. The choice of instrument would depend upon the examining body requirements. The point is that candidates are entitled to an explanation of how they achieved the target criteria, or, on the other hand, why they are being referred. Whenever possible, the rationale should be written using constructive and objective descriptors of accomplishments and should highlight areas for improvement.

*Feedback is clear, constructive and suitable to the individual's requirements*

Constructive feedback serves to **reinforce learning** and permits early correction of errors, provided it is received **soon after an event.** It should be **objective** and **descriptive** and must be soundly based upon the observation of performance. The **core process** of giving learners **timely feedback** on their progress and performance in a positive and encouraging manner is discussed in more detail in Chapter 11.

*The individual is encouraged to seek clarification on the reasons for the assessment decision*

Candidates need to win, and, with examinations and the like, winning means gaining credit for skills and knowledge demonstrated. Teachers must recognise this and reinforce success. If they do this their learners will come to realise that positive constructive learning behaviour will lead to rewards that will enhance their self-image, whereas 'failure' could result in loss of face and demotivation. It is for these reasons that teachers should encourage questions and requests for clarification during examination inquests, reviews and feedback sessions. Teachers must not punish candidates who fail to meet assessment standards but instead assign causes and give explanations so that people will not be labelled as failures. If they perceive themselves as failures they will probably start acting like losers, but if courses of remedial action are clarified and supportive comment is forthcoming, purposeful behaviour will supplant the tendency to give in or opt out.

*The consequences of the assessment decision are fully explained to the individual*

Feedback resulting from various methods of review and assessment gives information about a learner's progress. Assessment decisions will reflect the performance demonstrated and outcomes achieved by a learner. The consequences of decisions will be contingent upon the learner's degree of success and will range from progressing to more advanced work to termination of their learning programme. In either case teachers must be able to give feedback which will enable learners to take positive action to enhance their current achievement. However, feedback should not be perceived as being a 'one-way' or 'top down' process with the teacher at the top passing comments down the line or making only critical and subjective observations. The learners must be party to any decision taken. In the event of 'failure', teachers should make it clear why the learner has failed to meet the requirements specified and encourage them to shape their learning behaviour to better effect.

*Individuals are encouraged to seek advice on further action as a result of the assessment decision*

Steps should be taken to involve students actively in decisions about their learning. The need for joint negotiation throughout the training and assessment programme should be understood right from the start. Study guidance would include help for learners in deciding training top-up or remedial learning methods and resources to be used, the level of teacher support needed, the rate of learning and how this will be regulated. Where actions plans have been written it is helpful to review progress and bring into focus difficulties which are holding up progress. Subsequent discussion will allow possible courses of action to be considered and, where necessary, referral to others who may be better placed to handle the problems encountered.

*Feedback is recorded in the appropriate documents*

Results of assessment may be reported in the form of records of marks scored during tests or letter grades from A to E for written work. Formative or summative assessment records will represent individual and group achievement. Records may take the form of:

- **Records of achievement** showing learner attributes or performance against criteria.
- **Grid-style profiles** showing learner achievement, competences gained and clusters of core skills owned. Profiles are now widely used and play an important role in many vocational programmes now on offer.
- **Record cards** and report forms.
- **Graphical** methods of representation and ranking.
- **Group assessment profiles** representing test information.

Profiling and record keeping enables teachers and learners alike to identify where improvements have been or could be made, and can be used to authenticate achievement.

## Self-assessment questions

1  Give three important reasons for using testing and assessing in a teaching or training situation.

2  Define the terms 'validity' and 'reliability' and explain how they relate to assessment.

3  What is an 'assessment specification'? Why is it important to specify clearly and agree assessment tasks and their requirements with all relevant parties before commencing an assessment programme?

4  Why is it necessary to provide candidates with clear and sufficient guidance on assessment tasks before they start their assessment?

5 Describe how you ensure that you keep up to date with current assessment practice in your discipline.

6 Outline factors which could impact on your assessment practice.

7 Why do award bodies operate a quality-assurance system when appointing assessors to their organisations?

8 Outline the means by which you ensure that the confidentiality and security of assessment evidence is not compromised.

9 Describe the various aspects of guidance that you might be called on to provide for your candidates before they take an assessment or test.

10 Why is it important to provide clear instructions (a rubric) when administering tests?

11 Describe the techniques that you could use when observing candidates for assessment.

12 Outline important aspects of the interviewing technique used by teachers when carrying out oral tests. Explain the importance of having effective personal interaction skills.

13 In an oral examination relating to a 'design and manufacture' project a candidate scored high marks but did badly in written assessments for other parts of the syllabus. What are possible explanations for this?

14 Explain the value of preparing and using assessment checklists that are matched to award criteria when you are assessing candidates.

15 Construct a mark scheme for one or more of your assessment tests. Allocate a total mark for each question and apportion marks for each significant piece of information required in the model answer to each question.

16 What is the point in providing all appropriate people with a rationale for the assessment decision?

17 What is meant by the phrase 'the verification of assessment decisions'?

18 Why is it essential to record assessment decisions accurately?

19 Explain how information concerning learner achievement and other outcomes of assessment can be used to introduce improvements to subsequent teaching and assessment procedures.

20 Providing feedback to individuals on the assessment decision is a key feature of assessment. Go back to Chapter 11 and answer the 15 self-assessment questions provided at the end of the chapter.

## *Preparing for assessment: sample activities*

### *Activity 14.1 Planning and preparing assessment procedures*
For one of your courses, design an assessment plan and an assessment specification. Prepare assessment procedures, test papers and any other documentation. Relate the plan and assessments to course aims and objectives. Administer the assessment and evaluate the outcomes.

### *Activity 14.2 Preparing and using a marking scheme*
Once you have designed an assessment that is both valid and reliable, it is necessary to produce a marking scheme that will enable the marker to evaluate the candidate's responses as fairly and accu-

rately as possible. It is even more desirable to prepare a comprehensive marking scheme when the setting is done by one teacher and the marking by others. Use the checklist suggested by Frith and Macintosh when producing your checklist (see Figure 14.6, p. 203).

Administer the test paper and mark half the candidates' papers yourself, and ask a colleague to mark the remaining papers, using your marking scheme.

When you have both finished, exchange papers and check for consistency of marking standards against the marking scheme. Discuss any discrepancies and adjust the marking scheme in the light of suggestions made by colleagues.

### Activity 14.3 Designing a profile

Design a profile that will be suitable for recording the achievement of candidates undertaking one of your training courses. When considering what to include, take into account the information given in the text above and the following key criteria suggested by Garforth and Macintosh:[5]

- What are the main purposes of the profile?
- Who is to be profiled?
- What is to be assessed?
- How is the assessment to be undertaken?
- Who is to be involved in the assessment process?
- How are the results of the assessment to be recorded?

### Activity 14.4 Conducting non-competence-based assessments

Conduct at least two non-competence-based assessments and record how you:

- confirmed your own right to assess candidates or established the licensing arrangements and credentials of other assessors involved
- set assessment tasks or carried out assessments set by an external body
- implemented the assessments
- prepared a rationale for judging candidate performance
- provided feedback to individuals on the assessment decision
- reported on evidence collected from the candidate(s)
- completed the necessary assessment and achievement records
- implemented internal and/or external verification procedures.

### Notes

1 C. Ward, *Designing a Scheme of Assessment*, Stanley Thornes, Cheltenham 1980, p. 91.

2 D.S. Frith and H.G. Mackintosh, *A Teacher's Guide to Assessment*, Stanley Thornes, Cheltenham 1984, p. 84.

3 NATFHE pamphlet, *Assessment*, compiled by members of the ATTI Examinations Panel, O.E. Marston (Convenor), London *c.* 1979, p. 35.

4 D. Garforth and H. Mackintosh, *Profiling: A User's Manual*, Stanley Thornes, Cheltenham 1986, pp. 2–4. This is a valuable source of reference for those wishing to familiarise themselves with a variety of performance profiles.

5 Ibid., pp. 21–30.

# 15

# Assessing candidate performance

TDLB Units D32 and D33 have been designed to meet the needs of those seeking a qualification that will enable them to undertake properly the very responsible role of assessing candidates working towards NVQs, GNVQs, SVQs and GSVQs. Intending **assessor-candidates** will themselves need to have appropriate vocational qualifications and/or considerable experience of working in the chosen occupational area that they will be assessing in before offering an assessment service. By demonstrating the D32 and D33 units to national standards, assessor-candidates will prove their competency and gain a 'licence' to assess others and judge evidence that candidates present.

Assessment duties involve gathering performance and knowledge evidence which is then judged against national standards in the form of units and elements of competence defined by sets of performance criteria, range statements and specified evidence requirements. The assessment process requires an assessor to discuss the candidate's prior achievements with them and to devise an assessment strategy. An assessment plan for assessing differing sources of evidence to be presented by the candidate concerned can then be negotiated. Once the plan has been agreed, arrangements can be made for collecting and judging the mix of evidence demonstrated or presented by the candidate.

On assessment day the candidate is observed either while undertaking normal workplace activities that will allow them to demonstrate their competency, or while performing a preset task covering the relevant criteria. Questions are then put to the candidate by the assessor who judges responses given. Alternatively, the candidate may choose to present a variety of evidence from prior achievement; current performance, product and knowledge evidence; witness testimonies, records, written assignments and third-party reports. The assessor then makes an assessment decision following a review and feedback session during which the candidate is encouraged to self-assess, ask and answer questions and clarify doubts. The assessment decision is communicated to the candidate and achievement records are completed to meet awarding body and 'in-house' requirements.

## Importance of self-assessment and planning

I was recently engaged by a large organisation employing 2000 health-care professionals to assist with the training of their vocational assessors and a number of APL advisors and internal verifiers. The training officer, Nikki Glendening, decided to undertake the D32, D33, D34 and D36 units herself (constituting City and Guilds Vocational Assessor, Advising on Prior Achievement (APL Advisor) and Internal Verifier Awards), and she has kindly given permission for some of her recollections and file documentation to be reproduced in the *Documents Pack*. Before launching into the evidence-gathering phase, Nikki found it helpful to write an outline **personal action plan** and then carry out an **initial self-assessment** for each of the seven elements constituting D32 and D33. Detailed **assessment plans** were negotiated and agreed with her accredited assessor later. The action plan is reproduced in Figure 15.1 (see *Documents Pack*).

In the past many students have found it quite difficult to get started on the D32/33 units and to maintain progress. With this in mind it might be useful for assessor-candidates to read through Nikki's personal reflections (Figure 15.9 in the *Documents Pack*) of how she set about achieving the two units before going on to discuss the relevant performance criteria in detail.

**Note: There is considerable 'cross-over' of evidence between TDLB units D32 and D33. The following text (pp. 212–22) relates to both units, and in order to avoid repetition, elements and performance criteria (pcs) have been combined where overlap occurs.**

## Agreeing and reviewing a plan for assessing performance

*The opportunities identified are relevant to the elements to be assessed*

Assessors must provide evidence that they can identify and plan for equal access to fair assessment opportunities. In order to meet the relevant D32/D33 unit criteria they will need to agree with candidates (i.e. the persons wishing to be assessed) possible opportunities for collecting evidence that can be identified and evaluated against its relevance to the element(s) to be assessed and its appropriateness to the candidate's needs.

In order to establish a working rapport with candidates, the assessor or the assessor-candidate (i.e. the teacher wishing to gain D32/D33) will need to arrange a first meeting during which key features of the assessment process may be discussed. The elements of competence to be demonstrated will be decided, and appropriate opportunities for collecting the necessary evidence can then be identified. The evidence to be assessed will probably comprise a mix of performance-related activity backed by an evaluation of supplementary evidence presented. Plans agreed should cover the assessment of evidence from at least three different evidence sources.

To qualify for the D32 and D33 units, assessor-candidates will need to gather records of three completed assessment plans including a planned activity covering at least three elements of competence. A starting point would be to agree the elements to be assessed, and then using relevant standards (performance criteria), assessment plans could be negotiated with the candidate(s) concerned.

Sample plans are given in Figures 15.2 and 15.3 (see *Documents Pack*) and these illustrate ways of developing and agreeing plans which are relevant to different types of candidates. It is essential that the needs of candidates with special assessment requirements are considered at the planning stage. As much choice as possible should be given to candidates without causing insurmountable barriers to assessment.

*Best use is made of naturally occurring evidence and related questioning*

**Naturally occurring evidence** is presented when candidates are working normally in their regular employment. It is probably the most important source of evidence that may be assessed since it clearly reflects the candidate's level of attainment based on standards required in a particular work area. Relevant standards (such as NVQs) state the performance expected of the competent person and also detail the knowledge and understanding they must have in order to do their job safely and correctly. Assessment of candidates over a period of time in the workplace demonstrates that they can apply their skills knowledge and understanding in a variety of **real work** situations and to the standards of the qualification sought.

Different methods of collecting evidence may be employed, but **live observation** of the candidate undertaking the agreed work during the assessment session is probably the best means of gathering evidence of competent performance. Other possible sources of evidence of natural performance include video, simulations, examination of processes undertaken or products created by the candidate. The importance of **associated knowledge evidence** must not be overlooked, so that questioning and supplementary evidence of prior achievement and written testimony can also be used to support evidence of **natural performance**.

*Evidence collection is planned to make effective use of time and resources*

Assessment of individual candidates can take several hours to complete, given the time involved in travelling, discussing assessment plans, observing candidates performing tasks, reviewing, questioning, giving feedback and recording achievement. However, there is a need for assessors to gather evidence cost-effectively and efficiently and to find ways and means of conducting valid assessments in the least possible time.

It may for example be possible to assess **groups** of candidates or individuals on **several units** during a single visit; or to gather sufficient knowledge evidence by using assignments, computer-based testing or supervised written tests including multiple choice. Third-party evidence should be considered, especially validated reports and authenticated signed witness testimony provided by supervisors, peers and other responsible people.

*Opportunities are selected to minimise disruption to normal activity*

As previously suggested, natural performance in the workplace will tend to reduce the need to make special assessment arrangements. But in any event, preplanning and prior agreement are essential prerequisites to minimising potential disruption to normal work routines. Negotiations should include prior consultation with individuals involved directly in the assessment process and with other people who may be working nearby.

The assessor should keep a low profile while observing the candidate, and the feedback and review should if possible take place in a quiet area where disturbance can be minimised. If an office is used it may be possible to redirect telephone calls and place a 'please do not disturb' sign on the door while the review is taking place.

*Opportunities are selected which provide access to fair and reliable assessment*

Whenever possible, assessment opportunities should be matched to the candidate's needs, and this is equally applicable to the able bodied and to those with impairments or any other special requirements. Assessment requirements are **specific to the individual**, and assessors must recognise the rights of adults as individuals, not as categories of people with disabilities or special needs. **Special assessment requirements** may, for example, arise as a result of physical or sensory disabilities, learning difficulties or emotional and behavioural difficulties.

Candidates with special requirements may have significant difficulties in mobility or communication that prevent them from participating in the regular assessment provision within a college or commercial environment without additional help. In such instances assessors will need to support the candidate by helping to provide access to a fair assessment opportunity, possibly by enlisting the aid of specialist staffing or in some cases by arranging for the use of special equipment in the assessment environment.

The philosophy of equal opportunities requires assessors to eliminate unfair discrimination in their dealings with candidates, and if they are not aware of the implications they should find out who to approach for advice. The City and Guilds policy statement *Access to assessment – candidates with special needs* is given in Figure 15.4 (see *Documents Pack*).

*When simulations are proposed, accurate information and advice is sought about their validity and administration*

Preset simulation of workplace activity may occur where it would be insensitive or impractical to observe a candidate while they were actually carrying out such an activity in a workplace, college, training programme or laboratory.

When considering why and when simulations might be used Nikki Glendening gives examples in a health care context. Nikki suggests a counselling session between a care worker and a distressed client where it would be inappropriate for an assessor to be present as a third party. Similarly, emergency situations such as cardiac arrest or care of a candidate during seizure would be examples of when it would be advisable for assessors to stand back and not become involved, choosing to assess by simulation or otherwise. The acceptability of using a simulation can be established when, for whatever reason, the activity would be uncomfortable or unsafe for the candidate involved in the assessment, since their interests must always remain paramount.

Simulations might otherwise be justified on the grounds of **cost-effectiveness**, size and lack of **local availability** of actual equipment, **scarcity** of resources needed, or attendant but unconnected **safety** considerations.

In general, the internal verifier in consultation with workplace supervisors and awarding body representatives could probably confirm the **acceptability of simulation** as the source of evidence to be judged against criteria. Simulations and tests should be conducted under controlled conditions and records kept of procedures and outcomes. The administration of simulations is discussed later in the chapter.

*The proposed assessment plan is discussed and agreed with the candidate and others who may be affected*

Involving the candidate in negotiating and agreeing plan content is paramount in amicable and effective assessment planning. Indeed, while it is desirable to assess competence under normal working conditions it would be both undesirable and unreasonable for an assessor to suddenly appear in the workplace intending to assess some aspect of a candidate's performance against a prescribed standard. The importance of reaching agreement with candidates and others concerned in the arrangements and gaining their approval and consent cannot be overemphasised.

Evidence requirements and the availability of facilities and resources can be checked out at the planning stage, and it may be that supervisors, colleagues, candidates, technicians or others will need to be consulted and their support confirmed. The standard plan format shown in Figure 15.3 (see *Documents Pack*) has spaces where notes about others concerned and special assessment requirements may be recorded.

*If there is disagreement with the proposed assessment plan, options open to the candidate are explained clearly and constructively*

All candidates have the right to appeal against the content of a proposed assessment plan. The aim of the assessor should be to ensure that the principles of fairness, equity, reasonableness and honesty are consistently applied when initially writing the plan and particularly when and if disagreement arises. Rights should be explained and assessors should be aware of their duty to deal with questions, requests for clarification and disagreements at the earliest opportunity.

If in doubt, assessors could seek a second opinion or advice from other assessors or internal verifiers. If a satisfactory solution still cannot be found the candidate could choose another assessor willing to adjudicate in the matter. In either case a positive and constructive open approach should be followed, taking care to avoid adopting a defensive stance.

*The assessment plan specifies the target elements of competence, the types of evidence to be collected, the assessment methods, the timing of assessments and the arrangements for reviewing progress against the plan*

The assessment plan should include details of the target unit and elements to be assessed and information regarding the who, what, where, when, why and how of the assessment of the candidate's performance.

The plan should also give information about:

- the assessment location
- the conditions and circumstances that are relevant to the assessment
- the assessment methods to be employed
- other people who will be involved in the assessment or providing facilities
- special assessment requirements that will need to be addressed
- evidence that will be presented.

The plan should be dated and signed by both assessor and candidate, indicating that agreement has been reached regarding arrangements for the assessment. Typical plans are given in Figures 15.2 and 15.3 (see *Documents Pack*).

*Plans are reviewed and updated at agreed times to reflect the candidate's progress within the qualification*

An assessment specification giving details of how the candidate will achieve all the units making up an award is sometimes produced. This might take the form of an **action plan** that could be updated during tutorials or after regularly monitoring a candidate's progress during a training programme or course of study leading to assessment and unit credit. Often candidates will prefer to identify shorter term, readily achievable targets, and having gained the unit credit will move on to their next choice.

The assessor should complete a **schedule for assessment and review** when originating an assessment plan, and this should be updated to take account of a candidate's success or referral.

# Collecting and judging performance evidence against criteria

*Advice and encouragement to collect evidence efficiently is appropriate to the candidate's needs*

The assessor will select suitable efficient methods for collecting evidence specified in the candidate's assessment plans. The plans will be introduced and reviewed, and the methods to be used to gather evidence during the demonstration will be discussed before the assessment proper begins. This is a fair way to proceed as it gives the candidate time to settle down and provides an opportunity to refresh their memory about what they will need to do and what the assessor will be doing while they are performing the work or preset task.

215

When the assessor is dealing with candidates who are experienced in presenting evidence, less preparation time will be needed than when they are assessing those who are inexperienced or lacking confidence. Considerable tact will be required when working with nervous candidates. They will be quick to spot an impatient assessor and will react badly if rushed into making a start before they have gained their composure. Being inexperienced in presenting evidence does not imply incompetence, it merely indicates that candidates are feeling apprehensive about being closely observed and questioned about their work. The assessor should be tactful and take time to encourage unconfident or distraught candidates to play an active role when planning or making the assessment arrangements, and especially during review and feedback sessions following the live performance.

*Access to assessment is appropriate to the candidate's needs*

The concept of special assessment requirements has been discussed earlier in the chapter, and arrangements will have been noted on the assessment plans negotiated with candidates once their needs are known. What must now be done is to ensure that the special requirements sought are actually available on assessment day. This could involve having a communicator/interpreter available to a hearing-impaired candidate, or a translator for newcomers with limited English as a second language; someone to take down dictation; ramps for wheelchairs; large printed materials or braille for the visually impaired; platforms for shorter people needing to access machinery located at a high level; tape recorders to play back recorded assessment information where candidates find it difficult to read instructions; or legitimate support for people who are temporarily incapacitated. Access must be provided to physical and human resources needed for the candidate to carry out the specified assessment task fairly and effectively.

*Only the performance criteria specified for the element of competence are used to judge the evidence*

National standards such as NVQ/SVQs are the standards from which assessment procedures are derived and judgements made. Subsequent recording of achievement and submissions for certification are thereby made possible. The units of competence specify performance criteria, range statements, and knowledge and evidence requirements. These criteria are used by assessors when judging whether or not the candidate can perform the activity specified in the element. Assessors must ensure that all criteria listed in the standards are met, but must avoid introducing their own criteria or house standards when judging candidates against nationally agreed standards.

*When evidence of prior achievement/learning is used, checks are made that the candidate can currently achieve the relevant national standard*

When accrediting prior achievement, assessors must take account of the difficulty in **verifying** and **authenticating** evidence of the competence claimed by candidates. This can arise from differences in work practices and techniques, together with updated or revised underpinning knowledge essential to performing effectively the work for which a credit is sought. Previous course certification alone is not a valid measure of **current performance**, neither is the possession of dated qualifications. Claims of skills exercised in previous employments may need to be confirmed by the employer concerned. The transferability of prior achievement to the performance against criteria being assessed would need to be established. Relevant documentation would also need to be checked for authenticity and correctness.

Assessors will need to judge the **currency** of evidence presented and competency claimed. They will need to challenge evidence of underpinning knowledge and establish the extent of the candidate's knowledge and understanding by asking questions. Skills can be proved by the candidate giving demonstrations with explanations.

*Evidence is judged accurately against all the relevant performance criteria*

Performance criteria usually provide a description of conditions and standards against which competency will be judged. Evidence presented must therefore be relevant to *all* performance criteria and range statements. Competence is then confirmed by candidates' completing all the criteria for success on a 'can do' basis. This limits, to a considerable extent, subjectivity and variation in assessors' opinions and consequent judgements.

General factors that may affect reliability include the form and content of the assessment and the environment in which it takes place. This is one of the reasons why carefully negotiating assessment plans with candidates beforehand is so important.

*Requirements to assure the authenticity, reliability and sufficiency of evidence are identified. The evidence is valid and can be attributed to the candidate*

Evidence presented must be attributable to the candidate concerned, and assessors will need to demonstrate ways of checking for the **validity**, **authenticity** and **sufficiency** of evidence presented. Live demonstrations by candidates known to the assessor will ensure that the performance evidence is valid, but particular attention should also be paid to **product evidence** (material things) and also to **written evidence** such as testimonials, assignments and claims of prior achievement.

Authenticity can be confirmed by using questioning and answering techniques with the candidate and also by consulting third parties with regard to testimonials and written reports. Fundamental questions that assessors should ask themselves are:

- Is the evidence offered definitely the work of the candidate?
- Does the indirect evidence supplied support the candidate's claim of competency?
- Is there sufficient evidence to make a judgement? If not, what else do I need to see?
- How can I gather the required additional evidence?

It is of the utmost importance to ensure that candidates will be able to perform competently in their occupational roles, anywhere, to standards specified in award documentation. Assessments must be **reliable**. The extent to which an assessment of competence is consistently **dependable** and reliable when carried out by different assessors, by a single assessor with different candidates, or at different times of day and in different places, is a measure of the reliability of the assessment.

The reliability of judgements will depend upon the professionalism of the assessors making the decisions and on the effectiveness of the assessment process adopted when they are collecting assessment evidence and evaluating achievement.

*Any preset simulations and tests are administered correctly*

Preset **oral** and **written tests** are useful when knowledge evidence is being gathered, especially when groups of candidates are being assessed on the same unit. Oral and written questions should be clear and unambiguous.

**Practical work** designed to test psychomotor skills includes skills testing, trade tests and tests of hand/eye coordination which can be employed when specific abilities are tested. Test results can be helpful to assessors when judging how well a person can perform a given task.

**Simulations** and practical work used for assessment purposes could include **physical** laboratory work or **language** laboratory activity, audio and visual tasks, workshop exercises, surveying and site investigation, model making and physical education activities.

When writing simulations it is useful for the assessor to provide the candidate with relevant performance criteria and a brief rationale justifying the task, followed by clear candidate instructions, performance and outcomes checklists, and achievement record. **Feedback notes** or a 'comments' box should be completed during the review following the simulation demonstration. Examples of an assessment checklist and feedback notes are given in Figures 15.5 and 15.6 (see *Documents Pack*).

*The assessor is as unobtrusive as is practicable whilst observing the candidate*

Any work-based assessment should reflect as nearly as possible the normal workplace activity and environment. It is therefore important that the assessor does not put the candidate off, cause them distress, heighten their anxiety or upset them in any way before or during the assessment. Assessors should not overtly or covertly adopt the role of an 'inspector'. They should maintain a low profile during the observation phase and resist a tendency to 'hover', but nevertheless they must see everything. This means that assessors will need to move around and sometimes move in closer in order to maintain a clear view of the process and all candidate activity. This is acceptable provided that assessors have first clearly explained the observation procedure and assured the candidate that nothing is 'secret' and that everything recorded will be shared with them during the following review.

*Evidence is judged fairly and reliably*

Ensuring that all assessment decisions are based on the standards agreed is of the utmost importance. Moreover, an awareness and understanding of the possible pitfalls in assessment is advantageous. Assessors who believe that they are unable to fulfil their assessment role fairly or competently should withdraw and arrange for another assessor to undertake the assessment, subject to the agreement of the candidate. Assessors must not allow personal feelings and subjectivity to interfere with their work. The use of internally verified procedures and plans, written task instructions, assessment checklists and assessment questions will help to avoid bias being introduced into the assessment process.

A **positive bias** can be exemplified by the **'halo effect'** influencing assessors and their judgement decisions. In other words, if the candidate creates a good **initial impression** they will 'pass'. If the assessor makes an assumption that one piece of evidence is excellent then all the candidate's evidence will be judged equally good. Similarly, there may be a tendency to evaluate too highly on the basis of the candidate's **personal traits,** or the evidence may be judged favourably because the assessor perceives a strong similarity between the candidate and themselves. It is of paramount importance in minimising these effects that evidence should always be judged objectively against the relevant standards.

A **negative bias** can be illustrated by **stereotyping** where judgements made about a candidate's work are based upon an image or conception held by the assessor of the person concerned, rather than on the evidence presented. Furthermore, assessors may impose unrealistic and unfair expectations if the evidence presented is contrary to what they expect.

*Difficulties in judging evidence fairly and reliably are referred promptly to an appropriate authority*

Assessors should not rush into making an unsound decision when they experience difficulty in reliably judging evidence presented by a candidate. The assessment should continue, and all other evidence should be evaluated and judged against the standards. But the assessment decision will probably need to be postponed until the difficulty can be resolved.

The problem must be dealt with as soon as possible and the candidate must be kept fully informed of the action being taken to resolve the difficulty. People who may able to offer advice or clarification would be other assessors, the internal verifier, the training standards group manager, an external verifier or awarding body liaison person.

*The candidate is given clear and constructive feedback and advice following the judgement*

The process of giving constructive feedback and advice is considered in Chapter 11.

# Collecting and judging knowledge evidence

*Knowledge relevant to the element is identified accurately from the performance evidence*

Knowledge evidence requirements may be given in awarding body candidate packs or information packs held by the centres at which candidates are registered. Awarding body listings of knowledge evidence requirements will often be found in their candidate packs. Other sources include diaries, log books, assessment specifications and record of achievement booklets. The award standards are used to generate performance evidence checklists and assessor-devised checklisted questions for use when assessing candidate performance and collecting knowledge evidence.

*Evidence of knowledge is collected when performance evidence does not cover fully the specified range or contingencies*

Performance evidence alone may not be sufficient to enable assessors to make reliable judgements. They may also collect supporting knowledge evidence by examining items produced during the assessment and asking questions about the process operated or conditions under which the products were made. In service occupations the way candidates manage processes and procedures or handle clients' requirements will be an important aspect of their role and hence be subject to oral questioning by the assessor. Oral questioning will serve to fill in any gaps in knowledge evidence that cannot be confirmed by observing the candidate actually performing the assessment task.

*Valid methods are used to collect knowledge evidence*

Oral and written testing are valid methods of collecting knowledge evidence that will serve to check understanding. Questions may also be asked to clarify any doubts in the assessor's mind and hence support decisions made regarding a candidate's claim of competence.

Checklisted assessor-devised questions should be prepared in advance. The checklists should be matched to element criteria and checked for relevance and suitability. The level and scope of questions available should cover the range.

Written questions can be used to assess underpinning knowledge. Some candidates prefer this method because they are able to pace themselves when writing their answers and can go back to questions that they feel have not been fully answered. The multiple-choice test format may be preferred by people with limited writing skills, but authenticity must be assured by suitable confirmation questioning regardless of the method used to collect written evidence.

*When questions are used, they are clear and do not lead candidates*

Questions must be unambiguous. Short, snappy questions are more easily understood by candidates than lengthy ones covering several aspects. Questions covering only a single chunk of knowledge are therefore preferred. Language should be easily understood. If the candidate's expression signals confusion or concern, questions may be repeated or rephrased to relieve anxiety. However, assessors should avoid **leading** candidates step by step to the required answer. Positive or negative bias should be avoided.

*Access to assessment is appropriate to the candidate's needs*

Awarding bodies have clear and unambiguous policies regarding candidate rights to fair and suitable assessment opportunities. Assessors are required to follow the guidelines laid down, and candidate requirements and any special needs should be identified at the planning stage. Extra time may be needed to take account of an impairment or temporary incapacitation that would slow down the candidate. Tape recorders/transcripts, interpreters, mechanical and electronic aids, modified question papers, Braille keyboards and any other requisites will need to be arranged.

Effective assessment planning should ensure that appropriate provision is made, but contingencies may arise whereby the candidate could be disadvantaged, rendering it necessary to renegotiate facilities or reschedule the assessment. Candidates should not be made to go ahead regardless, as this may result in an unfair assessment opportunity, failure to achieve the criteria concerned and resultant loss of esteem and demotivation.

*The knowledge evidence conforms with the content of the knowledge specification and is judged accurately against all the relevant performance criteria*

The assessor should maintain a record of **oral** or **written questions** used to assess candidates' underpinning knowledge as defined in the knowledge evidence specification given in award standards. Preset question checklists are used by assessors during reviews and feedback sessions following live performance or examination of written work or third-party evidence. Candidates are normally asked to sign the listing of their responses to questions asked and to confirm agreement with the data recorded by the assessor. Frequent checks of the validity and reliability of questions used when assessing knowledge should be carried out by the assessor. The internal verifier should also monitor the process and examine question checklists in order to confirm the currency and sufficiency of questions asked and answered against the most recent award standards.

*Evidence is judged fairly and reliably*

Evidence collected and judged must cover the **contingencies** and **range** of performance or knowledge evidence specified in unit criteria. This is where 'What if . . . ?' type questions can be employed when performance evidence cannot reasonably be provided. Answers to questions are checked against 'model' answers prepared by the assessor in consultation with other assessors and subject specialists. Assessors must not go beyond the unit knowledge evidence requirements when questioning candidates. The standards define that knowledge evidence which 'must be demonstrated in order to perform competently' to the national standards. Any attempt by assessors to introduce the concept of 'excellence' or extend the range of questioning for **assessment purposes** by arbitrarily inventing additional knowledge requirements should be discouraged.

# Making assessment decisions using differing sources of evidence and providing feedback

*The decision is based on all the relevant performance, knowledge and other evidence available*

A candidate can only be judged as competent when the assessor is sure that *all* the performance criteria have been demonstrated to the required standard and that range statements and evidence requirements of a particular element or unit have been satisfied.

*When the combined evidence is sufficient to cover the range, the performance criteria and the evidence specification, the candidate is informed of their achievement*

Having reached an assessment decision after considering all the relevant evidence available the assessor will be able to tell the successful candidate that they have fulfilled all the unit criteria and will be credited with the unit concerned. Both candidate and assessor should sign the record of achievement and any other relevant assessment documentation. This confirms their agreement with decisions taken.

*When evidence is not to the national standard, or is insufficient, the candidate is given a clear explanation and appropriate advice*

Usually candidates will know whether or not they have performed to standard, and it will not normally be necessary to spell out where they have gone wrong. When a candidate fails to achieve all the specified criteria they must be given an opportunity to self-assess and comment on their performance before the assessor tells them objectively and descriptively precisely which criteria have not been met. Encouraging the candidate to have their say first will promote an honest response, and they will feel happier about a referral than they would if told that they have 'failed' or 'not met all the criteria'. Candidates are often more critical of their performance than the assessor concerned. They will usually respond positively to sympathetic but honest comment from the assessor provided that their self-esteem and self-image are preserved.

Candidates needing help should be offered advice on how they might accomplish the necessary top-up training and be given an opportunity to find a way forward. Records of advice offered and decisions taken during the assessment review should be signed by the assessor and candidate and stored securely. The candidate should be given a copy to take away.

*Feedback following the decision is clear, constructive, meets the candidate's needs and is appropriate to their level of confidence*

Assessors can make feedback constructive by adopting a clear, honest and positive approach. Feedback must be based only on what has been observed and examined and must be descriptive and objective. By starting and finishing with positive aspects the assessor can help the candidate to value their existing competence and to perceive areas where they are not yet competent as potential opportunities for new learning and personal development.

Feedback should be adjusted to meet candidates' differing levels of confidence and experience. Giving constructive feedback is discussed at some length in Chapter 11.

*The candidate is encouraged to seek clarification and advice. Any inconsistencies in evidence are clarified and resolved*

Inconsistencies in evidence must be clarified and resolved during the review and feedback session following a live performance or examination of APL or written evidence. The assessor will, however, meet with different types of candidates, some experienced and some inexperienced in presenting evidence, and will need to learn how to cope with them during reviews and feedback sessions.

There will be the **friendly types** who smile and nod in agreement with everything that is said. They may not be prepared to offer any comment and will not seek clarification at the time, but they may go away and complain to their friends about the assessor's domination of the session. If such candidates do not offer any comment they should be coaxed into describing what they did well or where they felt they could have done better.

**Talkative** candidates are often poor listeners. They can take over completely given half a chance, and the focus of the review can be quickly lost. They interrupt while the assessor is commenting on some aspect of the demonstration that is of particular importance, and miss the point being made. Assessors will need to redirect the candidate's attention towards making focused statements or listening to constructive comment.

The **silent** or **shy** candidate says very little but may listen carefully to all that the assessor says. Without confirmation of understanding or agreement from such candidates the assessor can quickly become frustrated. To break the silence open-ended questions must be asked in order to draw out some kind of response.

**Stubborn** candidates will stick to their opinions regardless of the circumstances. Nothing will make them change their minds. If they think they have met all the criteria they will switch off. Any form of rational discussion will fall on deaf ears. All that the assessor can do is to leave them with written comments to think about later.

Some candidates are extremely **busy** and can hardly spare the time to demonstrate the evidence let alone participate in the subsequent review. In such instances, in order to reduce interruptions it may be desirable to give the feedback somewhere other than their office or work station, away from people and telephones.

All candidates should be encouraged to self-assess, clarify doubts and ask pertinent questions.

*Evidence and assessment decisions are recorded to meet verification requirements*

The ability to maintain clear, accurate, legible and concise records is an essential aspect of the assessor role. Awarding body records and individual achievement records should be updated after each assessment decision has been communicated to the candidate. Individual and group achievement records are maintained by the assessor to support the verification process and are used to build up a picture of the candidate's progress towards their target award.

*Records are legible and accurate, are stored securely and are passed on to the next stage of the recording/certification process promptly*

Individual records, group records, registration documents and applications for certification such as the City and Guilds Form 'M' should be stored securely, and the confidentiality of candidates' personal details and achievements maintained. Achievement records should be updated frequently and information passed on to the responsible person according to award body or 'in-house' standards. Records must be stored securely and information should be made available on a 'need to know' basis only.

## Self-assessment questions

### Agreeing and reviewing a plan for assessing performance
1 What types of evidence could be used for assessment purposes?

2 What is meant by a realistic work environment?

3 Explain how naturally occurring evidence could be collected.

4 Why is it both preferable and important to assess candidates while they are performing their normal work role?

5 What steps should you take to minimise disruption to normal work routine when planning assessments?

6 What other settings or contexts are acceptable and under what circumstances would these be adopted?

7 How would you set about collecting performance evidence?

8 Give examples of supplementary evidence that you might also need to collect.

9 Why is it important to collect evidence of underpinning knowledge?

10 Why is it important to negotiate and agree assessment plans with candidates?

11 What other people might be involved at the assessment planning stage?

12 Specify the minimum number of elements to be assessed at one time.

13 What is meant by performing across the range?

14 What would you do if the candidate presented evidence that was not on your 'list' of acceptable evidence?

15 If you needed to assess a simulation, how would your plan differ from that of a 'natural performance' assessment plan?

16 How would you ensure access to fair and reasonable assessment?

17 In what circumstances and for whom might you need to make special assessment arrangements?

18 What important and relevant legislation protects people from unfair discrimination?

19 What options are available to candidates if there is disagreement when negotiating assessment plans?

20 When planning assessments how could you minimise the costs of the assessment process but still carry out a valid and reliable assessment?

## Collecting and judging performance evidence against criteria

21 When you are collecting and judging performance evidence against NVQ or other criteria why is it important to consult the assessment plan?

22 What is the point of using an 'assessment checklist' when you are collecting evidence?

23 How can you be sure that the candidate's performance activity meets all the performance criteria (pcs) being assessed?

24 Why is it important that the candidate takes responsibility for identifying and presenting relevant evidence?

25 How could you encourage candidates to collect their own evidence?

26 How would you gather performance and product evidence during a simulation?

27 Why is it important to remain unobtrusive (keep a low profile) when you are observing a candidate in action?

28 Explain how you would maintain a low profile and yet maintain adequate observation at all times.

29 What type of evidence would you expect to collect while the candidate is performing in the workplace?

30 Under what circumstances would you use preset tests or simulations when collecting evidence?

31 What important conditions must prevail when you are administering tests and simulations?

32  Why must standards be referred to when you are assessing a candidate's performance?

33  If there were difficulties in interpreting the pcs/standards to whom would you turn for advice?

34  If you were assessing product evidence only, how could you ensure that it was the candidate's own work?

35  Why should the candidate be allowed to complete the assessment task unaided?

### Collecting and judging knowledge evidence

36  Explain the importance of checking knowledge evidence during the assessment process. Why is it important to ask questions concerning underpinning knowledge?

37  What are the available sources of knowledge evidence?

38  Describe the range of questioning techniques that could properly be used by teachers when gathering evidence and give an example of circumstances where each would be used. Why would you use the methods described?

39  Specify any other types of questions and tests that you would need to use as a qualified vocational assessor.

40  Describe the type of preset questions and tests you would use for assessment purposes.

41  Where could you obtain other sets of preset tests if needed when assessing candidates?

42  List the assessment instruments you have in your bank.

43  In what circumstances would you need to construct your own assessment questions?

44  What is meant by the term 'validity' ?

45  When constructing tests how can you ensure that the questions are valid?

46  Why is it important to restrict the scope of questions asked to the unit that you are assessing?

47  What is meant by 'leading candidates' when asking questions?

48  Why must the adequacy of candidate answers be judged? How is 'judging' effectively carried out?

49  Why is it important to involve the candidates sufficiently in their own assessment?

50  What action would you take when certain pcs have not been met?

51  Why is it important to give feedback as soon as possible?

52  How are consistency and reliability maintained when different candidates are assessed?

53  How, where and when must candidate achievement be recorded?

54  Describe how your assessment provision allows access that matches individual candidates' needs and requirements.

### Making assessment decisions and providing feedback

55  Describe how the assessment specification ensures that the evidence selected will match the stated pcs.

56  What factors should be considered when you are choosing a location to share feedback with the candidate?

57  Why is it essential to reduce or preferably eliminate disruption in the workplace when you are carrying out an assessment and giving feedback?

58  What features of a normal work environment could adversely affect a candidate's performance?

59  How can you be sure that you use only the specified pcs when making your assessment?

60  What positive or negative biases to candidates might you experience?

61  How can you be sure that the candidate clearly understands which pcs have been met?

62  What action would you take when certain pcs have not been met?

63  Why is it important to give feedback as soon as possible after the assessment?

64  Why is it essential to give constructive feedback?

65  Why should you encourage candidates to ask questions about their assessment?

66  How might your approach change when dealing with candidates who were either very confident, or lacked confidence, or had special assessment requirements?

67  What benefits derive from keeping records of achievement/assessments?

68  Why is it important to complete records at the time of assessment?

69  How are your records transferred between different parts of the recording system?

70  How and where are the records stored?

71  Describe what is meant by the term 'verification'.

72  What is the procedure for obtaining counter-signatures?

73  What can be done to ensure that candidates will understand what they need to do in order to meet the required standard of any pcs that have not been met?

74  How can anxiety be reduced when candidates present themselves for assessment?

75  What is meant by the concept 'quality assurance in assessment'?

## Preparing for assessment: sample activities

### Activity 15.1 Building a portfolio of evidence for D32 and D33

Gather a full set of evidence needed for your D32 and D33 portfolio. Sample evidence that could be presented in your D32/D33 portfolio is presented in the *Documents Pack*. It is assumed that you already have the D32 and D33 standards. The examples of assessment documentation relating to the NVQ2 in Care Award have been provided by Nikki Glendening. A contents list is given followed by self-assessments and typical evidence required for the seven elements. Other relevant documents shown include a standard 'personal action plan', a 'witness status list', and a set of 'assessment check-lists' and 'summary of evidence sheets' completed by an accredited assessor.

As can be seen, apart from the need to write several assessment plans covering differing sources of evidence, and to assess the relevant evidence that candidates present, much of the D32/D33 evidence is common to both units.

When assembling your portfolio it would be helpful to include:

● your curriculum vitae
● a brief description of your 'occupational role and assessor duties' (see Figure 15.7 in the *Documents Pack*)
● a 'matrix' showing how your evidence file is cross-referenced to each of the D32 and D33 unit performance criteria (see sample 'evidence list', Figure 15.8 in the *Documents Pack*)

- 'initial self-assessment sheets' for each element and list of evidence thought to be needed
- 'summary of performance and supplementary evidence' sheets listing evidence presented for each element
- a diary or 'storyboard' recording how you went about gathering evidence and demonstrating your competency for the two units (see 'Personal Reflections', Figure 15.9 in the *Documents Pack*).

## Activity 15.2 Preparing written evidence of underpinning knowledge for D32 and D33

Richard L.K. Kosior is a highly motivated and experienced aircraft engineering supervisor with a proven track record in training and instructional presentations. He is responsible for conducting quality assurance checks of the maintenance and repair work of aeronautical engineers and is therefore committed to conducting the necessary assessments of competency of his colleagues to ensure that their performance on the job and the maintenance of aircraft is kept to a very high standard.

Richard decided to register for the D32 and D33 units and immediately set about getting to grips with the TDLB terminology. He felt that he needed to gain an overview of the C&G 7281/22 Vocational Assessor Award processes and criteria specified. Much of his current assessment practice was seen to be immediately transferable to assessing for NVQ/SVQs but he wished to gain a sound understanding of the required knowledge evidence. With this in mind he self-studied material[1] and questions provided by me and submitted the following provisional draft for review and comment.

Check out and where necessary correct Richard's responses to the questions listed, and supplement his answers where appropriate. In doing so you will gain considerable insight into the knowledge evidence required for Units D32 and D33.

### Questions and answers relating to underpinning knowledge for D32 and D33

draft answers provided by:
**Richard Laurence Kazimierz Kosior**
**Weymouth, Dorset, 1996**

*Questions and answers relating to underpinning knowledge for D32*

1. *WHAT TYPES OF EVIDENCE WOULD YOU LOOK FOR WHEN ASSESSING YOUR OWN VOCATIONAL AREA?*

   a. Observe candidate carrying out a task and give assessment.
   b. Give candidate oral questions from bank to assess knowledge, competence.
   c. Obtain from archive records written evidence of prior achievements and completion of tasks.
   d. Question candidate's supervisor/training chief.

2. *WHAT ARE THE MAIN FEATURES OF NVQs?*

   a. They recognise that people can be accredited for what they can do in the work place and recognise the skills they have learnt through their working lives.
   b. They are open ended, no formal studying required, no specified homework to do or final written examinations to take.
   c. They bring together all various certificates that may not be readily recognised under one umbrella that can be recognised.
   d. They are proof of demonstrated competence.

3. *HOW CAN VALIDITY BE ESTABLISHED?*

Validity of evidence can be established by observing, asking questions, checking written evidence, confirming evidence from previous employers. Assessment must meet NVQ unit standards and be based on the specified performance criteria and range statements. Objective assessment made. Subjectivity eliminated as far as possible.

*Good example.* Candidate giving demonstrations, observe candidate during normal work routines, by asking check questions. (*Seeing is believing.*)

Claims of expertise or skills from previous employment may need to be confirmed by the employer concerned; relevant documentation would have to be authenticated.

4. *HOW CAN RELIABILITY OF ASSESSORS BE ACHIEVED?*

Carry out quality assurance checks and employ assessments that will limit variance in quality accreditation. By the assessor working to set performance criteria that provide a description of conditions and standards against which competence can be judged and confirmed by completing all the criteria. Liaising with the internal verifier.

5. *HOW CAN THE CANDIDATE BE INCLUDED IN THE PLANNING PROCESS?*

On meeting, the candidate should be encouraged to put forward ideas of how best to demonstrate achievement, discuss and agree the plan, venue, time and what is required. Discuss the unit to be assessed, carry out a self-analysis to find out where they are and where they want to be.

6. *WHAT FEATURES WOULD YOU EXPECT TO SEE IN AN ASSESSMENT PLAN?*

Details of elements to be assessed, target date, context for assessment, evidence to be presented and action agreed.

7. *HOW CAN DISRUPTION AT WORK BE MINIMISED?*

Whenever feasible, having due regard for safety and cost, the basis of assessment should be performance in the work place and at a time mutually agreed, when it is not too busy as to provide distractions.

8. *WHO WOULD YOU GO TO FOR ADVICE IF THERE ARE ANY PROBLEMS IN THE PLANNING PROCESS?*

The candidate, line manager or internal verifier.

9. *WHAT POSITIVE AND NEGATIVE BIASES COULD ASSESSORS FACE?*

*Positive bias.* If candidate is perceived as being a similar person to assessor. Halo effect.

*Negative bias.* If candidate is a dissimilar person to assessor. Racism. Stereotyping. Gender.

10. *HOW CAN ASSESSOR BIASES BE AVOIDED?*

Only carry out the assessment against the laid down performance criteria for the unit involved. Do not home in on aspects of performance that only you are interested in. Avoid any kind of discrimination.

11. *HOW CAN AUTHENTICITY OF EVIDENCE BE ESTABLISHED?*

By asking questions, requesting further evidence or demonstrations to confirm competence. Seek confirmation from a third party.

12. *WHEN MIGHT A PRE-SET TEST BE USED?*

Prior to commencement of training course. To determine candidate level of knowledge, and as part of supplementary evidence presented by a candidate to support actual demonstration of competency or work-based performance.

13. *WHEN MIGHT A SIMULATION BE CONSIDERED?*

When the task to be carried out and assessed happens rarely or if it is too expensive or time consuming to use a live piece of equipment.

14. *HOW WOULD YOU ADMINISTER A PRE-SET TEST AND A SIMULATION?*

Carry out assessment of performance criteria that cannot be completed, ask questions on the elements that cannot be carried out and if possible carry out task on a training piece of equipment. A pre-set test may be carried out if none of the aforementioned can be completed to assess knowledge.

15. *WHY SHOULD THE ASSESSOR BE AS UNOBTRUSIVE AS POSSIBLE WHEN OBSERVING CANDIDATES IN THE WORKPLACE?*

So as not to interfere with the candidate and appear to be sitting on his/her shoulder – this may increase any nerves the candidate may already have. *You may get in the way.*

16. *WHAT TYPES OF QUESTIONS ARE MOST APPROPRIATE FOR COLLECTING EVIDENCE OF UNDERPINNING KNOWLEDGE?*

*Open.* A number of different answers available – What do you think? What if? Why? How does? When should?

*Closed.* Only one acceptable answer.

*Leading.* This attempts to get the candidate to answer the question as you wanted it answered – I think . . .

*Hypothetical.* This is a means of getting the candidates to expand on their knowledge and use their reasoning – What if?

The type of questioning most appropriate for collecting evidence of underpinning knowledge is the *open* and *hypothetical.*

17. *IN WHAT SITUATIONS CAN ORAL QUESTIONS BE CONSIDERED?*

a. When unable to observe actual performance of the candidate.
b. To confirm underpinning knowledge of subject.
c. To strengthen knowledge.
d. To gather supplementary evidence.

18. *IN WHAT SITUATIONS CAN WRITTEN QUESTIONS BE CONSIDERED?*

    a. During an assessment session where a large number of candidates are to be assessed at any one time.
    b. To improve cost-effectiveness of assessment.
    c. Where a candidate is asking for prior achievement to be recognised.
    d. During an assessment session to find out if the candidate has sufficient knowledge of the task to be demonstrated.
    e. To determine the level of understanding of the subject.
    f. To determine if the training methods need to be modified.

19. *WHAT ARRANGEMENTS SHOULD BE MADE FOR CANDIDATES WITH SPECIAL NEEDS?*

    Every effort should be made to ensure that the special needs of candidates are met.

    a. *Hearing impairments.* Use an interpreter/communicator, give extra time allowance and mechanical/electronic aids. If linguistic problems present, use question papers with modified wording as recommended by a specialist teacher of hearing-impaired candidates.
    b. *Visual impairment.* A reader, tapes, question papers with large print, Braille, extra time and mechanical/electronic aids.
    c. *Learning difficulties.* Extra time, tapes or readers should be made available.
    d. *Physical impairment.* As above, including special lifting equipment as required.

20. *WHEN CAN A CANDIDATE BE JUDGED TO BE COMPETENT?*

    When the candidate can carry out work, demonstrate knowledge, skills and understanding to set standards required and demanded by employers and customers in real work conditions.

21. *HOW SHOULD FEEDBACK BE MADE CONSTRUCTIVE?*

    Use objective and descriptive feedback relating to what you as the assessor saw. If feedback needs to be negative it should be shown to be capable of being converted into a positive – turn a weakness into a strength. Start by recounting good points of performance, give feedback to identify where further action is needed to meet required standards.

22. *HOW WOULD YOU DEAL WITH A CANDIDATE LACKING IN CONFIDENCE?*

    Encourage and explain clearly what is about to happen and why; carry out assessment in candidate's normal place of work under normal conditions. Ask open questions, be informal, give positive feedback.

23. *WHAT IS IMPORTANT ABOUT ASSESSMENT RECORDS?*

    a. *Formative.* This is ongoing assessment building up over time and can be used to provide information for training providers to overcome any problems.
    b. *Summative.* They can be used during the final assessment of competence and determining overall performance. They must be clear, accurate, legible and concise. They may be passed on to the internal verifier on request.

*Questions and answers relating to underpinning knowledge for D33*

1. *WHAT DOES VALIDITY MEAN WHEN IT IS RELATED TO EVIDENCE?*

   It means that it is current and only relates to that candidate. The evidence is authentic and it actually relates to the competence claimed, i.e: it relates to the pcs.

2. *WHAT POSSIBLE SOURCES OF EVIDENCE CAN BE IDENTIFIED?*

   Reviewing portfolios, oral question and answer sessions, projects and assignments, demonstrations in the workplace under natural conditions, skill tests, simulations, records of prior achievement, guided discussion, open-ended written answers given in short or long essay form, and reports from supervisors.

3. *HOW CAN TIME AND RESOURCES BE USED COST-EFFECTIVELY IN ASSESS-MENT?*

   Plan and carry out the assessment in the normal place of work at a practicable time. Ensure all concerned in the assessment are informed prior to its taking place of exactly what is going to happen. Make use of simulations or use only the resources necessary to carry out the assessment. Assess only what needs to be assessed. Arrange to assess larger groups by using paper-based knowledge tests to check some underpinning knowledge. However, this would need to be authenticated by checks. Performance would have to be observed.

4. *HOW CAN FAIR AND RELIABLE ASSESSMENT BE ENSURED?*

   The assessment should be approached systematically, a uniform standard maintained. Assessment should be made against performance criteria only and any bias must be avoided. Internal verifiers can confirm if set standards are being met or not. Fair access should be provided for people with special assessment requirements.

5. *HOW CAN CANDIDATES BE INVOLVED IN ASSESSMENT PLANNING?*

   By negotiating with and briefing the candidate on what is to be assessed, when, how and where. A mutually acceptable assessment plan must be agreed.

6. *HOW CAN CANDIDATES BE ENCOURAGED TO PROVIDE QUALITY AND NOT QUANTITY OF EVIDENCE?*

   The candidate should be informed that the evidence required to be produced should be current, relevant, authentic, accurate and concise. By suggesting the candidate makes an initial self-assessment of evidence to be gathered and discussing what is required of them. Sufficient evidence to meet evidence requirements must be provided by candidates but tendency to oversufficiency and inclusion of irrelevant material should be discouraged.

7. *HOW CAN RELEVANCE OF EVIDENCE BE ENSURED?*

   By ensuring it only relates to the performance criteria that are being assessed in all aspects.

8. *WHAT SHOULD CANDIDATES BE JUDGED AGAINST?*

The assessment specification, i.e: the laid down NVQ/SVQ performance criteria, evidence requirements and range statements.

9. *HOW CAN ASSESSOR BIAS BE AVOIDED?*

Avoid any form of discrimination; assess only what is required as laid down in the performance criteria. Assess objectively and avoid making irrelevant judgements.

10. *HOW CAN AUTHENTICITY OF EVIDENCE BE ESTABLISHED?*

By asking in-depth questions, checking records or requesting a direct demonstration of competence claimed. Obtaining confirmation by third parties.

11. *HOW CAN CANDIDATES BE ENCOURAGED TO USE EVIDENCE FROM PRIOR ACHIEVEMENT?*

Brief candidates carefully about the possibility of using valuable experience gained earlier. Explain the need to support claims with valid evidence. Explain to them this will enable them to obtain credit for competences they already have.

12. *HOW CAN CURRENCY OF EVIDENCE BE ESTABLISHED?*

Review candidate's portfolio of evidence to ensure it is valid, reliable and current. Ask questions and seek confirmation from sources of evidence. Candidates can be questioned or asked to demonstrate competence claimed and to ensure that they are up to date with techniques and knowledge.

13. *HOW CAN INCONSISTENCIES OF EVIDENCE BE RESOLVED?*

Consult the internal verifier. Request further evidence of achievement.

14. *WHEN CAN COMPETENCE BE AGREED ON?*

When the person has satisfied all the laid down performance criteria and is able to perform competently in all contexts in which they can reasonably be expected to work.

15. *HOW CAN FEEDBACK BE MADE CONSTRUCTIVE?*

Start with the good points observed, give positive aspects of candidate's performance, make specific points and avoid generalising. Be objective, give praise where it is due. Use descriptive feedback techniques and relate to instances that you have observed or products that you have examined.

16. *HOW SHOULD YOU GIVE FEEDBACK TO A CANDIDATE LACKING IN CONFIDENCE?*

Highlight the good points and strengths observed; let them know that they did something competently. If criticism needs to be given turn the negative into a positive and explain how things could be improved. Get the candidate also to give their views.

17. *HOW CAN TWO-WAY COMMUNICATION BE ESTABLISHED WHEN GIVING FEEDBACK?*

By asking the candidates what they thought were the good points, how things could have been done differently, was there anything they did that could possibly be improved. Let the candidate know of anything that can be done to help them achieve the level of competency required. Above all listen to what they have to say. By the use of open-ended questions candidates can be encouraged to say more.

18. *WHAT ASSESSMENT RECORDS ARE NECESSARY?*

Units achieved, dates achieved, units to be assessed and when, formative assessments, assessment check lists, individual record of achievement, group records of achievement.

19. *WHAT CAN YOU DO WHEN THERE IS INSUFFICIENT EVIDENCE TO ESTABLISH A CANDIDATE'S COMPETENCE?*

Administer a pre-set test covering the performance criteria of the unit or element being assessed. Ask questions, negotiate the next steps to take with the candidate. Identify the need for additional evidence matched against the standards.

20. *WHAT IS THE ROLE OF THE INTERNAL VERIFIER AND EXTERNAL VERIFIER?*

*Internal.* The awarding bodies' *quality assurance* agents. They confirm whether or not standards are being maintained within assessment centres and among assessors.

*External.* To ensure that *internal verifiers* are doing their job correctly, to clarify procedures, answer any questions raised, offer advice and ensure that national standards are met.

**Note**
1  See L. Walklin, *The Assessment of Performance and Competence*, Stanley Thornes, Cheltenham 1991 (reprinted 1994).

# Key Role E

## Managing relationships and evaluating developmental outcomes

# 16

# Evaluating training and development sessions

Systematic monitoring, review and evaluation of the quality of teaching and learning will need to be an integral part of a training provider's operations. There is a need to monitor, review and evaluate the responsiveness of any training programme to the learner needs identified and the quality, efficiency and effectiveness of outcomes achieved. Another check that is normally made is that of relating learners' actual achievements to original objectives. The review and evaluation process will identify the strengths and weaknesses of the programme and will give rise to modifications for future planning consideration.

The evaluators will need to make all of the programme team members aware of the modifications required and feed back information to all concerned in the operation. An element that is often overlooked is the degree of learner satisfaction: that is, whether or not they thought the training provision met their needs and expectations.

Teachers as evaluators will need to be able to assess the effectiveness of training methods employed and learner outcomes in terms of their performance against learning objectives. When judging accomplishment, teachers will need to satisfy themselves that candidates can perform safely at the requisite level of competence and are able to demonstrate the ability to operate equipment or control processes as defined by performance criteria and range statements. Work-related attainment can be evaluated by checking that learners have mastered individual elements of competence and integrated these into a whole, skilful demonstration that is judged by the qualified assessor to meet unit requirements.

During training, teachers will need to monitor continuously the learner's performance on each of the elements that make up a unit of competence. It is too late to put things right at the end of a training programme. Performance should be evaluated by the teacher and learner at regular intervals so that a smooth progression to higher level skills may occur. Routine assessment of learner achievement is essential to logical progression and success, but as in all learning situations, learners are individuals, each developing a style and rate of learning that suits them.

The teacher is responsible for the management of instruction and for the deployment of resources to the best effect, the aim being to arrange things so that learners may learn effectively. The quality of a programme can be judged against a prepared checklist of questions relating to each of the following six important elements:

- planning
- method

- feedback
- resources
- activities
- supervision.

Learners may be required to work with the teacher on a one-to-one basis, or individually, or together in small groups. There are many different training methods to choose from when selecting the one to use for a particular group of learners. Skill is needed in identifying, classifying and selecting methods that will be of most use to the teacher or particular learners. Teaching and learning methods may be grouped under three main headings:

- **Teacher-centred methods** based on exposition (teacher talking, telling and giving information), and formally directing and controlling the learners' activities.
- **Student-centred learning** where the learners control much of the action whether they are working in teams or as individuals.
- **Resource-based learning** where individuals may be using techniques, including computer-assisted learning, to master content or other theory; or forms of experiential learning (learning derived from experience); or distance learning. They may also be working on assignments or they may be involved in a personalised system of instruction.

The teacher will need to demonstrate insight when evaluating and comparing outcomes achieved by the use of varied teaching and learning approaches.

# Collecting and analysing information on training and development sessions

*The purpose and scope of the evaluation is clearly identified and agreed with the appropriate people*

The **purposes** of evaluation range from appraising classroom management and learning facilitation skills to evaluation of the overall effectiveness of the training provision. Other

---

- Recruitment, APL advice, initial assessment (guidance and support)
- Appropriateness and quality of the training programme (in meeting learner needs)
- Methods used (effectiveness, pacing, timing, learner support, learner-centred → didactic presentation)
- Operational expedience (administration, adequacy of facilities, physical and human resources, timetable)
- The reaction of learners to the training opportunities provided (warmly welcomed → unpopular)
- Retention rates (causes of attrition – early leavers, non-completions and other drop-outs)
- The reaction of teachers and support staff to provision (popularly accepted → strongly rejected)
- Staff development and training needs (in-service or external top-up training or updating)
- The attainment of learning/training objectives (including validity and relevance to learners)
- The new knowledge and skills gained by each learner (qualifications and certification of outcomes)
- The transfer of vocational skills gained to employment-related duties (relevant → little use)
- The cost-effectiveness of training provision (budget and comparison with other possible training solutions)

---

**Figure 16.1** *Checklist: purposes of evaluation*

important aspects of training and development evaluation include those given in Figure 16.1.

**Evaluation** is the process of judging the success of a programme of training in terms of its social, financial and developmental outcomes and/or its cost-effectiveness. Teachers who are able to appreciate the purpose and advantages of evaluation can use this knowledge to increase learner motivation, develop teaching skills and benefit learners through improved performance. At a basic level, evaluation is concerned mainly with estimating the degree to which the training provision has increased the knowledge, skills and experience of learners, and in the guise of 'appraisal' to assess the effectiveness of a teacher's performance at work.

Teacher evaluation is often facilitated by self-assessment or interview and review. The implementation of regular evaluations of instructional techniques and the use of resources can lead to more effective teaching inputs and learning outcomes. Written evaluations (or 'happy hour' sheets) can be completed by learners at the end of a session or programme, and a typical example is given in Figure 16.10 (see *Documents Pack*).

The **scope** of evaluations may extend to analysis of the features given in Figure 16.2.

---

- Training methods employed
- Organisation of sessions
- Training content
- Use of material and physical resources
- Learning opportunities, experiences and learner activity
- Teacher activity and effectiveness
- Effect of teacher behaviour on learners
- Outcomes of the training session

---

**Figure 16.2** *Scope of evaluation*

*Information required to evaluate training and development sessions is clearly specified*

Before conducting an evaluation it is necessary to identify the aspect of training and development that is to be evaluated and the processes involved. Valid and reliable evaluation can only be accomplished if suitable assessment criteria and a rationale for their selection are available. Sources of information such as those listed in Figure 16.3 will provide the basic standards against which to make your judgement.

*Information is collected using suitable methods and procedures*

If you intend to exploit the potential of monitoring and evaluation you will first need to consider how you can make it work for you. High up your list of considerations will be possible methods of evaluating your training and development sessions. Some teachers will opt for analysis of survey questionnaire completions while others might decide to rely on oral or written 'expert' observations and judgements, reports or discussions and inquests. Seeking the testimony and opinions of **empowered learners** will probably be the most valuable method of discovering the truth about programme suitability, content and methods; although teachers' own observations and self-assessments, if made honestly, could yield the best results.

| The aspect of the training and development to be evaluated | Information required to evaluate aspect specified |
| --- | --- |
| Planning and preparing learning opportunities | Syllabuses: breath, depth and relevance of coverage<br>Units, elements and pcs<br>Needs analyses<br>Task analyses<br>Programmes constructed<br>Schemes of work<br>Lesson plans and objectives |
| Managing learning opportunities | Classroom management<br>Facilitation skills: setting and progressing learner activities<br>Resourcing<br>Technical skills: operating equipment<br>Teamworking and liaising |
| Assessment and record keeping | Validity and reliability of marking and assessment judgements<br>Testing and assessing attainment<br>Liaising with other assessors and verifiers<br>Records of formative assessments and progress records<br>Summative assessment records<br>Internal and external validation and moderation<br>Applications for certification |
| Teaching practice assessment | Appraisals of teaching practice<br>Self-assessments<br>Peer-group reports<br>Mentor reports<br>Supervisor reports<br>Learner evaluation of teacher's performance |
| Training provision | Relevance of training opportunities to learner and employer needs<br>Efficient use of learner and teacher time<br>Consistency of standards<br>Cost-effectiveness of provision<br>Validation of mission and attainment of organisational objectives |

**Figure 16.3** *Sources of information*

Information-collection methods should be reliable, as there is a need to obtain explicit and unambiguous data so that interpretation by several people will yield the same results. Teachers can obtain such data by observing and recording the frequency of checklisted specific behaviour or events over a period of time. **Rating systems** where overall **impressions** are formed about some 'measure' such as classroom management can be suspect since they are often not founded on specific information recorded during an observation.

Teacher **self-evaluations** can be based on self-assessments of lessons and seminars using rating sheets such as that shown in Figure 16.4 (see *Documents Pack*), which uses a scale from 1 (poor) to 7 (excellent) to provide a qualitative estimate of performance. **Peer assessment** can be carried out by colleagues using the same rating sheets.

Members of the learner group can also be invited to make critical assessments of your performance. Suitable forms (sometimes called 'instruments') can be designed to be completed by members of a learner group who can make constructive comments regarding particular teaching and learning sessions. **Learner evaluations** of teachers can be most revealing providing that an atmosphere of trust can first be established. However, teachers are unlikely to hear the truth if the learners fear that they will be 'punished' in some way if they speak out. Typical **learner evaluation sheets** are shown in Figures 16.5 and 16.6 (see *Documents Pack*).

Appropriate use can be made of the **question and answer** technique to assess learner achievement of lesson objectives both during and at the end of a teaching and learning session. **Knowledge assessment** can also take the form of written feedback and results from multiple-choice tests, which have the advantage of producing data that can be analysed statistically, examined by others and where necessary used by candidates as tangible material for their evidence files.

**Skills assessment** has particular relevance when vocational 'hands-on' skills achievement is analysed. The effectiveness of a lesson where a demonstration followed by practice has been the main element may be judged to some extent on the performance of individuals who need to carry out similar tasks after such instruction. This is particularly relevant to preparing candidates for NVQ/SVQs, where they are assessed against predetermined performance criteria.

**Post-training assessment** against national standards for a particular award can fulfil two purposes: first to judge candidates' performances on a unit of competence, and second to check learners' progress and thus evaluate the effectiveness of the facilitator's training and development sessions. The **summative assessment** form given in Figure 16.7 (see *Documents Pack*) contains a listing of key result areas claimed by the candidate, and valuable comment on the degree of learner satisfaction derived and quality of programme management.

**Direct observation** of teachers in class can be carried out by assessors, mentors and peers who complete 'teaching practice' assessment forms giving their judgements about certain aspects of the session. A form such as the one given in Figure 16.8 (see *Documents Pack*) can be used to provide a record of the observer's perceptions of an event, but there is no opportunity for an 'action replay'.

**Video-taped** and structured observation sessions provide a more permanent record that can be discussed and reviewed later. When analysing periods of oral work the **Flanders' interaction analysis categories** can be used. The ten categories shown in Figure 16.9 were used by Ned Flanders to classify the statements and behaviour of teachers and learners. An observer sits in on a lesson and at the end of each three-second period categorises and records the communication behaviour of that session. Alternatively a recording may be made of the session and the communication behaviour categorised later. The results are then analysed and the percentage of time given over to each category is calculated. A high proportion of categories 5, 6 and 7 indicates a teacher-dominated presentation, whereas a high proportion of categories 8 and 9 would indicate a learner-centred session with a high level of learner participation.

*Questions asked during the evaluation are clearly phrased and unambiguous*

The basis of **valid** evaluation, audits and questionnaire design is the selection of sensible and worthwhile features to appraise. Attempting to measure the effectiveness of a programme against trivial criteria should be avoided, even though this may at first appear to be an attractive way of confirming the value of a programme. When training we like to be complimented on our efforts and to read flattering comments on evaluation sheets. This is good for our ego. But we must avoid the temptation to word questions so that the probability of obtaining only positive responses is heightened, as this says very little about the quality of the training process and outcomes.

| Flanders' interaction analysis categories | | |
|---|---|---|
| Teacher talk | Response | **1** *Accepts feeling.* Accepts and clarifies an attitude or the feeling tone of a pupil in a nonthreatening manner. Feelings may be positive or negative. Predicting and recalling feelings are included.<br>**2** *Praises or encourages.* Praises or encourages pupil action or behaviour. Jokes that release tension, but not at the expense of another individual: nodding head, or saying, 'Um, hm?' or 'go on' are included.<br>**3** *Accepts or uses ideas of pupils.* Clarifying, building, or developing ideas suggested by a pupil. Teacher extensions of pupil ideas are included but as the teacher brings more of his [or her] own ideas into place, shift to category five. |
| | Initiation | **4** *Asks questions.* Asking a question about content or procedure, based on teacher ideas, with the intent that a pupil will answer.<br>**5** *Lecturing.* Giving facts or opinions about content or procedures; expressing *his [or her] own* ideas, giving *his [or her] own* explanation, or citing an authority other than a pupil.<br>**6** *Giving directions.* Directions, commands, or orders with which a pupil is expected to comply.<br>**7** *Criticising or justifying authority.* Statements intended to change pupil behaviour from nonacceptable to acceptable pattern; bawling someone out; stating why the teacher is doing what he [or she] is doing; extreme self-reference. |
| Pupil talk | Response | **8** *Pupil-talk – response.* Talk by pupils in response to teacher. Teacher initiates the contact or solicits pupil statement or structures the situation. Freedom to express own ideas is limited. |
| | Initiation | **9** *Pupil-talk – initiation.* Talk by pupils which they initiate. Expressing own ideas; initiating a new topic, freedom to develop opinions and a line of thought, like asking thoughtful questions; going beyond the existing structure. |
| Silence | | **10** *Silence or confusion.* Pauses, short periods of silence and periods of confusion in which communication cannot be understood by the observer. |

Source: N. Flanders, *Analysing Teaching Behaviour*, © 1970, Addison-Wesley Publishing Company, Inc., Chapter 3, p. 34, Table 2-1: 'Flanders' International Analysis Categories (FIAC)'. Reprinted with permission.

**Figure 16.9** *Flanders' interaction analysis categories*

**Evaluations** can be facilitated either by using a set of clear objective and specific questions or by using more open-ended and subjective questions. Responses to unambiguous, objective questions will be capable of rigorous statistical analysis, while open-ended questions are more likely to generate detailed descriptions of feelings based upon conscious experiences during the programme or opinions resulting from participation in relevant learning experiences. Figure 16.10 (see *Documents Pack*) gives an example of a completed evaluation questionnaire. A set of these forms were completed by learners and analysed by Gary Miller (see the summary in Figure 16.16 in the *Documents Pack*). All too often, completion of evaluation forms is left to the last minute when people are packing up their things and are anxious to leave the session. When implementing evaluations teachers should give clear explanations on the purpose, method of completion and confidentiality of ownership of responses. Questions asked should be unambiguous and sufficient time allowed for the learners to think and respond properly.

In order to facilitate meaningful returns from learners, some questionnaires used may need rethinking in terms of language, presentation and in some cases purpose. If you find that your questionnaires tend to invite only negative and unhelpful comments from learners, changes will be needed to encourage unbiased objective and constructive criticism. Surveys conducted should be representative of all your learner groups.

*Information is recorded accurately and rules of confidentiality are followed*

The mode of completion of a programme monitoring and evaluation (M&E) questionnaire may affect the quality of responses, depending on whether or not the learners are supervised while form-filling. The issues of **trust** and **confidentiality** in respect of data gathered from learners must also be considered by teachers when they are handling data and reporting on outcomes. Information gathered should be accurately recorded against preset criteria. The validity and reliability of information collected can reflect differences in perception of those collecting and analysing data. Teacher **professionalism** should always come first, as opposed to **political considerations** such as the temptation for teachers (as the evaluators concerned) to succumb to the need to retain a teaching contract at any cost, or to conform to the vested interests of employers and funding agents. Factors such as these could lead to situations where the degree to which an evaluator is biased towards securing a particular outcome could seriously affect the reliability of any information collected.

*Information is assessed against clearly specified and agreed evaluation criteria*

Candidate assessment can be used as a form of evaluation criteria. If this method is used, information gathered should be based on quantifiable outcomes defined by criteria, and not subjective opinions about the processes involved in accomplishing particular tasks. Using approved preset standards will avoid introducing bias. When pretests and post-test scores are used as measures of success it is often assumed that candidate gain is attributable entirely to teacher facilitation, and not to unknown factors such as prior achievement or 'out of college' experiential learning. The reliability and validity of evidence collected must be assured, and this could be achieved, for example, by evaluating the performance of learners carrying out predetermined tasks (all learners would be required to attempt the same task). Only then would it be possible to assess programme performance objectively. Other criteria used for evaluation purposes are a variety of performance indicators, national standards and organisational standards.

When you are collecting information, excessively long questionnaires may be off-putting to the learners sampled, and you may be concerned about the considerable volume of information generated. Probably the most time-consuming element of the evaluation process will be extracting and collating information from the questionnaires for analysis. It could easily take an hour to extract information from a sample of 25 forms. The workload when scaled up on a pro-rata basis for all your students could call for computer, data-handling and processing skills.

When you are assessing information, positive and constructive views of the learning environment and justifiable criticism of programme delivery, style and content will impact on future course planning. Confirmation of the learners' high regard for a teacher's professionalism and appreciation of the quality of training provision are gratifying when forthcoming, but some comments made may be very controversial and of considerable concern if teachers are adversely criticised. When comments are critical of a particular teacher it is difficult to know how to handle such information. But viewing the facts with a degree of professional detachment, objectivity and sensitivity will enable the evaluator to see things clearly and to make suggestions or decisions that will benefit the learners and teachers concerned.

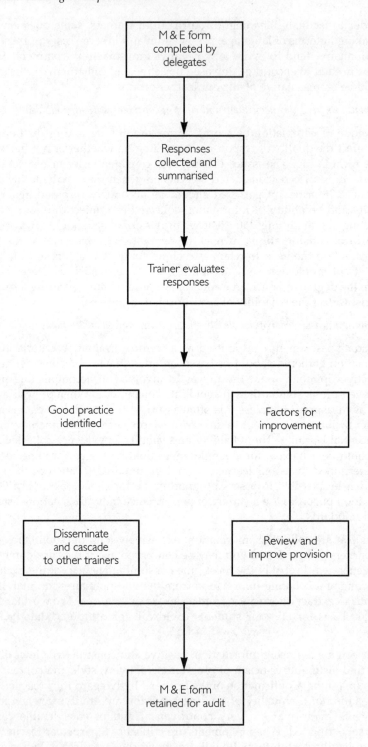

**Figure 16.11** *Evaluating training events*

*Respondents are informed of the purpose of the evaluation and encouraged to give their views*

Evaluations and the results of spot checks are used to inform teachers and other decision makers about the quality and suitability of provision and to justify any subsequent action taken. Audits may be based upon course team reviews, departmental programme reviews, external moderators' and assessors' reports, HMI reports, and course evaluations provided by learners or delegates. A systematic approach, such as that given in Figure 16.11, could be used to handle feedback provided by delegates who have completed an M&E form. Whenever possible, feedback should be gathered from participants and any others involved in delivering training. The need to evaluate your own performance may result from your need to take account of current relevant national and organisational debates relating to training and development. You will need to keep up to date.

*Results of the evaluation are used to improve training and development sessions*

Confirmation of the results of evaluation will take the form of reinforcement for effective teachers and the identification of opportunities for improving teaching techniques for those below par. Learners participating in the evaluation process may question the validity of collecting and analysing the information they provide if nothing appears to happen after their questionnaires have been completed. They should perceive that you have taken action and that benefits will accrue in response to their comments and suggestions. You will need to follow up evaluations by **implementing** improvements and by keeping the learners informed of progress made when improvements are delayed or when no observable action seems to have been taken.

The validity of your evaluation could be affected by the following factors:

- the learners' prior learning and achievement: existing experience and qualifications
- construction of the learning programme
- specific conditions and characteristics of the learning programme
- entry conditions: open access or prerequisite qualifications and experience
- venue, time and place of learning opportunities
- teaching and learning methods adopted
- mode of delivery: facilitation, didactic teaching, interactive learning or distance and open learning
- training methods used
- application of good practice in respect of employment and equal opportunities legislation.

The size of groups sampled may affect the reliability of information gathered, and conclusions drawn from relatively small and possibly unrepresentative samples may be invalid and open to misinterpretation. However, contributors to the evaluation are generally supportive and helpful and their comments useful when you are contemplating improvements in training provision.

# Improving training and development sessions

*All information required for improving training and development sessions is gathered and reviewed*

When evaluating training programmes teachers and their supervisors will need to audit the effectiveness of training provision and associated training strategies. The flow chart given in Figure 16.12 is concerned with **auditing training strategies**. A suggested starting point is the **identification of training needs**, and the training programme developed should match the learner's requirements. Outcomes can then be assessed against the programme objectives.

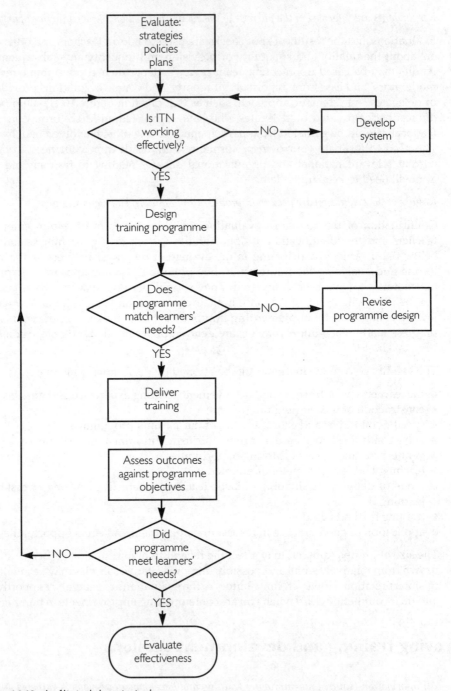

**Figure 16.12** *Audit: training strategies*

The **physical resources** needed to aid and support the learning opportunities can be evaluated against intended purposes. Additional resources may have to be provided where an audit, such as that given in Figure 16.13, reveals that programme objectives or learner requirements have not been fully met.

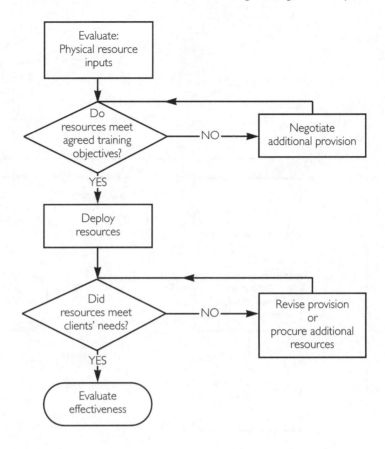

**Figure 16.13** *Audit: physical resource inputs*

**Human resources** are the sum total of all people involved in the delivery of the training programme. They provide the energy, effort, skills, knowledge and competence to drive the programme. A flow diagram that may be helpful when evaluating your own effectiveness and those of other team members is given in Figure 16.14. It is suggested that if your skills satisfy the present and predictable requirements of the training programme then nothing will need to be done other than to carry out ongoing evaluations. Where a training gap is detected, specific training needs will be identified and retraining or updating carried out.

Systematic monitoring and evaluation of training and development sessions is essential to effective classroom management and programme planning. Information is gathered in order to provide essential data needed to inform the teacher's or provider's management information system so that continuous improvements in training provision can be made.

When teachers are reviewing information gathered during training and development sessions and identifying areas for improvement the following points could be checked out:

● To what extent were the aims and objectives for the programme met?
● Were the chosen delivery methods suitable for the sessions? Was there enough learner activity? Should there be more practical work? Was sufficient time allowed for giving and receiving feedback?

243

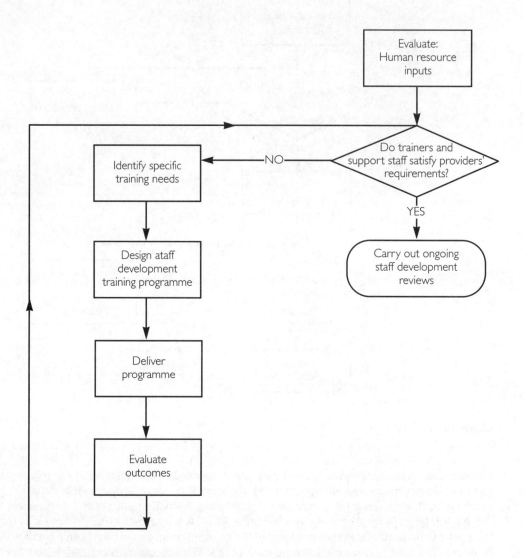

**Figure 16.14** *Audit: human resource inputs*

- Was appropriate use made of available resources? Was learning enhanced with their use? Was the teacher too dependent on them? Were more aids needed? Were aids correctly selected – matched to learning objectives?
- Was the session suitably structured? Good mix of activities? Breaks at the right time? Too much pressure put on self/learners?
- Was the environment suitable for the planned session? Room matched to activities? Size, layout, seating, facilities and temperature adequate?

- Were health and safety requirements met? Hazards identified and risks assessed? Warnings and advice given and protective clothing and equipment worn?
- Did the teacher have sufficient knowledge of the subject?
- Was the necessary level of motivation and enthusiasm demonstrated?

Self-reflection is one of the key underlying themes and concepts which are integral to all 7306 units, and City and Guilds suggest that a **personal account** of your teaching performance and preparation can provide a useful source of evidence. With this in mind Gary Miller wrote short descriptors of what he did when demonstrating various performance criteria, and cross-referenced the statements to the unit pcs concerned. The abridged statement given in Figure 16.15 illustrates how Gary supplemented his main **teaching diary** with focused comment on **what he did** in support of the **direct performance evidence** that he presented to the assessor.

An example of the completed evaluation questionnaires referred to in Gary's statement is shown in Figure 16.10 (see *Documents Pack*). The questionnaire was administered to a group of students undertaking an introductory education and training management programme at the end of their course in order to evaluate programme presentation and outcomes. The course team analysed the data gathered, which revealed the need to provide more books, to review programme content and to adjust the amount of out-of-college work set to better match the available programme hours and domestic circumstances. This would hopefully eliminate the sense of pressure felt by some learners. The summary of responses given in Figure 16.16 (see *Documents Pack*) was collated by Gary Miller, who was a member of the course teaching team.

*Potential improvements to training and development sessions are clearly identified*

Potential **improvements** in training methods will include **better organisation** of sessions, more **effective use of resources** (human and physical) and greater **relevance of content**. Information required for improving training and development sessions should be gathered using

---

I recorded all my teaching practice activities for each day I taught on the 'Introduction to Education and Training Management' course in my FAETC teaching diary. In addition I reflected on the activities and included such things as my thoughts, feelings and suggestions for future improvement. [Pcs (a), (b) and (d)]

I requested feedback from Mr Les Walklin (the NEBSM course tutor) and from Mr Bryan Rowbotham (a fellow FAETC student) regarding my formal presentations and any group work that I facilitated. Their comments were noted and incorporated into my events diary. [Pcs (a) and (b)]

At the end of the course group members were supplied with evaluation sheets containing a number of questions regarding course content, delivery, relevance to their needs, etc. These were completed anonymously so as to maintain confidentiality and to encourage freedom of expression and honest views. A summary of these responses was made together with suggestions for future improvements in the introductory programme.

Gary Miller
Evidence reference E231 (pcs a–f incl.)

**Figure 16.15** *Abridged statement: collecting and analysing information on training and development sessions*

ongoing self-assessment and learner feedback as the main sources. Learning outcomes will be affected by the effectiveness and suitability of the learning opportunity facilitated, and constructive feedback will reveal evidence of good practice as well as potential problems. The information gathered should be critically assessed and **potential improvements** identified. Improvements should be made if at all feasible but implementation would depend upon the degree of flexibility of each programme component and availability of desired resources. For example, the fixed layout of a room such as a lecture theatre with staged seating might present a potential barrier to interaction and learning, or the room used could be too large or too small to accommodate the group comfortably. The availability of suitable alternatives at the time you need them would dictate the outcome.

### The objectives of the potential improvements are clearly specified

Firstly, the areas where improvements will be made should be targeted. Then the **purposes** of potential improvements that will need to be implemented must be made clear to all concerned in the proposed changes. With this need in mind it is first necessary to decide on the overall purpose and then to define relevant **specific objectives** for the improvements envisaged. Where **quantitative** changes are focused on learner outcomes, proposed objectives should be fairly easy to define. For example, resultant learner achievement can be measured by examination results and the number of competence-based units achieved. However, **qualitative** objectives will be more difficult to specify and the outcomes of changes will be less easy to assess. Learners may not be very forthcoming about what they really think of their learning experiences, and changes in their attitudes may not be reflected in any evaluations attempted.

When you are negotiating and agreeing objectives there will therefore be a need to establish how improvements in 'before' and 'after' inputs and outputs may be measured or confirmed. Writing objectives for improving your own teaching performance can be very helpful, although it could be quite difficult to correlate your changes with subsequent improvements in learner outcomes.

### The feasibility and benefits of implementing potential improvements are accurately determined

Being realistic in what is possible, and knowing how to bridge the gap between what is theoretically possible and the concrete practical experience likely to be encountered when implementing change, is the key to successful implementation. Therefore, before agreeing to make changes or acting on suggestions for improvements you may need to ask several questions, such as:

- Is it feasible. If so, what is the priority? Might it be desirable to implement the request or should it definitely happen?
- Is the change realisable? Is it practicable?
- Is the change viable, reasonable and within reach? Do the proposals lie within the bounds of possibility?
- Are the suggested improvements permissible, allowable and legal?
- Shall I be empowered to make the changes?
- Will the improvements be contingent upon extra funding?
- What is the probability that the innovation will be introduced?
- What shall I tell the learners if I know that there is little or no chance of getting their wishes implemented?

Factors which impact on the introduction of improvements include the following:

- Finance to acquire additional resources to enhance a session may not be available because of cost/budget factors.

- Accommodation may not be suited to the preferred mode of delivery.
- There may be resistance to change because of the teacher's lack of knowledge or confidence.
- Colleagues may resist any proposed changes.
- Accessibility to information which would enhance a presentation may be restricted.
- Mode of delivery may be dictated by a superior,
- Course structure and timetable may be so rigid that change is neither feasible nor permitted.

*Introduction of improvements is planned and agreed with the appropriate people*

Nowadays teachers are habitually accepting change that is more often than not thrust upon them. But in order to keep up to date there is also a need to respond to necessary changes deriving from feedback from the classroom or training environment. Once the need to introduce improvements has been identified, a plan for implementing changes should be devised. However, if you are the person responsible for planning you should remember that for successful implementation of any improvements **those who implement the plans** must be consulted when **the plans are made**. Those concerned need to make the problem their own, and be aware of the 'paralysis by analysis' syndrome: i.e. too much talking and analysing often results in very little getting done. A suggested approach to the planning phase is given below.

- Recognise the need for change:

  - Identify and analyse desired improvements.

- Obtain an overview of the implications of the proposed change:

  - Diagnostic phase: establish what is the current position.
  - Who will benefit?
  - Who will be involved?
  - What changes will be made?

- Formulate a strategy for implementing the changes:

  - What do you want to change?
  - What are the available options?
  - Clarify priorities.
  - Generate solutions.
  - Consider how you/your team are going to implement the changes.

- Consider relevant economics of change:

  - Cost of doing nothing.
  - Cost/benefit of changing people, methods or buying in new resources/technology.

- Identify sources and causes of resistance to change:

  - Fear of unknown.
  - Lack of information.
  - Misinformation.
  - Threat to current status and competence level.
  - Intransigence.
  - Complacency.

- Specify factors that may help overcome resistance:

– Involve people concerned in the change process.
– Build a shared vision.
– Sell the benefits of changes.
– Provide support throughout.

● Keep notes on agreements made.

*Improvements are introduced at the appropriate time and in an effective manner*

Servicing improvements will mean providing help, back-up materials or resources to your customers, i.e. the learners who have enrolled for your current courses. Post-training learner support and follow-up are also important customer requirements and should form part of any curriculum quality management system.

When introducing necessary improvements there will be teachers who will readily become involved and there will be those who will resist the pressure for change. A good team leader will be able to harness the goodwill of the willing innovators to the latent potential of the others who may initially feel less inclined to become involved. Timing the implementation is of the essence. To be effective, changes made should benefit those already in the system as well as those who will follow. But choosing the right moment to implement changes may be out of your direct control, especially if you are dependent upon others to authorise finance for additional resources. What is important is to involve those concerned by identifying a common reference point and showing how changes could affect them. It is desirable to seek the cooperation of learners and colleagues alike, and to encourage them to come to terms with the need to change things. Once the relevance of the proposed improvements can be perceived a common accord will be reached and things will begin to move forward.

In order to introduce improvements effectively you will need to:

● establish a planning team (preferably involving the learners) that will design and steer activities
● be clear about your purpose
● assess the tasks that confront you
● plan for contingencies
● rate tasks for 'urgency' and 'importance'
● identify team subject specialists who will write learning materials and handle more specific detail relating to proposed changes
● focus team effort onto developing course materials and reviewing assessment systems
● prioritise: produce a timetable for implementation
● maintain a record of the improvements you have made.

## Self-assessment questions _____

1 Explain the main purposes of evaluating training and development methods, organisation of sessions, content and use of resources.

2 Produce a checklist of other valid purposes of evaluation.

3 Outline the sources of information required to evaluate training and development sessions.

4 Describe suitable methods and procedures for collecting information that could be used for evaluation purposes. Include methods such as discussion and written feedback in your description.

5 Why should questions asked during data collection and evaluation be unambiguous and clearly phrased?

6 Explain why information gathered should be accurately recorded.

7 Why should any rules of confidentiality be followed when evaluation documentation is processed?

8 Explain what is meant by the terms 'performance indicators', 'national standards' and 'organisational standards'.

9 Why is it necessary to assess information gathered against clearly specified and agreed evaluation criteria?

10 Explain why it is important to inform respondents such as participants and others involved in presenting the training of the purpose of the evaluation and encourage them to give their views freely.

11 Explain the importance of encouraging self-assessments, learner and peer evaluations and continuous monitoring of training and development programmes.

12 Explain how the results of an evaluation might be used to improve subsequent training and development sessions.

13 Why is it important for teachers to comply with employment and equal opportunities legislation and codes of good practice when evaluating training and development opportunities?

14 Explain why it is necessary to keep up to date with relevant national and organisational debates relating to training and development.

15 What benefits could be derived from specifying objectives for the implementation of improvements and agreeing proposals for change with those affected?

16 When you are making plans for the introduction of improvements why is it important to involve those who will implement the plans?

17 When you are planning and implementing improvements why is it important to keep records of any agreements you make with learners or other change agents?

18 Write a plan for introducing improvements to one of your training and development programmes.

19 Maintain a record of improvements introduced and present the report as evidence for this unit (E23).

20 Outline important factors which have impacted on the introduction of any improvements that you have implemented. List any other factors that could affect the change process.

## *Preparing for assessment: sample activities* _____

### *Activity 16.1 Analysing periods of oral work*
The typical analysis of classroom discourse given in Figure 16.17 shows that in a class of 40, on average, each learner talks for about one per cent of the time available while the teacher may be talking for 60 per cent of the lesson.

● For each of your own groups, estimate the time occupied by each category given in Figure 16.17.
● Using your values calculate the average amount of time each learner spends talking.

Having completed the analysis do you feel that any changes are needed in the discourse pattern of your classes?

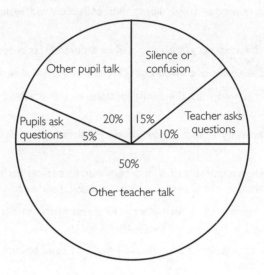

**Figure 16.17** *Typical analysis of classroom discourse*

### Activity 16.2 Analysing training sessions
Collect and analyse information from at least two training and development sessions. Use data gathered from self-assessments, peer assessments, learner assessments and written records of knowledge, skills and competence-based assessments to support your analysis.

### Activity 16.3 Designing and administering a programme evaluation form
- Design a programme evaluation form to suit one of your training programmes and candidate groups.
- Administer the evaluation and analyse responses gathered.
- Identify areas for improvements and suggest how these could be implemented.

### Activity 16.4 Improving training and development sessions
Provide evidence of improving at least two training and development sessions. Justify the changes you have made.

# 17

# Evaluating and developing own practice

Whenever possible, teachers should be encouraged to evaluate their own practice against self-set goals and targets which they have negotiated and agreed with their supervisors. Teacher appraisal is now widespread, and there is a need to operate a sound system of evaluating training needs backed up with a programme of personal development opportunities that satisfies both individual needs and the training provider's plans. However, the notion of teachers being accountable for their personal performance and for the level of service provided for their learners is still not readily accepted by every practitioner.

Innovation and the rapid rate of change in educational provision calls for relatively new roles for some as innovators or agents of change. Teachers need to be conversant with staff development policy and provision designed to satisfy training needs thrown up by new types of teaching and learning methods, together with advances in experiential and student-controlled learning such as open learning, computer-assisted learning and supported self-study.

Nowadays, teachers as managers of learning opportunities cannot afford to ignore the need to react to innovation in the education and training environment. Survival in today's fiercely competitive environment will depend on how well those involved identify the necessary changes and devise suitable strategies to ensure that developments in training need are properly implemented. By examining the strengths and weaknesses of existing provision teachers can identify the need for change: for example, there may be a need for practitioners to adapt their own practice to meet changes in training and development such as the implementation of NVQ/SVQs, the introduction of a modular curriculum, team teaching or cross-college integration of programmes. Colleges and training providers must be able to accommodate rapid change, and to do this teachers must be able to identify self-development needs and take the necessary action to update their knowledge, skills and attitudes accordingly.

But what factors must be taken into account when there is a need to adapt to changes in educational processes in your own organisation? Resistance to the implementation of change is a widespread reaction to unwelcome innovation, but the need for change should not always be viewed as a threat to one's security. The outcomes of change are not all bad. Adopting an optimistic attitude will often enable you to seize on opportunities to improve your facilities and gain some advantage from funding that normally supports innovations. Teachers can develop the capacity to change by taking the initiative and latching on to the necessary innovation while others are facing backwards and clinging to the old way. In the end teachers will have to adapt their own practice to meet changes in training and development, but better still they should be constantly improving the quality of their provision so that they will be able to respond to the pressures when confronted with imposed change.

# Evaluating own practice

*Own practice is evaluated against set goals and targets*

Whenever possible, performance should be assessed against measurable standards, but when these are not to hand teachers can usefully assess their performance against national criteria, self-imposed goals or organisational performance targets. They can then identify developmental needs to support the potential for improvement and diversification by judging achievement against the selected criteria and noting any deficiency. The rationale for evaluation of one's own practice may be contained in the criteria, range statements and assessment specification covering the requirements of a particular training and development programme, Training and Development Lead Body (TDLB) units or Management Charter Initiative (MCI) standards.

A self-analysis of interpersonal skills can be used to estimate your management of face-to-face encounters and social skills that are so important in teacher/learner relationships. Techniques used to analyse behaviours such as proposing, clarifying, seeking suggestions, suggesting, agreeing, disagreeing, seeking clarification, interrupting and responding have been suggested by N. Rackham and others,[1] while transactional analysis[2] may be used to study your interaction with learners and to establish your behaviour pattern, teaching style and preference for promoting a child, adult or parent relationship in class. Alternatively, published checklists of teacher competences and codes of practice suggested by researchers and authors may be used to provide features against which to compare your performance.

*A range of valid and reliable evidence is used for assessing own work*

**Appraisals** are used to assess performance and to talk about a teacher's recent accomplishments. Regular appraisals yield documented evidence of achievements and provide a means of monitoring the work of teachers and their learners, examination results, attrition rates, completions and many other performance indicators. **Self-assessment** techniques can be used to carry out formative assessments over a period of time, and these can be used to describe how strengths have been built upon and how the need for further development and improvement has been or could be addressed. **Peer-group assessments** and the views of colleagues and learners should also be sought, and any judgements made should be related to some kind of standards or to targets written into action plans.

*Evidence is interpreted with the support of others*

It is helpful to talk things over with a mentor or colleague when interpreting evidence of your own performance. People tend to look for the bad news, and can be rather harsh on themselves when self-assessing or reading appraisal reports and judging performance evidence. However, this tendency can be overcome if you ask someone you trust to help you interpret written criticism or the content of reports. The first question to ask yourself must be: 'Am I setting myself (or accepting) unrealistic targets that cannot be achieved?' If you are, then the reason for your underperformance will be obvious.

If you are falling down on the job, a strategy that could be adopted in order to soften the impact of adverse criticism is to bear in mind the overall **quantity** and **quality** of work produced. For example, are you trying to do too much too quickly? Or are you striving for perfection and setting yourself impossible targets in one area while neglecting another?

When deciding a course of action you will need to balance the good aspects of your work with the areas that need improvement. Try to avoid overkill on any one area and devote sufficient time to correcting shortcomings. In order to preserve your self-esteem you could, for example:

- look for some complimentary aspects in the report: find some positive aspects of your performance to start with
- relate your discussion to particular instances, evidence and comments written down
- make specific points and avoid generalities
- turn negative criticism into positive intent: decide to do something about your shortcomings
- look for ways forward
- decide a course for future action
- end your discussion on a high note.

*Interpretation of evidence includes an assessment of the impact of own behaviour and values on learners*

A suitable starting point when assessing the impact of your own behaviour on learners might be to consider whether your management style is satisfying their expectations. You could ask yourself whether or not the evidence gathered suggests that you are doing your best for them, and if so is your best good enough? You might consider whether there is any more that you could do to support the achievement of their personal targets and objectives or to make learning a really pleasant experience.

We all come from different social, economic, occupational and moral backgrounds, and these factors will influence the way we evaluate our performance and learner contributions. Our **expectations** of learner performance could be affected by the way we perceive their status in society; and our **value systems** will cause us to make personalised and often subjective judgements about information concerning our performance that we collect from learners and colleagues. The need for **impartiality** is an easy concept to understand, but it is not always easy to apply because we will have our **preferences** and could be inclined to judge others unfairly. We may stereotype learners and treat them unequally. Instead of accentuating our learners' strengths and minimising their weaknesses we could mistakenly be more inclined to highlight only weaknesses and thereby punish them. There are many ways in which our values and beliefs will impact on our learners. We should therefore attempt to reduce the tendency for our personal values to influence adversely our relations with learners. Instead, we should set about overcoming personal biases, building trust and commitment and valuing contributions from the group.

*Results of evidence of performance are used to reflect own practice and professional issues*

Feedback from learners and teaching practice observers can be of great value to any teacher, and a few areas that could reflect your current practice will now be discussed. For example, evidence collected could indicate that your teaching methods may be too pedantic and thereby encouraging learner dependency when a rather more learner-controlled self-directing approach might be more suitable for your group. If this is the case then a more democratic, collaborative and informal structure based upon negotiated and agreed objectives and a high degree of learner involvement could replace a formal, competitive and autocratic regime where the teacher is the predominant figure.

Programme planning may be seen as the province of the teacher, with learner involvement restricted to merely soaking up and regurgitating what is prescribed for them. Alternatively, a self-assessment of needs and diagnosis of what the group thinks will be most beneficial to them could lead to a mutually negotiated and highly prized developmental learning programme that best matches individual needs, award body standards and organisational requirements.

Lesson plans may be designed with rigid structures and fixed subject-related objectives promoting a direct transfer of essential knowledge from the teachers' notes to the learners' notebooks with little thought required by either party. While in some instances this might be a suitable approach, the group might prefer a logically structured and well-resourced problem-solving learning opportunity facilitated by the teacher acting mainly as a resource.

Information obtained during reviews could indicate that the teacher concerned values learner experience and constantly draws upon what they have to contribute throughout the learning session. On the other hand, learner inputs could be underestimated and disregarded or, even worse, thoughtless teachers might belittle learners' offerings or cut them dead in mid-sentence.

The suggestions given above cover but a few of the possible circumstances that could be highlighted during evaluations, and it might be helpful for readers gathering evidence for this unit (E31) to explain how they have used the evidence of their own performance to introduce changes. When reflecting on your own practice and professional issues you may wish to consider whether or not you are able to:

- put people at ease, quickly establish rapport and create a good working relationship
- show concern for your learners
- demonstrate that you 'know your stuff' and can relate theory to practice and teach for transfer
- show that you are assertive and confident in your approach
- show that you are flexible and open to suggestions and ready to change your approach or style to suit the needs or mood of the group.

A number of comments generated by adult learners participating in teacher-candidate evaluations are given below. They often include contradictory suggestions about how teaching provision might be improved.

- 'Could you please adopt a traditional teaching role – one that we feel comfortable with?'
- 'Increase the teacher inputs – we would like a basic framework within which to work and a set of handouts for reference.'
- 'Cut out the blow-by-blow feedback following sub-group activities. Just give us the key facts. We know that you will have already prepared them on handouts.'
- 'Tell us the truth. How well or badly did we do?'
- 'Regarding self-assessment we'd like you to assess us. We aren't really qualified to assess ourselves – we can only guess at it. You know the standard, we don't.'
- 'We'd like to identify our own objectives and decide how we'll achieve them.'
- 'Could you please make more use of small group work? We enjoy working in teams.'
- 'We prefer this collaborative activity-learning routine – we can all get involved.'
- 'The lessons are too rigid. Too much lecturing. Give us more problem-solving tasks.'
- 'Just give us a broad outline of what you want. We'll fill in the details.'

*Criticism is accepted in a positive manner and assessed for its validity and importance*

The style adopted when feedback is given on performance will affect the way it is perceived. Feedback in the form of unhelpful criticism may be greeted with a stonewalling reaction which helps no one. But when criticism is given objectively and descriptively, the likelihood of the recipient responding with an irrational emotional outburst is reduced. And if account is taken of the good aspects mentioned there will be a greater probability that the recipient will be able to accept the downside. Teachers should always adopt an open-minded attitude when receiving feedback from students and colleagues alike, and should judge the criticism levelled against the relevant standards. Only then can the validity of the comment be established and a willingness to respond positively be promoted.

*Goals and targets are revised as a result of reviewing all relevant evidence of performance*

Performance could be evaluated in at least two ways. Teachers could be assessed either against **key result areas** specified in their job description or against **attributes** thought to be required by today's teaching force. Their behaviour in each of these categories will impact on their learners. It follows that if teachers can understand what is required of them they can estimate just how well (or badly) they are fulfilling their responsibilities to their learners.

Teachers can only **revise** goals and targets after reviewing all relevant evidence of performance and comparing achievements against the indicators set. Formal **appraisals** will reveal items for improvement in key result areas but teachers can continuously self-assess against teacher rating scales and lists of teacher characteristics obtained from relevant textbooks. Student evaluations of teaching effectiveness should also be encouraged. In order to assess the impact of their behaviour and personal values on learners teachers will need to interpret evidence collected and determine problems highlighted. Any difficulties in achieving key result areas should be noted and development needs such as related coaching, training or counselling support should be requested. Poor performance causing learner distress would probably lead to the instigation of appropriate disciplinary procedures and ongoing reviews, or, in serious instances, to dismissal.

Some general questions concerning your behaviour that could usefully be considered when revising personal development goals and targets are set out below.

### Typical key result areas
- Am I providing adequate learner support and striving to improve the quality of my learners' experiences?
- Am I communicating effectively with my learners on an individual basis and as a group?
- Am I providing a satisfactory level of information and advice?
- Am I motivating my learners and assisting them to perform their learning activities?
- Am I actively promoting learner independence and esteem, and recognising individual capabilities?
- Am I planning, preparing, organising and resourcing learning opportunities that meet learner expectations?
- Am I maintaining my learners' records properly?
- Am I safeguarding learner information and respecting their right to privacy?
- Am I complying with health and safety legislation and providing a safe working environment?

### Other considerations
- Should I be acting purely as a resource person and facilitator or operating further along the continuum towards didactic teaching? Is my style of presentation best suited to the learners' needs?
- Do my preferences in respect of method, materials and resources match those of the learners concerned?
- Should I be adopting a more behaviourist, competence-based approach or a more academic style?
- Should the learners define the learning objectives or should I?
- Should I be encouraging greater use of reflection and qualitative methods of evaluation?
- Should I be taking more notice of the learners' perceptions of the value of the learning and experiences derived from participating in the activities provided?

# Identifying self-development needs

*Clear and realistic goals and targets for own development are set and prioritised*

Training outcomes should be matched to departmental objectives, learner requirements and your own felt needs. The staff development officer or training department will probably have designed a programme of open seminars that will meet key organisational and departmental needs, but your personal training opportunities could be arranged either in-house on a demand-led basis or by direct application to external training providers. Goals and targets can be defined after you have established your training requirements, checked on available resources and decided how best to meet the needs identified. Whenever possible, personal goals should be linked with organisational objectives.

In order to maintain credibility and be able to adapt easily to changing work-related demands, you will need to identify, diagnose and solve your training requirements proactively. You are the best person to influence decisions about matching personal development goals with new organisational requirements and maximising your contribution quickly and effectively. This is where there is a need to instigate a plan of action and keep track of your progress, recognise your strengths and limitations, record achievements and prioritise remaining development targets. Goals and targets set should be based on an accurate assessment of all relevant information available about areas for personal development, and some suggestions about where to look for inspiration are given in the next section.

*Goals and targets are based on an accurate assessment of all relevant information*

When goal setting you will need to attach more importance to significant and pressing training requirements than to perhaps more attractive but unimportant or non-essential matters. When you are seeking information there are four significant sources of information that will have a direct bearing on your personal development. They are:

- your own current competence
- the current and anticipated future demands of the job
- your aspirations
- overall organisational needs.

Some people find it difficult to identify areas that they will need to consider when appraising their performance. With this in mind it is suggested that you might consider factors such as those given below when identifying your own needs and preparing development targets:

- looking ahead and setting short-term, middle-term and long-term objectives
- identifying specific departmental objectives and targets
- specifying innovations that you wish to introduce
- setting personal objectives against standards supplied
- managing interpersonal relationships
- assessing the adequacy of your technical knowledge and practical ability
- assessing current work rate: productivity
- meeting deadlines and producing work on time.
- reflecting on your attitude towards quality assurance matters
- working on your own initiative and without supervision
- solving problems
- accepting the responsibility for your own actions and supervising others
- making decisions
- understanding and upholding current training-related legislation.

*Goals and targets take into account the need to keep abreast of developments in training and development and related areas*

Somehow teachers will need to keep abreast of new developments as they evolve. Every teacher has a responsibility to monitor current government policy and relevant debates relating to training and development, and to consider the ways in which they impact on their personal development needs. Staff development officers, supervisors and team leaders have a responsibility to keep their colleagues informed about relevant training opportunities available in-house and from external suppliers. This can be achieved by publishing programmes advertising a menu of topical events covering innovation and 'flavours of the month' and making it easy for delegates to access the events.

*Ways of achieving goals and targets are identified*

Once you have established what you wish to achieve you will need to devise an action plan covering the goals and target objectives to be met. This will involve prioritising tasks to be accomplished and working out a feasible timescale to completion for each objective. Using basic planning techniques it should be possible to schedule the sequence of tasks, calculate the resources needed and estimate the time each task will take to complete. Some tasks will follow on in a logical sequence, whilst in some instances it will be possible to overlap tasks and reduce time to completion. A suggested planning-led approach to achieving the goals identified is as follows:

- Identify personal development needs.
- Clarify your objectives.
- Break down your objectives into discrete targets.
- Analyse what must be done.
- Devise your action plan.
- Implement the plan.
- Monitor progress against targets.
- Revise targets as required.

Articles indicating possible ways of achieving your goals might be featured in journals or NATFHE publications. Other sources of information include professional bodies such as the Institute of Personnel and Development, staff development seminars and meetings, and union representatives.

When training on the job in a college or with external training providers is contemplated, the head of department or course tutor would probably be able to arrange a timetable of planned experience. Secondments to industry or commerce provide opportunities for retraining, updating and learning new skills. Coaching and shadowing other teachers are possible alternatives to in-house courses backed up with practice and mentor support.

*Methods of assessing own work and achievement of targets are identified*

A **functional analysis** of your work could provide the basis for assessment of achievement against job-related tasks. Self-assessment techniques are often employed in order to establish how well you are meeting job and organisational needs and also to validate existing techniques and to highlight areas for improvement, the object of assessments being to check on performance of key roles and to identify the need to change methods with a view to making improvements. Furthermore, by getting used to assessing your own efforts you will be better able to overcome defensive attitudes that might be demonstrated when receiving formative feedback from supervisors.

When assessing the achievement of targets teachers could usefully take account of cost implications, the effectiveness of the use of time and resources, and the impact of their teaching methods on the learner group. When judging your performance a balance should be struck between the quality of outcomes achieved and the overall cost-effectiveness of meeting your own objectives and those of the learner group.

Methods of evaluating performance include using inventories (see Figure 17.1 in the *Documents Pack*) and questionnaires to record achievement against factors that are indicative of effective teaching. Indicators of achievement against targets might include estimates of your effectiveness when:

- planning, preparing and facilitating training
- employing classroom management techniques
- organising learning
- managing the learning environment and resources
- administering programmes and departmental systems
- handling relationships with learners and colleagues
- coordinating the administration of learner assessments and interpreting test results
- evaluating the programme effects on learners: degree of satisfaction, enjoyment, ongoing interest, distress, desire to progress, employability, etc.
- monitoring drop-out rates
- using follow-up surveys to check the usefulness and utilisation of knowledge and skills taught.

Teacher behaviour in the classroom can be monitored using teaching practice assessments, student ratings, learner evaluations and self-rating sheets. The concept of self-assessment is discussed in Chapter 16, and an example of a teacher self-assessment sheet is reproduced in Figure 16.4 (see *Documents Pack*).

*Personal action plan is developed and regularly reviewed*

Further training and updating can help you to fulfil personal development goals and enhance your teaching skills. Having identified areas for improvement, rationalised your goals and set targets, you will need to prioritise self-development needs and find suitable learning opportunities that will enable you to meet your requirements. Once you have formulated the seeds of an idea of how you propose to respond quickly to your identified needs you could devise a suitable **personal action plan.** By writing a plan you will be able to decide where you wish to go, devise the means by which your targets will be achieved, allocate completion dates and initiate activity. The plan can be used to keep track of your progress.

There are many methods of personal action planning that could be used, but some teacher-candidates find the completion of standard proforma action plans rather limiting and prefer to draft their own versions. A sample action plan written by Gary Miller and presented as E312 evidence is given in Figure 17.2 (see *Documents Pack*). The plan details Gary's main goals and outlines actions he proposes to take in order to achieve them. A more detailed consideration of the specific actions he will take to improve his teaching skills is given in Figure 17.3 (see Documents Pack).

*Developments to own practice are tried out in ways which do not cause problems for others*

County in-service training (INSET) consortia and teacher centres offer facilities for initial training, updating and ongoing personal development. Other possibilities include INSET activities related to local colleges, teamworking and self-help groups. Some Scottish local enterprise companies (LECs) and training and enterprise councils (TECs) in England and

Wales administer NVQ/SVQ networks, and local training and development initiatives provide useful training opportunities and developmental support.

Teaching centres are ideal places in which to try out new methods. Staff will be there to help you and there will probably be other teachers who will be able to lend a hand when you are trying out new methods. You could develop particular teaching techniques by first watching films or videos illustrating examples of good practice of particular skills and then demonstrating the technique during a short **microteaching** session. Alternatively you could follow the observation of an experienced teacher in action with practice designed to develop those specific teaching skills where deficiencies have been noted. If possible you should arrange for your microteaching to be recorded on video which can be reviewed later. You could also complete a self-assessment form and obtain feedback from the 'learner' group. Documents that could be used for this purpose are given in Figures 17.4 and 17.5 (see *Documents Pack*).

### Microteaching procedure

- Specify your aim and objectives for the microteaching.
- Write a lesson plan covering the content.
- Set the scene for your input. Explain to the group of observers what you intend to cover.
- Make your presentation.
- Withdraw from the room and complete your self-rating sheet.
- Allow time for the group to review your performance and complete their group assessment form.
- Return to the room and share your self-assessment comments with the group.
- Receive feedback from the group.
- Update your self-rating form by adding any comments you wish to make following receipt of the group feedback of your performance.
- Upgrade your teaching accordingly.

Your teaching skills could be perfected by revising and improving your methods and taking account of feedback obtained during the microteaching. Short practice sessions could follow until you are satisfied with your performance.

*Developments to own practice are evaluated and the results used for continued self development*

Teaching practice assessments could be requested from colleagues, mentors or training department staff, and forms such as the one given in Figure 16.8 (see *Documents Pack*) could be used to record features of your performance. These forms normally have sections where the teacher observed can respond to comments made by the assessor and note actions to be taken where improvements are needed. When evaluating progress made to date you could rate your personal development on a scale ranging from 'exceeding requirements' to 'unsatisfactory' and react accordingly (see Figure 17.6).

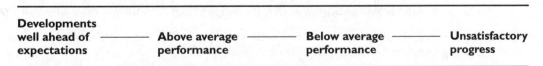

**Figure 17.6** *Personal development progress rating scale*

# Adapting own practice to meet changes in training and development

*Developments in training and development and related areas are regularly reviewed*

In the current climate of change, teachers are advised among other things to take account of the implications of the Education Reform Act 1988 and its consequent influence on national and local debates relating to organisational structures and development. Performance indicators are now widely used to assess a provider's efficiency, and often payment from stakeholders will be outcome-related (i.e. based on outturn). Whether the reader intends to work in a college, private sector training organisation, training department of the NHS or a large commercial company, there is a need to carry out reviews and interpretations of likely developments and suggested changes. Related areas for review could include:

- improving aspects of your own work
- introducing new facilities or resources
- reacting to demographic and labour market trends
- developing new courses
- marketing new products and developing new candidate bases
- developing new markets overseas
- promoting a philosophy of total quality management (TQM)
- introducing quality assurance systems (BS/EN/ISO 9000)
- restructuring (re-engineering) and 'flattening' the organisational structure
- introducing 'flexistudy' and distance learning projects
- managing personal and professional development
- maximising team performance.

Collections of articles relating to current or proposed government policy gathered from national newspapers and periodicals provide suitable portfolio evidence that demonstrates a commitment to keeping up with events leading to change. Teachers can help themselves to keep up to date with national events by reading *The Lecturer* published by NATFHE – the university and college lecturers' union; the *Times Educational Supplement*; magazines and relevant publications held in libraries and resource centres.

*Suggested changes are interpreted and considered critically in relation to the needs of existing and potential learners, occupational environment, and external factors*

While there may appear to be little reason even to think about how to **analyse change** in the context of your current work, things have a habit of catching up with you rather more quickly than you would wish. In some instances, practitioners will be happy to bury their heads in the sand and justify inactivity by convincing themselves that 'it's a management problem – leave it to the vice principals and heads, that's what they're paid for', but the perceptive teacher wishing to survive will anticipate a need to change in line with the provider's overall strategy.

Teachers will therefore need to devise methods of reviewing and interpreting developments in training and development, including changes in:

- organisational policy and practice
- training and development practices
- national systems (such as the National Curriculum)
- local systems
- procedures

● teaching and learning methods.

*Own resistance to change is recognised and steps taken to deal with it appropriately*

People tend to feel resentful if change is imposed without adequate consultation. Clear explanations must be given as to why proposed changes are necessary and how the individuals involved will be affected. They will need time to prepare a rationale for the way they will deal with new developments in training programmes or unwanted variations in timetables. For example, loss of esteem is felt when, because of poor enrolment, favourite 'high level' classes are replaced by less interesting 'low status' subjects which will require a lot of hard work in new preparation and updating. While some people seem to thrive on change and will welcome the challenge identified with a particular innovation, others will react adversely, especially when change is imposed at very short notice. People tend to feel insecure and can easily easily become depressed, especially when jobs are threatened or if overtime payments cease as a result of changes. Poor communication and lack of awareness raising are often the culprits promoting resistance to change, and this is especially true if the rate of change is perceived to be too rapid.

Ways of dealing with change include:

● taking the grapevine version with a pinch of salt
● avoiding arguments
● seeking factual information about the reasons for changes
● asking supervisors to explain how the proposed changes will affect you personally
● finding out how you can benefit from the forthcoming changes
● requesting personal development opportunities or retraining
● avoiding inactivity and feelings of inadequacy
● adopting a positive attitude and finding ways of accommodating the changes
● forming a curriculum development team to generate necessary teaching resources to cope with new training developments
● consulting your NATFHE representative if confused or threatened.

## Reflecting on resistance to change

**Resistance to change** is undoubtedly a widespread phenomenon, and people will often find it difficult to choose between alternatives that contain both positive and negative features. Emotion and tension often cloud the line dividing two alternatives: making a rational choice between going along with the proposed change and trying things out, and taking avoidance action. On a more personal level, the following extract from Gary Miller's reflections on his own experiences while achieving his C&G 7306 FAETC describes how he coped with changes in teaching and learning methods. It is interesting to note how Gary's earlier experiences coloured his approach to learning, and how he moved (perhaps at first somewhat reluctantly) towards a more learner-centred facilitative role.

### Reflecting on resistance to change

Having now been involved in adult and continuing education since August 1994, I have come to realise the changes in teaching and training methods that are taking place. My previous experience with adult education (as a student on BSc and MSc programmes) primarily revolved around formal lectures and pure practical sessions, with the occasional tutorial if there was time. Student participation and feedback was minimal, with learning outcomes assessed primarily using test papers and examinations.

My next involvement with training was in 1989 during the course of my employment with a large insurance company. Much of their training involved formal tasks, followed by (easy!) multiple choice test papers. Some learner participation occurred, primarily when students were asked to answer specific closed questions used to test theory. My own views and thoughts were not requested, in fact they were positively discouraged, and the statements 'What the trainers say is law' and 'Consultants are not paid to think' were heard on many occasions.

When, in August 1994, I attended a NEBSM Introductory Course in Educational Training and Management run by Les Walklin, it came as a bit of a shock to find that instead of sitting passively in the classroom and being talked at, I would have to actively participate! I felt extremely uncomfortable at first, being urged to give my views and opinions in small and large group situations. Similarly, I found group work and discussions completely alien in the early stages. However, I quickly came to appreciate the value of such teaching methods. The group work discussions helped build my confidence, although I still felt a little intimidated in large group discussions.

Following on from this, the FAETC 7306 course, due to its competence-based approach, involved considerable learner participation. Again, I found such activities stimulating, but I still felt reluctant to participate in large group discussions (fellow members said what I wanted to say before I had the chance!). I think this still relates back to my university education, where I could get on with the work but feel secure while keeping a low profile and hiding in the background.

Thus, during the course of my teaching practice I was acutely aware that I must allow the learners in my group to have their say and actively participate. However, with my background I found this extremely difficult to start with. I find it much easier to talk around a subject, since any learner participation (awkward questions) can throw me off track – but, for adults, the 'talk-mode' of delivery must be very boring. At first, I found that I had to consciously make myself ask questions designed to elicit a response from members of the group. I just hoped that I could handle the situation if my question led to requests for explanation and clarification that I had not fully prepared for. But I found that it did become easier with practice and it was gratifying when the group responded positively – which they always did.

In summary, I found the sudden change in my perceptions of teaching methods a complete shock. I therefore had to completely change my concepts and attitudes to the way I thought adult teaching could best be performed. I then had to apply these changes to my teaching practice. I now feel more comfortable acting as a facilitator of learning, but I realise that I require a lot more practice before I can say that I am an expert at it.

Gary Miller, December 1995
Evidence reference Element E313 (pc 'C')

*Resistance to change from others is identified and handled appropriately*

Sooner or later most teachers will be faced with need to change their own working methods or introduce new learning programmes. They must therefore have the skills needed to devise and implement a strategy which enables the required changes to take place without adversely affecting morale. The process of change may be perceived as a natural phenomenon and entered into willingly, or on the other hand change may be thrust upon people. An outline strategy for managing change is given in Figure 17.7, followed by a list of factors that could be considered when planning and implementing the strategy.

```
┌─────────────────────────────────────────────────┐
│                                                 │
│               Change strategy                   │
│                                                 │
│          Identify the need for change.          │
│                                                 │
│       Detail possible responses to that need.   │
│                                                 │
│       Consider implications of each option.     │
│                                                 │
│            Foresee likely outcomes.             │
│                                                 │
│     Identify sources of resistance to change.   │
│                                                 │
│          Analyse causes of resistance.          │
│                                                 │
│              Formulate remedies.                │
│                                                 │
│   Involve those affected by the change in planning │
│      and implementing the change process.       │
│                                                 │
│           Monitor implementation.               │
│                                                 │
└─────────────────────────────────────────────────┘
```

**Figure 17.7** *Change strategy*

### Factors which impact on own and other people's reactions to change include:

- fears – of being misled, caught out or abused
- unwillingness to discard the old way
- inability to become absorbed in a new project and to learn quickly and thoroughly understand new requirements
- inability to adjust to new procedures
- degree of willingness to conform or to accommodate change.

### Identify sources and causes of resistance to change such as:

- dissent and hostility
- silent protest evidenced by hindering the introduction of change, outright rejection or some kind of restraint
- inability to cope with the unexpected
- limiting factors: protectionism and monopolising certain aspects of the work
- evaluations of current achievement which could lead to unwanted reassignment or retraining.

### Prepare and manage ways of overcoming resistance:

- Realise that for every change decision there will be a reaction.
- Communicate the purpose of change and outline how this might be achieved.
- Map the current position and justify the need for change.
- Encourage your people to recognise the need for change.
- Find ways of opening the door and welcoming change.
- Sell the benefits of change.
- Check whether your people understand any new duties they will be asked to take on.
- Define the target outcome.
- Set a large number of lower priority attainable goals together with a few high-priority and more demanding goals.
- Share proposals and invite adaptations and suggestions for meeting goals.

- Identify obstacles and barriers to change.
- Prepare to handle reactions to change positively and supportively.
- Be flexible in your approach – be prepared to adjust your plans to accommodate changing circumstances and group needs.
- Encourage your people to be receptive to new ways of doing things.

**Identify likely responses:**

- Resistance: people setting their face against the proposed change
- Refusing to cooperate: vetoing action proposed by others

Identify other likely responses by carrying out a force field analysis.[3] (See Figure 17.8.)

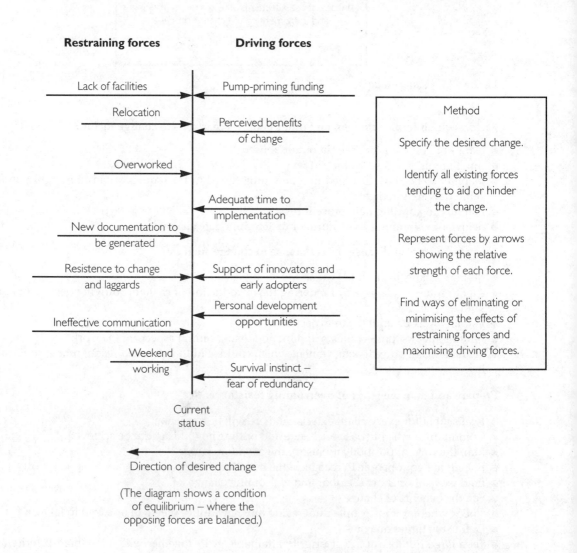

**Restraining forces**      **Driving forces**

Lack of facilities    Pump-priming funding

Relocation

Perceived benefits
of change

Overworked

Adequate time to
implementation

New documentation to
be generated

Resistence to change    Support of innovators and
and laggards    early adopters

Personal development
Ineffective communication    opportunities

Weekend
working    Survival instinct –
fear of redundancy

Current
status

**Method**

Specify the desired change.

Identify all existing forces
tending to aid or hinder
the change.

Represent forces by arrows
showing the relative
strength of each force.

Find ways of eliminating or
minimising the effects of
restraining forces and
maximising driving forces.

Direction of desired change

(The diagram shows a condition
of equilibrium – where the
opposing forces are balanced.)

**Figure 17.8** *Force field analysis*

**Involve those affected by change in the change process by:**

- seeking the cooperation and commitment of stakeholders, innovators and early adopters
- introducing the concept of synergy, team effort and joint ownership
- adopting an open-minded approach
- challenging existing practices
- looking for ways and means of making improvements
- critically analysing existing methods and suggesting improvements
- agreeing a timetable for action
- identifying their own relevant needs and developing new competencies
- promoting a willingness to try out new techniques, changed procedures or methods of working
- making it easy for the late adopters to accept the proposed change, fall in line and follow the crowd.

*Existing practices and systems are challenged where new ideas and practices have the potential to be more effective*

Existing practices and systems should be challenged whenever anything new is introduced and particularly when major facilities, systems or resources are to be introduced. Considerable changes will be required when, for instance, new ideas and practices have the potential to be more effective. Typical generators of the need for significant change include:

- setting up new departments
- installing new technology and equipment
- introducing new systems and procedures
- offering new qualifications
- implementing a new assessment philosophy
- introducing new staffing grades and job roles

Apart from the usual problems of insufficient physical and human resources, other typical indicators of the need for change might be:

- problems in pre-course activities such as clarifying programme intentions
- inadequate pre-programme counselling and guidance
- difficulty in agreeing and setting standards
- poor communications: lack of information and promotional materials
- selection procedures: difficulties in gaining access to programme
- unfriendly enrolment procedures
- mismatch between learner group needs and provision
- lack of learner support.

At individual teacher level the starting point for any review of existing practices will be the programme or **course evaluation**. The **programme aims** and objectives provide the standards or target areas against which performance indicators can be measured. Failure to satisfy **learner entitlement** will also signal the need to challenge existing practices and systems. Apart from the information derived from learner evaluation sheets, performance could be profiled against indicators such as those that follow (although there are many others to choose from):

- how well the course was managed
- suitability of teaching strategies
- matching teaching methods against lesson content
- linkages with work experience

- utilisation of latest technology
- achievement of programme objectives: qualifications awarded and referrals/examination 'failures'
- relevance of content
- perceived difficulty/level of work
- workload: too much/too little work involved
- registered absences from classes
- estimation of learner enjoyment and level of satisfaction with course
- number of early leavers
- attrition rate: number of non-completers
- provision for integrating disabled learners
- amount of help offered learners with reading, writing and numeracy problems
- level of learner autonomy/empowerment
- stakeholders' expressed satisfaction (or dissatisfaction).

*Benefits of change are actively promoted and presented in a positive manner*

It is said that in a commercial context, customers do not buy a service or product, they buy the benefits that the service or acquisition will bring them. This concept is transferable to the management of change. When thinking about effective ways and means of promoting change there will be a need to formulate a policy and agree clear objectives for implementing the change. But people may be unwilling to adopt or support change unless they can readily see that there is something in it for them. It is therefore sensible to establish the benefits to participants of becoming involved before launching into the implementation stage. A suggested approach to establishing the benefits to people who will be affected by the proposed change is given in Figure 17.9.

Identify benefits associated with the change.

Specify positive features of change.

Highlight advantages of seizing the opportunity.

Outline tangible benefits.

Explain how benefits can be realised.

Establish commitment.

**Figure 17.9** *Establishing benefits to participants*

Promotional activities can be devised that are aimed at gaining interest and developing positive attitudes towards the intended change. Any means of gaining support should be considered, including finding volunteers (innovators and early adopters) to influence the remainder by instilling confidence and emphasising the 'can do' aspects. Any expertise available to support people throughout the change period should be used, and efforts made to capitalise (but not rely too heavily) on people's goodwill. Throughout the implementation stage, successes could be reinforced by publishing newsworthy items.

*Disruption to learners from adopting change is minimised*

Deliberately disrupting learners' programmes or learning opportunities should be avoided at all costs. Making changes during classes will cause agitation or, even worse, create turmoil or disorder. Moving equipment around or making alterations to the room layout while learners are working will inevitably disrupt the learning process. Any form of upheaval should be avoided as this would lead to restlessness, thereby interrupting the progress of a lesson or programme and losing the learners' commitment to work productively.

Making changes at programme level could adversely affect the learners' level of achievement and lead to complaints, and in any case the learners are entitled to expect fair treatment and consideration. If unexpected disruption does occur make it clear that any problems are your problems not theirs – but nevertheless listen to their comments and welcome their suggestions. Don't blame others for difficulties holding up progress, and ensure that you clearly accept ultimate responsibility for any decisions taken.

*Results of change are reflected on and used to inform future action in promoting change*

However successful they are, all teachers need to change and keep changing. But change can be risky so it pays to find out what other teachers have been successful in achieving before going it alone. The evaluation of change can best be undertaken by those most closely involved in the innovation, and this, of course, will include the implementers and the end users of the service affected. Effective and **ongoing monitoring** of outcomes should be considered as an integral and essential part of the change process. Important aspects to be looked at will include the current **quality** of the changed provision and the **validity** of the change in terms of its **effects** on those involved.

Future action in promoting continuous improvement will be determined by first establishing what could usefully be changed and then gaining the knowledge required to facilitate the change. The logic of the proposition outlined in Figure 17.10 appears indisputable.

> Continuous improvement requires change.
>
> Change requires new knowledge.
>
> New knowledge requires learning.
>
> Thus rapid learning is required
> for rapid improvement.

**Figure 17.10** *Promoting continuous change*[4]

A framework for reviewing change outcomes could be devised in order to provide **indicators** that will **inform** future changes. For example, it could be useful to keep a diary of how the change was implemented and record key information about aspects such as the time expended and costs incurred, methods employed, staff and resourcing commitments, and records of investigations. Having collected relevant information and noted significant findings you will be able to draw conclusions and make recommendations about how best to **hold on to gains** made and **improve strategies** for managing future changes.

## Self-assessment questions

1　Why is it important to evaluate your own teaching practices against set goals and standards?

2　Draw up a list of sources of valid and reliable evidence that you could explore when gathering evidence for an evaluation of your own practice.

3 Why is it important to seek the views and support of others when you are interpreting evidence gathered?

4 Explain why it is important for teachers to consider the impact and effects of their behaviour on learners.

5 Explain the value of reflecting on your own practice and professional behaviour.

6 Explain the benefits of giving constructive, objective and descriptive feedback to colleagues, and why they should adopt an open and positive manner when receiving criticism.

7 Why may it be necessary to adjust goals and targets as a result of reviewing evidence of performance?

8 Explain how you can use the views of candidates and colleagues, and evidence of work results, appraisals and formative assessments when evaluating your own performance.

9 List the various methods of self-assessment that can be used when teachers are evaluating their performance.

10 Describe the value of completing checklists when you are collecting performance evidence.

11 Why is it important for teachers to keep abreast of government policy and current relevant debates relating to training and development?

12 Explain how clear and realistic personal development goals can be set and prioritised.

13 Draw up a personal action plan showing how your own identified personal development needs will be met.

14 Why is it important to review progress regularly against planned targets and update action plans accordingly?

15 Explain the possible undesirable effects on learners of experimenting and trying out new methods in the classroom or workshop.

16 Comment on the advantages and disadvantages of using evaluation sheets such as those in Figures 16.4–16.8, 17.1, 17.4 and 17.5 (see *Documents Pack*).

17 Explain what is meant by 'resistance to change'. Explain the steps you take (or would take) when dealing with your own resistance to change.

18 Devise a strategy for identifying and handling others' resistance to change.

19 Explain how to promote change effectively and minimise disruption to learners when implementing changes.

20 Explain the importance of taking account of the results of current changes when you are planning future changes.

## Preparing for assessment: sample activities

### Activity 17.1 Evaluating your own practice

Seek the assistance of learners and colleagues in gathering objective views about your teaching style and teaching methods. Use checklists or any other form of review instruments to collect evidence that can be used to evaluate your own practice. Write a personal action plan showing how you will meet any self-development needs identified.

### Activity 17.2 Monitoring current training and development debates

Research current news items and reports on government policy and current relevant debates relating to training and development. Summarise the key features that will affect your work and make notes on the ways in which any innovations or changes will impact on your own development needs.

### Activity 17.3 Responding to change

Describe two instances where you have adapted your own practice to meet the need to respond to changes in your training and personal development. Produce your own documentary evidence to support claims made, and also collect testimonies from employers, colleagues and candidates that will authenticate the adaptations made.

### Activity 17.4 Introducing change

Teachers are often required to take on the role of an 'agent of change'. Identify an area where you consider that there is a need for innovation and change. Reflect on the results of changes that have involved you either as someone who has been affected by the changes or as an agent of change. Consider how your earlier experiences can be used to inform future action in promoting change.

Draw up plans for implementing the innovation which you have identified. Your plans should cover the following objectives:

- Describe the need for the proposed innovation and change.
- Identify feasible change options.
- List the anticipated responses from those who will be affected.
- Forecast the likely outcomes, benefits and costs of the various change options.
- Identify likely causes of resistance to the proposed change and ways of overcoming resistance.
- Specify essential requirements for successfully implementing the changes. Include:
  - effective communication
  - awareness raising
  - selling benefits
  - involving those affected in planning and facilitating the changes
  - teamworking
  - monitoring progress and providing support
  - pacing and phasing change
  - following up.
- Evaluate outcomes.

### Notes

1 N. Rackham, P. Honey and M. Colbert, *Developing Interactive Skills*, Wellens Publishing, Northampton 1971.

2 E. Berne, *Games People Play: The Psychology of Human Relationships*, Penguin, Harmondsworth 1967.

3 Opposing forces are almost always present in times of change. There will be driving forces that tend to move the desired change forward and restraining forces that tend to maintain the status quo. When these forces are in equilibrium no movement may be perceived. For something to happen the restraining forces must be overcome or eliminated. A technique used to gain a clearer picture of the disposition of forces is a **force field analysis** (see Figure 17.8).

**Driving forces** relating to factors favourable to the proposed change are located on one side of the vertical datum line representing the **current status**, with the **restraining forces** on the opposite side. The analysis is carried out during the early stages of an assessment of what people's

269

attitudes and reactions will be toward a proposed change. It can be seen that the length of the lines of force drawn on a particular diagram is proportional to the perceived importance of the opposing factors. These factors are identified during an analysis of how people profess to feel about the change after careful explanation and discussion of what is involved. The analyst can prepare an action plan, and resources can be targeted after the main concerns and problems that have to be overcome have been idenfied. Priority is then allocated to the solution of each.

4    Source: Joiner Associates Inc., 3800 Regent Street, PO Box 5445, Madison, Wisconsin. 53703-0445 USA. Quoted by Tony Henry, Principal, East Birmingham College, during his TQM presentation at the Trainer Development Group National Conference 'Placing Trainer Training in the Future', held at Hotel Arcade, Birmingham, on 7 June 1991.

# 18

# Managing relationships with colleagues and customers

The ways in which teachers work with colleagues and customers will determine the success of the teaching team and the effectiveness and value of learning outcomes. Good communications and harmonious relationships can go a long way towards making up for deficiencies in resources, and can promote a high level of satisfaction and personal development for teachers and learners alike.

The bulk of our customers will be learners, although we may serve many other stakeholders. Today the term **internal customer** refers to any person who is receiving a service from people like you who are providing the required service. But at the same time we could be customers of another supplier such as the reprographics supervisor. It can be seen that all customers and colleagues are interdependent, and therefore in order to be successful we need to communicate well. This will involve an ability to manage our relationships with colleagues and customers so as to share common goals and effectively meet agreed aims and objectives.

Colleagues and customers alike can expect to receive our support when they need it, and we in turn can expect their support too. Ethical aspects of professional teaching practice are accounted for by establishing good working relationships, and are reflected by high standards of teacher conduct and by placing a great deal of importance in satisfying the interests of our learners. This entails demonstrating professional values and giving colleagues and learners a high level of support when and where they need it. This in turn requires that we have regard for the psychological and social effects that our behaviour may have on those with whom we interact on a daily basis. When we notice signs of distress, overload or pressure on the people around us we need to offer our support and not stand back or look the other way. We need to offer advice and help where we can; to aim to work together in cooperative and collaborative ways; and act in ways that will safeguard the interests of our customers. But we can only do this by working hard at establishing and maintaining constructive relationships with our colleagues and customers.

## Managing relationships with colleagues

*Time is taken to establish and maintain constructive relationships with colleagues*

Building constructive relationships with colleagues is the key to successful team teaching and other forms of cooperating and working together. Cooperating is much better than competing, and efforts should be made to achieve mutual respect and trust so that optimum working practices result.

As teachers we must realise that we are all different. Differences in background, temperament, personal characteristics and preferred teaching style will all affect the way we get along with each other. Networking with colleagues with whom the practitioner works closely on a regular basis, and those with whom the practitioner works with occasionally, should be based on openness and honesty. Respect for the other's point of view should be demonstrated, and opinions should be exchanged without fear of ridicule or loss of face. Where views conflict, a suitable compromise should be sought – for there is always a middle way.

*Behaviour towards colleagues is open, honest and friendly*

We can demonstrate open, honest and friendly relations with colleagues by always doing the right thing and behaving decently towards one another. We are morally bound to conduct ourselves according to the ethical principles, college rules and codes of behaviour appropriate to our position as teaching professionals. These codes, written or unwritten, govern our behaviour towards our colleagues and students alike.

We should demonstrate an altruistic approach in our relationships with colleagues, and be seen to be virtuous and to be setting a good example when dealing with our learners. When it comes to anti-discrimination, equal opportunities and health and safety matters we need to be beyond reproach in what we say and do. But teaching is a stressful occupation, and at times we can forget all about ethics and become so wrapped up in our own troubles that we ignore the needs of others and forget our team obligations. We become short tempered and seek to unload our problems on whoever happens to be nearest at the time. This does nothing to preserve good relationships, and should be resisted. By all means seek help from your colleagues but do not try to make your worries theirs.

Other factors impacting on relationships with colleagues include:

- age differences
- differences in socio-economic status
- grade or position in hierarchy
- level of qualifications and experience
- differing views on equal opportunities and anti-discrimination practices
- a teacher's own values and beliefs
- having or lacking the ability to say 'No' when this can be justified
- win/win or win/lose orientation.

*Support is sought from an appropriate person in dealing with difficulties with colleagues*

Situations may arise during daily interaction with colleagues whereby you are confronted with difficulties that you cannot handle yourself. People with personal agendas that do not coincide with your needs can cause obstruction and incidents that result in conflict. For example, how do you handle less-than-cooperative colleagues who reject outright sensible suggestions put by yourself or other team members? How do you cope with outright hostility or rejection? How can you deal with team members who are not contributing much to agreed team targets and not completing tasks allocated?

Newly appointed teachers may be considered too keen – taking on extra work and volunteering for anything as long as they can catch the head of department's eye. Established teachers may be perceived as competitors in the promotion stakes. Others may opt out and concentrate on protecting their own interests, guarding jealously the niche they have painstakingly carved out over a long period. If their current status is challenged teachers may resort to backbiting – talking about others behind their backs and blaming them for anything they can hang on them. Clashes over timetabling, classes allocated, level of work and overtime can also lead to disagreements.

Appropriate sources of support for dealing with difficulties with colleagues arising from the causes listed above will have to be found. The **timetabler** is an obvious target for people seeking to resolve a good many sources of conflict. Immediate 'superiors', team leaders and course tutors may be able to offer guidance and advice on other matters. **Experts** in specific areas who may be more qualified to sort out the problem could be called upon to help, as could your personal **mentor**.

If you need support in dealing with difficult staff you should target your confidant carefully. Don't go about involving anyone who will listen to your story. If you involve too many people the responsibility for taking remedial action will be shared and this can lead to opt-outs. To maintain harmonious relations and team spirit will be the desired objectives of any advice given.

*Opinions and information are exchanged and shared with colleagues*

It is important to realise the benefits of shared ownership of strategies and proposals. You can encourage ownership and commitment on the part of colleagues by exploring the suggestions they make and seeking their opinions about matters of mutual interest. Think about how you have offered advice to colleagues and the ways in which differences in opinions have been handled. Do you agree that by pooling ideas a broader perspective of any topic can be obtained, and that this is much better than basing opinions on supposition or unsupported assumptions?

You can help to develop the full potential of small teams by gaining support and commitment to an endeavour and working together with other team members to avoid pitfalls. Managing relationships with colleagues involves looking at several dimensions of any problem and seeking a wide body of opinions. When people contribute to the decision-making process interest is taken in the notion of shared accountability for decisions taken. You can facilitate cohesion and team development by actively trying to see things from the others' point of view and taking account of their feelings and emotions when giving your opinion or exchanging information with colleagues.

*Differences of opinion are dealt with in ways which try to avoid offence, and conflicts are resolved in ways that maintain respect*

Collaborative, cooperative and harmonious working of the teaching team is desirable if learners are to get the best out of any learning opportunity. Providing the appropriate quality of learner support is a shared responsibility which to be successful will depend on the **avoidance of conflict** among team members. In order for teamwork to be effective there must be mutual understanding, trust and respect between the team members. Unfortunately, from time to time individuals do have differences of opinions and conflict may result. In this instance, both sides of the argument should be heard and recognised even when those concerned do not particularly admire one another. It is no use adamantly sticking to a single point of view and hoping to browbeat the other person into submission. All that would happen is that individuals would stick to their own personal objectives at the others' expense, or if in a position of power would press ahead regardless while ignoring other opinions.

Professional codes of conduct require that this kind of outcome does not result. Teacher accountability demands that the rights and responsibilities of other teachers are respected and that high standards of interpersonal relations are maintained. Offence and conflict must be avoided at all costs, and the assistance of an unbiased advocate should be sought if agreement cannot be reached individually or within the team.

*Colleagues are encouraged to feel comfortable to express opinions, concerns and to ask for help*

Enlightened education and training providers are now introducing the 'delayered' management structure. They are replacing yesterday's strictly hierarchical and forbidding style of management with a somewhat more open and democratic approach to teamworking. The climate is now right for adopting the 360° approach to appraisal and support whereby teachers can benefit from feedback from many sources: supervisors, peers, learners, support staff and other stakeholders. The flatter organisational structure also encourages people to feel comfortable when expressing opinions, making suggestions, asking for team support or seeking advice from individual colleagues. This enables teachers at all levels to maximise their contribution to the teaching and learning programme, to derive satisfaction from helping others and to benefit from adopting an open-minded attitude to coaching and counselling given and received. However, colleagues will only give their support to this new-style open approach if they can be assured of obtaining a fair hearing and can feel that any confidential information concerning them is protected.

*Advice and help are offered with sensitivity*

Stress can result from a person's inability to cope with the demands encountered within the environment in which they work. The effects of distress caused by overwork, pressures in the classroom, pain inflicted by tactless supervisors and the resulting stress are felt by many hard-pressed teachers. The kind of situations frequently met within the educational world that call for teacher support and advice include the following:

- being landed with a tough assignment, feeling well out of your depth and being beset with difficulties
- having your work cut out to maintain your basic timetable let along bearing the brunt of an additional workload
- being allocated dead weights or unmotivated helpers who lack initiative
- being given a formidable problem that is more easily specified than done, and getting into a muddle
- thinking about your problems, feeling puzzled, worrying and having difficulty in getting to sleep
- being hampered by a lack of resources, minimal budget or unrealistic timescales and conditions
- teaching unreasonably large groups and facing severe cuts in programmed hours allocated to complete the work
- taking up a lot of time and nervous energy sorting out new equipment that is suffering teething troubles, and making do with older or inadequate resources
- experiencing friction between yourself and learners or other members of staff
- reaching an impasse with an obstinate or ill-behaved student who is hard to deal with
- feeling that you are batting on a sticky wicket or sailing close to the wind
- dealing with borderline students and worrying about making doubtful assessment judgements; feeling the pressure brought about by your employer's fixation on performance-related payments and fearing repercussions if you are honest in your decisions.

Advice should be given tactfully to colleagues in an open and friendly manner. Suitable choices of options should be offered to reduce potential embarrassment or conflict. Advice should be provided in private and never within earshot of students, and confidences should not be openly discussed with other colleagues. If you find yourself in circumstances such as those listed above you would be well advised to seek advice and help from someone who is able to offer support sensitively. Likewise, as a teacher you would be expected to demonstrate a knowledge of appropriate sources of advice and help and how to match them with individual colleagues' needs. When giving advice, a counselling approach could be used to allow your colleague to reflect on any potential problem and hopefully to avoid it or solve it for themselves. Suitable sources of information could be offered, or other personnel could be introduced who may be better qualified to deal with their problem. The abridged statement given in Figure 18.1 illustrates how Gary Miller supplemented his main teaching diary with comment on how he sensitively offered advice and help to a colleague. He used this statement to supplement other relevant direct performance evidence contained in his **critical incident log and analysis**.

> During the course of my teaching practice I did, on occasion, offer help to Bryan the co-facilitator. I made suggestions about session content, sequencing and alternative delivery modes in a constructive manner. At all times I was mindful of the need to give advice that would hopefully enhance the process for learners and make things easier for Bryan. Any potential disagreements or differences of opinion were always resolved privately before the session commenced and reviewed afterwards. Finally, if it became clear that Bryan was still not entirely happy with my proposals I would suggest that he consulted Les, the course tutor.
>
> Gary Miller
> Evidence reference element E321 (pc 'g')

**Figure 18.1** *Abridged statement: offering advice and help*

*Division of work with colleagues takes account of complementary skills, knowledge, experience and individual development needs, where possible*

**Division of work** involves the allocation of different parts of a task or training programme to different teachers. This implies the need to work openly and cooperatively with colleagues and to foster a constructive working relationship with them. When allocating work you will need to acknowledge your own inadequacies and limitations and avoid taking on duties or responsibilities that you feel you are not qualified to carry out safely and properly. **Specialisation** results from training and qualifying in a particular area of study and leads to gaining occupational area skills that will enable a teacher to undertake certain work more efficiently and effectively. You will need to collaborate with your colleagues and recognise and respect the skills, knowledge and experience that they are able to transfer into the programme. You will also need to take account of their potential involvement in programme delivery, assessment and evaluation when devising the scheme of work at the planning stage.

*Promises and undertakings to others are honoured, taking account of other priorities and commitments*

Showing enterprise can be very commendable. But being overambitious and having too many irons in the fire can lead to overload and failure to get any task done to the required standard. New teachers may find it hard to say 'No'. They sometimes volunteer their services and launch into an undertaking without considering their existing commitments which should really take precedence. Having made a promise they feel committed and assume an obligation to take on the associated responsibility for the programme or project. They make an unwritten contract and then find that they have taken on more than they can cope with and are unable to honour their promises. The result: they become distressed and let down their colleagues.

Before giving any undertaking you need to take a realistic view of what you can manage to do and you need to prioritise. If you find that you cannot honour your obligations you should tell those concerned without delay while there is still time to formulate contingency plans. If it is not possible to contact the people concerned a report should be made to a responsible person who could help. Under no circumstances should the welfare of your learners be put at risk or team standards compromised because you are unable to honour your promises.

## Managing relationships with customers

*Time is taken to establish and maintain constructive relationships with customers*

A **customer** can be any person who receives a service from a training provider, and the aim should be to foster good relations by maintaining a personalised, warm, friendly and welcoming atmosphere supported by interested and committed people. First impressions count. As media advertisements pronounce: 'You never get a second chance to make a good first impression.' When customers need you, will you be on hand to attend to their needs? Will you greet them with a smile? If they interrupt while you are working will you stop what you are doing and listen carefully to what they have to say? Or will you be so busy and stressed that you will transmit your anxieties to them and terminate the conversation before getting a clear picture of what is needed? To build constructive relationships you have to do better than this. Customer enquiries should not be viewed as an interruption to your work: you are dependent upon their business.

Adult learners can quickly identify with teachers who show genuine interest in them, and once this is perceived they will respond with loyalty and enthusiasm. Credibility must be established as soon as possible with a new group of learners. The effectiveness of teaching and learning will depend not only on adequate preparation of subject matter, but also on the way your learners evaluate you on day one. If you are seen to be credible, that is reliable and qualified by experience and ability in the task area, then there is a high probability that you will be accepted. But if the learners form the opinion that you lack the necessary assertiveness or subject expertise they will be quick to notice shortcomings and you will be off to a bad start. A teacher is more likely to establish a constructive relationship with learners if they can win the group's confidence and approval very early in the programme.

**Internal customers** include all who receive or make use of services you provide. This applies whether you are working with regular customers or working with occasional customers. Everyone you interact with will be either a customer or supplier, and customer requirements can only be met when their specific needs are communicated and correctly perceived by their suppliers.

*Customers are addressed and described in the manner which they prefer*

Suitable icebreaker activities introduced early during the first meeting can be used to break down barriers, and the opportunity used to match names with faces. The appropriate use of humour will assist in building learner confidence and overcoming inhibitions. It is especially important to demonstrate a caring attitude when addressing learners for the first time. Each customer should be addressed by name and should be given a clear indication that their views and comments are required and valued. Suitable praise, reinforcement and public acceptance helps build rapport. However, emphasis should be placed on finding out essential information about every individual, such as their preferred manner of address in relation to their name and title. Some learners prefer a more formal style of address such as Mr, Mrs or Miss Wyatt; others are happier if first names are used; while some prefer nicknames such as Chippie Wood or Smudger Smith. But the choice must be theirs, and it would be wrong to assume that it is OK to use labels that you think will be acceptable – you must check first.

*The manner of communication and interaction with individual customers is appropriate*

The manner of communication will be either informal or formal, and how you perceive the current situation when interacting with a particular individual will lead to the arousal of motives for communicating with that person in a certain way. Your actions will probably be triggered by a combination of your customer's approach to you and your recollection of similar past events with other people. Prejudices, assumptions and expectations are aroused by the tone of the interaction, and this will affect the way you respond.

Interactive behaviour is influenced by your own personality traits that have developed over time. Factors which impact on the manner of communication and approach you adopt might include your perceptions and patterns of thinking, motives, emotions and the effect of conflict experienced when interacting with people. These factors may include commonly held cultural and social perceptions which you share, as well as your own attitudes, values and beliefs based on past experience. Racism evidenced by racial prejudice and stereotyping, although illegal, may negatively affect the manner of interaction with others. On the positive side, having a knowledge of **community languages** spoken by some ethnic minority groups will be useful when you are communicating with individual customers whose first language is not English.

Over time we each tend to develop ways of responding to others and controlling our behaviour towards them. In general when communicating with learners a 'the customer is always right' policy could be a useful starting point. By taking an interest and listening carefully you can find out what your customer really wants. However, if having heard what they have to say you cannot agree with them, do not tell them that they are wrong or they will lose face. Always remember that the way people respond to what you have to say will depend on the way that you say it.

*Customers are given clear and sufficient information about the service they can expect*

Customers have at least one thing in common: they expect to get value for money. They will judge the training provider on the quality of service received and the extent to which their expectations are consistently met. A **mission statement** defines the philosophy that underpins the provider's training operations, and a short mission similar to that given in Figure 18.2 expresses in the broadest terms the kind of service learners can expect.

When learners need more detailed information than the mission provides, it becomes necessary to disseminate more information about learner entitlement; you can assist this process by drafting a **customer's charter** giving details of the service learners can expect. A typical charter is given in Figure 12.3.

**The type of information which customers need is:**

- learning opportunities available
- student entitlements and agreements
- support services available
- student handbook.

---

**Mission**

● To satisfy local, regional and national employment needs for people educated to various levels of creative sensibility and technical competence to carry out work-related activities in a variety of occupations dependent on their particular area of specialisation.

● To provide each customer with an accurate and realistic insight into work-related employment opportunities, requirements and prospects.

● To structure learning opportunities so as to provide the educational and professional experiences necessary to enhance customers' employment prospects.

● To develop customers' creative, intellectual and craft skills to a high level, and to aid personal development and the ability to adapt to changing circumstances.

● To provide encouragement, advice and assessment in order to help each customer fully realise individual potential.

---

**Figure 18.2** *Short mission statement*

### Customers can reinforce and supplement the information given by:

- speaking to other customers or any of the training provider's teachers or support staff
- reading printed information provided in the form of handbooks, handouts or charts
- watching demonstrations and videos
- asking further questions about the programme and training methods employed
- consulting with advisory staff.

### Customers can find out information and interpret instructions for themselves by:

- speaking to other candidates
- consulting written sources
- observing others
- interpreting spoken instructions
- interpreting written instructions
- finding out the needs of others in the group
- finding out the facts about things that have gone wrong
- finding out the needs of other customers.

*Constraints on communication with customers are identified and minimised*

Language is the characteristic feature of communication and it is the means by which thought processes are manifested. Languages are sets of rules, and the application of these rules makes possible the formation and understanding of sentences. If the rules are known and the appropriate vocabulary is available to listeners, then they will be able to interpret sentences that they have never heard before. Similarly they will be able to assemble words in a form that will be readily understood by others with access to the same language.

Many teachers are of the opinion that differences in educational opportunity are manifested by the ability or lack of ability of their customers (students) to form concepts, ideas and attitudes, and to use vocabularies – mental and verbal – that they possess. Differences in socio-economic status and cultural influences will invariably affect life chances and the quality of written and oral communications when in an educational environment. Language deficiencies resulting in impaired progress and development are influenced by many factors, including level of intelligence, degree of verbal stimulation at home, and social dialects resulting from the origin and social environment of those concerned.

Basil Bernstein[1] refers to two main language codes: the **restricted code**, which is characterised by the use of short, simple and unplanned sentences, thereby limiting the scope of expression; and the **elaborate code**, used by middle-class speakers who have access to a large number of alternative words, which enables them to understand elaborate statements, frame complex messages and make clear their intended meanings. The differences in language codes greatly affect the quality of communication and what can be learned in class. Consequently, if the language used by teachers is not understood by learners then the concept being taught will not be internalised and many levels of abstraction will be beyond their capacity.[2]

**Underachievement** is a term used to describe achievement that is below par when compared with expectations. Performance that does not match expectations may be associated with factors such as problems at home, lack of drive and poor motivation, which may induce problems that could be mistaken for lack of ability. Literacy and the influence of language on communication may also be influenced by:

● the effects of home life and schooling on linguistic development
● language competence potential: the ability of the customer to learn
● the effects of acquisition by imitation.

*Requests from customers are handled promptly and within agreed timescales*

The personal touch is very important in any relationship and especially when handling requests from customers who need help. The aim should be to earn yourself a good name for dealing efficiently with customer requests. Make it easy for them to reach you. Get a clear picture of their needs by asking sufficient questions to clarify and check that you have heard and understood correctly what the customer is requesting. Avoid the risk of sending them away to run the maze or get caught up in bureaucratic procedures. Make fast decisions and keep the customer informed.

Teachers should be seen to be acting in the customer's interest and injecting a standard of excellence into their handling of requests. Acting impersonally makes it easier to pass the buck when customer requests have not been met. You will on occasion need to act as an honest broker and call in other teachers or support staff to help out. In such instances it will be better for customers to deal directly with the person who will handle their request. Suggestions for gathering evidence to show how requests from customers are handled promptly and within agreed timescales are given in Activity 18.5.

*Difficulties with customers are dealt with in ways which try to avoid offence, and are resolved in ways that maintain respect*

Issues of equality of opportunity, non-discriminatory practice and the maintenance of customer self-esteem must be foremost in our minds when we are dealing with people who are experiencing learning difficulties or problems relating to the training provision. In any interaction the preservation of positive aspects of our self-image is an all-important consideration whether we are teachers or learners. So if difficulties are to be overcome we must preserve and if possible boost the customer's self-image and ensure that we do not cause them to lose face. An explanation of a manner of interaction with customers that could be adopted, and the way in which difficulties could be resolved, is given below.

Firstly, greet the customer by name. Smile, put them at ease and avoid giving any suggestion of confrontational behaviour. Encourage them to talk about their difficulties. Give them your full attention. Listen sympathetically, taking careful note of what they are saying, and identify what they need that isn't being provided. Once this is established you can use your knowledge of the programme or available resources to give your customer the best information and advice available.

Probe for their wants and needs. While they are talking, mentally match what is available with what they need. The better you meet their individual needs the greater will be the chance of maintaining the customers' goodwill and retaining a good team. Show that you want to help them by responding quickly to their needs and by telling them what you **can do**, not what you cannot do. State the alternatives. Find an acceptable solution by suggesting what is feasible, and obtain their agreement on a way forward. Sell the benefits of what is immediately available. And if you can provide the opportunity and the means for them to sort out their own complaints by allocating the resources needed to resolve their difficulties, so much the better.

Handle your customers' objections by readily agreeing with their point of view and using the 'Yes, I can appreciate your concern and I agree that . . . but . . .' technique. Then make your suggestions. Never argue with people for this will surely lead to conflict. Treat customers as special people with unique requirements rather than as stereotypes with standard complaints. If you can do this they might come around to allowing themselves to see the benefit of what you have offered. You might even both agree to call in satisfied customers or others in the group who have experienced similar difficulties. But if in the end you cannot resolve the problems you should explain why, offer to refer them to someone who might be better placed to help them, and close on a positive note.

If you feel that you just do not have what it takes to handle situations such as this you might improve your personal effectiveness by:

- gaining confidence in yourself and seeing the effect it has on your customers and the way they respond to your suggestions
- asking other people in the group for help
- noticing the needs of others and offering help
- reacting appropriately to requests from others
- discussing with others how things are to be done
- reacting appropriately to complaints from others
- converging with others in order to establish or maintain an appropriate relationship
- noticing when people behave exceptionally and whether action is required
- gaining satisfaction from helping your customers meet their individual wants and needs
- learning to demonstrate an 'inspired leader' approach.

*Difficulties which cannot be resolved are promptly referred to an appropriate person*

From time to time there will be a need for teachers to handle grievance situations and assess the causes and consequences of learner difficulties or inter-group conflict. Each party will have a different perception of the situation as seen from their point of view. It is how the teacher interprets the relationship between the reality and what is in the mind of the complainant that will impact upon the approach to be adopted. We are all human, and teachers like learners will be subjected to a variety of emotions that directly affect their behaviour when dealing with others. Rigid attitudes may have been formed on the basis of unpleasant past experiences. Responses may be logical and rational or they may be irrational and based on emotions rather than objective facts. If we are to influence others' behaviour then we must be first able to control our own.

It is no good blundering into a potentially emotive situation without having any idea about how to manage the event. Teachers must be prepared to explore with customers the sources and causes of their difficulties, and must have available for use a number of resolution strategies and tactics for taking the heat out of an unpleasant incident. This could mean exploring with the individual concerned personal or organisational barriers that are standing in the way of an amicable solution. Teachers must be able to adopt a variety of conflict management styles, and should therefore practise and develop personal skills and responses to aggressive behaviour which can facilitate sound relations with the customer and maintain their self-respect.

Confrontation in a group situation should be avoided since this may well undermine trust and lower credibility with a learner group. Bearing this in mind the teacher should:

- not make threats
- not deliberately embarrass the complainant
- attempt to reason
- remain unbiased
- allow other group members to influence positively the resolution of conflict.

When confronted privately by an individual customer the teacher should:

- remain calm and avoid the temptation to argue
- attempt to relieve any tension
- acknowledge that the customer has a problem
- attempt to define the problem using open, but probing, questions
- attempt to reach an outcome that is acceptable to both parties

Being able to judge when to seek advice is one of the key requirements for teachers who are attempting to resolve conflict with customers. After all reasonable avenues have been explored with the customer there will be little else to do but contact appropriate sources of support for dealing with any unresolved difficulties.

## Self-assessment questions _____

1 Describe the importance of establishing good relations with customers and colleagues.

2 Describe how to build constructive relationships with customers and colleagues.

3 Why should customers and colleagues be addressed in the manner which they prefer?

4 List the possible benefits of shared ownership of strategies and proposals.

5 Explain how differences of opinion could be dealt with so as to avoid offence and conflict.

6 Why is it important to actively encourage colleagues and customers to express their opinions freely and openly without fear of retribution?

7 Explain the effect of cultural factors and your own values and beliefs on your relationships with colleagues.

8 Explain what is meant by the terms: 'delayering' and 'the 360° approach to appraisal'.

9 List the sources of support available for dealing with difficulties with colleagues.

10 Explain how issues of equality of opportunity and non-discriminatory practice could affect relationships with colleagues.

11 Explain what is meant by the terms 'division of work' and 'specialisation'.

12 Why is it important to honour promises and undertakings made to others?

13 Why should customers be given clear and sufficient information about the service they can expect?

14 List the types of information that your customers are likely to need.

15 Explain the purposes and benefits of mission statements and a customer's charter.

16 List the sources of constraints on communications you have experienced when dealing with your colleagues and customers.

17 Explain how to judge when to seek advice in dealing with customers on a one-to-one basis and also in a group situation.

18 Explain how you might improve your personal effectiveness when handling customers' objections.

19 Why should confrontation and altercation with a student in the presence of a group be avoided?

20 Explain how you would go about referring to an appropriate person a customer with difficulties that you cannot personally resolve.

## Preparing for assessment: sample activities

### Activity 18.1 Working with colleagues

Describe how you have built constructive relationships with colleagues that you work with on an occasional basis and those that you work with regularly.

### Activity 18.2 Giving advice and handling differences of opinion

Outline the different approaches you might use when offering advice and help to colleagues

Write an account of instances where you have offered help and advice to colleagues and matched your support with their individual needs.

Outline the various sources of support available for dealing with difficulties with colleagues in your workplace.

### Activity 18.3 Effective two-way communication

Identify and analyse some significant problems of communication you have encountered in the context of teaching your learner group.

Consider how you might improve your person-to-person and person-to-group communication, and in particular ask yourself whether you are:

● asking the right questions in the most effective way
● recognising and correctly interpreting the signals emanating from the group
● listening and using silence effectively
● talking the students' language.

### Activity 18.4 Improving the effectiveness of student (customer) communications

Check whether your manner of communication and interaction with your individual customers is appropriate to their needs. List the ways in which students (customers) may be assisted to communicate effectively during a training programme.

Assess the quality of your own students' communication skills and decide whether any of the ways of increasing effectiveness that you have identified above can be introduced in your classes.

Discuss your list with colleagues and your student groups and evaluate the feasibility of actually introducing the new methods and the likely benefits of the innovation.

### Activity 18.5 Handling customer requests

Describe how you handled requests from customers with difficulties promptly and within agreed timescales. A possible approach to this activity might be to keep a record of requests from your customers. Make a diary entry or maintain a log of events, meetings and agreements reached for several instances where you have handled requests. Agree an action plan, or at least agree timescales for implementing any action needed to meet the request. Explain how you used your records to monitor progress or referred to the record of interaction later.

Describe how you offered continuing support and followed up by checking the implementation and suitability of the service provided.

### Activity 18.6 Managing relationships with customers

Provide evidence of managing relationships with at least two customers. Explain how you dealt with the customers' differing needs, expectations and approaches.

### Note

1 B. Bernstein, 'Social Class Language and Socialisation', in S.A. Abramson (ed.), *Current Trends in Linguistics*, Mouton Press, The Hague 1971.

2 Trying to make sense of the effects of language on relationships in classrooms and on the process of teaching and learning has occupied much time. Many researchers have studied the mental processes involved in the acquisition of language and its application in the social context and specifically to its role in education. Two approaches to studying educational language, 'logical-empirical' and 'intepretive', are described by Young, Arnold and Watson in a paper entitled 'Linguistic Models':

> To some extent these two traditions have been associated with two different styles of research. The first of these (the logical-empirical) drew its methods from the behavioural sciences and attempted to apply objective categories to counting instances of behaviour ... The interpretive method applied a more intuitive approach aimed at understanding the meaning of language.

They later specify some researchers who have been involved in work associated with the study of language in an educational context:

> The first tradition may be exemplified by the work of Romiett Stevens (1912) and later work by Flanders (1970), Bellack (1966), Smith and Meux (1962) in the United States, and Sinclair and Coulthard (1975) in the United Kingdom. The second tradition may be exemplified by the early work of Barnes et al. (1969) in the United Kingdom and more recently by the more systematic work of Hugh Mehan and his colleagues in the United States.

Obviously, the material presented here is somewhat limited, but its purpose is to heighten awareness of the importance of teachers' presentations and of the relatively short time students may spend talking. It will be of value to interested readers to examine the research of those mentioned above, and also of pioneers such as Rosen and Gumperz, Labov, and Hymes.

# Bibliography

S.E. Asch, *Social Psychology*, Prentice-Hall, New York 1952.

R.M. Belbin, *Management Teams: Why They Succeed or Fail*, Butterworth-Heinemann, Oxford 1981

E. Berne, *Games People Play: The Psychology of Human Relationships*, Penguin, Harmondsworth 1967

B. Bernstein, 'Social Class, Language and Socialisation', in S.A. Abramson (ed.), *Current Trends in Linguistics*, Mouton Press, The Hague 1971

City and Guilds, *7306 Further and Adult Education Teachers Certificate (NVQ) Candidate Pack*, London 1995

M.J. Dunkin (ed.), *The International Encyclopaedia of Teaching and Teacher Education*, Pergamon Press, Headington 1987

Employment Department Group, *Labour Market and Skills Trends 1992/93 (SEN 32)*, Sheffield 1991

F.E. Fiedler and J.E. Garcia, *New Approaches to Effective Leadership*, John Wiley, New York 1987

J. Fish, *Special Needs Occasional Paper*, Longman for the Further Education Unit, Longman Resources Unit, York 1989

N. Flanders, *Analysing Teaching Behaviour*, Addison-Wesley, Reading, Massachusetts 1970

D.S. Frith and H.G. Macintosh, *A Teacher's Guide to Assessment*, Stanley Thornes, Cheltenham 1984

R.M. Gagné, *The Conditions of Learning*, Holt, Rinehart and Winston, New York 1965

D. Garforth and H. Macintosh, *Profiling: A User's Manual*, Stanley Thornes, Cheltenham 1986

P. Hanks (ed.), *Collins Dictionary of the English Language*, William Collins, Glasgow 1989

J. Heron, *Six Category Intervention Analysis*, Human Potential Research Project, University of Surrey, Guildford 1975

D.A. Kolb, *Experiential Learning: Experience as the Source of Learning and Development*, Prentice-Hall, Englewood Cliffs, New Jersey 1984

J.S. Kounin, *Discipline and Group Management in Classrooms*, Holt, Rinehart and Winston, New York 1970

D.R. Krathwohl, B.S. Bloom and B.B. Masin, *Taxonomy of Educational Objectives: Handbook 2 Affective Domain*, McKay, New York 1964

R.F. Mager, *Preparing Educational Objectives*, Fearon Publishers, Belmont, California 1962

Margerison-McCann, *Team Management Systems*, TMS Development International, York 1995

O.E. Marston, *Assessment*, NATFHE pamphlet, London *c.* 1979

S. Milgram, 'Behavioural Study of Obedience', *Journal of Abnormal and Social Psychology*, vol. 67, 1963

N. Rackham, P. Honey and M. Colbert, *Developing Interactive Skills*, Wellens Publishing, Northampton 1971

N. Rees, *The Politically Correct Phrasebook*, Bloomsbury Publishing, London 1993

W.P. Robinson, *Language and Social Behaviour*, Penguin Books, Harmondsworth 1972

L. Walklin, *The Assessment of Performance and Competence*, Stanley Thornes, Cheltenham 1991 (reprinted 1994)

L. Walklin, *Instructional Techniques and Practice*, Stanley Thornes, Cheltenham 1982 (reprinted 1994)

L. Walklin, *Instructional Techniques and Practice for Driving Instructors*, Stanley Thornes, Cheltenham 1993

L. Walklin, *Putting Quality into Practice*, Stanley Thornes, Cheltenham 1992

L. Walklin, *Teaching and Learning in Further and Adult Education*, Stanley Thornes, Cheltenham 1990 (reprinted 1995)

C. Ward, *Designing a Scheme of Assessment*, Stanley Thornes, Cheltenham 1980

# Index

Note: DP = Documents Pack